Strictly
DISHONORABLE

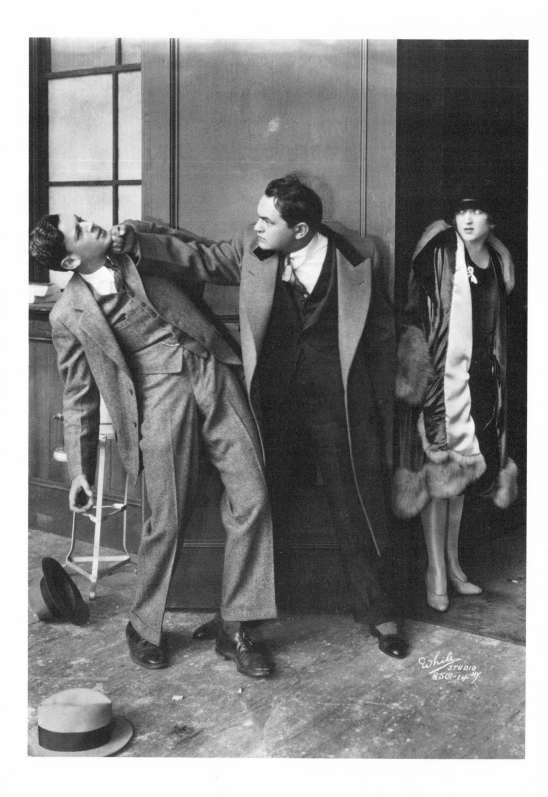

White Studio
8501-14 N.Y.

Strictly

DISHONORABLE

AND OTHER LOST AMERICAN PLAYS

Selected and introduced by
Richard Nelson

STRICTLY DISHONORABLE
Preston Sturges

THE RACKET
Bartlett Cormack

A SLIGHT CASE OF MURDER
Damon Runyon and Howard Lindsay

THE GHOST OF YANKEE DOODLE
Sidney Howard

Theatre Communications Group   New York   1986

Strictly Dishonorable and Other Lost American Plays is published by Theatre Communications Group, Inc., the national organization for the nonprofit professional theatre, 355 Lexington Ave., New York, NY 10017.

Library of Congress Cataloging-in-Publication Data

Strictly dishonorable & other lost American plays.

      Contents: Strictly dishonorable / by Preston
Sturges—The racket / by Bartlett Cormack—
The ghost of Yankee Doodle Dandy / by Sidney
Howard—[etc.]
      1. American drama—20th century. I. Nelson,
Richard, 1950-   II. Title: Strictly dishonorable
and other lost American plays.
PS634.S86   1986   812'.52'08   86-5782
ISBN 0-930452-55-0 (pbk.)

FIRST EDITION

Contents

Introduction
by
Richard Nelson

A number of years ago, while sitting in a thirty-pence seat with a partially obstructed view of London's Old Vic stage, I first began to discover for myself the joys of the American drama of the late twenties and thirties. In front of me was Michael Blakemore's National Theatre production of Hecht and MacArthur's *The Front Page*, a play I had read but until then had not at all understood. I think I must have expected some sort of "genre" farce, full of forced situations and caricatures; what I found was a mean and angry play—a comedy, yes—but one which seemed to live and breathe on the fringe of common morality. In this production, which layered on no preconceived style but rather let the play "be" (and run an unfarce-like three hours), the evening was electric, even dangerous. But even more amazing, especially as I was in England, it was very, very American. Precisely why I felt this I cannot say; I only know that there is something unique to the American character that allows profound innocence and cold ruthlessness to inhabit the same being. It was this characteristic that was finding such perfect expression on the stage before me.

Years later, I was asked to become the literary manager of the theatre company at the Brooklyn Academy of Music, and one of my first assignments from David Jones, the artistic director, was to nose around libraries, used book stores and manuscript collections in search of "forgotten" American plays that our company could produce. As the intention of BAM was to build a large classical company with as many as thirty actors in residence, plays from times when large casts were common could again be seriously explored for production. Therefore, thanks to BAM and David's encouragement, mine was a unique opportunity in the American theatre, and my hunt for the "forgotten" filled most of my time. I dug through plays of the eighteenth century, of the forties and fifties, of the teens and early twenties; but with my *Front Page* experience still so strong inside me, it was the world of the late twenties and thirties that I most closely explored. In it, I feel I found my best rewards.

There is Charles MacArthur's *Johnny on a Spot*, about the election of a politician who has died in a brothel, and which BAM presented in its first season; there is Hecht and Gene Fowler's *The Great Magoo*, with its bizarre ending in which an old lady comes out from behind a curtain "with a douche-bag dangling from her hand" and says to the ingenue, as she is about to walk off into the sunset with her boyfriend, "Hey, Cinderella. You forgot your pumpkin!" And curtain. There's the original script of George S. Kaufman's *Coconuts*, with this speech for the Groucho Marx character:

> Remember, there's nothing like liberty. That is, nothing like it in this country. Be free. Now and forever, one and indivisible, one for all, and all for me and me for you, and tea for two.

And there is this exchange in Ben Hecht's *To Quito and Back* (which, though produced in the forties, is still spiritually a part of the thirties), between a Latin American revolutionary and an elderly Italian countess, as an American writer looks on:

> PIZARRO: You are a radical, are you not, Mr. Sterns?
> COUNTESS: He's an American author and he's got a right to have moods.

And there are the four plays in this volume. Each, in its own way, is rooted in the late twenties and thirties; each is an expression, I believe, of that innocence mixed with ruthlessness found in *The Front Page*, though the way in which this is expressed differs radically from play to play; each is profoundly American; and it is my hope that each will not only be read here in this volume, but will again find a place on the American stage.

Before making a few comments on the plays and their playwrights, I would like to point out one possibly inescapable fact. David Jones, referred to above, is English, a former director with the Royal Shakespeare Company; Michael Blakemore, though Australian, lives and works in Britain; the National Theatre I mentioned is the National Theatre of *Great Britain*; the policy of searching out "forgotten" American plays is one first articulated by the RSC with such productions as Bronson Howard's *Saratoga*; recent successes at the National and the RSC include *Guys and Dolls* and Kaufman and Hart's *Once in a Lifetime*; the English actress, Glenda Jackson, has lately starred in O'Neill's *Strange Interlude* on Broadway; the 1984 Broadway production of *A Moon for the Misbegotten* was staged by a young British director; and a series of critical books recently published by New York's Grove Press includes a volume on O'Neill with Laurence Olivier on the cover, one on Arthur Miller with the National Theatre's production of *The Crucible* on its cover, and one called *American Dramatists 1918-1945* with the RSC's production of *Once in a Lifetime* on its cover.

Well, I can guarantee that Theatre Communications Group, the publisher of this collection, is a decidedly *American* outfit. My hope is that this volume will be only the beginning of increased support and encouragement on the parts of American publishers and theatres for the uncovering of the treasures of our culture.

MCQUIGG (After a moment): I'm licked again by due process o' law, uh? Well—
(Seizing and tearing up the writ) I'm sick o' the law. We'll fight this out here.

—from *The Racket*

The career of Bartlett Cormack was, as they say, short and sweet. By the time of his death in 1942 at the age of forty-four, Cormack had long since given up the stage for Hollywood and the movies. *The Racket*, which opened on Broadway on November 22, 1927 and ran for 119 performances, was Cormack's only play ever to reach New York. (The only other two to be produced were *Painted Veil*, a comedy about Hollywood that closed in Princeton in 1931; and *Hey Diddle Diddle*, an adaptation of a Somerset Maugham story that ran only in London in 1937.)

Born in Hammond, Indiana, Cormack's life seems in some ways archetypal of several writers of his generation, such as Ben Hecht, Charles MacArthur and Gene Fowler. Chicago reporter, New York playwright, then Hollywood screenwriter, his movie credits include *The Beachcomber, Fury* (Fritz Lang's first American feature), the film of *The Front Page* and *This Day and Age*, which was directed by Cecil B. DeMille. It is this last film which most relates to *The Racket* or, rather, to the gunslinging morality of the play's leading character, the police captain, McQuigg.

In *This Day and Age*, some civic-minded boys take the law into their own hands and torture a known gangster into confessing his heinous crimes. When the film came out in 1933, it was strongly criticized abroad and was even banned in Holland for its "fascist tendencies." *The Racket* takes place in "The central room of the Tenth District police station far out on the southwest side of Chicago. The station is an old, remodeled Victorian house. . . . " This is a rich and meaningful setting indeed, for a play that seems to lament the loss of simpler times and to cry out in disgust at the corrupt present.

The world of the play is neither a police station nor a home, but rather a place unsettled, in transition, perhaps even in revolution (albeit right-wing revolution in this case). Its characters, gangsters and corrupt politicians trying to wait out the week's election, the captain who takes the law into his own hands as if he were the sheriff of a mythical Dodge City, the naive reporter with a textbook knowledge of justice, have all been displaced and find themselves struggling "far out on the southwest side of Chicago." Like the very best of the genre that *The Racket* most closely resembles, the movie Western, it finds its force by starkly delineating the moral questions of its violent situation. From its opening image to its last line (one of the greatest I know in the American theatre), its situation never relaxes for one second.

ISABELLE (Picking up a hair pin): I didn't know women used hairpins anymore.
GUS: Probably my cleaning woman dropped it.
ISABELLE: Probably. Is she blonde?
GUS: I ... ah ... never noticed. ... She wears a dust cap.
ISABELLE (Pushing a cigarette end from the ashtray): Well, you ought to tell her
   to stop smoking your cigarettes. It doesn't look nice to see the ashtrays all full
   of cigarette-butts with ... lip rouge on them.
GUS: Darling—are you jealous?
ISABELLE: Me? No, just neat.

—from *Strictly Dishonorable*

Whereas Bartlett Cormack has been long forgotten, his one success languishing for years out of print and unproduced, Preston Sturges's fame seems to be on the rise, what with the recent publication of his biography and a selection of his screenplays. But it is not the successful playwright that he first was that is being remembered. Rather, it is the screenwriter and film director of a string of highly successful "satirical" comedies in the forties, including *The Great McGinty*, *Christmas in July*, *Sullivan's Travels*, *The Palm Beach Story*, *The Miracle of Morgan's Creek*, and *Hail the Conquering Hero*. In fact, Sturges's success in Hollywood has all but eclipsed the fact that *Strictly Dishonorable*, which opened on Broadway on September 18, 1929, ran for 557 performances and became one of the great successes of the decade. It is hard to fathom how this wonderfully charming, beautifully written play could have become so "forgotten."

Like so many playwrights of the period, Sturges was born in Chicago, though, unlike Hecht and MacArthur, his route to New York and Hollywood did not take him through the world of Chicago journalism. Possessed of a mother who was a fierce disciple of Isadora Duncan, Sturges had a quixotic education, lived in Paris, ran a perfume company, all the while carrying out a search for his true calling that did not end until September 1929, when Brooks Atkinson joined others in singing the praises of the thirty-two-year-old playwright:

> *Strictly Dishonorable* reveals a native understanding of the theatre that may be ripened and developed by constant labor in the writing and producing of plays, but cannot be acquired by those who lack it. ... His gift for playwriting quickens interest in his future.
>
> (*New York Times*, September 1929)

Strictly Dishonorable was actually Sturges's second produced play; his first, *The Guinea Pig*, had opened the previous January and run for sixty-four performances. Still, the craft and sophistication of *Strictly Dishonorable*, Sturges's ability to allow his characters to speak for themselves, reveals a knowledge far beyond his experience.

There is, however, one world of experience that, because of Sturges's background, we should not be surprised to find in the play—the realm of travel, world culture, internationalism. Unlike any other writer in this volume, Sturges expresses an international point of view and sympathies. This simple comedy about an innocent Southern belle and an experienced Italian opera star in fact turns on the conflict between staying safe and protected, and "seeing the world" and growing, and concludes on the side of expanding one's horizons. For this reason, I do not think it outrageous to suggest that *Strictly Dishonorable* is a wonderful expression of that great debate which raged across America in its decade (and which finds direct expression in another play in the volume, *The Ghost of Yankee Doodle*): the clash between those urging America to remain isolated and those arguing for America to accept an international role as an active participant in world affairs.

MARKO: We'll give him No Nose Cohen—he's the handsomest!

—from *A Slight Case of Murder*

At the time that they came together to write *A Slight Case of Murder*, Howard Lindsay was the successful collaborator (with Russel Crouse) on the book for *Anything Goes*, and Damon Runyon, the "Balzac of the racetrack," as Brooks Atkinson once called him, was a wildly successful journalist, columnist and writer of short stories. Whereas Lindsay would go on to co-author such hits as *Life with Father*, the book for *The Sound of Music* and the Pulitzer-winning *State of the Union* (all with Crouse), Runyon never wrote another play. But it was an unpublished Runyon story that inspired *A Slight Case of Murder*, and it is Runyon's "world" that the play most vividly portrays.

Already in his fifties when he collaborated with Lindsay, Runyon was by far the oldest of the playwrights in this volume and as such, he seems to express a somewhat different perspective on the changing world of the thirties. Whereas the central characters of the other three plays all actively deal with the way in which society is changing, the "retired" gangster/bootlegger, Marko, in *A Slight Case of Murder* seems to think himself unable to change, and pins any hopes he might have for true respectability on his daughter. The situation, then, is that of a "foreigner"—Marko—finding himself in a new world (post-Prohibition) from which there is no going back. He feels uncomfortable, but knows there is nothing he can do about it beyond hoping that his daughter might be able to assimilate. In other words, at its center, Runyon's play is an immigrant play, and its perspective is that of an older generation toward changing times.

While the gangsters of *The Racket* fight to keep their power, those in the Runyon/Lindsay play have only nostalgia for the "Good Old Days." And while Isabelle struggles with the question of remaining protected or seeing the world in *Strictly Dishonorable*, it is a given in *A Slight Case of Murder* that travel and world culture are things to be valued. And the ruthlessness that is virtually worn as a badge in *The Front Page* and *The Racket* is here hidden in the past, while the innocence that energizes Isabelle and attracts Gus to her is here assigned to the offspring. In essence, this world of the immigrant is one of faith—faith that things are getting better, if not necessarily for the parents, then certainly for the children. And this faith, though the play never says so, seems also to be in the country itself. I can't help but think that the world of *A Slight Case of Murder* is in fact infused with patriotism, a sentiment that was to blossom in the forties when America went to war.

One short note on the production history of *A Slight Case of Murder*: It opened on September 11, 1935 and ran for only sixty-nine performances. The reviews were mixed at best, yet by the time the Sunday *Times* came out, Brooks Atkinson was already moderating his criticism. "On the first night," he wrote, "the performance was strident and disjointed, although it is said to be now improved." Improved in just a few days? It makes one wonder if the failure of the play might perhaps have been due to something going wrong on opening night, and not the play itself. Well, it wouldn't have been the first—or last—time.

SARA: It's rather nice, I find, to be with a man who isn't suffering from ideological jitters.

—from *The Ghost of Yankee Doodle*

Whereas the characters in the three other plays all appear to be oblivious to the larger themes of their dilemmas, those in *The Ghost of Yankee Doodle* face them dead on. Isolationism, internationalism, pacifism, the possibility of moderation in a crazed political climate, are not submerged themes here but rather issues discussed by the characters. And whereas Cormack settled for a kind of melodrama form for his morality tale, and Sturges chose romantic comedy, and Runyon a kind of farce, Sidney Howard has subtitled his play "A Tragedy."

Howard was only forty-eight when he died in 1939, after being crushed by a tractor on his farm in Massachusetts, yet he was already considered one of our finest playwrights; his premature death was mourned as a great loss to the American theatre. His plays include *They Knew What They Wanted* (for which he received the 1924 Pulitzer Prize), *Silver Cord*, *Lucky Sam McCarver* and *Yellow Jack*. His screenplays include the phenomenally successful *Gone with the Wind*. A year before his death he founded The Playwrights Company, along with Maxwell Anderson, Robert E. Sherwood, Elmer Rice and S. N. Behrman. Howard was actually more than a writer: he was a force in the theatre, arguing for more serious work dealing with large subjects. *The Ghost of Yankee Doodle*, which ran for only forty-eight performances in 1937, represents a major effort toward achieveing the kind of theatre in which Howard so firmly believed.

The characters in the play are not immigrant types or gangsters or talented singers; they are the monied WASPs of Middle America, the country's real movers and shakers. As they discuss the direction and needs of the United States, one is made to believe that they can effect their conclusions. In other words, here is a political play in the best sense: a play about people dealing politically in a context where such dealings can matter. The topics broached in *The Ghost of Yankee Doodle*—jingoism, patriotic confusion, capitalist greed—have become no less important over time; only, perhaps, less fashionable. In part, the play is a study in the pain of argument and the exasperation of the intellectual in complex times. It is the fate of liberalism that is being debated, while the ability to "walk the middle way" is being questioned. By the end, we come to believe that the choice faced by America is between ruthlessness and innocence. And it's not only the characters who will have to choose.

Now, forty-five years later, having elected a President whose popularity is in part based upon his uncanny ability to delineate the ruthless and innocent strains within himself, it is clear that America has never made the choice between these two character traits. Instead, we continue to allow them to cohabit and, in fact, to be the source of much of our self-image. It makes sense, therefore, to hope that such plays as these and others of their time will not be seen as dated artifacts of a bygone era, grown estranged from the central concerns of American society, but as part of that continuous evolution that is American culture.

Richard Nelson is the author of numerous plays, including *The Vienna Notes*, *Jungle Coup* and, most recently, *Principia Scriptoriae*. He has translated and adapted the works of Molière, Goldoni, Beaumarchais, Chekhov, Brecht, Erdman and Fo. A volume of Nelson's original works, *An American Comedy and Other Plays*, has been published by PAJ Publications, and his *Between East and West* is included in TCG's *New Plays USA 3* anthology.

STRICTLY DISHONORABLE

A Comedy in Three Acts

by

PRESTON STURGES

Preston Sturges

The original production of *Strictly Dishonorable* opened at the Avon Theatre in New York City on September 18, 1929. It was produced by Brock Pemberton, who directed it with Antoinette Perry. Raymond Sovey designed the sets and J. N. Gilchrist served as stage manager.

Isabelle (Muriel Kirkland) restrains Henry (Louis Jean Heydt) as the rest of the original cast looks on.

The Original Cast

Giovanni . . . . John Altieri
Mario . . . . Marius Rogati
Tomaso Antiovi . . . . William Ricciardi
Judge Dempsey . . . . Carl Anthony
Henry Greene . . . . Louis Jean Heydt
Isabelle Parry . . . . Muriel Kirkland
Count Di Ruvo . . . . Tullio Carminati
Patrolman Mulligan . . . . Edward J. McNamara

Place

The speakeasy of Tomaso Antiovi and an apartment above it, on West 49th Street in New York City.

Time

Saturday night and Sunday morning of a day in early autumn.

Characters

(In order of appearance)

GIOVANNI, a lookout

MARIO, a waiter

TOMASO ANTIOVI

ISABELLE PARRY

HENRY GREENE

COUNT DI RUVO

PATROLMAN MULLIGAN

The Play

ACT ONE

The Italian speakeasy of Tomaso Antiovi on West 49th Street at 11:41 p.m. on a Saturday evening in autumn.

One door leads into the kitchen. Another leads into a hall which connects the kitchen and the street door. An arch leads into the hallway and to stairs to the apartments. Upstairs can be seen through the arch. Two windows are covered with heavy drapes and cannot be seen. There is a bar with one stool behind, and one in front of it. Mirror between the two windows. Two tables before banquette. Chairs next to the tables. Wall telephone next to banquette. Hall rack in hall, and between rack and stairs, a small chair. Slot machine. Portable phonograph on stool near mirror. A radio next to arch.

MARIO, a waiter, is reading a tabloid newspaper at a table. The radio is playing. GIOVANNI is seated in the hall listening to the music.

GIOVANNI: La musica é una gran bella cosa.
[Music is a wonderful thing.]

MARIO turns off radio angrily, then reads. GIOVANNI enters, puzzled turns on radio and goes back to his seat.

MARIO: Com'e possibile sentire questa robaccia?
[How can anyone listen to this garbage?]

6

MARIO *turns off radio.* GIOVANNI *rises and comes into room.*

GIOVANNI: Che diavolo succede. Bado che nessuno la tocca.
[What the devil is happening? I'll see that no one touches it.]

GIOVANNI *turns on radio and hides behind arch.* MARIO *tears paper in rage, then turns off radio just as* GIOVANNI *looks in and catches him by wrist.*

A lazzarone! Ti ho detto che non la tocca.
[You cad! I told you not to touch it.]
MARIO: Questa maladetta radio mi fa avere i nervi.
[This damn radio irritates me.]
GIOVANNI: Ma io ho lo stesso diritto di sentire la radio come tu di leggere il giornale.
[But I have the same right to listen to the radio that you have to read the paper.]

TOM *enters.*

TOM: Silenzio! What's a matter with you people? You make all noise when it's near to close. E questa tavola qui senza sparecchiare.
[And with this table here not cleared off yet.]

GIOVANNI *goes into hall. The iron gate is heard to slam and* GIOVANNI *goes off to answer it.* MARIO *folds napkins and sets table, then sits and pulls tabloid from pocket and begins to read.*

GIOVANNI (*off*): Good evening, Mister Judge.

JUDGE *enters and starts to stairs.* GIOVANNI *sits in hall.*

TOM (*Goes upstage toward arch*): Oh, Mister Judge, could you come in one minute, please?
JUDGE: I'm pretty tired, Tom. I want to get upstairs to bed.
TOM: Only just one little minute.
JUDGE (*Entering*): What is it?
TOM: I make you one drink, huh? Then you no feel tired.
JUDGE: No. I've had a devil of a siege in court today and I'm tired and weak.
TOM: I make one little Old-Fashioned.

TOM *starts to bar;* JUDGE *follows to front of bar.*

JUDGE: I know your Old-Fashioneds; don't make more than one.
TOM (*Behind bar*): All right, Mister Judge—all right. (*Starts to mix drink*) Judge, I got today a bigga trouble. I gotta paper.
JUDGE: What sort of a paper?
TOM: I don't know, Mister Judge. A man leava dis paper—(*Takes summons from pocket*) Suh—suh—summons to appear before the presiding mag—magistrato. I don't understand. I no do nothing. (*Hands* JUDGE *summons*)
JUDGE: Let me see it. (*Reads summons*) Why—this is for contempt of court!

TOM: Me?

JUDGE: Sure. Tomaso Antiovi.

TOM: Corpo di Bacco! Contempt of court? Why, I do nothing. What means contempt for court, Mister Judge?

JUDGE: Contempt? Why, it means you have no respect for the court—that you—ah—spit on it.

TOM: I spit? Cristo Santo! Never could I do such a thing, Mister Judge. I spit on the court? I do not even spit on the floor. I have admiration for the court. I love the court and all the fine judges—like you, Mister Judge.

JUDGE: Yeah—I know. Well now, let me see—you were summoned to appear on Tuesday. Why didn't you go instead of being in contempt?

TOM: I have no contempt. Why must I go last Tuesday?

JUDGE: Because you were caught speeding on Sunday.

TOM: It say that?

JUDGE: Sure it does.

> MARIO *rises guiltily and starts to straighten table, moving around slowly as scene progresses.*

TOM: Me make too much money to go joy ride. I no use the car on Sunday, Mister Judge.

JUDGE: You didn't lend your car to anybody, did you?

TOM: Lend my—? (*Looks at* MARIO *and crosses to him*) Mario—Mario! You took my automobile—

MARIO: Si l'ho preso, ma non é successo niente.
[I had it, but nothing happened]

TOM (To JUDGE): Yes, Mister Judge, he took the automobile, but he say nothing happen.

JUDGE: Did any policeman give you a paper?

MARIO: No, Mister Judge—only one small very little ticket.

TOM (*Mimicking* MARIO): Only one very little ticket—

JUDGE: Were you speeding?

MARIO: No, Mister Judge, no. I went so slow—like a snails I went—a sick snails.

JUDGE: You must have been obstructing traffic. Well, I guess it'll be all right.

> *Gives* TOM *summons.*

TOM (*Returning to behind bar*): You fix it up, Mister Judge?

> MARIO *picks up glasses and bottles from table.*

JUDGE: Yes, I'll fix it up.

TOM: Thank you, Mister Judge—I'm very sorry.

GIOVANNI (*Appearing in arch, mimicking* MARIO): I went slow—like a snails, Mister Judge. Animale!

MARIO: Tartaruge! Lumacha!

TOM: Piano! Ssh! Ssh!

THEY *stop abruptly.* GIOVANNI *returns to chair in hall;* MARIO *exits. The telephone rings.*

This is a *speak*easy. You make it sound like a *loudspeaker!* (HE *answers phone*) Allo. Yes. His Excellency no come in yet, Miss Lilli. No. . . . No. . . . No. . . . I don't know. . . . Any time now. . . . Yes, Miss Lilli. You call again . . . all right. Goodbye. (*Hangs up and goes to table. Takes pencil and makes note of call*) Alla time—alla time—womens call up—Miss Lilli—Mimi—Miss Katie—Susie—Tessy—alla time—too much for a singer!

JUDGE: Is Di Ruvo singing tonight?

TOM: No—no sing tonight. Sing last night. Pagliacci. I go. Ah, Dio mio! The whole Metropolitan. Everybody, he weep like an onions when he sing—(HE *sings*) *Ri di Pagliacci.* (*At finish of a snatch of song*) Ah, he is grand!

JUDGE: Where is he? I want to congratulate him.

TOM: He go on big party, but he should be home now. (*Looks at his watch*) He stay out too late. No good.

JUDGE: Why shouldn't he stay out late if he wants to? He isn't a child.

TOM: Ah, to me, il Signorino is always a child—a little child. I remember in Sorrento when he first arrive—when the stork bring him and his father, il Signor Conte, come all smiles and tell us servants: "Open the wine, my good friends, and drink to the health of my son who just now, this minute, I have the pleasure to meet."

JUDGE: Yes, but he's grown up now.

TOM: Ah, grown up. To me who see him so—and so—and so—well, now he is so. But still he is not grown up. When I tell him instructions from his mother, La Signora Contessa, you know what he do—he laugh at me.

Bell rings. GIOVANNI *rises and exits.* TOM *looks at his watch again, shakes his head sadly as* HE *returns behind bar.*

Ah, too late—too late!

JUDGE: Nonsense, nonsense!

TOM: No nonsense, Judge—no good.

JUDGE: He can take care of himself.

GIOVANNI (*Appearing in arch and holding up small card*): Customers, Signor Tomaso.

TOM: Who are they?

GIOVANNI: Man and a lady—no come before.

TOM: They got card?

GIOVANNI: Yeah.

TOM: All right.

GIOVANNI *exits.* JUDGE *starts to arch.*

JUDGE: I guess I'd better disappear.

HENRY *appears in arch and looks in room.*

Oh.

JUDGE *returns and sits at bar.* HENRY, *not pleased with place, starts to leave.*

TOM: Come in, Mister—come in.

HENRY (*Turns to go; meets* ISABELLE): Naw. I'll come back some other time.

Sound of gate off. ISABELLE *appears in arch and enters room slightly, looking around.*

TOM: What's the matter? You no like?

ISABELLE: What a lovely place, Henry. And look at that quaint little bar. Can we sit down?

TOM *exits.*

HENRY: No. This isn't the place I thought it was. This is dead. I guess I got the cards mixed.

ISABELLE (*Crossing to a table*): I—I like it here, Henry.

HENRY: I tell you the other place is the one we're looking for. The whole gang from the office goes there. They'll be there with their wives.

ISABELLE: Let's not bother. It took an hour to park the car this time. (*Goes to chair*) Let's sit down for a minute, anyway.

HENRY (*Coming in slightly*): I tell you if you saw the other place . . .

ISABELLE: I wouldn't even know the difference, Henry. I've never been in a speakeasy before and I'm afraid if we leave this one, you'll just carry me home.

HENRY (*Comes to table and sits*): Oh—all right. But we'd be better off if we were home.

ISABELLE (SHE *sits*): Aw, no, we wouldn't. You gotta have a little fun sometimes. (SHE *opens pocketbook, takes out mirror and looks at herself. Powders nose. Leaves pocketbook open with* HENRY's *list easily accessible*)

HENRY: What's the matter with home?

TOM *enters with bottle of cherries, placing them on bar.*

Don't you like it there?

ISABELLE: Of course I do, Henry.

HENRY: Well, don't—talk that way about it then. (*To* TOM) Hey, there—how about some service?

TOM (HE *rings bell*): In a moment.

MARIO *enters.*

MARIO (*Crossing to table*): You like a drink?

HENRY (*Mimicking*): Yes, I like a drink. What do you think I came here for? Bring me a double Scotch! What do you want, Izzy—a liqueur?

ISABELLE: Whatever you say, Henry. It's all the same to me.

HENRY: And a crème de mint!

MARIO (*As* HE *crosses to upper end of bar*): One double Scotch—and one benedictine.

HENRY: I . . . SAID . . . CRÊME . . . DEE . . . MINT! Now get it straight!

MARIO: No got any. S'alla same, anyway.

TOM: Maybe I got! (HE *exits*)

MARIO *starts to read tabloid.*

HENRY: Well, make it snappy!

ISABELLE: Don't get angry, Henry. You never used to get cross so easily. Why . . . when . . . when I first knew you, you were always smiling and . . . and sweet. What's the matter with you, getting cross all the time?

HENRY: You didn't think I was going to be as sappy all my life as when I first met you, did you?

ISABELLE: Well, I hoped so. You said you'd be always like that and I'd . . . learn to love you 'cause you were going to be so good to me. You weren't just making believe, were you?

HENRY: Of course I wasn't. But when a fellow's courting a girl, naturally . . . he puts his best foot forward . . . and . . . puts up with a whole lot of damned nonsense he . . . he wouldn't stand for all his life. Now when I sell bonds—

ISABELLE: You . . . you're not going to be nice to me any more?

HENRY: Of course I am, Isabelle. But you've got to be more *serious. Life* is serious. You Southerners are all alike. You think the sun shines just to make a nice day for you to go picnicking. It doesn't! It shines to germinate the wheat kernels to make your bread. It shines so you can have vegetables—fresh squash, beans, spinach—

ISABELLE: I hate spinach!

TOM *enters.*

HENRY: Well, you don't eat the right food. But you will! (*To* TOM) Say, do I have to wait here all night?

TOM: Just a minute, Mister, I got other customer. Must serve him first.

HENRY: You seem to be taking a long time about it.

TOM: An Old-Fashioned take a lot of stuff.

ISABELLE: We're not in any hurry, Henry.

HENRY: Who said we're not? I want to get home.

ISABELLE: Not just yet, please. You know . . . New York thrills me so, I'm happy. . . . just to be in it.

HENRY: Yeah? Well, it doesn't thrill me. (*Drums table and looks over at* TOM) Hey!

TOM: In a moment, sir.

ISABELLE: Could we—could we have our drinks at the bar, Henry?

HENRY: The bar is for men; you'd better stay at the table.

ISABELLE: Oh, but I wanted to . . . (*Resignedly*) Oh, all right.

JUDGE (*To* TOM): They must be married.

ISABELLE: Not yet. (*To* JUDGE) But this is part of my trousseau.

JUDGE: Take your time, young woman, take your time. S'like going to jail: S'easy to get in, but hard to get out. I know. I'll tell you how I know. . . .

JUDGE *rises and starts toward them.* HENRY *scowls at him menacingly.*

HENRY: Yeah?

JUDGE (*Crosses to bar*): Some other time, my dear, some other time.

TOM: Mario!

MARIO: Subito! (HE *picks up tray of drinks, crosses to table and serves them—then exits to kitchen*)

HENRY (*In an ugly mood*): Well, it's about time . . . and say! Tell your friend the jailbird to keep away from this table.

JUDGE (*Crossing*): Jailbird! Are you referring to me?

TOM: Ssh! Ssh! Ssh!

JUDGE (*In a voice like thunder*): Answer my question!

ISABELLE (*Looks up at* JUDGE *and makes a pleading little gesture with her hands*): Please. . . .

JUDGE: At your service, Madam. (*Turns to* TOM) You know, Tom, I seem to be the only sober person in this place—(*Turns to* ISABELLE *and bows*) And you, Madam—and you. And this is no place for a sober man. (*Starts to door*) I'm going into the kitchen—(*Turns at door*)—where the eggs aren't boiled so hard.

HE *exits.* TOM *exits.*

ISABELLE (*Rising*): I suppose we'd better get out of here, Henry. (SHE *starts getting her things together*)

HENRY (*Sullenly*): There's no hurry. That old . . . Turk isn't going to drive me away!

ISABELLE: No, Henry . . . (*Coaxingly*) . . . but let's go anyway . . . and not have any more rows this evening.

HENRY *pounds table.* TOM *enters.*

HENRY: Bring me another Scotch.

TOM: S'pretty late . . . Well . . . one more maybe . . . all right.

HENRY: Don't do me any favors.

TOM (*In doorway*): Don't worry, Mister, I won't.

ISABELLE: Really, Henry, I'd much rather go.

TOM *rings bell.*

HENRY (*Harshly*): Well, I'd rather stay.

MARIO *enters and goes to upper end of bar.*

I suppose I'm in the wrong again.

TOM *exits.*

ISABELLE: No, you aren't!

HENRY: I suppose I should have let that old booze-hound get away with that stuff. . . .

ISABELLE (*Sitting at table*): No, Henry. You were perfectly right . . .

MARIO *starts across to serve drink.*

I mean it . . . but sometimes I . . .

HENRY: But sometimes you what?

ISABELLE (*Desperately*): I mean . . .

> MARIO *serves a double Scotch.*

Thank you very much. . . . Now let's be happy. Here's to you, Henry. Here's to us.

> MARIO *exits.*

HENRY (*Doggedly*): Sometimes you what?

ISABELLE: Huh? Oh, I don't remember. (*Sweetly*) Let's forget about it.

HENRY: Let's *not*. If you've got any private thoughts about me, I'd rather know them . . . *before* we're married. If I had any private thoughts or criticisms of you, I'd tell you about them.

ISABELLE: I'm sure you would, dear, you're so . . . frank.

HENRY: Well, you be frank, too!

ISABELLE: It's nothing really, except that I'm not used to all the ways up here.

HENRY: Well, the people are different.

ISABELLE: Oh, not really, I guess, but . . . down home everybody's sort of friendly-like . . . that's all.

HENRY: That's only because it's a little town. You'll find the same thing once we're settled in West Orange. . . .

ISABELLE: I . . . I don't think we'll find it in West Orange, Henry.

HENRY: What's the matter with West Orange?

ISABELLE: Oh, nothing.

HENRY: Isn't everybody there friendly to you? The family's certainly been nice to you, hasn't it?

ISABELLE: Of course, Henry. Naturally everybody I've *met* has been nice. That isn't what I'm talking about. It's the whole *feeling* out there that isn't . . . cordial. Don't you see?

HENRY: Frankly, I don't.

ISABELLE: No . . . I don't suppose you do. But. . . . but . . . that's why I don't want to live in New Jersey.

HENRY (*Facing her across table*): You . . . you . . . don't . . . want . . . to . . . live . . . in . . . New Jersey!

ISABELLE: No, Henry, I don't.

HENRY: But that's . . . ridiculous! I've never *lived* anywhere else. I've never *considered* living anywhere else.

ISABELLE: I know, dear.

HENRY: All my family's lived there always. I was born there. Why, it's *beautiful* in New Jersey.

ISABELLE: Yes, Henry . . . but I don't like it.

HENRY: I suppose you're going to tell me Yoakum, Mississippi, is a better town than West Orange. That little dump!

ISABELLE: I never said I wanted to live in Yoakum all my life. . . . I don't boast about it.

HENRY: You don't bo. . . . Well, I should say you wouldn't. Good Lord! You come from Yoakum to West Orange. . . .

ISABELLE: From hell to heaven?

HENRY: Well, I wouldn't have said it. . . .

ISABELLE: Of course not, dear, you're too polite. (SHE *smiles at him quizzically*) Aw, listen to me, Henry. I'm not ungrateful. It was sweet of your mother to ask me to visit you all and give me those two pretty dresses. I think you're all just as nice as you can be; sweet and thoughtful and . . . and very elegant and . . . and . . . honorable and . . . and . . . (SHE *makes a hopeless gesture*) . . . but I don't want to live in New Jersey, Henry.

HENRY: Where *do* you want to live?

ISABELLE: Couldn't we have a tiny little apartment here? I've seen pictures in *House and Garden* of such cunning ones . . . with little kitchenettes and . . . and . . . built-in washtubs and things. Couldn't we afford that, Henry?

HENRY: Of course I could afford it . . . but you couldn't run it. You can't even take care of your own stuff, let alone manage a whole apartment!

ISABELLE: I could manage it.

HENRY: No, you couldn't! (HE *takes list from her pocketbook*) How about this little list of things I asked you to do yesterday?

ISABELLE: I did 'em.

HENRY: Yeah? (*Reading from list*) "Purchase six white broadcloth shirts for Henry. Size fifteen and 34 inch sleeve. . . . "

ISABELLE: I got 'em.

HENRY: Yeah . . . you got 'em! Thirty-five and a half inch sleeves so Mother had to sit up half the night shortening them . . . you can't even sew.

ISABELLE: I can embroider.

HENRY: That's practical! And another thing . . . did you go to the Insulex Office and get their booklet on heating an eight-room house all winter on a ton of coal?

ISABELLE: I don't think you can.

HENRY: Never mind what you think, did you?

ISABELLE: I . . . I forgot.

HENRY: Check! (*Checks off item*) Now did you go up and look at that lot?

ISABELLE: Uh-huh.

HENRY: Well?

ISABELLE: I don't like it.

HENRY: What are you talking about? Why, that's one of the finest lots in town. In the heart of a restricted neighborhood, near a playground . . . for the kiddies, only a block from Mother's, a block-and-a-half from the church . . . what's the matter with it?

ISABELLE: It hasn't got any trees on it.

HENRY: Good! What are trees good for, anyway—except for a lot of damned birds to roost in and wake you up at four o'clock in the morning!

ISABELLE: Oh, Henry . . .

HENRY: Besides, you'll be a lot better off near Mother, so she can show you how to manage things.

ISABELLE: I want to live here, Henry.

HENRY: I've already told you I don't like New York . . . rotten, dirty place. I want to be someplace where I can exercise and take long walks, where I've got room to *breathe*.

ISABELLE: Don't you think you could do that here? Everybody looks as if they breathe all right.

HENRY: Yeah—carbon monoxide!

ISABELLE: I don't know anything about that, but I read in a paper where people out in the country die much sooner than people in a big city.

HENRY: That's not statistics!

ISABELLE: Well, it said so in the paper. (SHE *looks away despondently*) Aw, Henry, couldn't we live here for a while anyway?

HENRY (*Disagreeably*): Well, you can live where you like . . . but *I'm* going to live in West Orange.

ISABELLE (*After a pause*): Then I will too, Henry . . . (SHE *smiles with an effort*) . . . and . . . and maybe it'll be very nice.

HENRY: You bet it will! (*Patronizingly*) Well now, that's settled! You just leave your happiness to me, and you won't have a thing to worry about.

ISABELLE: I . . . I know I won't, Henry.

HENRY (*Pompously*): That's the way to talk.

ISABELLE *rises and starts toward the bar.*

Where are you going?

ISABELLE (*Stopping*): Just over here . . . I want to put my foot on the rail.

HENRY: I think you'd better stay at the table.

ISABELLE (*Over her shoulder*): Please, Henry. Let me do a little bit what I like—till we get married.

SHE *goes to bar, putting foot on rail and laughing. Her arm hits bell accidentally.* SHE *laughs and rings bell again, then pounds twice on bar.* TOM *enters.* HENRY *rises— goes up to Victrola and starts to wind it.*

TOM: Yessir?

ISABELLE (*Pretending to be an old souse*): Gimme a drink.

TOM (*Smilingly*): Yessir, what you want?

ISABELLE: What've you got?

TOM: Baccardi, Manhattan, Bronx, Silver Fizz, Golden Fizz . . . Old-Fashioned.

ISABELLE: *Ooh!* I think I'll go back to my boyhood days and have an Old-Fashioned.

TOM: Yessir.

ISABELLE: Will you join me, Henry?

HENRY: No, thanks—I've got a Scotch. You'd better stick to crême de mint.

ISABELLE: But that just tastes like sugar water. Henry, I'd like to have something real while we're here.

HENRY: You want to get drunk, huh?

ISABELLE: Course I don't—it's only an Old-Fashioned—and old-fashioned people never got drunk—leastways, that's what I always heard.

HENRY: By the way . . . who's paying for this?

ISABELLE (*Looking in pocketbook*): Oh, I forgot, I haven't any money, Mister.

TOM: Don't you worry, young lady—no pretty girl has to go thirsty in Tom's place.

ISABELLE (*Toward* HENRY): There, Henry. You see? That's what I call friendly. Thank you, Tom, very much.

TOM: 'S all right, lady, any time.

HENRY (*Back at the Victrola*): Oh, I'll pay for it.

ISABELLE: No, Henry. (*Back at the bar*) We couldn't allow that. Could we, Tom?

TOM: Yes, mam. (HE *puts the completed drink before her*)

ISABELLE: You should say no.

TOM: Yes, mam.

ISABELLE: Well, anyway . . . here's to you, Tom. (SHE *drinks*) That was *delicious*.

TOM (*In a whisper*): You want another one?

ISABELLE: Yes.

JUDGE (*Enters, goes to bar*): Say, Tom . . . (JUDGE *sees* ISABELLE) Make me one of those too.

ISABELLE (*Feeling slightly emancipated already*): They're mostly fruit juice, anyway.

TOM (*Smiling wickedly*): Mos'ly.

HENRY (*Looks up and sees his enemy, the* JUDGE, *at the bar.* HENRY *stiffens*): Haven't you been at the bar about long enough?

ISABELLE: No, Henry—I'm having a lovely time. (SHE *sits on stool, upper end of bar*)

JUDGE (*Goes to table*): Whyn't you get wise to yourself, Henry? I'm not trying to swipe your girl.

HENRY (*Meets* JUDGE): You'd have a swell chance.

JUDGE: Well . . . well, I guess you're right. There is something about your manner that . . . ah . . . must be very fascinating . . . to some people.

HENRY: You're very quick on the repartee, aren't you?

JUDGE: No . . . not quick, Henry . . . but sincere, Henry. Come on—let's bury the hatchet—come and have a drink.

ISABELLE: Come on, Henry.

HENRY: Oh . . . all right. (THEY *cross to bar*) But we'll make this the last. (HENRY *goes to lower end of bar*)

JUDGE: Nonsense. Who's tired? Make that three, Tom . . . on my bill. What do you want to go home for? It's early.

HENRY: Well, it may be early for you, but it's pretty late out in New Jersey.

JUDGE: Why? Do they have different time out there?

HENRY: Of course not. But we live pretty far away. And we might be locked out.

JUDGE (*To* ISABELLE): Oh, do they lock you out, too?

ISABELLE: Why . . . I'm . . . living with him.

JUDGE: But you said you weren't married.

HENRY: We're not, but—

JUDGE: But you're living in the same house?

HENRY: Yes, but—

JUDGE (*In horror*): Slightly irregular—

HENRY: Not at all—not at all!

JUDGE: Now let's get this straight; you're living together in New Jersey, aren't you?

HENRY: Yes, but . . .

JUDGE: Just a minute. . . . Under the same roof?

ISABELLE: Oh, yes.

JUDGE (*Moving away slightly*): Well? There y'are. S'all right. S'none o' my business. (*Turns*) Say! You must think I'm drunk. Ha, ha, ha.

HENRY (*Coldly*): You're quite right. However, since you *will* mix into other people's affairs. . . . Listen carefully: This young lady is engaged to marry me. She is living with my parents in West Orange, New Jersey. Is that clear?

JUDGE (*Bowing low to* ISABELLE): I beg your pardon . . . a thousand times.

ISABELLE: That's all right.

JUDGE (*Turns to* HENRY): And whom are *you* living with?

HENRY (*Somewhat startled*): Why, I live with them too. Naturally.

JUDGE: What do you mean, naturally? I don't live with my parents. Tom, here, doesn't live with his parents. The young lady don't live with her parents. (*To* HENRY) Why should *you* live with *your* parents?

HENRY: Well, I do.

JUDGE: Very suspicious. (*To himself*) Very suspicious.

HENRY: Time we were home.

JUDGE (*To* HENRY): Say, Henry, how is everything out there? Huh? How're the crops?

HENRY: The what?

JUDGE (*Sits on edge of a table*): The waving wheat fields—the waving onion fields, all the little radishes—and things like that. *Say!* What do you want to live in a place like that for, anyway? S'terrible!

ISABELLE: That's just what I was saying.

JUDGE: Whassa name?

ISABELLE: West Orange.

JUDGE: Wes' Orange. S'awful. (HE *mimics*) Where d'ya live? I live in Wes' Orange. Where's that? Why, it's just beyond South Banana before y' get to Eas' Pineapple. Nothin' but fruit stands. All Greeks.

HENRY: Yeah? Well, it was good enough for the men who fought the Revolution.

JUDGE: Certainly it was good enough for 'em. Anybody'd start a revolution if he lived in Pineapple, New Jersey. I'd start one myself—throw fruit at everybody— that's what I'd do. Say, now I'm beginning to understand, he's a revolutionist— dangerous character. You want to be very careful of a man with whiskers.

ISABELLE (*Laughing*): But Henry hasn't got any whiskers.

JUDGE: Oh, yes, he has, he's fooling you. Shaved 'em off. Probably got a pocketful of bombs. (*Picks up drink at bar*) Well, here's to a merry life in West Orange— New Jersey!

Bell off rings. JUDGE *sits.*

HENRY (*Starting to table*): We'd better get started.

ISABELLE (*Crosses to mirror*): Please, not yet, Henry. I'm having a beautiful time.

HENRY: You know the family will expect us to go to church in the morning.

ISABELLE: Oh, yes—I'd forgotten . . . still, let's stay a little bit longer.

HENRY: Well, make up your mind. A few moments ago you said you wanted to leave.

ISABELLE: That was when you were cross. But now I'd like to stay. Sometimes you're very sweet, Henry.

GIOVANNI (*Off*): Buona sera, Signor Conte.

HENRY: That's more like it. (*Goes up to slot machine*)

GUS: Buona sera. (AUGUSTINO CARAFFA, *Count of Ruvo, appears in arch. The sound of the gate closing is heard*) Good evening.

MARIO *appears in arch, takes* GUS's *coat and muffler,* ISABELLE *is at mirror and sees* GUS. HENRY *starts to play slot machine at intervals throughout scene. On* GUS's *entrance* HE *looks over shoulder at him.* TOM *crosses to welcome* GUS.

TOM: Oh! Eccellenza . . . *cosi tardi!*
[So late!]

(HE *looks at his watch and holds out his arms in a supplicating gesture*)

E le raccomandazioni della Signora Contessa? Cosa posso scrivere alla Signora Contessa. . . . *Bugie!*
[And the reports to the Countess? What can I write to the Countess. . . . Lies!]

GUS (*To* TOM, *placatingly*): Andiamo, Tomaso! (HE *points to his own watch*) Non é ancora mezzanotte!
[It's not midnight anymore]

TOM (*Grumbling*): E . . . ma . . . peró. . . .
[But . . . but. . . .]

GUS (*Holding up his hand*): Oh, falla finita.
[Oh, just stop it]

JUDGE: What's the matter?

GUS: It appears, my dear Judge, that I am very wicked . . . because I stay out too late.

JUDGE (*Looking at his own watch*): Well . . . I think he's right.

GUS: What!

JUDGE (*Puzzled,* HE *looks at the watch again, then listens to it.* HE *starts to wind it*): Well, I think he's right anyway.

GUS: This is a conspiracy. . . . You're all against me. How are you, Judge?

JUDGE: Never felt better in my life—I'm on the wagon. Not drinking anything except a few Old-Fashioneds.

GUS: Oh—just a few lemonades. (HE *turns again to* TOM) Tomaso, did any letters come for me?

TOM (*Crossly*): No, Eccellenza . . . but a call from Miss Lilli—and some packages. . . . *No buy* so much. Spenda too mucha money! (TOM *exits*)

GUS (*To the* JUDGE): Maybe my old Tomaso will forgive me when he sees what I have in the packages.

JUDGE: Why? What did you get?

GUS: Some surprises for him.

TOM (*Entering*): Here are the packages for you. (HE *carries two packages, placing them on a table*)

GUS (*Crossing to* TOM): Not for me, Tomaso, but for you.

TOM (*Opens packages*): Come?

GUS: Yes! For you, old brontolone. (*Gives stick and hat to* MARIO, *who exits up steps with them*)

TOM (*Pointing to himself and smiling*): For me?

GUS: Yes. And never again let me hear you complain about your rheumatism.

TOM (*Opens box with violet ray lamp. Puzzled,* HE *picks it up*): Cos' é questo? [What is it]

JUDGE: What's that?

GUS (*Taking lamp from* TOM): You shine it so . . . (HE *demonstrates on* TOM) . . . where it hurts . . . and then it doesn't hurt any more.

ISABELLE *drifts toward table.*

TOM (*Beaming*): Oh . . . grazie, Eccellenze, ma perche spenda so mucha money per me?

GUS: Never mind that . . . now look in the other box. (*Toward* JUDGE *slightly*) Now watch him . . . he will be like a cat with a . . . catnips.

TOM (*Opens box and discovers it is full of India Figs, a sort of cactus*): Ah! *Santo Dio!* . . . *Fichi D'India!* (*Displays them to* JUDGE) You—you like to eat some with me?

JUDGE: What—a cactus? Never!

TOM (HE *licks his lips greedily*): Good! I go eat 'em right away to your health, Eccellenza.

TOM *exits.* GUS *goes to door, watching him.* ISABELLE *is near table.*

GUS: Yes, but think of *your* health, and don't eat them too much. Funny old man . . .

HENRY *goes up to arch and gets change from* GIOVANNI.

. . . but very nice. Now we are friends again.

JUDGE (*Rising*): Gus, I want you to meet a very old friend of mine. This charming little lady is Miss . . . ah . . . Miss . . . what's your name?

GUS *looks at* ISABELLE *and starts toward her slowly.*

ISABELLE: Isabelle . . . Isabelle Parry.

JUDGE: Of course, Miss Isabelle Parry. The flower of the South, Gus. Miss Parry, the Count Di Ruvo. (JUDGE *goes behind bar*)

GUS (*Facing* ISABELLE): How do you do, Miss Parry. (HE *bows low*)

ISABELLE (*Looking intently as if trying to place him*): How do you do?

GUS (*Turning to* JUDGE): Judge, this is most unkind of you.

HENRY *returns to slot machine.*

JUDGE: Huh?

GUS: I mean, a true friend, as you pretend to be, would not have kept anyone so charming and beautiful all for himself. It was very selfish of you not to give me this great pleasure before.

JUDGE: I want you to meet her fortunate escort, Mr.—ah—Henry.

GUS: Oh, how do you do?

ISABELLE: Oh, Henry.

GUS: Not my favorite author, O. Henry?

HENRY: I'm not an author and my name is Greene. How do you do?

GUS: I am well, thank you.

HENRY *exits to hall, speaks to* GIOVANNI, *then exits.*

JUDGE (*Back of bar*): Have a drink, Gus.

GUS (*Crossing*): Since when have you taken up bartending, Judge? The Bar Association should see you now.

JUDGE: *Sh!* don't remind me of my duties.

ISABELLE *and* HENRY *look at him in astonishment.*

You'll spoil the evening.

ISABELLE: Are you a *real* judge?

GUS: Why, certainly—

JUDGE: Certainly not, my dear, certainly not. That's only the courtesy title. I'm a . . . I'm . . . a . . . a . . . judge at the dogshow.

ISABELLE (*Sits at table*): But you said—

GUS: Oh—but, Miss Parry—didn't you know? He's a famous expert—the world famous expert on Pekinese—oh, he *loves* dogs!

JUDGE (*Coming from behind bar*): Yessir! You can't fool me on a Pekinese—or a bulldog—or a collie—or a—

GUS: Or a schnauzer.

JUDGE: What's that?

GUS: Schnauzer.

JUDGE: What?

GUS: Well, make it a spitz then.

JUDGE: Make it yourself!

GUS: I mean, Judge, there is a dog also called the spitz.

JUDGE: Is that so! Well, the way these new dogs spring up overnight! They don't give you time to brush up on the old ones. (*As* JUDGE *goes to bar*) Anyway, I know my Pekinese.

Telephone rings.

GUS: I think we should offer a toast to such an expert and to our beautiful guest.

Telephone rings again. TOM *enters.*

Tomaso must find some champagne to celebrate the presence here of—someone so lovely. And some Italian chocolates.

MARIO *enters and goes to phone.*

TOM (*As* HE *exits*): Subito, Eccellenza—I go downstairs.

MARIO (*At phone*): Allo—yes—one minute, please. (*Crosses to* GUS)

GUS (*To* ISABELLE): Do you like some champagne, Miss Parry?

ISABELLE: I've never had any.

GUS: You've never had any!

MARIO: Eccellenza la Signorina Lilli al telephone.

Angrily, GUS *goes to telephone and* MARIO *exits.*

GUS (*At telephone*): Hello—Hello—Who?—Oh, hello, Lilli—Not just now—I am in conference—No, don't come—I explain to you tomorrow—all right, I call you back in half an hour—good-bye.

HE *hangs up.* ISABELLE *rises.*

ISABELLE: But, Mister Count—

GUS (*Coming to her*): Di Ruvo.

ISABELLE: I know I've seen you before—it was recently. I'm sure we've met—I wonder where it was.

GUS: No, Miss Parry. I'm sorry to say we have not met. I wish we had.

ISABELLE: Thank you. But I know I've seen you—

JUDGE: I guess it was in the Lucky Strike advertisement.

ISABELLE: The Lucky—? Of course—that was it.

GUS: Such is fame.

HENRY *appears in arch.*

But we've never met. If we had—how could I have forgotten?

TOM *enters.* ISABELLE *goes to her table.* TOM *goes to other table and places champagne there.*

TOM: Here is the champagne.

ISABELLE (*Seeing* HENRY *in mirror as he comes to the table*): Henry, you've seen those Lucky Strike advertisements.

HENRY: I don't like that guy! (HE *sits*)

GUS (*Toward* ISABELLE *with box of chocolates*): Will you have some Italian chocolates, Miss Parry?

ISABELLE: Thank you.

TOM: There! One bottle of happiness! It turns your tears into laughter—makes you forget all your troubles. The sunshine of Italy in a bottle of Cinzano.

TOM *takes glass to* HENRY. GUS *goes up to tray and takes a glass for himself and* ISABELLE. JUDGE *gets glass of champagne and returns to bar.*

JUDGE: Let's have some music, Tom—something romantic.

TOM: Sure, Judge—what do you want—something hot?

JUDGE: Play a love song.

TOM (*At phonograph*): Sure.

ISABELLE: Are you romantic, Judge?

GUS (*Giving* ISABELLE *her champagne*): How could he help to be—this evening.

ISABELLE *sits. Phonograph starts and plays "La Maison Blanche" from Manon.*

ISABELLE: That sounds like Caraffa. It is Caraffa, isn't it?

GUS: Yes. . . . I think so. How do you like the chocolates?

HENRY: That's a good phonograph.

ISABELLE (*Closing her eyes*): What a heavenly voice. There's nobody else like him.

JUDGE: So you have heard him?

ISABELLE: Oh, yes, I've been to the Metropolitan three times to hear him sing.

GUS: Did you like him?

ISABELLE: He was marvelous. It was such a thrill! Of course I couldn't see him very well from where I sat . . . (SHE *points to the ceiling*) . . . but they say . . .

GUS: Perhaps it is just as well you couldn't see him . . . so you can keep your illusions. Most of the singers are a little . . . débordant. Only the birds can sing . . . and keep their shape.

THEY *all listen in silence till the record ends.*

TOM (*Stands lost in the music, comes to with a start and shuts off the machine. Then* HE *turns and speaks to* GUS *with pride*): Ah, my little Signorino, how you sing! I could listen to you all night. (*To* ISABELLE) He's some singer, huh?

ISABELLE (*Dumbfounded.* SHE *stares at* GUS): You! . . . But that's Caraffa!

GUS (*Giving* TOM *a dirty look*): Yes.

JUDGE: Oh, yes, he sings a little . . . when he isn't posing for Luckies. (HE *smiles sardonically at* HENRY)

ISABELLE (*Still staring fascinatedly at* GUS): But I thought you said Caraffa . . .

GUS (*Very quietly*): I am Tino Caraffa. That is my stage name.

ISABELLE (*Rises*): You! How wonderful!

GUS (*Slightly embarrassed*): Thank you very much. . . . May I give you a little more champagne?

ISABELLE (*Still in the land of dreams*): If you please.

GUS (*Serving her champagne*): Have you still . . . some illusions?

ISABELLE: More than ever.

HENRY (*Who has not been enjoying this*): Don't drink too much of that stuff, Isabelle.

GUS *puts glass on table.*

JUDGE (*In mock surprise*): Oh, there you are, Henry!

Bell rings.

I thought you were lost.

HENRY (*With meaning*): I stick around pretty well.

JUDGE: Yes. . . .

GUS: Put on some jazz, Tom.

TOM: Si, Signor Conte—right away—

GIOVANNI *enters from hall and beckons to* TOM.

GIOVANNI: Signor Tomaso—

TOM *and* GIOVANNI *exit.*

ISABELLE (*To* GUS): I didn't know opera singers liked jazz.

GUS: Why, it's new, interesting, courageous! I think young people should like jazz.

JUDGE: How about old people who like it?

GUS: It shows they're still young, Judge.

HENRY: Yeah? Well, how about young people who *don't* like jazz?

GUS: The conclusion is obvious, Mr. Greene.

HENRY: Is that so! Well, let me tell you . . .

TOM (*Entering*): Excuse me—Nobody here got a car outside with a Jersey license, have they?

ISABELLE *puts drink on table.*

HENRY: I have. What about it?

TOM: The policeman outside wants to see you.

JUDGE (*Steps forward slightly*): Perhaps if I . . .

HENRY (*Rising*): I can manage all right, thank you. (*To* TOM) How much do I owe you?

TOM: Two Scotch—one-fifty, one benedictine fifty cents—altogether two dollars.

HENRY: You mean to say you charge seventy-five cents for that lousy Scotch?

JUDGE: That's all right, Tom—this is my party.

HENRY: Here you are. (*Hands* TOM *a bill*) Leave the change on the table.

HENRY *goes into hall and gets his hat.* TOM *puts change on table.*

HENRY: Come on, Isabelle.

ISABELLE: Oh, please, let's stay a little longer, Henry. I'm having such a nice time. See if you can fix it up with the—

JUDGE: If you'll allow me to say a word to the policeman . . .

HENRY: I don't need *any help* . . . from you.

JUDGE: But I think if I spoke to—

HENRY: There's nothing you could do, I couldn't do.

JUDGE: This isn't West Orange, you know.

HENRY (*Picking up his change*): I'll say it isn't. Come on, Isabelle!

ISABELLE (*Coaxingly*): Oh, Henry, please! Just a little . . . (*Then, seeing that* HE *is adamant,* SHE *shrugs and begins slowly to gather her things*)

The bell rings violently three times. Someone bangs the gate.

TOM: You better hurry, Mister. I think Mulligan is getting mad.

HENRY: To hell with that guy!

ISABELLE: You'd better go, Henry!

HENRY (*Looks furiously at* ISABELLE *who is still taking her time*): All right. . . . But I'm coming right back. And then we're going home. Do you understand?

HE *stalks out—followed by* TOM. *There is an embarrassed silence.*

ISABELLE (*Looks at the two men pleadingly.* SHE *is ashamed*): He isn't . . . always that
   way.

GUS (*Consolingly*): Of course not, my dear. We understand.

JUDGE (*Returns to bar*): A charming fellow . . . at heart.

ISABELLE: Oh, yes, he really is, but—

   TOM *enters in arch.*

TOM: They're having a lovely argument. The car is sitting in front of a . . . water
   faucet. (HE *exits at once*)

ISABELLE (*Goes up to arch*): Perhaps we could help.

JUDGE: He said he didn't need any help. He's so sure of himself. Aw, he'll get out
   of it all right.

ISABELLE (*Returning to table for cape and bag*): Good-bye! It's been mighty nice to
   meet you both. I never met anybody famous before—I thought it would be
   different—

GUS: But why?

ISABELLE: Oh, I don't know. I thought a famous person would be very grand . . .
   and . . . and . . . but you're just . . . like the people I like.

GUS: I am very glad you like such people . . . because I . . . like you. . . . very much.

ISABELLE: Thank you.

GUS (*Crossing to phonograph*): Do you think we could dance once before you go?
   Or would Mr. Henry object?

JUDGE: Oh, Henry would be delighted.

ISABELLE: Well, Henry's outside . . . he isn't here . . . and I'd like to dance with you.

GUS: Will you then?

   SHE *nods.* HE *starts phonograph.* THEY *meet and dance.*

JUDGE (*As* HE *exits*): Playing with dynamite—playing with dynamite.

GUS: You are very lovely!

ISABELLE: You shouldn't say that.

GUS: Why not?

ISABELLE: Because it isn't true.

GUS: But aren't you beautiful?

ISABELLE: No.

GUS: Very well. (HE *laughs*) I . . . I love to dance with you, because you are very
   ugly. Is that better?

ISABELLE: I'm not so terribly ugly.

GUS (*In feigned astonishment*): Aren't you?

ISABELLE: No. . . . I'll get by.

GUS: Really!

ISABELLE: Oh, yes. But I'm not beautiful.

GUS: To me, Miss Parry, you are more beautiful than . . . than . . .

ISABELLE: Than what?

GUS: Than I could ever imagine anyone to be.

ISABELLE: You shouldn't say that to me.

GUS: You are right. I shouldn't.

ISABELLE: And I ought not to like to hear it.

GUS: No.

ISABELLE: But I do. (THEY *both laugh*) Aren't we wicked? (SHE *trips and hurts her ankle*) Oh! (SHE *looks down at it*)

GUS: Oh, my dear, did you hurt yourself?

ISABELLE: It's all right.

GUS: We must not let anything happen to something . . . so adorable. (HE *is kneeling; kisses his fingertips and touches them to her ankle*) There. Now, it is well again.

ISABELLE: I think you are a very bad man.

GUS: I? A bad man? But why?

ISABELLE: Well . . .

GUS: Do you really dislike me?

ISABELLE: I . . . I don't know. (SHE *tries to walk; ankle causes her to limp slightly*) Oh—

GUS: It still hurts? I'm so sorry (*Gets a chair from table*)

ISABELLE (*Sitting in chair*): I think if I take my weight off—it'll be all right.

GUS (*Beside* ISABELLE): There. (*Pause*)

ISABELLE: Who is Lilli?

GUS: Who?

ISABELLE: Lilli—the girl you spoke to on the telephone. Is she a singer?

GUS: No . . . no . . . she's a cousin of mine. (HE *laughs*) How observing you are! Was your papa on the police force? A detective, maybe?

ISABELLE: No, no—Papa never did any work. Work irritated him terribly.

GUS: But how did you live?

ISABELLE: Plantation. Cotton, you know.

GUS: Oh, yes—I know. I sing some plantation songs.

ISABELLE: They're pretty, aren't they?

GUS: Beautiful.

ISABELLE: I love to hear darkies sing 'em at night. Funny people! Don't have anything . . . never did have anything . . . never will have anything. And just as happy. . . . You ever been to Mississippi?

GUS: Where?

ISABELLE: Mississippi.

GUS: Mississippi?

ISABELLE: Yes.

GUS: Is that near Buffalo?

ISABELLE: You've never been there. We used to have a nice place. And then, just when cotton got high, women stopped wearing underwear.

GUS: Did women wear cotton underwear?

ISABELLE: Silk underwear is immoral. That's what Papa always said. He tried to get us all to wear cotton stockings, too, but we wouldn't do it.

GUS: I don't blame you. . . . Ah—were you a large family?

ISABELLE: No, just an ordinary family—four boys and seven girls.

GUS: Salute!

ISABELLE: Oh, that isn't big. Down home when they raise families, they raise *families*.

GUS: And how!

ISABELLE: Well, they don't have much else to do.

GUS: And you are the most beautiful of the seven Parry sisters.

ISABELLE: Oh, no—they're all better looking—except one. One is uglier than me.

> HENRY *and* GIOVANNI's *voices are heard in altercation off.* ISABELLE *rises, goes to table and picks up bag.*

But Mother is more beautiful than any of them.

> HENRY *rushes into room, followed by* TOM *and* GIOVANNI. *Door in hall left open.* GIOVANNI *remains in arch, leaning against it. Gate is heard to slam.* JUDGE *enters and goes behind bar, sitting on stool and watching fight progress.*

HENRY: Just what I thought. A grafting cop sees a New Jersey car parked near a hydrant, so he pushes it up in front of it, and then works a little blackmail.

JUDGE: How do you know he pushed it?

HENRY: Because I know he did! (*To* ISABELLE) And you want me to live in this rotten town! Come on, let's get out of here!

TOM: You like to stay and dance before you go?

HENRY: No! Who wants to dance?

TOM: The young lady—she dances good.

HENRY: What! (*No reply*) What!

GUS (*To* TOM, *reprehensively*): Tomaso!

HENRY: Oh! So that's what you do the minute my back's turned?

ISABELLE: Please, Henry. . . .

HENRY: That's why you wanted me to go out, huh? So you could make a fool out of me. . . .

GUS: But, Mr. Henry—we only—

HENRY (*Looking her up and down*): What a fine wife you'd make!

ISABELLE: But, Henry! I didn't do anything.

HENRY (*Sneering*): Oh, no. Maybe it isn't anything where *you* come from. But the women in *my* family don't pick up with the drunken bums they meet in a speakeasy.

ISABELLE (*Aghast*): Henry . . . please!

> MARIO *appears in arch.*

HENRY: You heard me. It's a good thing I wasn't gone longer. What do you *mean* by dancing with that lousy wop?

> MARIO *and* GIOVANNI *move forward angrily, talking in Italian.*

GUS (*Jumping to his feet*): You—

ISABELLE (*Turning to* GUS *and the* JUDGE *with a helpless gesture*): I'm . . . I'm sorry.

GUS (*Bowing to* ISABELLE): It's perfectly all right. (*Then to* MARIO *and* GIOVANNI *who are talking angrily*) No, no, ragazzi. That was for me. (HE *waves them back*)

HENRY: Yeah, that was for you, you dago!

> HENRY *starts to cross and bumps against a chair.* HE *falls to his hands and knees.* MARIO *and* GIOVANNI *laugh loudly.* HENRY *is beside himself.*

Shut up! You rats.

> ISABELLE *intervenes, coming between them.*

GUS (*Perfectly calm*): Why not address your remarks to me?—Mr.—Greene!

HENRY: Did you think you weren't included? What I say goes for everybody.

GUS: Splendid!

HENRY: Yes . . . you're very brave, aren't you?

GUS: No . . . not unusually so.

HENRY: I'll say you're not!

GUS: You say so.

HENRY: YES! And I'll tell you something else, you greaser!

GUS: Continue, please . . . don't hesitate.

HENRY (*Advances menacingly. Then* HE *looks back at* MARIO *and* GIOVANNI *and hesitates*): If there weren't so many dagoes around here to stick knives in my back, I'd give you something to remember me by.

> MARIO *and* GIOVANNI *threaten* HENRY.

GUS: One moment, Mr. Greene. (HE *turns to* TOM) Tomaso, porta via i ragazzi— [Take off, guys]

> MARIO *and* GIOVANNI *exit, followed by* TOM.

You see? . . . Now, Mr. Greene, I am at your service—you have only *one* dago— to face.

HENRY: Yeah! I'm apt to trust you and your gangster friends.

> ISABELLE *goes to table.*

Come on. Get your things and get out of here.

> ISABELLE *looks around helplessly, then begins to gather her things very slowly.*

(*Savagely*) Do you hear me?

> HE *goes to leave and turns.* ISABELLE *clenches her fists and doesn't move.*

DO YOU HEAR ME? Get your stuff together and come on or, by God, I'll . . .

ISABELLE: You'll what?

HENRY (*Toward her*): I'll teach you to behave like a little tart!

ISABELLE (*Furious*): You'll WHAT?

HENRY: You heard me. I'll give you one more chance. Now, snap into it or you can stay—for good!

ISABELLE *puts bag on table defiantly.*

(*Somewhat less blusteringly*) You—you know what this means?
ISABELLE: Perfectly.
HENRY: If you don't come now . . .
ISABELLE: I understand.
HENRY: I . . . won't come back. . . .
ISABELLE: I know everything you're thinking; that I have no money . . . to go home . . . and that . . . that my mother . . . hasn't any to send me. It's all right. I'm glad. I'll . . . manage without you. Now . . . (SHE *takes off her engagement ring*) . . . take your ring. (*Crosses to* HENRY, *hands him ring*) TAKE IT, I SAY!

Dazedly, HE *does so.*

HENRY: Now, wait a minute.
ISABELLE (*Working herself into a frenzy*): Now, go back to *West Orange* . . . and tell them about me. That I wasn't good enough for you. And while you're at it, you can tell them I'd rather scrub floors than be married to such a . . . such a . . . GENTLEMAN.
HENRY: Yes, and it would suit you better too. You and all the other lazy white trash like you.

HE *strides to the door and exits.*

ISABELLE: Thank you, Henry.

The iron gate clangs.

Well . . . now I've done it. (SHE *starts to laugh hysterically. Turns back to audience*)
GUS (*Rushes to her side*): I'm very sorry—Miss Parry—I feel so guilty about this.
TOM (*Coming in*): Nice fella. (*Straightens chair and table and exits*)
JUDGE (*Rises and stands behind bar*): Everything will blow over. Things like that always do. Don't be unhappy.
ISABELLE (*Facing front*): Who's unhappy? (SHE *breaks into a peal of laughter*)
JUDGE: There, there.

SHE *continues to laugh.*

Now, now.

Still, SHE *laughs.*

Everything will be all right.
GUS: We must make it all right.
ISABELLE: Everything *is* all right. Hooray! (*Crosses to bar*) Oh, Lordy, give me a drink!

JUDGE *serves her with a soft drink.*

Do you know, there's been something the matter with me for months, and I've just this minute found out what it was.

GUS: What was it?

ISABELLE: It was Henry! Entirely too much Henry. And that family in West Orange. Oh, Lordy, give me another drink.

GUS: Please don't drink too much.

JUDGE (*Displaying soft drink*): It's all right.

GUS: I'm afraid we've made you a lot of trouble, Isabelle.

ISABELLE: Trouble? You darling—you've saved me from trouble—and a lifetime of boredom. I thank you.

SHE *kisses* JUDGE *as* GIOVANNI *and* MARIO *appear in arch, dressed for street.*

MARIO: Good night. That fellow no mean any harm.

GIOVANNI: After all, he's not a bad fellow.

MARIO (*As* HE *exits*): Buona notte ragazzi.

[Good night guys]

GIOVANNI (*As* HE *exits*): Buona notte.

ISABELLE: Good night.

The gate clangs.

Now, that's what I call friendliness. Like we have down home. The darkies say: "How do, Miss Isabelle, this sholy is a pow'ful fine day." It don't mean anything, but it sounds nice.

JUDGE: I think we can easily arrange to send you home.

GUS (*Crossing to her*): But, not right away—I hope. We must talk these things over. I cannot lose you so soon. (*Is now at bar*)

ISABELLE (*Crossing to table in front of* GUS): He seemed so different from everybody down there that I thought he was different than they were. And I just this minute woke up. They were lazy and he was industrious. They liked to make love, gamble and likker up. Oh, they were bad all right and compared to them he was upright and honorable. But I guess honor isn't everything—do you think so, Judge?

JUDGE: Well, now, let me see. Speaking ex officio, I should say that honor . . . or righteousness . . . should be tempered with the milk of human kindness— that is if you can temper anything with milk. But I think too much honor is apt to curdle the milk.

TOM (*Enters*): That fella come back. He wanta talk to you. I no let him in.

ISABELLE (*To* JUDGE *and* GUS): Shall I talk to him?

GUS: Do you want to?

ISABELLE (*To* TOM, *with great finality*): Tell him to go away.

SHE *leans on a chair and smiles triumphantly at her companions.* TOM *exits.*

JUDGE (*Sits on stool behind bar, back to audience*): Cruel woman.

ISABELLE: Tell me I was right, Gus.

GUS: I am afraid that I could not give an honest opinion. I want so much for you to stay. . . .

ISABELLE (*Looking at him sweetly*): Oh!

GUS: Yes.

ISABELLE: That's nice of you to say so.

GUS: I would not say so if it were not true.

ISABELLE: Do you always tell the truth?

GUS: Well—nearly always.

ISABELLE: I wonder.

TOM (*Reappearing in arch*): He's mad as hell. I tell him to go away. He say: No . . . he stay. I say: All right, good night. He say: Listen, you wop, you, I break down the door. I say: I ain't no wop, go ahead and try. He say: All right, then, you dago, I go get an officer and make you all arrest for a-kidnap the young lady. So I say: I ain't no dago, I'm Siciliano and I poosh the door in his face. That's what I do! (HE *exits*)

ISABELLE (*Running to bar*): Do you suppose Henry will get an officer?

GUS: Now, Judge, we're in your hands.

TOM (*Appears in arch*): He's out there with Mulligan the cop. Mulligan says what's goin' on here. What'll I do, Judge?

JUDGE (*Rises*): Just a minute. (HE *thinks, then speaks to the other two*) Gus, you take Isabelle in the dining room, and keep quiet.

THEY *rise, and exit.* SHE *takes all her things.*

Now, Tom, bring Mulligan in here, but leave the young man outside. If he asks you why, tell him he isn't a member of this club. (*Puts bottle of Scotch and two glasses on bar, then comes front of bar*)

TOM (*As* HE *exits*): All right, Judge.

MULLIGAN *appears in arch.* TOM *follows, standing next to him.*

MULLIGAN: Where is she?

TOM: Who?

MULLIGAN: The young lady.

TOM: No lady come to my speakeasy.

MULLIGAN: Don't use that word! How many times do I have to tell you I don't know what this place is?

TOM: I'll tell you.

MULLIGAN: Shut up! Now, where is she?

TOM: I don't know.

JUDGE (*Turns*): Officer! What are you doing in a speakeasy?

MULLIGAN: Well, bless my soul, if it isn't my old friend Judge Dempsey. Shure, your honor, I'm here in pursuance of my duty.

TOM *exits to hall.* JUDGE *starts toward* MULLIGAN.

JUDGE: And what duty are you pursuing?

MULLIGAN: I'm pursuin' a kidnapper, your honor.

JUDGE: Are you sure, now, that you're not pursuing an alcoholic beverage?

MULLIGAN: Shure, Judge, my tongue is hangin' out a foot, but I'm on the trail of a dangerous kidnapper.

JUDGE: A dangerous kidnapper, huh? My, what a wicked world. And who is this kidnapper?

MULLIGAN (*Toward* JUDGE, *slightly*): Ther're two of thim, your honor. One of thim is a young Eyetalian, and the other one is an old, broken-down barfly, a regular bum.

JUDGE (*Starting*): Huh?

MULLIGAN: That's what the other fellow said. And they've stolen a girl!

JUDGE (*Slightly vexed*): Huh! Is that so? And where did you get this information?

MULLIGAN: The young fellow who lost the girl is outside. Shall I bring him in?

JUDGE: Don't bother. He's outside, huh? Well, well. And why does he suspect that the damsel is secreted in this establishment?

MULLIGAN (*Puzzled*): Yes—indade—to be sure.

JUDGE: I'm asking you: Why does he think the girl is here?

MULLIGAN: Oh! He says he lost her here. He was here earlier in the evening.

JUDGE (*Puzzled*): Oh, he was!

MULLIGAN: Yeah!

JUDGE: What does he look like? Was he a tall man, with a beard?

MULLIGAN: No, your honor, he's clean shaven.

JUDGE: With a broken nose?

MULLIGAN: No, not atall, he wears glasses.

JUDGE (*Thinking hard*): With glasses, huh? . . . Oh! *That* fellow—that Orangeman.

MULLIGAN: That what?

JUDGE: That Orangeman!

MULLIGAN (*Stiffening*): Oh, is he, now?

JUDGE: Oh, yes. He was talking about it all the time he was in here.

MULLIGAN: And I thought he was a dacent young fella.

JUDGE: You never can tell.

MULLIGAN: That's a fact. (HE *eyes the bottle surreptitiously*)

JUDGE (*Crosses to bar*): Would you like a little drink, Mulligan?

MULLIGAN: Shure, your honor, an' me tongue is like blottin' paper, but I never touch a drop whilst pursuin' a criminal.

JUDGE: And a very good rule, too. How about a little ginger ale, out of a non-refillable bottle? That's what I'm having.

MULLIGAN (*Crosses to bar—eyeing the bottle*): Oh, ginger ale! With pleasure, your honor.

The JUDGE *pours two stiff drinks.*

Well, here's to Prohibition, sor: a noble law.

JUDGE: Experiment.

MULLIGAN: Whatever it is.

THEY *drink.*

And what a wonderful improvement they've made in these soft drinks since the law went in.

JUDGE: That's progress for you.

MULLIGAN (HE *thinks a second, then scowls*): An Orangeman, huh? And makin' all that trouble. (HE *pounds on the bar*) They *always* make trouble.

JUDGE (*Tapping his forehead*): I think he's crazy.

MULLIGAN: Naturally, your honor.

JUDGE: He was a terrible nuisance in here, always losing things.

MULLIGAN: Besides the girl, what else did he lose?

JUDGE: Well . . . well, first, he lost a dog.

MULLIGAN: You're sure it wasn't a horse?

JUDGE: No, it was a dog! That's what he said, and we believed him.

MULLIGAN: Never believe an Orangeman.

JUDGE: Of course not. But we didn't know he was one then.

MULLIGAN: I'll bet there wasn't any dog.

JUDGE: That's what I suspect.

MULLIGAN: Just a liar.

JUDGE (*Starts to arch, slightly*): Yes, and when he came back from the street *he told* such a *story,* such a pre*posterous,* ri*diculous,* unbe*lievable* story, that we *knew* he was a liar. (*Comes back to* MULLIGAN)

MULLIGAN: What did he say?

JUDGE: *He said . . .* Well, he said, the *officer* on this *beat . . .*

MULLIGAN (*Thinks this over. Suddenly* HE *frowns*): HUH!

JUDGE: Yes, the officer on this beat had deliberately, and with malice aforethought, pushed his car—

MULLIGAN: Pushed his car—

JUDGE: In front of a municipal hydrant.

MULLIGAN: With malice aforethought—

JUDGE: And then—you won't believe your ears, Mulligan—had tried to extract from him a certain amount of United States currency, in other words, held him up for a bribe—not to arrest him.

MULLIGAN: Oh, he said that, did he? Well, he'll be lucky this night if he doesn't lose some of his teeth!

JUDGE: Of course, after that, we didn't believe anything he said.

Bell and pounding heard off. Also HENRY's *voice.*

MULLIGAN: I think I hear a disturbance on the public highway. (HE *starts toward arch*) Some drunk, no doubt. Perhaps a few hours in the cooler. Well, good night, sir, and many thanks for the ginger ale.

JUDGE: Don't mention it. Oh—and Mulligan!

MARIO: Yes, sir?

JUDGE: Observe the law!

MULLIGAN: To the letter, your honor. (*Starts off, stops*)

JUDGE (*Crossing to* MULLIGAN): You go ahead—but I'm coming right out to see that no murders are committed.

MULLIGAN: All right. But you could trust me to do the right thing.

JUDGE: That's just what I'm afraid of. And Mulligan!

> MULLIGAN *stops.*

Don't use that stick!

MULLIGAN: Only in case of a tie.

> HE *exits. Gate is heard closing.* JUDGE *calls off.*

JUDGE: Gus! Isabelle! It's all right. Come on back.

> THEY *enter.*

ISABELLE: What's happened?

GUS: I am sorry to have made such complications.

ISABELLE: Are we to be arrested?

JUDGE: I don't think so. In fact, I think by now Henry has probably changed his mind. Almost certainly has changed his mind.

ISABELLE: I guess he's cooled off.

JUDGE: I think Mulligan did say something about the cooler—(*Goes to arch*)

ISABELLE: The what?

JUDGE: Nothing—nothing. But I'll just go out and see that Mulligan doesn't get too excited.

ISABELLE: I'm sorry to be such a nuisance.

JUDGE (*As* HE *exits*): It's no nuisance—it's a pleasure.

GUS (*To* ISABELLE): Isabelle—may I call you Isabelle?

> SHE *turns and faces* GUS.

ISABELLE: Uh-huh.

GUS: Can you possibly forgive me? I'm terribly sorry for you, but very happy for me. To think—you are alone—with me. Do you know that you are adorable?

ISABELLE: Am I?

GUS (*Very passionately*): Yes.

> HE *kisses her.* SHE *fights a little, but not much.*

I am mad about you.

ISABELLE: You're very convincing.

GUS: But, now, where are you going for tonight?

ISABELLE (*Moving away*): I . . . I don't know.

GUS (*Follows her*): You must . . . stay here.

ISABELLE: Huh?

GUS: With me.

ISABELLE (*Looking into his eyes*): What do you mean?

GUS (*Slightly ill at ease, looks away*): I mean, I . . . I hope you will accept my hospitality—until you find what you wish to do.

ISABELLE: For tonight?

GUS: For so long as you will honor me as my guest.

ISABELLE (*Very slowly*): But . . . have you room for me?

GUS: Certainly! In my living room is a divan so comfortable . . . so embracing—so soft—it longs for somebody to repose on it.

ISABELLE: Somebody like me?

GUS: Nobody else, Isabelle.

ISABELLE: But I don't want to be any more bother.

GUS: You—bother? Sweet child—will you be my guest?

Gate is heard off. Then JUDGE *enters through arch, speaking as he comes.*

JUDGE: Well, Mulligan pointed things out to Henry very clearly. And now, young lady, to find a place for you.

ISABELLE: Well, he just said—he was kind enough to offer me—he said I could stay in the living room of his apartment for tonight.

JUDGE: But you're not going to?

ISABELLE: Yes—I am.

JUDGE (*Glancing from one to the other*): Well, in that case, I wish you a very good night then.

Goes up to arch on way to staircase. ISABELLE *follows slightly.*

ISABELLE: Judge!

HE *stops and turns.*

JUDGE: Yes?

ISABELLE (*Hesitating*): Good night.

JUDGE (*Mumbling indistinctly*): Good night.

HE *goes upstairs.* SHE *watches him a moment, then comes to* GUS.

ISABELLE: The Judge is afraid for me.

GUS: Yes.

ISABELLE: What are your intentions toward me?

GUS (*Smiling*): Strictly dishonorable, Isabelle.

End of Act One

ACT TWO

The living room of GUS's *rear apartment, upstairs over the speakeasy. It is a few minutes later—12:40 a.m.*

French windows and window seat on one wall. Covered canary cage hung on section of window. Doors leading to hallway of building, to bath, and to bedroom. Grand piano and stool. Keyboard set with music on it. Props to dress. A love seat set in curve of piano. Table next to this with teddy bear and picture of woman in frame. A small stand with stockings in boxes in the drawers. Bookcase next to door and table between doors to bedroom and bathroom. On table, phonograph and telephone. Small bed table against other wall. Small bed lamp on same. Lamps on piano and on phonograph. Large armchair next to divan, with cover, and fully made up with sheets and pillows. Foot of divan, small cushioned seat. Bathroom fixtures in bath, chest of drawers in bedroom.

Stage is dark, except for moonlight coming through French windows. GUS *enters, turns and calls off.*

GUS: Come in, Isabelle. Are you afraid?

ISABELLE (*In doorway*): Put on the light, please.

GUS (*Switching on lights*): Certainly. There. (HE *crosses to bed table and turns on light*)

ISABELLE (*Entering*): So this is what it's like.

GUS: What what is like?

ISABELLE: A man's apartment.

GUS (*Closes door and hooks chains*): Yes . . . it is not so terrible . . . is it?

ISABELLE: No, it's lovely. Is this your own furniture—or do you rent it?

GUS (*Closes curtains on window*): No, it is mine. Tomaso—he is my landlord, you know—his taste in furniture is different.

ISABELLE: I suppose it is.

GUS: Yes. He likes . . . ah . . . massive mahogany . . . carved very elegantly with lions' heads and such things . . . and covered in green . . . how you say . . . ploosh?

ISABELLE: I know. We've got that kind down home . . . in the parlor. But ours was red plush.

GUS: In red it's more beautiful, no doubt.

ISABELLE: I think it's awful.

GUS: Do you? I am very glad then.

THEY *laugh.*

Will you give me your things, please?

SHE *hands him cape and bag, which* HE *places on piano.* SHE *crosses to love seat.* SHE *notes teddy bear.*

ISABELLE: Oh, what a darling teddy bear.

GUS: It was given to me for luck—and right away I meet you.

ISABELLE (*Picking up a hairpin on love seat*): I didn't know women used hairpins any more.

GUS: Probably my cleaning woman dropped it.

ISABELLE: Probably. (*Crosses to small stand*) Is she blonde?

GUS: I . . . ah . . . never noticed . . . She wears a dust cap.

While ISABELLE *is examining ashtray,* HE *sees photograph of woman on table next to love seat.* HE *turns it down quickly.*

ISABELLE (*Pushing cigarette end from tray*): Well, you ought to tell her to stop smoking your cigarettes. It doesn't look nice to see the ashtrays all full of cigarette butts with . . . lip rouge on them.

GUS: Darling—are you jealous?

ISABELLE: Me? No, just neat. You get that way when you've got four big brothers tearing 'round the house and upsetting things.

GUS (*Sits in love seat*): You say your brothers are . . . *large?*

ISABELLE: Oh . . . not large. Why, the biggest one is only six feet two, and Charley, the baby, I don't think he's even quite six feet.

GUS: Practically . . . a midget.

ISABELLE: No, but Papa always said he'd be puny.

GUS: What a man. Your papa.

ISABELLE: Papa was a real man and when he died it took ten men to carry him.

GUS: I'm sorry.

Telephone rings. HE *smiles nervously, rises.*

Er—excuse me just a moment.

HE *goes to telephone.* SHE *goes to window and looks out.*

Allo. . . . Oh, yes, Lilli. I am still in conference. . . . We moved upstairs. . . . I don't know, probably very late. We are hardly beginning . . . no, I wouldn't come . . . it would not amuse you. . . . Yes, dear . . . yes . . . yes . . . yes . . . I do . . . I do . . . I do . . . very much . . . yes . . . good night.

ISABELLE (*Closing window*): Your cousin again?

GUS: Oh, yes. . . . She . . . ah . . . she is one of those women who wastes much time on the telephone . . . other people's time.

ISABELLE: What is she like?

GUS: I don't know. She's really very charming. You must forgive my telling lies, but she wishes always to talk about family matters. . . . (*Crosses to* ISABELLE)— and I do not like to talk about family matters . . . tonight. (HE *embraces her*)

ISABELLE: Uh-huh.

GUS: Yes. How lovely you are . . . so young . . . so pliant . . . so intoxicating. . . . So sweet—so gentle—

ISABELLE (*Breaking away slightly*): I'm so pleased to hear you say nice things.

GUS: Darling, I'm so happy to have you alone with me—all alone.

SHE *breaks away from him nervously.*

ISABELLE: Uh-huh, uh-huh, uh-huh—(SHE *is at piano keyboard.* SHE *looks at a piece of music*) Oh—this is your music?

GUS: Yes, darling.

ISABELLE: Will you—sing something for me?

GUS (*Sitting on love seat*): No, no, Isabelle.

ISABELLE: Why not?

GUS: Because, I am not Caraffa now. I am only me, Di Ruvo, Gus, who—who is so happy to be alone—with you.

ISABELLE: But I—

GUS: No, no, no. Caraffa belongs to everybody. He is hanging in his dressing room with his costumes. He waits for his sweethearts—for Mimi, for Tosca, for Manon. He is not lonely. It is Di Ruvo—Gus—who *was* lonely—until he found his Isabelle.

ISABELLE: Is it like that to be famous?

GUS: Yes, it is like that to be alone, nearly always. To own a talent like singing is like to own maybe a trained bear that dances to make people laugh. The owner, he is nobody, but the bear, he is everybody. The poor man is invited to a party. What happen? So soon he arrives, they say: Did you bring the bear? Or: Will you sing for us a song? It is the bear, the talent, they want. For him they care nothing.

SHE *crosses to him and stands there.* HE *takes her hand.*

ISABELLE: I never thought of that.

GUS (*Draws her to him slightly*): No. Nobody thinks of it. But what do I care. Perhaps you like a little Di Ruvo, huh? A little bit?

There is a pounding coming from floor above. THEY *break in alarm, and* SHE *turns toward window.*

ISABELLE: What's that?

GUS: It is the Judge—signaling to me from upstairs.

More pounding, then the JUDGE *calls down.*

JUDGE: Gus. Gus.

GUS (*As* HE *crosses to window*): Proprio al momento opportuna.
[At just the right moment]

(*Calling out window*) Hello.

JUDGE: Say, what's the date today?

GUS: The day?

JUDGE: The date.

GUS (*Looking at watch*): Sunday—since half an hour—already.

JUDGE: What?

GUS: Sunday. (*Turns to* ISABELLE) What is the matter with him?

JUDGE: No, no—not the day—the date.

GUS (*To* ISABELLE): What date is today? (*Calls out window*) The ninth.

JUDGE: Thanks. (HE *slams window*)

GUS (*Crossing to divan angrily*): Seccatore, noioso.

[Nuisance, bore]

ISABELLE (*Watching* GUS): I wonder what he wants so badly.

GUS: Oh, he probably suffers from curiosity.

ISABELLE: I like him. I wish he weren't angry with me.

GUS: I wish he would mind his own business. They are all the same—these busybodies. Tomaso tells me how to live; the Judge would tell me how to love. And neither knows—they have already forgotten. (HE *crosses to her*) Believe me, darling—believe me and you will know happiness.

Footsteps heard outside door.

ISABELLE: I wonder what that is? Do you suppose Henry—

GUS: Ssh.

Three raps on door.

JUDGE (*Off*): Say, Gus—

GUS *takes chain off door.* ISABELLE *turns and as* JUDGE *enters, goes to love seat.* GUS *goes to armchair angrily.*

May I come in? (*Comes in*) Say, are you positive this is the ninth?

GUS: Absolutely.

JUDGE: S'my birthday. What do you know about that?

ISABELLE: Many happy returns of the day.

GUS: Congratulations.

JUDGE: Thank you—thank you both. (*Sits in love seat*) And now—now I'm going to save you both from a very dull evening. We're going to celebrate.

GUS: Here?

JUDGE: Now, don't apologize—this is good enough for me. I'm an old-fashioned man—don't like anything fancy. Tom will be right up with the champagne.

GUS: You—ah—told Tom to bring the champagne here?

JUDGE: Yeah, I telephoned down to him.

GUS *laughs mirthlessly.*

GUS: Oh.

JUDGE: This is my party. I'm taking care of everything.

GUS *laughs again.*

You—ah—didn't mind my giving a party here, did you, Gus?

GUS: Of course not, my dear Judge—I'm delighted. (HE *laughs again and sits angrily in small seat at foot of divan*)

ISABELLE: Me, too.

JUDGE: Good. Let's have some music. You know, a party without music is like an egg without salt.

HE *goes up to phonograph, but before* HE *can get it in readiness,* TOM *enters with champagne and glasses.*

TOM: Here is the champagne, Mister Judge. I am sorry it take so long, but that fellow come back. (*Leaves door open and places tray on small table near love seat*)

ISABELLE (*In alarm*): Who? Henry?

TOM: The policeman—Mulligan.

JUDGE: What does he want?

TOM: He look for somebody.

GUS (*Rising*): Who is he looking for, Tomaso?

TOM: Looking for la Signorina.

GUS: La Signorina?

TOM: Il suo capolo l'ha mandato a cercarlo e dice che e qui, e va di la di qua, di su di giu.

[His sergeant sent him to find you and tell you the man from West Orange sent him and he's going here and there and up and down]

GUS: Calma. Calma, Tomaso. It would seem that Mr. Henry also told the sergeant that Isabelle has been kidnapped, so the officer—

JUDGE: Mulligan—

GUS: —has come back again with orders to search the house.

JUDGE: Oh, he has, has he? Tom!

ISABELLE: What shall I do?

TOM: Hide in the Judge's room.

JUDGE (*Alarmed*): Not on your life! (*Turns to* TOM) Where is Mulligan?

TOM: When I come upstairs, he say he go look in the yard—behind the house in the back-house. (HE *points to window and crosses to it*)

JUDGE (*Crossing to window*): I'll get rid of him all right. (*Calling out window*) Mulligan! Mulligan! Mulligan.

GUS *follows* JUDGE *to window.* ISABELLE *is behind* GUS. MULLIGAN *enters.* HE *watches them at window.*

ISABELLE (*Starting toward window*): Do you suppose he'll find me?

GUS (*Holding her back*): No, darling, never! But don't show yourself at the window.

ISABELLE: Could he come up here?

TOM: If he do, I kill him!

JUDGE: I'll have him broken!

GUS: He wouldn't dare.

JUDGE *almost falls out window.*

ISABELLE: Catch him, Gus.

GUS (*Holding* JUDGE *back*): I've got him.

TOM: Me, too.

JUDGE: It's all right. I see him. Do you see him, Tom?

TOM: Yes.

JUDGE: That thing that looks like a horse over there?

TOM: Yes—like a horse.

ISABELLE (*Turns and sees* MULLIGAN): Oh! (SHE *recovers*) Fancy seeing you here. (SHE *nudges* GUS)

MULLIGAN: Fancy!

GUS (*Turning*): Oh.

HE *laughs nervously and nudges* JUDGE, *who turns.*

JUDGE: Oh—you!

MULLIGAN: Yes—the horse, himself.

TOM (*Crossing to* MULLIGAN): I no mean to kill you, Mr. Mulligan.

JUDGE: What are you doing in here again?

MULLIGAN: The desk sergeant sent me back here to find her.

JUDGE: To find whom?

MULLIGAN: The young lady I was looking for.

JUDGE: It seems to me, Mr. Mulligan, you're always running after young ladies when you should be pounding your beat.

MULLIGAN: Judge!

JUDGE: Very suspicious. Very suspicious. I think you're lascivious.

MULLIGAN: Well—er—only on rainy days.

JUDGE: What about this young lady?

MULLIGAN: Your honor, it's just like I told you. I'm pursuing a dangerous—

JUDGE: Stop! Remember the straw that broke the camel's back—remember the heel of Achilles!

MULLIGAN: I will! I've got fallen arches, myself. But I'm looking for a young lady held against her will by villains!

JUDGE: Do you see any young lady being held against her will by villains?

MULLIGAN: Not a sign of one, your honor.

JUDGE: You didn't think for a moment it was this young lady, did you? Come here, my dear—

ISABELLE *goes between* MULLIGAN *and* JUDGE.

—show the officer your wrists and ankles aren't tied.

MULLIGAN: Ah, the Judge is having his little joke.

ISABELLE (*To* GUS): Perhaps the officer would like some of your Italian chocolates.

GUS: I think he would much rather have a drink. Tomaso!

TOM *starts to pour champagne.*

ISABELLE: But policemen never drink on duty!

MULLIGAN: It just seems like never.

GUS *takes drink from table.* ISABELLE *hands drink to* JUDGE *and one to* MULLIGAN.

GUS: Here's to the police!

MULLIGAN: And here's to the people that send the police out on false clues. Bless their little hearts!

JUDGE (*To* MULLIGAN *significantly*): And here's to a long farewell.

THEY *all drink and put glasses down.*

MULLIGAN: Well, thanks very much for the ginger ale. And excuse me coming in like this—it was orders.

Starts to leave; JUDGE *stops him.*

JUDGE: You'd better run around to all the other speakeasies and see if you can find any kidnappers there.

MULLIGAN: All the other speakeasies? What do you take me for—Paul Revere?

HE *exits.* JUDGE *sits on divan.*

TOM: I go let him out. (*To* ISABELLE) Oh—la Signorina like tea or coffee?

ISABELLE: What?

GUS (*Sitting on love seat*): Do you like tea or coffee?

ISABELLE (*Nodding toward champagne*): Why can't I have that?

GUS: For breakfast.

ISABELLE: Oh. . . . Oh . . . coffee . . . please.

TOM: Grapefruit?

ISABELLE: No, thank you.

TOM: And an egg.

ISABELLE: No, thank you.

TOM: Sausage?

GUS (*Reprovingly*): Tomaso.

TOM: No hungry, huh? Tt. Tt. Too bad. You get sick. What time you want?

GUS: Finiscilla di parlare, Tomaso!
    [Stop talking, Tom]

TOM: Va bene Eccellenza. Good nigh', good nigh'. . . . Buona notte a tutti! Sleep good. (HE *exits*)

ISABELLE (*Sitting on arm of armchair*): He's nice. Have you known him long, Gus?

GUS: All my life. He was what you call . . . chamber valet . . . in my father's house.

ISABELLE: Chamber valet?

GUS: Yes. You know . . . he makes the beds and dusts . . . with a feather.

JUDGE: Housemaid?

GUS: The same work. But later he came to America. He's a rich man now. The food in his restaurant is famous.

JUDGE: That's why I never moved out of the house when he bought it and opened up his café.

ISABELLE: I see! It was very nice of you to come and live with him.

GUS: Well, my mother wanted me to. She's funny, my mother. Every month she writes a long letter to Tomaso, telling him what I should eat, and how it must be cooked and am I wearing my flannels and, I suppose, do I brush my teeth.

ISABELLE: How sweet of her.

GUS: Ah, well, to our mothers we are always little children, also when we get old.

JUDGE: Don't talk about being old on my birthday.

TOM (*Knocking, then entering hurriedly*): Eccellenza, Eccellenza! Signor Conte!

GUS: Ma cosa c'é?

[But what's happening?]

TOM (*In a whisper*): La signorina Lilli. (HE *describes her presence downstairs with pantomime*)

GUS (*Starting to door*): Ah, I must go downstairs . . . excuse me a moment.

JUDGE (*Stops him*): Has Henry—

GUS: No, it is not Henry this time.

ISABELLE: Your cousin again?

GUS: Yes, Lilli—

ISABELLE: Why don't you ask her to come up?

GUS (*Going to door*): No. She is too old. You know—two flights of stairs is—

HE *exits.* JUDGE *rises, crosses to table, fills glass and crosses to love seat.*

JUDGE: Now we can celebrate. Here's to you, my dear—look well before the leap. (*Sits on love seat*)

ISABELLE: Judge—I'm in love with him.

JUDGE: Isn't this rather sudden?

ISABELLE: I don't know. I've never been in love before.

JUDGE: But—this other fellow?

ISABELLE: Henry?

JUDGE: Yes.

ISABELLE: I didn't love Henry.

JUDGE: Was that quite—fair?

ISABELLE: I told him I didn't love him.

JUDGE: Oh.

ISABELLE: He said I'd learn to love him—little by little.

JUDGE: Oh—an optimist.

ISABELLE: I think he read it in a book somewhere. I never heard of anybody learning to love little by little, like it was playing the piano or something. Did you?

JUDGE: I—ah—never studied the piano.

ISABELLE: I always thought it was *bang*—all at once, or not at all. And now, I know it's bang.

JUDGE: A big bang.

ISABELLE: Uh-huh. So much so that nothing else matters very much.

JUDGE: How did you ever get engaged to Henry—although it's none of my business.

ISABELLE (*Sitting in armchair*): Well, I had to get married some time; and my sisters all got the pick of the boys 'cause they were prettier—

JUDGE: Aw—

ISABELLE: Oh, yes, they were. So that only left Willie Borelle and Chet Lee when it came my turn to pick, and Willie's got the jitters—

JUDGE: Jitters?

ISABELLE: You know, he makes faces all the time—like this. (SHE *distorts her face*)

JUDGE: Oh, my God.

ISABELLE: And both Chet's parents died in the state asylum, and he said if I didn't marry him he'd shoot me, so I didn't marry him.

JUDGE: You were very brave.

ISABELLE: Well, he'd already told that to all my sisters, so I reckoned he was pretty safe. Besides, Papa always said: Never let anybody bluff you.

JUDGE: Your father was right.

ISABELLE: Uh-huh—he played poker that way. By the time he died our plantation was so small, we didn't know whether to try and grow cotton on it, or turn it into a croquet grounds.

JUDGE: And then along came Henry.

ISABELLE: Uh-huh—in a big shiny Buick. He was visiting over at the Sawyers's. Went to college with Buck. He liked me right away.

JUDGE: Can't blame him for that.

ISABELLE: Thank you. Had to carry me up to show me to his parents right off. They're all right—if you like that kind of people. Think they're better than my family. He was so sweet to me down home and then, soon's he got me North you'd 'a' thought I belonged to him. (SHE *rises—goes toward door and looks at it as if waiting for* GUS *to return*) And I know now I couldn't belong to anybody—unless I loved him.

JUDGE: And you think you're in love with him?

ISABELLE: I don't think, Judge. When I heard that record and I saw him standing there like a bashful little boy, I said: Woman, prepare to see your dreams come true.

JUDGE (*Rises—looks at her a moment, then goes to phonograph table*): Young woman—

SHE *turns to him.*

Tonight you're going to a hotel—to the Martha Washington! And tomorrow you're going home!

ISABELLE: No, I'm not!

JUDGE (*Goes to piano and picks up her wrap and bag, then putting them down again*): Do you hear me? Put on your things!

ISABELLE (*Backs away*): I won't.

JUDGE: You will!

ISABELLE: I won't.

JUDGE: You're very unreasonable. (SHE *smiles at him*) I'll have you arrested.

ISABELLE: You can't do that.

JUDGE: Oh, *can't* I?

ISABELLE: No. You haven't got a warrant.

JUDGE: Ha-ha! I'll *show* you . . . (HE *starts for secretary*) . . . just give me a fountain pen and a piece of paper, and I'll . . .

ISABELLE: You can't fool me. You're not a real *judge.*

JUDGE: I'm not, hah? Well, by God. . . .

ISABELLE: It's just a . . . courtesy title.

JUDGE: Oh, it is, is it? Well, there are a lot of people in Sing Sing right this minute who'd be glad to hear that . . . to wish I hadn't shown them so much courtesy.

ISABELLE (*Sitting on love seat*): Judge!

JUDGE (*Very suspicious*): What is it?

ISABELLE: Even if you are a real judge, come and sit here . . . beside me.

JUDGE (*Starts to sit—checks himself*): No, no! You can't weaken me with *that stuff.*
No bribes. That's been tried before. They're all in jail! (*Crosses away*)

ISABELLE (*Sniffles*): I think . . . I'm going to cry.

JUDGE: Has no effect on me whatsoever!

ISABELLE *sobs.*

Women's tears leave me cold. I hate women! I like to see them cry. I enjoy it! (*In back of love seat*) For God's sake, stop it!

ISABELLE (*Still sobbing*): Come here!

JUDGE (*Crossing away*): I will not!

SHE *sobs again.* HE *stops.*

All right—stop it! (*Crossing and sitting next to her*) Stop it, I say! (*Pats her*) There, there.

SHE *stops crying as* HE *pats her, looks up at him with a broad smile.* HE *realizes* SHE *has deceived him.*

ISABELLE: I wonder where Gus is.

JUDGE: I don't want you to see him again!

ISABELLE: You can't send me home!

JUDGE: But I tell you—

ISABELLE: But, darling, you don't understand.

JUDGE: What! I don't understand WHAT!

ISABELLE: That I *can't* go home. I went away to be *married.*

JUDGE: What of it?

ISABELLE: I can't go back like—*damaged goods.* You can't *do that* in a little town, no matter how innocent you are. They'd think there was something *wrong* with me. Why, the whole of Yoakum would sit with its eyebrows up in the air for nine months just waiting and hoping for the worst.

JUDGE: They could wait as long as they liked—nothing would happen.

ISABELLE: Then they'd say nothing could happen. (SHE *laughs*) I know my own home town.

JUDGE: Then what *are* you going to do?

ISABELLE: Gonna stay here . . . with Gus.

JUDGE: But . . .

ISABELLE: He *said* I could stay . . . as long as I liked.

JUDGE: Of course you know he won't marry you.

ISABELLE (*Placidly*): I don't expect him to marry me.

JUDGE: He'll never marry!

ISABELLE: He's probably right.

JUDGE (*Pounding love seat*): I . . . won't . . . have . . . it!

ISABELLE: Now don't start again, darling. If I want to be foolish, let me be foolish . . . for once. I've always been sensible and good . . . you know it isn't much fun to be a girl . . . sometimes . . . and now I'd just like to drift with the current and not struggle any more . . . and for a little while . . . be happy.

JUDGE: I think you're immoral.

ISABELLE: Well, I read in a book of psychoanalysis that nothing is immoral except—

JUDGE: Except what?

ISABELLE: Oh, Lordy—I've plumb forgotten.

GUS (*Entering and crossing to bedroom door*): Ah, forgive me—that Lilli—she makes me tired and hot. Women are so illogical—

ISABELLE: Oh!

GUS: Except you, darling—except you. (HE *exits*)

JUDGE (*Rises, goes to armchair and stops, turning to her and pointing his finger at her*): And suppose you *do* have a baby!

ISABELLE (*Very amiably*): And *suppose* . . . I don't. They're not compulsory, you know.

JUDGE: What! Why . . .

ISABELLE: In the movies, darling. Only in the movies.

JUDGE: Where did you learn such things!

ISABELLE: Well . . . I've got five married sisters.

JUDGE (*Starts to door, stops*): Well . . . remember . . . I *warned you!*

ISABELLE (*Rises*): Of what? You haven't warned me about anything.

JUDGE (*Indignantly*): *What?* Didn't I *tell you* that you're taking the first downward step . . . didn't I tell you that you're treading . . . *the road to hell?*

ISABELLE: Why, *no.* You didn't say anything about it . . . you must have forgotten. (*Crossing toward* JUDGE) Judge! You're a darling . . .

JUDGE: Forgive me. I'm just an old busybody. I've no right to tell you how to find happiness . . . when I never was able to find it for myself.

ISABELLE: Do you think I will be unhappy, Judge?

JUDGE: I don't know. You always hear of these things ending up . . . in sorrow.

ISABELLE: Maybe you don't hear about them when they end happily.

JUDGE: Maybe.

ISABELLE: You see, I've never been very happy, Judge. I mean like I am now, because I never felt about anybody, like I do about Gus. Don't you think, it's better to be very happy for a little while . . . than never to be happy at all?

JUDGE: I don't know. I don't know anything about it. All I know is you've spoiled my birthday—

ISABELLE: I'm sorry.

JUDGE: But I wish you'd give it a little more thought—will you?

ISABELLE: I will, Judge.

HE *goes to door.* SHE *follows slightly.*

Good night.

JUDGE (*Opens door*): Good night. (*Starts out door and turns*) But if you do have a baby, I'll adopt it.

> JUDGE *exits.* SHE *trails him to door, lingers, then goes to piano and picks up cape and bag.* SHE *looks toward bedroom then starts to door as* GUS *enters.* SHE *puts her things back quickly.* GUS *is in pajamas and lounging suit.*

GUS: Where's the Judge?

ISABELLE: Gone to bed.

GUS: Good! What was he talking about so long?

ISABELLE: Oh, happiness—and things like that. He—he wanted me to go away from you.

GUS: And you?

ISABELLE: I didn't want to go. (*Pause*) But I think I'd better.

GUS: Darling!

ISABELLE (*Warding him off*): Don't you think I'd better?

GUS: Yes—I think you had.

ISABELLE: But I don't want to.

GUS: Come here!

ISABELLE: If I stayed—would you promise not to say sweet things to me?

GUS (*Holding her hands*): But, darling, I won't say sweet things to you if you don't want me to.

ISABELLE: But I do want you to!

> HE *starts to embrace* HER.

Gus, couldn't you overpower me?

GUS (*Backs away a step in surprise*): What!

ISABELLE: Then it wouldn't be my fault.

GUS: Darling, you must not say such things.

ISABELLE: But I think 'em.

GUS: Listen to me, darling! A great man once said: "Thought is the eternal rival of love." When you love, don't think—just drift with the current of your heart.

ISABELLE: But that's just it. I'm a little frightened. (*Starts to back away slowly through next speech*)

GUS: Frightened? You? A great big girl like you? Who came from Mississ—well, where you said—here to New Jersey to live with those cold storage family—and after weeks with these ice boxes, you had the courage to face Mister Henry. You are not frightened; I'll not let you be frightened.

> ISABELLE *is by piano keyboard.*

ISABELLE: Stop scolding me—stop it, I say. I won't let you scold me. (*Defensively,* SHE *picks up music and looks at it*) Oh, it's in Italian. I always wanted to travel. Sing it for me!

GUS (*Crossing to piano*): You're trying to be clever to avoid me.

ISABELLE: No, I'm not—honest. Please sing it for me.

GUS: Do you think you will understand?

SHE *smiles.*

Perhaps you will like Caraffa then—better than Di Ruvo.

Takes music, sits at piano and sings. SHE *is listening to him.*

Donna Vorrei Morir!
Donna Vorrei Morir!

GUS *rises and crosses to her, taking her hands.*

ISABELLE: What does it mean, Gus?

GUS (*Taking her in his arms*): It means I adore you!

ISABELLE: I wonder why that sounds so nice—even if it isn't true.

GUS: But it is true! Isabelle, kiss me!

THEY *kiss and break.*

ISABELLE: Don't lie to me, Gus. The thing I like best about you is you've told the truth.

GUS: You are a strange little girl—I'm not sure I understand you.

ISABELLE: I'm not sure I understand myself. I only know—that I'm happy to be here.

GUS: Thank you.

ISABELLE (*Pointing to divan*): Is that where the guest sleeps?

GUS (*Crossing to divan*): Yes, darling. It's more comfortable than my bed and it's all ready—(*Pulls cover back, disclosing bed made up*)—see!

ISABELLE: Pink sheets, ruffles and everything. Always made up . . . in case of emergency!

GUS (*Fixing sheets*): Sometimes a friend may want to stay . . . if he misses a train.

ISABELLE: And have you pajamas for the friends who miss trains?

GUS (*Solemnly*): I think I can find a very nice pair of pajamas . . . that shrunk in the wash . . . they should be just about right.

ISABELLE: And *slippers*?

GUS (*Pensively*): I think it is just possible . . . *yes!* When my sister was here she forgot a pair . . .

ISABELLE (*Merrily*): I *thought* you probably could find some. *Somebody* must have forgotten some sometime.

GUS (*Looking at her feet*): What adorable feet! . . . You must wear about size three.

ISABELLE: Good heavens! Have you them in different *sizes*? *What* a man!

GUS (*Crossing to embrace her*): *Darling!* You must not say such things . . .

ISABELLE: I wouldn't have you any different.

HE *puts his arms around her.* SHE *holds him off.*

Now, go and get the p.j.'s and things.

HE *exits to bedroom.* SHE *starts to untie belt of dress.* HE *enters with pajamas and a pair of slippers.* SHE *puts belt of dress on arm of armchair.*

GUS (*Coming to* ISABELLE): Here are the p.j.'s and things. May I help you?

ISABELLE: Uh-huh.

GUS (*Looking dress over*): Where does it unbutton?

ISABELLE: You see where it unbuttons.

GUS: Shall I then?

ISABELLE: Uh-huh.

HE *starts to unhook dress. When* SHE *lifts dress over shoulders,* SHE *starts to speak.*

I used to love to have my clothes taken off when I was too little to know how.

HE *takes dress and hangs it on screen.* SHE *is now in teddy, stockings, and shoes.* SHE *sits on arm of armchair, dropping stockings to below knees.* HE *comes down, sits on seat, foot of divan and takes shoes and stockings off.*

I used to wear a lot more clothes when I was little . . . and Mama wore more than I did . . . and Gramma wore more than all of us put together.

Stockings, garters and shoes are laid on a small seat at foot of divan. GUS *puts slippers on.*

Gramma said when she was a young girl, she wore three times as much as when I knew her—

GUS: Really.

HE *rises.* SHE *drops straps of teddy over her shoulders.* HE *takes top of pajamas and puts it over her head, teddy drops at her feet.*

ISABELLE: I'll bet the men back in Gramma's day used to get awfully impatient waiting for the women to get undressed . . . (SHE *picks teddy up and places it on back of chair. Then she sits on arm of chair again*) . . . to go swimming. But maybe they didn't swim much in those days—

GUS *has pajama pants.* SHE *slips her feet into them as* HE *draws them up and over pajama coat.*

I used to wear things like that when I was a little girl only they had feet in 'em. (*Pajamas on,* SHE *rises, fixes her hair, then looks down at herself, slapping thighs of legs in protest*) No, no, no—the top goes on the outside.

GUS (*Drawing top out of pajama pants and laughing*): I must patent this.

HE *goes between foot of divan and small seat;* SHE *ties belt of pajama coat.* HE *holds his arm out to her.*

Ah, Isabelle—my lovely Isabelle—come and sit beside me.

HE *sits at foot of divan,* SHE *sits on small seat, reclining in his arms.*

GUS: Piccola, amore cara, tell me—what can you see in this ugly old opera singer?

ISABELLE: You're not ugly.

GUS: Do you like me a little?

ISABELLE: More than a little.

GUS: Why?

ISABELLE: I don't know—I don't think any woman knows. But it's like heaven to be near you—just your hand on my arm is like—I can't explain what it's like—

GUS: Don't explain. Words cannot explain such things. Words are only good for "How do you do?" — "Will you have some sugar in your tea?" Only for things that do not matter. No one must ever try to explain miracles with words. Darling! (*Kisses her*) I am mad about you.

Kisses her again. ISABELLE *rises, a little bewildered.* SHE *crosses to table next to love seat.* HE *follows her.*

ISABELLE: I guess I—I'd like a little more champagne. (SHE *hands him glass of champagne*) Here's to you.

GUS: Here's to you!

THEY *drink. Then put glasses down.* HE *tries to take her in arms.* SHE *breaks away defensively.*

ISABELLE: Now—put out the lights.

GUS *goes up to switch. Lamps on piano and table between bath and bedrooms doors go out.* HE *starts to bed lamp;* SHE *stops him.*

Except that one.

GUS (*Starting to her*): Angel!

ISABELLE (*Meeting him in embrace*): Oh, Gus, I am happy!

GUS: It is I who am so happy.

ISABELLE: I love you.

GUS: But, darling, you are trembling. Are you then so afraid?

ISABELLE: I'm a little bit afraid.

GUS: But you must not be. Life is beautiful . . . and its most beautiful moments are called . . . love. They are very rare, my Isabelle, such moments as this . . . to be accepted tenderly . . . and without fear.

ISABELLE: Don't ever let me go.

GUS: No, no—let you go? I'll hold you close—close to me. My baby—like a child—

SHE *breaks into sobs.*

But you are crying.

THEY *break.*

But you are a baby!

SHE *crosses to love seat, her back to him and still sobbing.*

ISABELLE: No, I'm not . . . don't girls usually cry?

GUS: Yes.

ISABELLE: Well . . . I'm no different from anybody else. (*Then, out of a clear sky*) Do you think I'm pretty?

GUS: Hein?

ISABELLE: Do you think I'm pretty?

GUS: Of course I think you're pretty. You're lovely.

ISABELLE: Well, why don't you say so, then? (*Turns to him angrily*) Isn't this the time
to say sweet things to me? What are you staying over there for? Don't you
like me?

GUS (*Rather emotionally*): It is because I like you so much . . . that I'm staying here.
You little . . . foolish! (*Suddenly* HE *makes up his mind*) Now come here! (*Crossing to her and taking her hand*) Come here, I say! (*Leads her to divan*) Now
get into bed!

SHE *gets into bed and* HE *stands over her.*

(*Angrily*) Now listen to me. Never in my life before . . . have I done anything
so stupid as now I am about to do. . . . Do you understand? Never! Not
once . . . I . . . I cover myself with ridicule . . . and I am . . . positive . . . that
I will regret it forever. *All my life.* I will be angry for this moment. I . . . I . . .
am CRAZY! (HE *strides over to table and picks up teddy bear.* HE *returns to the
bed and puts it down beside her*) There! So you won't be frightened.

ISABELLE (*Clutching at the teddy bear*): I'm not frightened.

GUS (*With an effort*): Now. . . . Good night.

ISABELLE: What do you mean?

GUS: I mean . . . I will sleep tonight in the Judge's apartment. And you . . . *you*
are going home tomorrow. Where your mama can take care of you.

ISABELLE: I won't. (*Then* SHE *sobs*) Oh, Gus, you're horrid.

GUS: Yes, I knew you would thank me. Good night. (*Goes to door*) Come here!
Come here!

ISABELLE (SHE *crosses to him, dragging teddy bear*): What do you want?

GUS (*Picking up chain on door*): So soon as I have gone, you will place this end
of the chain in this receptacle . . . do you see? (HE *indicates it*) . . . So if I change
my mind, if I weaken, this chain will be stronger . . . than my resolutions.
Do you understand?

ISABELLE (*Mulishly*): I won't do it. I hate you.

GUS: You are a very bad girl. Good night.

ISABELLE: Aren't you even going to kiss me?

GUS: No.

ISABELLE: Aren't you going to put me to bed?

GUS: No!

ISABELLE: Then I'll scream!

SHE *starts to scream.* HE *picks her up and starts to divan.*

GUS: Am I a nurse-maid that I have to take care so of babies? (*Puts her on divan*)
Good night.

ISABELLE: Now kiss me!

GUS: Just a little one.

HE *leans over.* SHE *grabs him and kisses him soundly. With difficulty,* HE *breaks away.*

Now—hook the chain on the door, baby!

HE *starts for door.* SHE *picks up teddy bear and throws it on floor, crying as* SHE *does so.*

ISABELLE: I'm not a baby! I'm not a baby!

End of Act Two

ACT THREE

*Same as Act Two, except that the hangings on the center section of French windows
have been drawn. It is ten o'clock the next morning and the sunlight can be seen
stealing through the curtains.*

ISABELLE *is lying on divan, sleeping. There is a soft rap on door and* TOM *enters,
dressed in the uniform of a valet de chambre.* HE *carries a breakfast tray, which
he places on table next to love seat.* HE *picks up tray with champagne and glasses
and exits.* HE *returns at once, crosses to French windows and pulls drapes open.
Then* HE *takes cover off canary cage. The bird whistles.* HE *silences bird.* HE *crosses
to divan, picking up teddy bear from floor and placing it at* ISABELLE's *side.* HE
goes to armchair, takes chemise and places it over small seat at foot of divan. HE
looks at stockings on arm of chair and finding a hole, HE *crosses to small stand.
Opens drawer, takes out several boxes, looking at them until* HE *gets right size.
Throws old stockings in drawer, crosses to chair and puts new ones on arm of chair.
Goes to bedroom door, then down to bed, touching it to see if* GUS *is there.* SHE
wiggles her feet. TOM *returns to bedroom door, raps. No reply; looks puzzled. Raps
on bathroom door. No reply. Opens it and looks in. Enters, turning on light. Looks
at shower curtains to see if* GUS *is behind them, then turns on water. Enters leaving
door open.*

TOM (*Calls softly*): Signorina—signorina—signorina.

> SHE *pulls cover over her head.* HE *goes to phonograph and plays record— "Stars
> and Stripes Forever."* SHE *sits up angrily and throws teddy bear on floor.* HE *picks
> it up and places it on piano, then closes phonograph.*

Good morning, Signorina.

ISABELLE: Good morning.

TOM: I no see his Eccellency . . . anyplace.

ISABELLE: He's not here.

TOM: Not here?

ISABELLE: No.

TOM: That's very funny.

ISABELLE: He's sleeping in the Judge's apartment.

TOM: Well, chi va piano, va seno, e va lontano.

[What goes slowly, goes well and goes far]

ISABELLE: Please don't play the piano.

TOM: No, I no play the piano. I go get your breakfast.

ISABELLE: I'd like a cup of coffee, if it isn't too much trouble.

TOM: No trouble—(*Takes tea to her*) I got for you a nice cup of tea.

ISABELLE: Are *you* going to boss me too?

> HE *hands her a cup of plain tea.*

I'd like some cream and sugar, please.

TOM: No, no. No cream and sugar . . . make you sick. Taka plain. Maka stomach swell up . . . maka room for the eggs.

ISABELLE: I *hate* eggs. I won't eat any eggs.

TOM: Very good for you. You eat eggs, and I give you sausage to poosh 'em down. *Then* you feel fine.

Canary starts to sing.

ISABELLE: Oh, Lawdy, couldn't you tell him to sing a little later?

TOM: You no like music?

ISABELLE: Not just now . . . *please.*

TOM: I turn him off. (TOM *crosses to cage*) Silenzio! Ssh! Ssh!

Canary stops. A cat begins to meow. HE *hurries to table next to love seat and fills saucer with milk.*

Ah, poosy, poosy, poosy.

ISABELLE (*In despair*): Bring him in. Bring him in. Let's have a party.

TOM: He's hungry.

ISABELLE: Well, for heaven's sake, give him those sausages. I hope he chokes on 'em.

TOM: I give him a little cream. Here, poosy, poosy, poosy!

Puts cream out window. Cat stops. Then HE *looks at her a moment.*

Ah, Cristoforo Columbo—what's the matter with you? You getting fat again, huh? (*As* HE *crosses toward bathroom door*) It won't be long, it won't be long. (*Suddenly* HE *rushes into bathroom*) Every morning I forget. (*Turns off water and reenters*) The bathtub ready, Signorina.

ISABELLE: I'll take a shower later.

TOM: Si, Signorina.

ISABELLE: You're not going to wash me, I hope!

TOM: No, no—no. (*Takes toothbrush from drawer in table*) I got for you a nice tooth-brush. (*Crosses to her with it*)

ISABELLE: It's not Lilli's, I hope.

TOM (*Hands her toothbrush*): No, it's a new one. You will find all different tooth-paste in the bathroom. Well, I go wake up Mr. Augustino now, g'bye.

HE *takes her teacup and puts it on tray and goes to door.* SHE *stops him at door.*

ISABELLE: Tom!

TOM: Yes, Signorina.

ISABELLE: Do—many young ladies come here?

TOM: No—just a few cousins and aunts.

HE *exits.* SHE *rises. Cat has begun to meow.*

ISABELLE: Hello, Cristoforo Columbus.

Cat meows. SHE *crosses to window and looks out.*

You happy? (*Cat meows*) You're going to have a lot of little pussies, huh? (*Cat meows*) How many you going to have? (*Three short meows*) You're going to have a whole family. Gee, you're lucky.

Cat meows. Rap on door. SHE *goes to door.*

Who is it?

JUDGE: It's I!

ISABELLE: Come in.

HE *enters and sees her in pajamas.* HE *is about to leave at once.*

Oh, I don't mind.

JUDGE: Well! And how is our little guest this morning?

ISABELLE (*Listlessly*): M'all right . . . thank you.

HENRY (*At door*): I was glad . . . mighty glad . . . to learn that you had come to your senses last night . . . but I always knew you would. You can't fool me on *character* . . . that's my business.

ISABELLE: I guess it would be hard . . . to fool you.

JUDGE: *Impossible!* . . . practically. And when Gus knocked on my door and told me that you had sent him away . . . I wasn't a *bit* surprised. . . . *He* was, but *I* wasn't . . . because I always *knew* you would.

ISABELLE: Did you?

JUDGE: *Oh*, yes! You know . . . there's something about a decent girl that . . . shows in the eyes.

ISABELLE: Is there?

JUDGE: *Oh, my,* yes. To an expert, there is no mistaking the good . . . for the bad.

ISABELLE: I guess you know quite a lot about women.

JUDGE: Yes . . . ah . . . I do. (*And* HE *adds hastily*) About *good* women.

ISABELLE: Judge, maybe good women are good because . . . because it takes two to be bad . . . and they can't find anybody . . .

JUDGE (*Angry*): Rubbish!

ISABELLE: Well, of course you *know*, Judge.

JUDGE: Yes, yes. Of course. (*Starts to her with ticket*) I took a little walk down to Grand Central this morning, heh, heh. (HE *laughs nervously and produces an envelope*) . . . and while there, heh, heh, I . . . ah . . . I bought you this little present. (HE *hands it to her*)

ISABELLE (*Hardly audible*): Thank you, Judge . . . I . . . I . . . thank you. (SHE *fumbles with the envelope and pulls out about a yard of green ticket, starts to look at it*)

JUDGE: I think you'll find it all there. There's quite a lot of it, isn't there. Yoakum must be at some distance from here. You know your home must be very beautiful this time of the year. The fleecy clouds, the giant redwoods, the sparkling Pacific—

ISABELLE: Oh! (SHE *drops down into love seat*)

JUDGE (*Crosses to her*): Now, now, Isabelle . . . be reasonable.

ISABELLE (*Through her tears*): How *can* I be reasonable . . . I don't want to go to Oregon when I live in Mississippi. You're just trying to get rid of me. (SHE *throws ticket on love seat*)

JUDGE (*Picking up the ticket and looking at it*): Is it possible there can be *two* places with such a name. S'ridiculous!

ISABELLE: You don't have to insult me. Is it my fault, where I was born?

JUDGE: Now, now, Isabelle, I didn't mean that. The mistake is easily rectified. (HE *stuffs the tickets in his pocket*) Now be a good girl and get dressed, and we'll go down there together, in a nice taxicab, and we'll fix it all up.

ISABELLE (*Rises*): Does . . . Gus know that you're sending me home?

JUDGE: It was he who told me to get the tickets.

ISABELLE: Gus!

JUDGE: Yes. I forgot to mention it—it's a little present from both of us.

ISABELLE: Oh—oh, yes.

JUDGE: Yes.

ISABELLE (*After a pause*): I . . . I don't want to go home, Judge. I . . . I can't go home. I told you so last night.

JUDGE (*Distressed*): What *are* you going to do then?

ISABELLE: I don't know. I guess I'd better get dressed though.

JUDGE (*At door*): Yes . . . yes. And in the meanwhile I'll see if I can think of something. Don't be long. (HE *exits*)

SHE *walks into the bathroom. The telephone rings.* SHE *reenters and goes to phone slowly, not knowing whether to answer it.*

ISABELLE: Hello . . . Yes. . . . Yes, this is Mr. Caraffa's apartment. . . . Oh! . . . Oh, hello . . . Henry . . . how did you find it? . . . Oh, in the phone book . . . that was right smart of you . . . Yes. . . . Yes. . . . Yes . . . you certainly were. . . . I think you'd better quit drinking . . . all right . . . all right . . . I'll see you. (*For the last word* SHE *drops her voice*) . . . all right.

SHE *hangs up very slowly.*

JUDGE (*Off*): Isabelle?

ISABELLE (*Going to bathroom door*): What is it?

JUDGE (*Entering*): Isabelle, I've been thinking and really the best thing you can do is to go home to your mother.

ISABELLE: You won't have to worry about me anymore, Judge. I've made up my mind.

SHE *goes into bathroom and* JUDGE *crosses to foot of divan. Rap on door. It is* GUS.

GUS: Isabelle! Isabelle!

Enters hurriedly. Sees JUDGE.

Oh—you are here. (*Looking around the room*) Where's the child?

JUDGE: She's dressing. (HE *indicates the bathroom*)

GUS (*Smiling happily at the bathroom door*): I can't wait to see her. Oh, Judge! Congratulate me, felicitate me, shake me by the hand, kiss me on both cheeks, I'M IN LOVE!

JUDGE: *Huh?*

GUS (*Ecstatically*): Oh! It's *wonderful*, it's *marvelous!*

JUDGE: When did this happen?

GUS: This morning. About two o'clock. I couldn't sleep. I couldn't think. I got up, I listened to you snoring, *still* I couldn't sleep. I thought I was going crazy. I thought: Am I *sick?* No. Am I *hungry?* No. *Thirsty?* No. Well, what *do* I want? (HE *smiles languorously*) And *then*, Judge, *then* I knew. *Oh, it's wonderful* to feel such a *pain* in the heart.

JUDGE (*Sourly*): It must be.

GUS: So *then*, what do I do? I take the telephone, I say give me Western Union, I say take a cable, please. And to my Mother I say: Mama Mia, I am in *love*. With the most beautiful, adorable, enchanting, exquisite, lovely, pure, intelligent, remarkable, educated . . .

JUDGE: At fifty cents a word?

GUS: It was on your telephone.

JUDGE *sits on divan.*

Faithful, obedient and irreplaceable maiden in the entire world and I humbly beg your permission to marry her. Answer immediately. Urgent. The answer should be here now . . . let me see: Two o'clock here is . . . seven o'clock in the morning in Italy. . . . The cable would get there about nine . . . Mama would faint once with excitement . . . that takes about an hour . . . then she composes her answer . . . that takes another hour . . . then Giulio goes down to the telegraph office with the message . . . it isn't far, but he's old . . . that's another hour . . . then two hours for transmission, that makes nine o'clock. . . . What time is it?

JUDGE (*Looking at his watch*): Eleven minutes past ten.

GUS: Aie . . . Santo Dio. One hour and eleven minutes . . . late. They have *no* consideration. It would be quicker to send a *letter*. Or to go by street car—

JUDGE (*Rises*): Now don't get excited, it'll be here. Hold your horses.

GUS: What do I want with horses? I want telegraphs.

JUDGE: There, there. Go and get dressed. It'll be here by the time you're ready. You're not going to propose in that, are you?

GUS (*Hugs* JUDGE): I'm a little bit excited . . . *oh, it's marvelous.*

JUDGE: Suppose she refuses you?

GUS: My God, I never thought of that. I must look my best.

HE *starts to bedroom, singing. Enters bedroom.* GUS *returns with clothes. Shower increases in volume.* HE *goes to door. Stops. Hears shower and comes toward bathroom door slightly.*

Oh! She's in my little bathtub.

JUDGE: Well, go and use mine.

Shower stops.

GUS: Thank you. (*Starts to go—stops*) And, Judge—if she comes out—don't tell her anything—let me surprise her.

JUDGE: You can trust me.

GUS *exits.* JUDGE *goes to bathroom door and raps.*

ISABELLE (*Offstage in bath*): Don't come in.

JUDGE: Isabelle!

ISABELLE: What is it?

JUDGE: I've been thinking . . .

ISABELLE: So early?

JUDGE: I say I've been thinking . . .

ISABELLE: Just a minute. (SHE *opens the door a little*) What did you say?

JUDGE: I say I've been thinking . . .

ISABELLE: Drinking?

JUDGE: No! Thinking . . . with the brains . . . about you.

ISABELLE: Would you pass me that pink thing up there? What have you been thinking with your brains about me?

JUDGE: Well . . . after much thought, I've come to the conclusion that perhaps you may be right.

ISABELLE: And now the stockings, please.

HE *gets stockings.*

Don't forget the garters!

HE *picks up garters, returns to door and hands them in.*

These aren't my stockings.

JUDGE: Well, it's a cinch they aren't mine!

ISABELLE: I guess they must be Lilli's. They're very nice though.

JUDGE: I have come to the conclusion . . .

ISABELLE: The what?

JUDGE (*Shouting*): The CONCLUSION . . . THE END.

ISABELLE: The end? Have you finished?

JUDGE (*Paces back and forth front of door*): No!

ISABELLE: Then why do you stop?

JUDGE (*Tearing his hair*): Oh, GOD!

ISABELLE: What?

JUDGE: Nothing. Now listen carefully . . .

ISABELLE: Will you pass me my dress?

JUDGE (*Looks around room for dress*): Dress? Dress? (*Sees it on screen and takes it*) Dress! (*Takes it to bathroom*) Here you are.

ISABELLE: Thanks. Now go right on—don't let me interrupt.

JUDGE (*Wearily*): Well, as I was saying . . .

ISABELLE: Yes, go on.

JUDGE: I have been thinking, and . . .

ISABELLE: Just a second, darling, would you please—

JUDGE (*Anticipating her*): All right—I'll get them. (*Gets slippers from upstage end of divan and hands them in to her. Then starts to love seat, exhausted*)

ISABELLE: Now, go on.

JUDGE: No, I'll wait until you're finished. (*Sitting*)

ISABELLE: What did you say?

JUDGE (*Wearily*): I said . . .

ISABELLE: What?

JUDGE: God give me strength!

ISABELLE (*Enters dressed*): *There!* That didn't take long, did it?

JUDGE: Nooooooo! Not when you think of all the things I handed you.

ISABELLE: You were sweet. Would you . . . would you hook me up?

JUDGE (*Rising*): Certainly. (*Goes up behind her and hooks her up with difficulty*) There! You should have zippers on here.

ISABELLE: Thank you. Now what were you trying to say while I was in there?

JUDGE: What I was trying to convey, with remarkably little success, was, that after thinking matters over carefully, I've decided you were right.

ISABELLE: Of course I was right. What about?

JUDGE: About going home.

ISABELLE: You think I'd better not go?

JUDGE: To put it in a nutshell, yes.

ISABELLE: But if I don't go home, what *will* I do?

JUDGE: *Stay here and get married.*

ISABELLE (*Crosses to window*): That's what I thought. (*After a long pause*) Even if I don't love him? . . .

JUDGE: Great guns! What's happened now?

ISABELLE: Maybe you're right. There doesn't seem much else to do.

JUDGE: He would be flattered if he heard you.

ISABELLE: I don't care . . . I don't care about anything.

TOM (*Knocking and coming right in*): Signorina . . . that young man . . . who come with you last night . . . he's downstairs . . . insists he wants to see you. I no tell him you're here yet.

ISABELLE (*Sighs*): Tell him to come up.

JUDGE: What!

TOM (*Exiting*): Yes, Signorina.

ISABELLE: I don't think Gus would mind . . .

JUDGE: What do you mean—he wouldn't mind—he'd be furious.

ISABELLE (*Crossing to divan*): No, he wouldn't.

JUDGE (*Crossing to other side of divan*): He would—

THEY *start to straighten cover of chair.*

He would.

ISABELLE: I know.

JUDGE: Oh, I don't understand anything anymore.

> ISABELLE *crosses to love seat.* JUDGE *puts two pillows on divan.* HE *is about to get others when* SHE *turns and sees him as* SHE *sits.*

ISABELLE: Never mind about that.

> *Raps on door.*

Come in.

> HENRY *enters.* JUDGE *brushes by him with a snort and exits.*

HENRY: I . . . I came to apologize . . . Isabelle.

ISABELLE: That's all right, Henry.

HENRY: I said some rotten things. I'm sorry.

ISABELLE: I said things, too.

HENRY: I was pretty drunk, I guess.

ISABELLE: I guess so.

HENRY (*Eyeing the room surreptitiously*): Did you . . . sleep . . . here?

ISABELLE: Yes, Henry. *There!* (SHE *points to the divan*)

HENRY (*From the chair*): Nice apartment . . . in a flashy way.

ISABELLE: Do you think it's flashy?

HENRY: Yes—ostentatious.

ISABELLE: What's the matter with it?

HENRY: Ostentatious—woppish.

ISABELLE: Well, I like it and the Count Di Ruvo said I could stay as long as I liked.

HENRY (*Viciously*): Damn nice of him. And where would *he* stay?

ISABELLE: I didn't ask him that.

HENRY: No . . . you wouldn't. But I can tell you where he'd stay, if you're anxious to know.

ISABELLE: I'm not.

HENRY: Where did he stay last night?

ISABELLE (*Smiling slightly and looking at him*): Where did *you* stay?

HENRY: Never mind where *I* stayed . . . where was *he*?

ISABELLE: With the Judge . . . your friend.

HENRY: How do I know he was?

ISABELLE: You don't . . . you never will.

HENRY (*Toward her slightly*): What do you mean?

ISABELLE: Just that! If you don't believe me *now*, you never will, that's all. About *this*, or anything else.

HENRY (*Narrowing his eyes*): If I thought . . .

ISABELLE: You can think anything you like. I know how your mind works.

HENRY: Naturally, I . . .

ISABELLE: I *still* have my virginity, if that's what's worrying you.

HENRY (*Shocked*): *Isabelle!*

ISABELLE: Don't be a hypocrite . . . that's what you were thinking . . . though why they make so much fuss about it is more than I can understand.

HENRY (*Thunderstruck*): *Fuss about it!*

ISABELLE: You heard me. As if it mattered to anybody but me. By the way, I forgot to ask you! Are *you* pure?

HENRY: *What?* Why . . .

ISABELLE: You needn't bother to answer. I'm not curious.

HENRY: It's *entirely* different anyway.

ISABELLE: Well, I don't *really* know anything about it, so you may be right.

HENRY: Now you're being sensible. (*Smiles—several steps toward her*) I . . . ah . . . hope you didn't take our little lovers' quarrel . . . too seriously.

ISABELLE *looks away, but says nothing.*

We're . . . still engaged, I mean.

ISABELLE *remains silent.* HENRY *edges closer.*

Aren't we?

TOM (*Is heard pounding up the stairs yelling*): Signor Conte, Signor Conte. (HE *bursts into the room with a cable in his hand.* HE *stands panting and looking around*)

ISABELLE: I guess he's in the Judge's apartment, Tom.

TOM: Thank you, I look. (HE *rushes out*)

HENRY (*Watches him go, then*): Isabelle!

ISABELLE: Yes?

HENRY: You didn't answer my question.

ISABELLE (*Vaguely*): Huh?

HENRY: Are you still my fiancée?

ISABELLE: I . . . I suppose so.

HENRY: I knew you didn't mean it . . . you couldn't.

ISABELLE *turns and looks at him without a trace of a smile.* HENRY *advances.*

Well, aren't you . . . aren't you going to kiss me?

ISABELLE: Yes, Henry.

SHE *is taken in his arms and kissed.*

GUS (*Off*): Isabelle!

GUS *bursts into room with cable. Sees* HENRY *kissing* ISABELLE. SHE *backs up against piano.*

I beg your pardon. The Judge said you wanted to see me.

HENRY (*All smiles*): It's quite all right, Count. It's *our* fault. By the way, Count, I want to thank you for turning over your rooms to my fiancée last night. It was very kind of you. I appreciate it.

GUS: I was only too happy.

HENRY: I also want to straighten out our little difference. I'm afraid I was intoxicated.

GUS (*Stiffly*): It is not necessary to mention it, sir.

HENRY: Well, then I guess . . . that's all. (*Turns to* ISABELLE) Are you ready, Isabelle?

ISABELLE: Yes, Henry.

HENRY *goes to door and opens it.* SHE *picks up cape and bag, sadly crosses toward* GUS.

Good-bye, Gus.

GUS (*Bowing*): Good-bye, Miss Parry.

HENRY: Well, so long.

ISABELLE *starts to go, and is stopped by* GUS's *words.*

GUS: If you please . . . I would like to speak with you . . . for one minute.

HENRY: Well, the fact is . . . we're in pretty much of a hurry . . .

ISABELLE: What is it, Gus?

HENRY: Well, I suppose we *can* spare a couple of minutes.

GUS (*To* ISABELLE): Alone.

HENRY (*Belligerently*): Say! What's the idea?

ISABELLE (*Turning coldly to* HENRY): This gentleman has shown me the greatest courtesy, Henry. More than you can possibly realize. You have nothing to fear in leaving me alone with him.

HENRY: I didn't mean that.

ISABELLE (*Still in the same level tone*): Will you wait for me in the car, please?

HENRY: Yeah, but—

ISABELLE: Are you going to start all over again, Henry?

HENRY (*Going to door*): Oh—all right. (*Turns*) But it's a damn funny idea. (HE *exits, leaving door open*)

ISABELLE (*Looking at* GUS *uneasily*): What is it, Gus?

GUS (*Closing door. Very gravely*): I came here just now . . . to ask you to marry me.

ISABELLE: Oh! (SHE *turns away from him*)

GUS: Yes.

ISABELLE: When did you get that idea?

GUS: This morning . . . after I left you. I couldn't sleep. I lay in bed wondering . . . wondering.

ISABELLE: What to do with me?

GUS: Yes.

ISABELLE: Then you thought of this . . . solution.

GUS: Yes. Always you see, I thought marriage was not for me. For a woman, such life would be . . . hell. Here a few months, then quick to Milan, a week at La Scala, then two, maybe three days at home, then a rotten trip to Spain . . .

ISABELLE, *who has been only to Excelsior Springs, West Orange, N.J., and New York, listens to this itinerary breathlessly.* SHE *dreamily contemplates the wonders of such a trip.*

. . . one week in Barcelona, one week in Madrid, then off to South America for the season. *It's terrible!*

ISABELLE: Yes . . . it must be.

GUS: *It is. It's awful.* So always I put behind me thoughts of marriage, so that some poor woman would not have to . . . share my sufferings.

ISABELLE: That was very thoughtful of you.

GUS: But bad as it would be for the woman, think what it would mean for the children.

ISABELLE (*Turns to him*): Yes, I suppose it would be hard for the children.

GUS (*Toward her slightly*): *Terrible!* But I will *not* be separated from my wife and children. I am, by nature, a family man. All my ancestors, on both sides, had families.

ISABELLE (*Wistfully*): I guess mine did too.

GUS: So can you see what it would be like . . . to travel? Nurses, valets, governesses, maids, toys, animals . . . tutors, little boys, little girls . . . it would be like traveling with a menagerie!

ISABELLE: How many children did you expect to have?

GUS: I haven't decided yet.

ISABELLE: Oh!

GUS: But then this morning, I said, what the hell, we only live once . . . if I can travel, the family can travel. So I put on my best suit, and came to tell you. And I find—

HE *extends his arm towards where* SHE *stood with* HENRY. ISABELLE *looks away from him.*

So now . . . before you go . . . out of my life into the arms of . . . a younger man, I want you please to remember that I loved you, Isabelle.

ISABELLE: You don't.

GUS (*Unheeding*): . . . that I loved you. Very real . . . very fine . . . very honorable love. And when I lose you, I am losing something . . . (HE *taps his heart*) . . . of me. Something . . . I am afraid I will not find anymore. (*In a more matter-of-fact tone*) Something I did not deserve, Isabelle, because I have been a very wicked man. But that is no consolation for me now. You must go now. (HE *turns*) You must not keep Henry waiting . . . the wife must be obedient and thoughtful. (*Looks around at her*) But if sometimes you hear me sing . . . you will know I am singing for you, Isabelle, only for you, and . . . and . . . that is all.

ISABELLE (*Facing him*): You don't love me.

GUS: Would I then have asked you to marry me? The only time in my life I ask anybody.

ISABELLE: And you were sure I'd say "Yes," weren't you?

GUS: No, Isabelle, but I hoped.

ISABELLE: Oh, yes, you were.

GUS: No, my child.

ISABELLE: You were sure I'd say yes because I couldn't do anything else. You felt sorry for me, and out of the kindness of your heart, you said, well, nobody else wants her, she's in trouble. *I'll* take her. Well, I don't want your charity. I won't have it, yours or anybody else's.

GUS: But, I love you, baby—

ISABELLE: No, you don't.

GUS: But, Isabelle.

ISABELLE: You don't, you don't. (SHE *is practically sobbing by now*)

GUS: I do . . . and you know it.

ISABELLE: You don't. *You don't.* If you did you wouldn't have left me . . . last night, with that stuffed teddy bear. (SHE *goes up to door and opens it*)

GUS (*Putting up his hands*): Baby!

ISABELLE: You're just trying to make me unhappy by telling me this now. That's what you're doing. Well . . . it's too late. I *don't* love you . . . I . . . I love Henry. You saw me kissing him just now. You know what that means? It means . . . that for the rest of my life . . . I'm going to live . . . in *West Orange* . . . New Jersey!

SHE *exits.* JUDGE *appears in door, watching* ISABELLE *leave. Then* HE *enters and comes to* GUS. GUS *passes cable to* JUDGE, *who looks at it a moment, then hands it back.*

JUDGE: What does it say?

GUS (*Reading*): Figlio mio: tu hai il mio permesso e la mia benedizione . . .

JUDGE *interrupts.*

Oh—excuse me— (*Translates*) My son—you have my permission and my blessing but . . . there cannot be no such person . . . you must be dreaming. (*Looks up*) I guess she is right . . . my mother. I was dreaming.

The canary begins to sing. HE *crosses to front of love seat, back to audience. Throws cable down.*

You can sing, Caruso, but I . . . I will never sing again.

Canary stops singing.

JUDGE: Oh, for God's sake, let's have a drink.

Phone starts to ring as HE *starts to door.*

I have something in my room.

JUDGE *exits.* GUS *goes to telephone reluctantly.*

GUS: Yes? Who? Oh, hello, Lilli, but the conference has just ended. No, it was not a success. I had hoped it would mean a long contract, but it was a complete failure. . . . Yes, Lilli . . . no, Lilli, I cannot see you.

JUDGE *enters, leading* ISABELLE. GUS *sees her and puts receiver down. Then* HE *rushes down to her.*

JUDGE: Gus! Gus! Look what I found crying in my room! Isabelle!
ISABELLE: It wasn't true. I lied to you. I do love you.

> *Telephone starts ringing in jerks, then begins to ring regularly.* THEY *embrace and break.*

GUS: But I warn you—I must have four sons and seven daughters—
JUDGE (*Starting to exit*): In that case I'll tell Henry not to wait.

END OF PLAY

THE RACKET

by

BARTLETT CORMACK

"Bloody instructions, which being taught,
return to plague the inventor. . . . "

—*MACBETH*

Bartlett Cormack

The Racket was originally produced by Alexander McKaig at the Ambassador Theatre, New York City, on November 22, 1927. The sets were designed by Livingston Platt.

Police inspect the body of fellow officer, Johnson (G. Pat Collins), as Irene Hayes (Marion Coakley) looks on.

The Original Cast

Pratt . . . . Willard Robertson
Miller . . . . Hugh O'Connell
Sergeant Sullivan . . . . Mal Kelly
First Patrolman . . . . Charles O'Conner
Lieutenant Gill . . . . Harry English
Assistant State's Attorny Welch . . . . Romaine Callender
Turck . . . . Harry McCoy
Detective Sergeant Delaney . . . . Fred Irving Lewis
Patrolman Johnson . . . . G. Pat Collins
Captain McQuigg . . . . John Cromwell
Dave Ames . . . . Norman Foster
Joe . . . . Edward Eliscu
Irene Hayes . . . . Marion Coakley
Sergeant Schmidt . . . . C.E. Smith
Clark . . . . Jack Clifford
Sam Meyer . . . . Ralph Adams
Alderman Kublacek . . . . Louis Frohoff
An Unidentified Man . . . . Edward G. Robinson
Second Patrolman . . . . Mike Flanagan
Glick . . . . Robert Le Seuer

Place

The central room and captain's office of a police station on the outskirts of Chicago.

Time

A Friday night at midnight and the next afternoon, in early November.

Characters

The play is dedicated to Adelaide.

The Play

ACT ONE

The central room of the Tenth District police station far out on the southwest side of Chicago.

The station is an old, remodeled Victorian house, and so this room is large, with a high ceiling, smoky old wainscoting, and soiled kalsomined walls on one of which there is a streak of fresh plaster that has lately repaired a crack. Two high, arched windows without blinds, their panes grimy and streaked with rain, are back left and right of a double door that leads out through a storm entryway down a short flight of steps to the street. (The stage directions throughout are right and left from the audience's, not actor's, point of view.) The door to the Captain's office is halfway down left; another, to the Lieutenant's office, is up right; and a swing door leads to the interior of the station down right. An old telephone booth encloses a pay phone in the corner back left. A small blackboard on which orders are posted and chalked is on the wall between the booth and the Captain's door. There is a radiator under the blackboard, and a water-cooler and glass back by the door to the street.

A breast-high partition of the same wood as the wainscoting and doors juts from the right wall, forming an enclosure that is the desk sergeant's "office." Swing gates enter it up and down. Inside are a desk and chair, and on the desk the usual station arrest and complaint books, three desk telephones—one rings, the others jingle—

70

and a teletype machine that now and then whirs and writes off reports from head-quarters downtown. There is an old bench against the wall this side of the Captain's door, and over it a NO SMOKING placard in red block letters signed by the City Fire Commissioner. An old-fashioned brass and glass chandelier hangs from the center of the ceiling, and an electric light in a green glass shade over the desk. Down left are an old kitchen table and two chairs, and nearby an iron spittoon, politically large, its inner surface of white enamel mostly scarred away.

It is shortly before midnight of a Friday in early November.

The lights are lit. PRATT *and* MILLER, *reporters, are at the table, playing rummy.* MILLER *is thirty-two, robust, unkempt, and now, as usual, slightly drunk.* HE *is wearing the old topcoat* HE *never is without, and in its pocket a copy of the* American Mercury. *A pint bottle of whiskey, a third full, is at his elbow.* PRATT *is twenty-nine, and debonair. His overcoat is folded on the bench, and his hat is at the correctly cocky angle on his head.* THEY *are cynical fellows—*PRATT *lightly, amusedly;* MILLER *heavily, bored.* PRATT *is softly humming, whistling, and dum de-da-da-ing a snatch from a popular song as* HE *plays.* SERGEANT SULLIVAN, *a fat, white-haired old-timer in uniform, is busy at the desk.*

MILLER *takes a card from the pack, grimaces wearily at it, and discards it.*

PRATT (*Taking* MILLER's *discard, discarding, and slapping down his hand*): Out. Pay me—double. (*Going to the desk,* PRATT *takes a phone and jiggles the receiver hook*)

MILLER (*Staring at his beaten hand*): Horses! (HE *throws down his cards, rises, and shoves a hand down in a pocket to push down his constricting pants*) I told you—I'd rather play bridge, with the cops.

PRATT (*At the phone*): Wire, darling.

MILLER (*Irascibly*): Where is this captain?

PRATT (*At the phone*): Superior oh one hundred.

MILLER: God, I'm tired. Up all day. I'm goin' to get out o' this comical business.

SULLIVAN: I never saw a reporter that wasn't, an' I never saw one that did.

The teletype whirs and writes.

PRATT (*At the phone*): Give me the desk.

SULLIVAN *tears off the teletyped sheet.*

Anything doing, Sarge?

SULLIVAN: No. A stick-up.

MILLER: In this godforsaken zone o' quiet?

SULLIVAN: No.

PRATT (*Amusedly*): Who'd stick-up what, out here?

MILLER: Listen, baby—trade follows the flag. With this McQuigg captain here now, anythin's liable to happen.

SULLIVAN: We can stand it. I ain't used to nothin' ever happenin' anymore'n you.

MILLER: No kid?

SULLIVAN: In the old days they was some use for policemen. Now pipe me—wet-nurse to a whole ward, an' gettin' a belly on me, cause *police*men 're out o' style.

MILLER: You got a policeman in your new captain. There's plenty o' sand in his spinach.

PRATT: Don't let him get your hopes raised, Sarge. He's worked on that sheet of his so long his imagination runs in purple headlines across a yellow sky.

MILLER: I suppose somethin's not liable to break here with McQuigg and Nick Scarsi itchin' to have each other's eyes for grapes?

SULLIVAN: I heard somethin' about the Captain an' that mug.

PRATT (*To* MILLER): You don't expect to see any Scarsis out here, do you? A cow would moo and scare those gangsters to death.

MILLER: McQuigg's here, ain't he? (HE *flops into a chair, hoisting his feet to the other one*)

PRATT (*At the phone*): Bob? . . . Pratt, on the McQuigg interview.

MILLER: Where the hell *is* McQuigg?

PRATT (*At the phone*): Sure. But all he does is quote his transfer order—you know: that "for-the-good-of-the-department" stuff.

MILLER: "For the good o' — " Nuts.

PRATT (*At the phone*): Damn right he's mad.

MILLER: He's bloodshot.

SULLIVAN: Who? The Captain?

MILLER: Don't kid me.

PRATT (*At the phone*): All right. I'll call you back. (*Replacing the phone*) No, Sarge—mustn't kid him. He knows! (HE *goes to the table*)

MILLER: Who don't know why McQuigg got dropped out here?

PRATT *jerks the chair from under* MILLER's *feet.*

(*Rising*) Jeez, you would! (MILLER *goes and takes the phone*)

SULLIVAN (*To* PRATT): It was Scarsi got the Captain transferred, uh?

PRATT: Shh. Mustn't gossip, Sergeant! (PRATT *deals and plays solitaire*)

SULLIVAN: That Scarsi! (HE *grunts*) Why somebody don't *get* him—

PRATT: Nobody gets a chance.

MILLER: He's got a horseshoe. After he banged his last competitor the corpse's whole family got in a frenzy at Nick's gyppin' 'em out o' their gold mine—you know, there's a *seventy* percent profit in liquor up north there in McQuigg's old district, where the high-class people live. They took a shot at Nick every time he went to Mass. Not a scratch. (*At the phone*) Greetin's, Genevieve. How was that nap? . . . You win. Main five thousand.

FIRST PATROLMAN *comes from the captain's office in shirtsleeves and suspenders, carrying a mop and a scrubpail, and goes out right.*

PRATT: Didn't the Captain say when he'd be back?

SULLIVAN: No.

MILLER (*At the phone*): Give me the desk.

PRATT: He's sleeping here till he gets moved, isn't he?

SULLIVAN: Yeh.

PRATT: How he must love that.

MILLER (*At the phone*): Boss, this is Miller again, out to hellangone on that McQuigg interview. . . . No, he won't talk. . . . But the *City Press*'ll be here. They'll get it if he does. . . . Yeh-h-h, the *Tribune*'s here. . . . Allri— Say! . . . They made some more o' those pre-election raids here tonight—those cathouses out South. . . . Wait a second. (*To* SULLIVAN) How many from those raids you got downstairs?

SULLIVAN: Seven.

MILLER (*At the phone*): Seven. . . . No, just bewildered little tarts. . . . No, for pictures you can get better ones at the stations downtown . . . 'right. (*Replacing the phone*) If that office o' mine calls me again, tell 'em I'm gone. They're not goin' to have me runnin' down tips on that Higgins story again tonight.

SULLIVAN: Did you find anythin'?

MILLER: On what?

SULLIVAN: Didn't you say Higgins—that private sec'etary o' the Old Man who disappeared?

PRATT: "Disappeared." Ha!

SULLIVAN: They've even had us lookin' for him.

MILLER: You all better quit lookin', or somebody just might find somethin' of him, and that'd reach high up.

PRATT: And that *would* blow to hell the Grand Old Party's chances of staying in after this election Tuesday.

SULLIVAN: I heard them rumors about what happened to Higgins.

PRATT (*Smiling*): You don't believe rumors, do you, Sarge?

SULLIVAN: About politicians, I'd believe anythin'.

MILLER *opens the door to the street and peers out.*

PRATT: Aren't you going to stick?

MILLER (*Slamming the door*): Have to, till the *Press* comes. That half-wit we got on the desk can't think fast enough to say anythin' but "stick around awhile."

HE *gets out his cigarette package, discovers it to be empty, crumples it, and throws it to the floor as* LIEUTENANT GILL *comes from his office—a stocky, stolid, unimaginative man of forty-eight, with a short black mustache, and a manner that* HE *conceives to be professionally hard.* HE *is in uniform.*

Give me a cigarette.

PRATT *gives* MILLER *his cigarettes.*

GILL (*Picking up the cigarette package*): Here! (HE *tosses it to* MILLER) There's a wastepaper place out back.

PRATT (*To* MILLER): Certainly. T't-t-t! (*To* GILL)

Lieutenant, I've been wanting to tell you what a relief it is to be in a clean station nowadays.

GILL: This district's as clean outside as the station is in. That's why we're not in your papers all the time. (HE *starts out*)

MILLER: Why don't you extend the good work to take in that cell those women are in downstairs? God!

GILL: We haven't facilities for women here.

PRATT: Do you know when the Captain will be—?

GILL: He just phoned he's on his way. (HE *goes out*)

MILLER: McQuigg'll unwind his red tape. (HE *drinks the rest of the whiskey with a shudder and a wrenching clearing of his throat*)

PRATT: You'd better cut that stuff.

MILLER: It's cut plenty before I get it. (HE *goes to the water-cooler and gets a drink*)

PRATT (*To* SULLIVAN): What time's the *City Press* get here?

SULLIVAN: He phoned he'd be late. He had to cover a campaign meetin' up at the other end o' the ward.

ASSISTANT STATE'S ATTORNEY WELCH *comes in from the street, followed by* TURCK. WELCH *is forty-two, pale, and tight.* TURCK *is large, hard, impassive.* HE *is lazily chewing gum.*

MILLER: Hi.

WELCH (*Going to the desk*): How are you, boys.

PRATT: What's the hanging prosecutor doing out here?

WELCH: The Old Man spoke at a meeting of ours out here tonight.

PRATT (*Smiling*): But that was at the other end of the ward, wasn't it, Mr. Welch?

WELCH (*To* SULLIVAN): The Captain in?

SULLIVAN: What can I do for you?

WELCH: I'm Assistant State's Attorney Welch.

PRATT: You know, Sarge—the Old Man's nominee for county judge Tuesday, on the—ah—Gluttonous Republicans's ticket.

WELCH: What?

PRATT: Oh, just my way of telling you two Republican factions apart. It does seem rather gluttonous not to give the Reform gang at least a couple of bones to gnaw. Their tongues are hanging out after the famine they've been through.

WELCH: You're the *Tribune*, aren't you?

PRATT *bows.*

I thought I recognized the air. Fresh. (HE *turns back to* SULLIVAN)

PRATT: The difference *is* striking, after you've been used to the other kind.

WELCH (*To* SULLIVAN): This is Sergeant Turck, of my office. He'll be here for these raids.

SULLIVAN (*To* TURCK): Out back.

TURCK *goes out.*

WELCH (*To* SULLIVAN): Do you know where the Captain went?

SULLIVAN: No, sir.

PRATT: Wasn't he at that revival of yours?

MILLER (*After an exasperated look at* PRATT): How's it look for Tuesday, Welch?

WELCH: It's a cinch.

PRATT (*Smiling*): Who for?

WELCH (*To* SULLIVAN): Tell the Captain I was in.

SULLIVAN: Yes, sir.

WELCH *goes out to the street.*

MILLER (*To* PRATT): Askin' him if McQuigg wasn't at that meetin' o' theirs! To kiss the hand that slapped him, I suppose.

PRATT: Oh, Welch is nothing but a frightened little yes-man, anyway.

MILLER: Who ain't?

DETECTIVE SERGEANT DELANEY *comes in from the street—a smooth-faced, athletic, good-looking man of thirty-seven, in plain clothes, a topcoat, and soft hat.* HE *goes alertly to* SULLIVAN.

DELANEY (*To* SULLIVAN): The Captain in?

SULLIVAN: He's on his way.

PRATT: *Hello,* Delaney!

DELANEY (*Abstractedly*): Hi, scribe. (*Back to* SULLIVAN) Any alarms?

SULLIVAN: Nooo.

DELANEY: There may be. There's a mob o' strangers to this peaceful little community out here tonight, so you better tell the men out back to ditch their cards and get the lead out o' their pants. (*To* PRATT) We all have to be on our toes now, with McQuigg.

PRATT (*Shaking hands*): How long have they had you here?

DELANEY (*Drily*): Since the last election.

MILLER: Jeez, you can't collect out here, can you?

DELANEY: No, this district drinks milk.

One of the desk phones jingles.

SULLIVAN (*Answering*): Tenth District—Sullivan.

PRATT: Play some rummy, Sarge?

DELANEY: Shoot 'em. (HE *goes to the table and they play*)

SULLIVAN (*At the phone*): Yes, lady.

MILLER: Where is—that—City—Press? (HE *drops to the bench, and dozes*)

SULLIVAN (*At the phone*): Yes'm. I'll have an officer right over.

DELANEY *twists around to him.* SULLIVAN *replaces the phone and goes to the door to the back.*

DELANEY: What is it?

SULLIVAN (*Pushing open the door*): Johnson!

JOHNSON (*Off*): Yes, sir.

DELANEY: Sullivan! What is it?

SULLIVAN (*Returning to the desk*): Nothin'. Some kids in an automobile disturbin' a lady's peace.

DELANEY *turns back to the game.* PATROLMAN JOHNSON *comes in—a tall, blond, powerful young man, buttoning his uniform coat.*

Drop over to eight nine one six Catalpa. Householder there can't sleep on account of a pettin' party parked out front. Prob'ly some o' them kids from the university, drunk an' raisin' hell.

MILLER: If they're collegiate, they're prob'ly raisin' a family.

JOHNSON *starts for the street.*

SULLIVAN: Just give 'em a spankin' and send 'em home.

JOHNSON: Yes, sir.

DELANEY: And keep your eyes open.

JOHNSON (*Cockily*): Me? Why?

DELANEY: There's a new crowd moved out here tonight. You might bump into somethin'.

JOHNSON (*Grinning*): Anythin' that bumps me ain't goin' to get up first. (HE *goes out*)

DELANEY: Look out they don't bump you from behind!

One of the desk phones rings.

SULLIVAN (*Answering*): Tenth District—Sullivan. . . . Yeh, right here. (*To* MILLER) You, Miller.

MILLER (*Rousing*): Huh?

SULLIVAN (*Setting the phone atop the partition*): Your office wants you.

MILLER (*Rising*): I told you I left, didn't I? (HE *goes to the phone*)

SULLIVAN: You haven't, have y'?

DELANEY (*As* PRATT *takes his discard*): You would save aces.

MILLER (*At the phone*): Yeh? . . . Yeh-h. . . . Yeh-h-h. . . . All right. (HE *hangs up viciously, and makes a note on copy paper pulled from his overcoat pocket*) Up at eight this mornin', up all night, and have to be in the speeders' court at ten t'morrow to fix another one. (*Stuffing the copy paper away*) The wife of a friend o' somebody who's a friend o' God, the city editor, just got a ticket for tryin' to beat a moonbeam across Michigan Avenue bridge. If a few more friends o' friends o' people who know somebody who works on a newspaper get on to this racket, somebody in that court's liable to retire a millionaire. (HE *sags to the bench again*) I hope the crime wave's quiet tomorrow, anyway.

PRATT: It will be, till after election, anyway. (*To* DELANEY) Eh, Sarge? (*To* MILLER) Haven't you noticed, bright boy—being on the inside of everything as you are—how quiet crime's been for the last few weeks, how hushed, so that the people may be lulled into a little additional stupor, and on Tuesday sleepwalk to the polls in such a glow of sweet security and peace that they'll vote to retain the—uh—heroic administration that put down crime, till after election?

MILLER (*With a tired wave of an arm*): H'ray!

PRATT *begins to whistle his tune again.* MILLER *jumps up.*

'Ave you got to memorize that dirge? (HE *gets out his bottle, discovers it to be empty, and throws it on the table*)

DELANEY (*Tossing him the bottle*): Here.

MILLER (*Catching it*): It's empty.

DELANEY: That's why it don't belong in here. The visitin' public might take it as evidence o' that rumor that policemen drink.

MILLER *goes into the entryway, throws the bottle out and returns.*

DELANEY (*Slapping down his hand*): There you are.

PRATT: You caught me with a fistful that time.

The door from the street is flung open and CAPTAIN McQUIGG *comes in in uniform— a man of burly virility, smooth-shaven, ruddy, with close-cropped, iron-gray hair and steady eyes.* HE *is fifty-three.* HE *has the bottle* MILLER *threw away.*

PRATT (*Rising, and tossing* DELANEY *some change*): Here.

DELANEY *rises.*

MILLER: Hi, Captain.

McQUIGG (*Extending the bottle*): That's a fine thing to come sailin' out of a police station in this God Almighty respectable ward. Whose is it?

MILLER: You can have it, Captain.

McQUIGG: I thought it'd be you boys. (*Going to the desk*) No policeman'd drink that class o' goods. (*Setting the bottle on the partition*) Get rid of it, Sergeant.

SULLIVAN: Yes, sir. (HE *takes the bottle and starts out*)

McQUIGG: Delaney, see if the Lieutenant's got those raid orders.

DELANEY: Yes, sir. I want to see you, Captain. (HE *goes into* GILL'S *office*)

PRATT: Captain, about that interview—

McQUIGG: Oh, uh—Sergeant! (SULLIVAN *turns*) On your way back, stop at your locker and bring the boys a shot o' whiskey that can stand up for itself. They deserve it, havin' to spend the night so far away from home.

SULLIVAN: I've no whiskey, sir!

McQUIGG: Go along, Sergeant, or you'll have me believin' this station's the old man's home they say it is.

SULLIVAN: Yes, sir. (HE *goes out*)

PRATT: Captain—

McQUIGG: No story.

PRATT: There is for my paper, if you'll talk.

MILLER: Yeh. "Something must be done."

McQUIGG: Start another anti-smoke campaign.

HE *starts for his office.* GILL *comes in, characteristically distressed.*

GILL (*To* McQUIGG): This—

SULLIVAN *comes in hesitantly with a glass of whiskey in each hand.*

This havin' liquor in the station's news to me. I've never stood for it.

McQUIGG: Maybe that's what's the matter with this station. (HE *motions* SULLIVAN *to the table*) All right, boys. Get warm.

SULLIVAN: There was a smidgeon, sir, we took off some joy-ridin' kids one night, so's they'd be able to drive home.

McQUIGG: Thank you, Sergeant. Did you take those glasses off somebody, too?

SULLIVAN: No, sir. There's nothin' in the Constitution about them. (HE *returns to the desk*)

MILLER: Here's to birth control!

HE *and* PRATT *drink.*

McQUIGG (*To* SULLIVAN): Anythin' new?

SULLIVAN: An assistant state's attorney is in.

PRATT: Welch.

McQUIGG (*Half to himself*): What's he want?

GILL (*To* SULLIVAN): Bring in the books.

SULLIVAN: Yes, sir.

GILL *goes into his office,* SULLIVAN *following him with some station books.*

PRATT: Captain, about your transfer?

McQUIGG: What're you up to? Policemen've been transferred before.

MILLER: You haven't.

McQUIGG (*Starting for his office*): The hell I haven't.

PRATT: Not since you've been a captain. We'd like a—

McQUIGG (*Turning*): I know what you'd like, knowin' the papers. You'd like me to let out a bray that'd make an election issue for you and a jackass out o' me.

MILLER: Oh, no, Captain, we wouldn't want you to—

PRATT: *We* would. Where did your transfer order come from?

McQUIGG: From the Chief's office, didn't it?

PRATT: Through the Chief's office. It had to, to be signed. But who—

McQUIGG *turns for his office.*

Captain, we've got this story now! But we have to have somebody to quote.

McQUIGG: Have all the cemeteries run out o' names? (HE *unlocks his office door*)

PRATT: Captain, suppose one of our leading gangsters—?

McQUIGG (*Sharply*): Who?

PRATT (*Smiling*): Well, perhaps I should say one of our leading big businessmen—a nice, new model big businessman with all the latest Republican improvements and accessories—a punk with about nine murders and no convictions against him—with a liquor and blackmail and graft racket that's a gold mine, and a lot of protection for helping the boys out at elections—a cocky, all wrapped-up-in-cotton-batting big businessman—like Nick Scarsi, say—?

McQUIGG: What about him?

PRATT: Suppose the policeman in command of the district that Scarsi's richest liquor territory was in had been fighting his lordship over who'd run that district, Mr. Scarsi, or the police . . .

McQUIGG (*His eyes pinching*): Well?

PRATT: And then one of Scarsi's important men got in a jam on a charge that wasn't bailable, like rape? And that in view of this approaching election, the powers-that-be thought the charge ought to be changed to contributing to the delinquency of a minor, because that charge is bailable, and probational, and in every way a much nicer charge than rape? But that the policeman who'd caught Scarsi's man, and knew he could make the rape charge stick, got his back up, and swore he'd send him down if it was the last thing—

McQUIGG: That's strong, for a policeman, these days.

PRATT: Suppose he was a captain, and that he worked so fast he yanked Nick's man up before a Reform judge and *did* send him down? And then he got exiled to the sticks. Wouldn't that be a story?

McQUIGG: For the movies. (HE *goes into his office and slams the door*)

MILLER: Flop.

PRATT: He's got something in the back of his head.

MILLER: You knew he wouldn't talk. You think he's crazy? They can't transfer him any farther away. But, no, you make speeches till I'll never get home tonight. (HE *starts for the door right*)

PRATT: Where are you going?

MILLER: Sullivan's locker. (HE *goes out*)

McQUIGG *comes from his office with some reports and goes to the desk.*

PRATT (*Following* MILLER): Wait for baby. (HE *goes out*)

McQUIGG: Delaney!

DELANEY (*From* GILL's *office*): Yes, sir. (HE *comes in*)

McQUIGG: Want to see me? (HE *goes over the reports*)

DELANEY: I made some trucks comin' out o' that old brewery a mile west o' here tonight, and nosed around the works. They're runnin' full blast on near-beer permits, with a detail o' those mugs from the Prohibition Department to give it a legal air.

McQUIGG: Anythin' else?

DELANEY: Who do you think's in charge? Himself.

McQUIGG (*Turning sharply*): Don't tell me—Nick?

DELANEY: Personally.

GILL *comes in, followed by* SULLIVAN, *who returns to the desk.*

McQUIGG: Was that all you saw?

DELANEY: That was enough for me.

McQUIGG (*To* SULLIVAN): Any squads out?

SULLIVAN: Schmidt's. They'll be in at midnight, and then we're clear.

McQUIGG (*To* GILL): General order for all shifts—watch that brewery.

GILL (*Staring*): At Ninety-first and Western there?

McQUIGG: I'm glad you know where it is, anyway.

GILL: Why, that brewery's been abandoned! The federal authorities padlocked it.

McQUIGG: Well, Mr. Nick Scarsi's opened it up again.

GILL (*Worriedly*): He oughtn't to come into this district.

McQUIGG: He is in.

GILL: What'll we do about that brewery?

McQUIGG: Nothin'. I'm after Nick. And if he thinks he can lick me again, in this district—(*To* DELANEY) Get back to that brewery, Jim, and find if Nick's stayin' here. He may be for awhile, till he gets his truck routes set. Buzz one o' that Prohibition detail about what he's goin' to do.

DELANEY: Give one o' those babies a dollar and he'd make a confession against himself. (HE *goes out to the street*)

McQUIGG (*Starting for his office*): You don't know Nick Scarsi, do you, Lieutenant?

GILL: Not me!

McQUIGG: You may. He don't like me. And when he's around me he usually drops in to tell me so. So as long as he's in the neighborhood keep the men inside the station awake, as well as those out on beats. It'd be a shame, havin' your station all mussed up. (HE *goes out*)

PRATT *comes in.*

GILL: All the responsibility back on me! (HE *goes into his office*)

PRATT: McQuigg putting him to work?

DAVE AMES *comes in from the street, his topcoat turned up about his neck.* HE *is twenty-three, eager with young enthusiasm, and full of an inexperienced, romantic capacity for surprise.*

AMES (*Going to the desk*): Hello, Sarge. Anything doing?

SULLIVAN: Haven't turned a wheel.

MILLER *wanders in.*

AMES: It's getting cold. And windy? In this town you're always getting roasted, frozen, soaked, and street stuff blown in your eyes!

MILLER: Alice in Wonderland. Kid, you *City Press*?

AMES: Yes. I'm supposed to be here earlier, but I had to cover a campaign meeting. Of all the bunk!

PRATT (*Advancing, and putting out a hand*): Pratt's my name. *Tribune.*

AMES (*Shaking hands*): Dave Ames is mine.

PRATT (*Waving at* MILLER): Mr. Brisbane of the *Herald-Examiner.*

AMES: I'm supposed to interview the Captain on—

MILLER: Fancy that.

PRATT: So were we.

AMES: Then he hasn't given it out yet?

MILLER: No, he's been waitin' for you.

AMES: Then can we see him now? What's he like?

MILLER: Well, David, he's kind o' like Goliath. So you beat it in there and slay him with your questionnaire, and then skip back and tell us cubs who've only been in this business fifteen 'r twenty years the news, so's we won't get

scooped, and have to tell our city desks that David did it wiv 'is li'l questionnaire. (HE *goes out to the street*)

AMES: What did I do?

SULLIVAN: Don't mind him. He's one o' these *vet*'rans!

PRATT: Oh, he's all right.

AMES: Sure. (*Taking off his overcoat*) I'm almost used to it now, anyway.

*There is the sound of a flivver turning into and coming up the alley alongside the
station, right.*

That the wagon, Sarge? Maybe they've got somebody!

SULLIVAN: No, Schmidt's squad checkin' in, that's all.

AMES (*To* PRATT): Don't you think the Captain might say *something*?

PRATT: He can't. *Lèse majesté.* You're new to the newspaper business, aren't you?

AMES: Yes, but I've studied it a lot, so—(*As* PRATT *smiles*) In school, I mean. I took
journalism.

PRATT: Illinois?

AMES: No, Nebraska—where I live. When I graduated, my dean told me Chicago
was the best newspaper town in the world, so I stopped off for experience.
Of course, from here I'm going on to New York.

PRATT (*Drily*): Of course. Well, we're still salty here. But you'd better forget
everything you learned in journalism school. They have journalism in New
York, I guess, but not here.

AMES (*Grinning*): I'm finding that out. But what I don't understand, is—

PRATT: You'll catch on.

AMES: I mean about the Captain's transfer. If what they say downtown's true—
How do municipal authorities get away with that stuff?

PRATT: It's all regular.

AMES: It's wrong, isn't it?

PRATT (*Startled*): What?

AMES: I mean—(*Embarrassed*) Well—

PRATT: Where they erred with McQuigg was trying to make a goat of a mule, that's
all. This captain's no reformer, kid. He's taken his "legitimate," like everyone
else. It's just that—you know who Nick Scarsi is, don't you?

AMES: I've read about him.

PRATT: Well, Nick's so cocky he gets on these old-fashioned policemen's nerves.
McQuigg's pretty cocky, himself.

AMES: I know, but—how does Scarsi control voters? You'd think a criminal—

PRATT: He gives them their daily beer, so hallowed be his name. Anyway, weren't
you always fascinated by pirates rather than saints? (*To* SULLIVAN) Come on,
Sarge, give the press the gossip, and we'll trek. (HE *goes to the desk and looks
through the complaint book*)

AMES *abruptly goes to* McQUIGG's *office and knocks.* McQUIGG *opens the door, a
report in his hand.*

AMES: Captain—(*Putting out a hand*) Ames is my name. *City Press.* We supply all the papers with news, you know.

McQUIGG (*Shaking hands*): How are you, son?

PRATT (*Starting out*): Good night, Captain.

McQUIGG: Good-bye.

PRATT (*Smiling*): No. *Au revoir.* (HE *goes out*)

AMES: Captain, if you're going to give out anything about your transfer—

McQUIGG: I'm not. (HE *turns back*)

AMES: But, Captain—

McQUIGG (*Turning*): Now, now, there's nothin' unusual—

AMES: Yes there is. Excuse me, but I've got all the dope.

McQUIGG: You have, have you?

AMES: Yes, sir. And the public's got a right to know—

McQUIGG: *What?*

AMES: Well—Maybe if the public knew about things like this they'd clean them out.

McQUIGG: Son, the public don't know it's alive, and don't care. I been workin' for it for thirty years. I know.

AMES: It might care if somebody would stand up and give it an example.

McQUIGG: Well, well! Give it an example o' what?

AMES: Well, of—(*Grinning*)—Standing up! Telling the facts about these things.

McQUIGG: Is that what you're goin' to do?

AMES: Sure. Except that my office told me the papers wouldn't print what you'd say if you did talk. They ought to print it.

McQUIGG: They can't.

AMES: That's what they're for, aren't they?

McQUIGG: Not here. This is a growin' town. Nobody'll listen to anythin' but boosts. However, go to it, son—if you can take it on the chin. But I can't give you that interview. (HE *turns*)

AMES: I don't agree with you.

McQUIGG (*Turning*): You'll learn to—and get hurt.

AMES: That's all right.

McQUIGG: This standin' up for things and fightin' other people's battles 'll only get you a smack on the nose.

AMES: You're pretty cynical. Well, I'm not.

McQUIGG: Yet. (HE *starts back into his office*)

AMES (*Smiling*): I don't have to be, do I?

There is the careening rumble and crash of a heavy truck tearing past outside, the sound of a shot, the crash of shattered glass in the entryway. As McQUIGG *jumps to and jerks the door open, disclosing broken glass on the floor and a broken pane in the window facing the street, there is a shout of raised, tough voices, "Hi-i-i, McQuigg!"* SULLIVAN *has jumped up.*

Must have been some of those campaign meeting drunks. There were some shots fired up there.

McQUIGG (*Drily*): Yeh. (*To* SULLIVAN) That's it. Let it go.

SULLIVAN *resumes his work.*

(*To* AMES) If you want an interview, we've got some girls downstairs.
AMES: Girls?
McQUIGG: I suppose they were, once. We tip the keepers off to these raids, but the keepers don't tip the girls.

AMES *cocks his hat and goes interestedly out.*

Campaign drunks, hell!

McQUIGG *goes to and looks up at the inside of the door. A bullet is embedded there.* HE *digs it out with a key, and bounces it in a hand.*

Some o' the Scarsi mob, leavin' Nick's callin' card. Sweep it up!
SULLIVAN: Yes, sir. (HE *starts out*)
McQUIGG: When Delaney comes in, have him report to me.
SULLIVAN: Yes, sir. (*Pushing open the door*) Healy! Get a broom in here. (HE *returns to the desk*)
McQUIGG (*Starting for his office*): Damn their cocky souls.

WELCH *comes in from the street.*

WELCH: Mac! (McQUIGG *turns*) Glad I caught you.
McQUIGG (*Shaking hands*): How are you, Judge?
WELCH (*Laughing shortly*): We'll wait till after Tuesday for that.
McQUIGG: Well, Mr. Assistant State's Attorney, then. (*Drily*) Has the Old Man located that missin' secretary o' his?
WELCH: You mean Higgins? Oh, he'll turn up.
McQUIGG: In what condition?
WELCH: These rumors about what happened to him are nonsense, Mac.
McQUIGG: As far as that Organization of yours goes they'd better be, hadn't they, till after election, anyway?
WELCH: There's always dirty gossip. Why, Higgins was the Old Man's confidential—
McQUIGG (*Interrupting*): Yeh, what you are now, uh? Is that why you're talking to me?
WELCH: I can tell you better in your office.
McQUIGG: This'll do. The city hasn't gotten around to installin' me a conference table yet.

HE *sits down at the table.* FIRST PATROLMAN *comes in with a broom and dustpan, goes to the entryway, and sweeps up the glass.* SULLIVAN *takes some reports into* GILL's *office.*

WELCH: You're not still hot under the collar about your transfer, are you? (*As* McQUIGG *does not reply*) The Old Man thought you might be, when you didn't show up at that campaign meeting of ours tonight.

McQUIGG: I never make those charivaris. They give me stomach trouble.

WELCH: Now, now. That attitude won't get you anything.

McQUIGG: That's where I've got it on you, Welch—I don't want anythin'. Come on! What'd they send you to tell me? I'm not a jury. You don't have to soft-soap me.

WELCH (*After a moment*): All right. You'll go back to your old station if you behave out here.

McQUIGG: What's the "behave" mean?

WELCH (*Agitation characteristically breaking through his tight control*): Good God! You know! (HE *sits and draws his chair up to the table*) Nick's taken over a brewery.

McQUIGG: Yeh?

WELCH: A mile west of here.

McQUIGG: Yeh?

WELCH: Just got it through Washington. I don't know how.

McQUIGG: No?

WELCH: We told him to wait—to stay away from you. The Old Man ordered him, himself. But he wouldn't. Not him! So it's up to you. Let him alone.

FIRST PATROLMAN *comes in with the swept-up glass and goes out right.*

McQUIGG: The hell I will.

WELCH: You've got to lay off till after Tuesday, Mac. We need Nick's river wards. (McQUIGG *snorts*) You know what this election means to us.

McQUIGG: Yeh. Whether *you* Republicans have to take your head out o' the feed bag. But I don't care which o' you get in. You all smell the same to me, so long as you tend to your business and let me tend to mine.

WELCH: Nowadays our businesses mix.

McQUIGG: I haven't had a general order about it yet.

WELCH: It's your business to lay off Scarsi now!

McQUIGG: Is that what the Old Man told you to tell me?

WELCH: I'm asking you, myself. I'm running in this primary.

McQUIGG: Welch, you've always been decenter than most o' that crowd o' yours. Why do you stick to Scarsi?

WELCH: I'm not sticking to Scarsi. I'm sticking to the Old Man. (*His voice rising*) Why shouldn't I? He's helped me—put me on the ticket for county judge. This is for him. And the quieter things are till after Tuesday—Nick's too influential to fuss with, that's all. And how he knows it! Last month he damn near kicked over the traces when they wouldn't let him be one of the official welcoming committee and ride down the boulevard in a silk hat with Queen Marie. Yes! And socially ambitious, too—changing that gold tooth of his for a white one! Sending that young brother of his to that snob college, East. Nick's got so big—

McQUIGG (*Interrupting*): By usin' politics that are crazier that he is, and a public that takes the performance as a hell of a funny show and don't know enough to come in out o' the rain. (*As* WELCH *starts to speak*) But that's all right! That's the game.

WELCH (*Rather wretchedly*): Yes.

McQUIGG: But Nick Scarsi's personal with me.

WELCH: Oh, it's all in the—

McQUIGG (*Cutting him short*): I'd been runnin' that district o' mine for nine years when Scarsi moved in and made a monkey o' me by protectin' his rackets and his mob so close I couldn't even get murderers to trial. (*Rising*) I fought that. That district was mine! But I got shot at from closed cars. A bomb blew off the porch o' my house. My wife's still gettin' phone calls tellin' her I'm goin' to be killed. (*After pacing a moment*) One day Mr. Scarsi strolled into my station tellin' me to lay off one o' his men I had, and I threw him out. Then my good men got transferred. And when I got one o' his vice presidents for rape—

WELCH (*Interrupting*): We know that.

McQUIGG: *I* got transferred.

WELCH (*Rising*): You'll go back. If you forget Nick, that's all.

McQUIGG: With him spittin' on my doorstep here? I will not.

WELCH: You've got to.

McQUIGG: If I get my hands on him—

WELCH: They'll break you.

McQUIGG: Who?

WELCH: The Organization. And what else can you work at? Think of your family. Do you want them hit—hard—by this? (SULLIVAN *returns*) And here's another tip—when you can't lick an organization, join it. Use your head. You can't just jam things through anymore.

McQUIGG: What?

WELCH: Nowadays, things operate (*Tapping his forehead significantly*) upstairs. (*After a moment*) Glad I saw you. Good night. (HE *goes out to the street*)

McQUIGG *scowls after him a moment, then strides to the door to the street, looks up at the bullet-gash there, slams the door, and goes quickly to his office.* PRATT *comes in right, followed by* AMES. McQUIGG *bangs out.*

AMES: Is he mad?

There is the grinding whir of a high-powered automobile turning into and up the alley alongside the station.

What's that?

MILLER *comes in from the street.*

MILLER (*Starting for the door*): Some cop's made what might be a good arrest. Man in a limousine. They were fightin' at the wheel as they turned in and damn near knocked over a lamppost.

The door is kicked open. MILLER *jumps back.* PATROLMAN JOHNSON *shoves* THE ARREST *through and, following, spins him on to bring him up with a crash against the desk—a young, bit-too-flashily-dressed, Americanized second-generation Italian, nasty in his arrogance, mean, flushed with drink. One side of his face is scratched and swollen. Seeing him,* MILLER *starts and frowns, trying to place him.* JOHNSON *is without his cap, and is panting happily.*

JOHNSON: There's your pettin' party, Sergeant. He had a hot car.

SULLIVAN: Yeh? Things are pickin' up. (HE *goes into* GILL's *office*)

THE ARREST: It ain't my—

JOHNSON: Shut up. (*To* AMES) Hello, Pr'fess'r.

AMES: How are you, Carl?

JOHNSON (*Grabbing* THE ARREST's *arm*): What's your name? Come on. Spill it.

GILL *comes in, followed by* SULLIVAN.

Hot car, Lieutenant.

GILL: Yeh?

JOHNSON: Yes, sir. That stolen Rolls that come in over the ticker this afternoon.

GILL (*Glowering at* THE ARREST): Oh—ho!

JOHNSON: Had another guy and a girl with him. They were havin' a scrap over the broad, I guess. The other one'd blown by the time I got there, and the girl beat it while I was gettin' this one under control.

GILL: Did you bring in the car?

JOHNSON: We had a little argument about it, but it's out back. (HE *takes a small loose-leaf notebook from his pocket, tears out a sheet, and hands it to* GILL) There's the motor number, sir—the same as reported for that missin' Rolls.

GILL (*To* SULLIVAN): What's the license number o' that Rolls?

THE ARREST: Jeez, Lieutenant, I told him it ain't my—

JOHNSON: Shut up!

SULLIVAN *hands* GILL *a slip of paper.*

GILL: Uh-huh! Keep him here till I verify that car. (HE *starts for the door right*)

JOHNSON: It's that Taylor car, all right, Lieutenant. It's got his initials, W. K. T., on the doors.

GILL *goes out.*

PRATT: Warren Taylor! (HE *takes the phone from the desk. At the phone.*) Wire.

MILLER (*Snapping a finger in sudden remembrance of* THE ARREST): I know you! Joe.

THE ARREST: Damn right.

JOHNSON: Who?

MILLER: I'll use the booth! (HE *hurries into the phone booth*)

AMES: Carl, did you hit him?

JOHNSON (*Grinning*): No. He fell.

PRATT (*At the phone*): Superior oh one hundred.

MILLER (*In the booth*): Main five thousand.

AMES (*To* MILLER): Hurry up, will you?

SULLIVAN: What's your name, you?

THE ARREST *sneers.*

JOHNSON (*Advancing on him*): Lockjaw, uh?

SULLIVAN: What's your name?

THE ARREST: Wait'll I tell it to you, you big balloon! You'll burst.

MILLER (*In the booth*): Give me the desk. . . . Well cut in on 'em! I got to make the Home with this. (HE *closes the booth door, so that his voice is muffled*)

GILL *returns.*

GILL: That's it. There was a special out for that car.

PRATT (*At the phone*): Give me the desk.

GILL (*To* PRATT): Taylor's a big bug downtown, eh?

PRATT: Just a millionaire.

GILL (*To* JOHNSON): Did you fan him?

JOHNSON: Yes, sir. (HE *takes a small, pearl-handled automatic revolver from his pocket, and hands it to* GILL) Nothin' but this, and a wad o' bills.

PRATT (*At the phone*): Bob? . . . Pratt. They just picked up that Warren Taylor car that was stolen. . . . Yes. . . . What? . . . No, some kid and a girl. . . . Well, the *Herald-Examiner*'s making it for the Home. . . . All right. . . . Give me a rewrite man.

JOHNSON: He's got the money. No identification.

GILL *empties the bullets from the automatic into his hand.* JOHNSON *goes through* THE ARREST's *pockets, takes out a large silver flask and a roll of bills.*

AMES (*to* MILLER): Give me a chance, will you?

GILL (*Inspecting the bullets*): Nasty, eh? (*To* THE ARREST) Knock 'em over for good with them, eh? Eh? (*Handing the bullets to* SULLIVAN) File these.

SULLIVAN *spills the bullets into an envelope, makes a notation on it, and seals it.*

JOHNSON (*Unscrewing the flask*): That's where you get your guts, uh?

GILL (*Taking the flask*): Hittin' it heavy, eh?

THE ARREST: Oh, for Christ's—

JOHNSON: Shut up!

GILL *passes the flask and money to* SULLIVAN.

PRATT: Officer! What's your name?

JOHNSON: C. Johnson. Write that in. My mother'll like it.

GILL: Come on now, you! Let's have a name and all about it, now!

THE ARREST: Lis'en, I never took that car!

JOHNSON: Maybe he'd talk to me, in the back room.

GILL: He'll talk to me. (*Edging closer, his voice rising*) What's your name, you— (*Grabbing him by the collar and shaking him*) Come on! And without any duress.

THE ARREST (*Knocking his hands away*): Keep your hands off me, you stuffed shirt bastard!

GILL *precipitately steps back.*

JOHNSON: Wai-i-t a minute. (HE *steps to* THE ARREST *and slaps him swiftly, first with*

one hand, then the other, then an uppercut) And don't tell your mouthpiece
there was any duress in that.

THE ARREST: You'll get yours for that, you dirty—

Enjoying himself, JOHNSON *cuts him off with a slap across the mouth.* THE ARREST
springs at him, but JOHNSON *pinions his arms, and laughs.*

PRATT (*At the phone*): Murph'? . . . Pratt, at the Tenth . . . McQuigg's new district.

THE ARREST (*Stiffening*): Is McQuigg captain here?

JOHNSON: That's who.

PRATT (*At the phone*): That Taylor car. . . . Yes. Story in the afternoon papers. . . .
Patrolman name of C. Johnson picked it up with a kid and a girl in it— . . .
No, she got away. . . . No name yet. . . . I'll call you back for the Final. (HE
replaces the phone)

THE ARREST (*Suddenly*): Wait a minute, Lieutenant. My name's Camino.

GILL: Camino, eh?

THE ARREST: Yeh. But lis'en, I never took that car.

GILL: What's your first name?

THE ARREST: Joe.

GILL: Where do you live?

JOE: Two one six six Artesian.

GILL (*Threateningly*): How old are you?

JOE: Twenty-one. Lis'en, Lieutenant, I'm clean on that car. Fellow that was with
me—he said it was his, see? He was out with a girl o' mine and I—

GILL (*Roaring*): Who was the other fellow?

JOE: Well, he was— (HE *stops*)

GILL: He'll remember it. (*To* JOHNSON) My office.

JOHNSON: Come on, Joey. (HE *takes* JOE *by the arm and shoves him on into* GILL's *office*)

GILL (*To* PRATT): Ever see him before?

PRATT: Nope.

GILL (*To* AMES): Did you?

AMES (*Astonishedly*): Me? (HE *shakes his head "No"*)

PRATT: Oh, your Camino's an amateur, Lieutenant. Stealing a Rolls when there
are only about nine of them in town? And carrying one of those boodwah
thirty-twos! Why, anybody who carries less than a thirty-eight in this town's
a fairy.

GILL: Book him, Sergeant.

PRATT: I'd wait if I were you. (GILL *turns*) Didn't you see him collapse when I mentioned the Captain's name? He thought fast, but his name's not Camino.

GILL: Huh? (*After a moment. To* SULLIVAN) Hold that up. (HE *goes into* McQUIGG's
office)

AMES *takes the phone.*

AMES (*At the phone*): Line, please (*To* PRATT) Who's this Taylor?

PRATT *is eyeing* MILLER *in the booth.*

Pratt?

PRATT: What?

AMES: Who's Taylor?

PRATT: Big contractor downtown. Society. His wife danced with the Prince of Wales when he was here.

McQUIGG *comes in, followed by* GILL.

GILL: There's somethin' funny. He was scared when he heard your name. (HE *goes into his office*)

McQUIGG (*To* AMES): You callin' your office?

AMES: Yes, sir.

McQUIGG: Stop it.

AMES *surprisedly replaces the phone.*

(*To* PRATT) Did you turn this story in?

PRATT: Not the name.

McQUIGG: Who's in the booth?

PRATT: *Herald-Examiner.*

McQUIGG: Did he see the pinch jump when he heard my name?

PRATT: He didn't see anything.

McQUIGG: Neither did you. (*To* AMES) Or you. (JOHNSON *comes in*) Johnson, keep this quiet till I see how funny it is. Anyone who's afraid of me's got lots of friends downtown. And I'm handlin' this station, myself. (HE *goes into* GILL'S *office*)

JOHNSON: Yes, sir. (HE *starts for the street*)

PRATT: Johnson? That girl in the Taylor car. Did you see what she looked like?

JOHNSON: No.

PRATT (*Starting after him*): Where are you going now?

JOHNSON: To find my cap! (HE *goes out*)

AMES (*Taking the phone*): Line, please.

JOE (*From* GILL'S *office*): I won't.

AMES: What are they doing? Third degree?

PRATT: Save your imagination till you're writing the stories. They'll pay you for it, then.

MILLER *comes from the booth and starts for the door.*

MILLER (*Jauntily*): I told you somethin' would break out here, with McQuigg on deck.

PRATT: What's delighting you?

MILLER *goes out.*

AMES (*At the phone*): State eight one hundred.

JOE (*A strained cry*): I won't!

AMES: Now what about that third degree? (*At the phone*) Give me the desk!

SULLIVAN: (*With a nod at* GILL's *office*) Don't turn that in.

PRATT: Just give them a flash. Here (*Taking the phone*) Do they know your voice?

AMES: I don't think so. They never listen to me long enough.

PRATT (*At the phone*): The desk? . . . This is Ames. (HE *stops, then replaces the phone*) They said to call back.

AMES: That's what they tell me!

PRATT (*Smiling*): Well, maybe they won't in New York.

AMES: Go on. Kid me. But I'll be a reporter in New York, and a good one!

JOE: *Stop!*

> *There is a short scream of agony, followed by a dull crash, and then silence.* PRATT *makes for* GILL's *office and goes in.* AMES *starts after him, when* IRENE HAYES *comes in from the street.* SHE *is twenty-eight, beautifully bodied, sophisticated, hard, wearing a large solitaire diamond ring, and carrying an expensive purse and silver fox.* AMES *stops, recognizing her.* SHE *goes to the desk, but* SULLIVAN, *busy does not notice her.*

IRENE (*After a moment*): Information, please.

SULLIVAN (*After a look at her*): Lost your dog or somethin', I suppose.

IRENE: Not yet.

SULLIVAN: Well, then—?

IRENE: Didn't you just get a boy with an automobile? One of your officers came up about—parking, so—

SULLIVAN: Yeh?

IRENE: Yes, so the boyfriend, he thought I'd better go. (SULLIVAN *rises*) But he told me if he had to go to the station to come over and meet him here. He said he'd only be a minute.

SULLIVAN: See the Captain. (HE *goes into* GILL's *office*)

AMES (*Removing his hat*): How do you do?

IRENE: What are you in for?

AMES (*Grinning*): I'm a reporter.

IRENE (*Bowing slightly with characteristic ironic amusement*): I'm Irene Hayes.

AMES: Sure, I know who you are.

IRENE: I've heard that one.

AMES: I mean, I've seen you at Weiberg's. You sing there, don't you?

IRENE: Yes, I sing there.

AMES: Well—don't you like it?

IRENE: Would you?

AMES: I can't sing.

IRENE: Neither can I.

AMES: Oh, go on! I thought you were great. I was going to ask you to dance with me.

IRENE: Why didn't you?

AMES: Oh, there were a lot of men at your table, and—

IRENE: They're part of the job. From ten to two!

AMES: Then I will come in. Some night next week.

IRENE: Yes? (*Coldly*) What for?

AMES: Why, I'd like to see you again, that's all.

IRENE: I was waiting for that one.

AMES: What do you mean?

IRENE: And all you want's a nice, sweet friendship, eh?

AMES: With you?

IRENE: That's how they usually start. But, of course, you're not after anything more?

AMES (*Backing away*): No! That's the trouble with you women. I say hello to you or something, and you think I want to— (HE *stops embarrassedly*)

IRENE: Excuse me!

AMES (*Jerking on his hat*): I'd like to know somebody in this town, that's all!

IRENE: Heavens! Why?

AMES: I'm tired of being on the outside of things.

IRENE: So am I. That's why I'm engaged to Joe Scarsi—to get on the inside, quick.

AMES: Joe—who? (*After a startled look at* GILL's *office*) Are you engaged—?

IRENE (*Interrupting*): Well, of course, darling, that was before I met you.

AMES: Is he—in there—some relation to Nick?

IRENE: His baby brother. Didn't he tell them who he was?

McQUIGG *comes in*, PRATT *after him.*

McQUIGG: No, I'm tellin' you—Camino's the name. Full confession, and voluntary. He says he was out ridin' so's he could make some girl.

IRENE: He didn't.

McQUIGG *turns.*

Where is he?

McQUIGG: If you mean this Camino—

IRENE (*After a laugh*): Don't you think I know who's my fiancé?

McQUIGG: Maybe he gave you a phony name. They do that regular now.

IRENE: Not with me. No, he told me to meet him here. He said he'd only be a minute.

McQUIGG: He's goin' to stay.

IRENE: Oh. (*After a moment*) Then I won't wait. (SHE *starts quickly for the street*)

AMES: Tell him.

IRENE (*Stopping*): Keep quiet!

McQUIGG: Tell me what?

AMES: She's engaged to that fellow in there. He's Nick Scarsi's brother.

PRATT *grabs the phone.*

McQUIGG (*To* PRATT): Stop that!

PRATT *replaces the phone.*

(*To* IRENE) So you're the girl in the car, uh? Then you can tell me somethin' about that boy.

IRENE: No, Policeman. I'm tongue-tied.

McQUIGG (*Going to her*): You'd better talk to me.

IRENE (*Backing away*): I'm liable to. Maybe you're framing him, but you'll not me. Listen! You get off base with Joe Scarsi and you'll get tagged out, like the last one who tried to take one of Nick's friends for a ride. Don't make any errors—

McQUIGG (*Cutting her short*): Well, if you won't talk to me— (*To* SULLIVAN) Get a couple of men in here.

He seizes IRENE's *wrist.* SULLIVAN *goes to door right.*

IRENE: Let me go!

SULLIVAN (*Pushing open the door*): Schmidt! Clark! (HE *returns to the desk*)

IRENE: Stop it, you—

DETECTIVE SERGEANT SCHMIDT *and* DETECTIVE CLARK *come in.* THEY *wear plain clothes and soft hats.*

McQUIGG: This young lady's visitin' us awhile.

IRENE (*Trying to pull free*): Let me go.

AMES (*Protestingly*): Captain—

McQUIGG (*Swinging* IRENE *across to* CLARK): Take her downstairs and put her in with the other guests.

AMES: Captain, those others are nothing but—

McQUIGG: Orders on her'll come from me.

CLARK: Yes, sir. (HE *touches* IRENE *on the arm, and jerks a thumb at the door*)

IRENE (*Rubbing her wrists*): I'll telephone first.

McQUIGG: No, you won't. That service don't come out this far.

IRENE: It will. (SHE *starts out*)

AMES (*Going to her*): Wait, I'll make a call for you if you want me to. I'm sorry! I didn't know they'd keep you.

IRENE: You little fool.

SHE *goes out,* SCHMIDT *and* CLARK *after her.*

McQUIGG (*To* PRATT): Now get this. (*To* AMES) You too, son! Maybe the fellow Joe Scarsi says was with him did steal that car. But I've got him, and I'm goin' to get him for that theft. If it gets out downtown he's here I won't be able to hang onto him an hour. They'll spring him on a writ o' habeas corpus or, if I book him, get him out on bail. I'm holdin' that girl as a witness, and I'm keepin' you here till I get this case set. Then you can phone your heads off.

AMES (*Exhaling*): Whew!

PRATT (*Looking after* IRENE): His fiancée, eh? Well, Nick will spank brother's bottom for that. (*To* McQUIGG) You know, women are poison to Nick.

McQUIGG: Maybe this one'll be dynamite. (*To* SULLIVAN) Get Delaney back. I want him here. (HE *starts for his office*)

SULLIVAN: Yes, sir.

PRATT: Where do we sleep?

MILLER *strolls in.*

MILLER: Hi, Captain.

McQUIGG *turns.*

How's young Scarsi takin' it?

PRATT *jerks alert.*

Jeez, he's all Nick cares about—that kid. And him droppin' into your hands! We're playin' it big, too, believe—

PRATT: Did you know who he was?

MILLER: Say, I made that "Camino" for Nick's brother the minute I came in. We'll be on the street downtown with the story in less than a half an—

PRATT (*To* McQUIGG): You'll never hold him now!

McQUIGG (*To* MILLER): Get out o' here!

MILLER: What's the ma—?

McQUIGG (*Going to the desk*): All o' you!

PRATT (*Grabbing* AMES's *overcoat, throwing it to him, and starting for the street*): Come on. There's a phone at the Greek's.

HE *goes out,* MILLER, *then* AMES, *after him.*

McQUIGG (*To* SULLIVAN): Keep two squads on station duty. Throw another one around that brewery.

SULLIVAN: Yes, sir. (*Goes out right*)

McQUIGG *starts for his office again.* WELCH *comes in from the street, breathing hard.*

WELCH: Mac!

McQUIGG *turns.*

I just called downtown. The *Herald-Examiner*'s got a story that you've got Joe Scarsi here.

McQUIGG: I have.

WELCH: Better—Better let him go before Nick hears—

McQUIGG: I want Nick to hear.

WELCH: Mac, he's Nick's one soft spot—this boy.

McQUIGG: Then this ought to make him squirm.

WELCH (*Excitedly*): You'll get yourself a suspension—

McQUIGG (*Sharply*): What?

WELCH: I—(HE *stops*)

McQUIGG: You cracked about me gettin' suspended.

WELCH: I cracked too fast. But you are greased for a suspension, and—now the order *will* go to the Trial Board.

McQUIGG: What's the charge?

WELCH: What's the difference?

McQUIGG: Who fixed it?

WELCH: Nick. (*Hastily*) But I'll quash it, if you'll let Joe Scarsi go.

McQUIGG: I'll mix with Nick to the finish now. Tell that to the *people's* Trial Board.

WELCH: Now, Mac!

McQUIGG: Tell it to the Old Man.

WELCH: Wait a min—

McQUIGG: Tell it to Scarsi!

> SULLIVAN *comes in and returns to the desk.*

Sullivan!

WELCH: What are you going to do?

McQUIGG (*Tapping his forehead*): "Operate upstairs." (*To* SULLIVAN) Put that girl in a crowded cell. That'll make her mad enough to talk. And book that boy— grand larceny, and carryin' concealed weapons, too.

WELCH: Nick will start something now!

McQUIGG (*Striding to his office*): I'm starting somethin' myself. I'm ripe to fight. (*Turning*) It's this country air! (HE *goes out*)

End of Act One

ACT TWO

The same as Act One, late the next afternoon. The order "Raincoats today" is chalked on the blackboard. SULLIVAN *is busy at the desk.* GILL *is in front of the desk inspecting the complaint book.*

GILL: More trouble in twenty-four hours than I've had in years.

SULLIVAN: This auto theft's the first excitement I've had since we got that body that was dumped out o' that car on Western Avenue a year ago. An' that crime only stopped off while passin' through! (*Half to himself*) Maybe we can use *police*men 'round here from now on.

GILL (*Tossing the book to the desk*): Is the night shift on?

SULLIVAN: Yes, sir. Except Johnson. He's late.

GILL: Fine him. (*Starting for his office*) My discipline—everythin'—turned upside down.

McQUIGG comes in from the street wearing a police rubber raincoat over his uniform and a soft hat. There is a day's beard on his tired, set face.

Any more raids tonight?

McQUIGG: What? (*After a moment*) Oh. Yeh. (HE *takes a long envelope from his pocket, and hands it to* GILL) The houses are standin' for 'em, so don't let the boys get too much exercise. And this time don't bring in any exaggerated drunks, especially women—they get sick all over the station. (HE *sinks to a chair at the table*)

GILL (*To* SULLIVAN, *inspecting the order he has taken from the envelope*): Bring Schmidt's squad in.

SULLIVAN: Yes, sir.

McQUIGG: There'll be an assistant state's attorney out to lead the damn things, for the publicity. (*To* SULLIVAN) Is Delaney back?

SULLIVAN: Yes, sir.

McQUIGG: Get him.

SULLIVAN goes out right.

GILL: Now—uh—(*Importantly*) about these raids—

McQUIGG: Get the time right. (*Indicating the order*) It's there—early, to catch the Sunday papers.

GILL: These newspapers ought to throw away their hammer and get a horn. They're makin' a stink-pot out o' this city.

McQUIGG: Which, however and thank God, still has the finest park system in the world.

GILL (*Approvingly*): Right.

McQUIGG: Have they bailed out Joe Scarsi yet?

GILL: No.

McQUIGG: They will. But he goes up for trial on Wednesday, and by that time I'll have his case set.

GILL: Are we keepin' this Hayes girl?

McQUIGG: You're damn right.

> DELANEY *comes in right, followed by* SULLIVAN, *who returns to his desk.* GILL *gives* SULLIVAN *the raid order, and then goes into his office.*

(*To* DELANEY) Is Nick Scarsi here at that brewery today?

DELANEY: Yeh, and stayin', they tell me, till he gets his truck routes fixed.

McQUIGG: Who's with him?

DELANEY: A driver for his own car, his personal barber—he's leery o' lettin' just anybody shave him now'days—and five or six of his "guns."

McQUIGG: Are they behavin' themselves?

DELANEY: They were south tryin' to fix the county patrols last night.

McQUIGG: Anythin' else?

DELANEY: Somebody stuck up that German's delicatessen on Sangamon Street this noon. But when all he could find was eight dollars, he left the money, gave the old Dutchman a crack on the jaw, and laughed like hell.

SULLIVAN: An' that German's yellin' yet.

DELANEY: They got a great sense o' humor, Captain, this Scarsi mob.

McQUIGG: Yeh. Like that callin' card they left for me last night. (*Grimly*) Well, Joe Scarsi goes up for trial next Wednesday, not next year. It took me all night and this mornin' to throw the switches for that. Did you get us set with a judge?

DELANEY: Yeh. Sherman. Nobody can get to him.

McQUIGG: Then if Miss Irene Hayes'll swear Joe stole that car—

DELANEY: Nick'll get to her.

McQUIGG: I hope, by God, he tries it.

DELANEY: Well— (*Drily*) the Alderman's been in.

McQUIGG: An Organization man?

DELANEY: Yeh?

McQUIGG: Who?

DELANEY: Kublacek. He rode in last election on that hundred percent American campaign.

SULLIVAN (*To* McQUIGG): He said to tell you he'd be back.

McQUIGG (*Rising*): Scarsi goin' into action, uh? Sergeant, is that patrolman—Johnson—in?

SULLIVAN: I'm never able to keep track o' him.

McQUIGG (*To* DELANEY): How is Johnson, Jim?

DELANEY: He's all right. (*Drily*) He's young.

McQUIGG (*To* SULLIVAN): Better keep him inside for awhile. (*Starting for the door right*) Bein' the witness against a Scarsi, if he's on a beat tonight he might be on a slab by mornin', with those "guns" out here. (HE *goes out*)

SULLIVAN: I told Johnson to be careful, myself. But do you think these bantams'll listen to me!

PRATT *and* MILLER *come in from the street.* MILLER *is bedraggled from the rain, and extraordinarily tired.*

PRATT (*To* SULLIVAN): Hi, Sarge.

MILLER (*To* DELANEY): Hi.

DELANEY *nods, and lights a cigarette.*

PRATT (*To* SULLIVAN): Anything doing?

SULLIVAN: Haven't turned a wheel.

MILLER: I told you we were nuts to lope out here.

PRATT: Why did you come then?

MILLER: Well, bright boy, 'cause you did. Every time that half-wit we got on the desk hears of a *Tribune* man takin' a streetcar he gets all a-twitter.

DELANEY (*To* PRATT): What's new on the election, scribe?

PRATT: Nothing. Oh, a couple of women's clubs petitioned the Governor to send up the militia to guard the polls.

McQUIGG *comes in right, carrying his raincoat.*

McQUIGG (*Stopping short. To* MILLER): You, uh?

HE *starts for him,* MILLER *warily hastening around the table for the door to the street.*

ALDERMAN KUBLACEK *comes in from the street—a heavyset politician of the servile sort, exuding an air of excessive good-fellowship and sweat.* HE *is neither well-dressed nor well-washed, but carries plenty of cigars.*

DELANEY: The Alderman, Captain.

MILLER: Just in time, Alderman.

KUBLACEK *automatically hands him a cigar.*

KUBLACEK (*With a wave of the hand to* DELANEY; *hoarsely*): Thanks. (*Going to* McQUIGG) Your Alderman, Captain. (HE *hands* McQUIGG *a cigar*) Glad to meet y', at last.

THEY *shake hands.*

McQUIGG: The Press, Alderman.

KUBLACEK (*Going to* MILLER *and* PRATT): All the newspaper boys're frien's o' mine. (HE *hands them cigars*) Captain, I looked for y' at that meetin' of ours last night. (*To* MILLER *and* PRATT) I got the Old Man himself out for that one. The church was jammed! (*To* McQUIGG) When I read about your pickin' up that auto theft last night I told the boys, "There y' are," I said, "what'd I tell y'? McQuigg'll give the taxpayers the pr'tection they deserve." Not that we got crime here, y'understand. I guaranteed the people a clean home neighborhood, an' they got it—not a speakeasy in the ward. But they got a right to efficient p'lice pr'tection, an' when they get it—like you're givin' it to 'em, Captain—it's like I said to the boys, I said, the community ought to show their appreciation.

McQUIGG: How?

KUBLACEK: I'm droppin' in to shake hands with y', an' that officer—Johnson—o' yours.

JOHNSON comes in down right, panting.

SULLIVAN: Where've *you* been?

JOHNSON: Grabbin' myself a couple o' hours sleep. I spent all night and this mornin' on a case o' my own I found. I'll clean it up in a couple o' more hours, the way I work, and then—

McQUIGG (*Drily*): Fine, officer.

SULLIVAN: What're you workin' on? A kid swipin' an apple, I suppose.

JOHNSON: Yeh? If I wanted to talk now—

MILLER: Why don't you?

McQUIGG: Are you startin' again? (HE *rises and starts for* MILLER)

MILLER (*Rising hurriedly*): I got somethin' for you tonight, Captain. (HE *pulls back his overcoat, exposing a bottle of whiskey in its inside pocket*) Just off the boat.

McQUIGG: Come in, I need it.

HE starts for his office followed by MILLER, PRATT *and* KUBLACEK.

Jim?

DELANEY: Nope, I'm on diet, of beer. (HE *goes out to the street*)

McQUIGG unlocks his office door and MILLER *and* PRATT *go in.* KUBLACEK *starts to follow them.*

McQUIGG (*Barring* KUBLACEK'S *way*): There's your Officer Johnson, Alderman. You can give him that "appreciation" o' yours direct. (HE *goes into his office*)

KUBLACEK (*Going to* JOHNSON): Glad to meet y', Johnson! (*Handing him a cigar*) That was a fine thing you did.

JOHNSON: Thanks.

KUBLACEK: Huh?

JOHNSON: For the smoke.

KUBLACEK: That's all right, m'boy. (HE *gets a cigar for himself from a different pocket*) I was sayin', that was a fine job 'y did last night. This ward's full o' respectable home-folks and healthy for kids, an' we can't have it polluted by lawbreakers an' crooks. (HE *lights his cigar*)

JOHNSON: There wasn't anything about last night—

KUBLACEK: You don't have to be modest with me.

The teletype whirs and writes. SULLIVAN *tears off its sheet and takes it into* GILL'S *office.*

JOHNSON: There wasn't anythin' to be modest about, or to brag about either. That's what a policeman's for, ain't it?

KUBLACEK: Sure, m'boy. But I wanted to drop in an' give y' the community's thanks.

JOHNSON: Anythin' else?

KUBLACEK: Well, now y' mention it, I remember some o' the more prominent citizens sayin' they hoped y' wouldn't be too hard on that lad y' picked up.

JOHNSON: I'm fryin' a bigger fish right now. Anyway, what happens to young Scarsi's up to the Judge.

KUBLACEK: But then you bein' the only witness—

JOHNSON: Yeh, that's what this other buzzard I got told me last night.

KUBLACEK (*Hurriedly*): But as I told 'em, I said, that's your business.

JOHNSON: It's the public's, too, ain't it?

KUBLACEK: That just exactly, Johnson, what a lot o' people who got influence feel about this Scarsi boy—that it's their business to give young delinquents a helpin' hand.

JOHNSON (*Meaningly*): How?

KUBLACEK: Mind y', I don't say it! But some o' the citizens—

JOHNSON: Drive on, Alderman.

KUBLACEK: O' course, if it'd been a murder—anythin' serious—

JOHNSON (*Sharply*): What d'you mean, murder?

KUBLACEK: This auto theft.

JOHNSON (*Relaxing*): Oh.

KUBLACEK: I mean, if it'd been anythin' *serious* like that—

JOHNSON: I'm tickled to death it wasn't a murder. There's some chance o' him gettin' a couple o' years for stealin' a car. Listen, Alderman, I know what you're up against—all you COD boys who have to do the dirty work for the Organization. So I won't ask you to come out with your proposition to see I get slipped somethin' good if I throw Joe Scarsi's case. One o' Nick Scarsi's own men tried that last night, and instead o' him gettin' me, I got him.

KUBLACEK *hurriedly gestures "Quiet."*

Joe ain't a drop in the bucket to the case I'm finishin' up tonight, so you just tell that big brother o' his to go to hell, will you? And tell him I told you! (HE *starts for the street*)

KUBLACEK: Officer—

JOHNSON *turns.*

I want to tell y'—if I don't put this over with you, they'll knife me, next election. And if this Scarsi kid even gets fined, I got to pay it out o' my own pocket. They told me. (HE *drops to a chair at the table, the ash from his cigar spilling over his vest*)

JOHNSON (*After eyeing him a moment*): Christ.

HE *goes out.* KUBLACEK *starts after him.* SULLIVAN *returns. Seeing him,* KUBLACEK *stops.*

SULLIVAN (*Going to the desk*): You can't bribe the young ones. They get insulted.

DELANEY, WELCH *and* TURCK *come in from the street.*

DELANEY: Alderman! You ought to know Mr. Assistant State's Attorney Welch.

KUBLACEK (*Hastily*): Always an honor to meet the brains o' the Organization! (HE *hands* WELCH *a cigar, feels for another to give* TURCK, *but finds none*) Well—G'bye! G'bye! (HE *goes out to the street*)

DELANEY: What've you got on for tonight, Welch?

WELCH: Nothing. Some more raids.

DELANEY: Yeh?

SULLIVAN: How are y', Turck?

TURCK: Overworked. (HE *goes out right*)

DELANEY (*With a nod and smile after* TURCK): So you're all set for Tuesday, eh?

WELCH: We're over, with the river wards.

DELANEY: Scarsi'll swing those for you, won't he?

WELCH: Yes, but I've promised those thirsty foreigners there enough beer and wine myself to float the City Hall. They think they'll get it! Our names are on the top of the ballot this time. That's twenty-five thousand votes. And we'll get the nigger vote—that's sixty thousand, there.

DELANEY: But the Reform gang'll get the—let's see—Swedes, Norwegians, Czechs, Hungarians, Lithuanians, Croatians, and whatever Americans vote. The Germans'll split. And the Democrats'll get the Irish, Bohemians, and Poles.

WELCH: But we'll stay in. The Captain here?

DELANEY (*Going to* McQUIGG's *office*): How you going' to fix Joe Scarsi's case? (HE *opens the door*)

WELCH: It will be legal, anyway.

DELANEY: Welch, Captain.

McQUIGG *comes to his door, an official paper in his hand.*

McQUIGG: Well, Mr. Welch?

WELCH: How are you, Mac?

McQUIGG: I'm gettin' better.

WELCH: You'll have a relapse if you go through with this Scarsi boy.

McQUIGG: I'll be ready to go through with him by Wednesday, when he comes to trial.

WELCH: Wednesday trial?

McQUIGG: Yeh. They had to give me that much, or I might talk about why I got dropped out here.

WELCH: They may have to give you more than that suspension, if you do talk. Mac, I told you—when you can't lick an organization, join it. You'll only get hurt—more, bucking Nick.

McQUIGG: I haven't been hurt yet.

WELCH: Neither has Nick. (*Smiling*) Or Joe.

McQUIGG: By God, you'll've earned that county judgeship, if they're not. (HE *returns into his office*)

WELCH (*After a moment, briskly, to* DELANEY): Well! How's the district?

DELANEY: We'll have more noise complaints after bedtime. Scarsi's got thirty trucks on tonight. Welch, why don't you get Nick to cushion his trucks? Don't you know some company that'd slip you some graft for a nice order of springs?

SAM MEYER, *an unkempt, shifty little Jew, comes in from the street.* HE *is in a state of perpetual anxiety, harassed.*

SULLIVAN: What can I do for you?

MEYER: Sam Meyer, Sergeant. From Reilly, Platka, and Cohn. You got Joe Scarsi here?

At his mention of JOE, DELANEY *goes into* MCQUIGG's *office.* WELCH *goes out right.*

(*Feeling through his pockets*) I thought I had a cigar.

SULLIVAN: You goin' to bail the kid?

MEYER: I got his bond.

DELANEY *comes in.*

DELANEY: The Lieutenant'll fix him up. (HE *goes into* GILL's *office*)

SULLIVAN: What are you, a bondsman and a lawyer, too?

MEYER: I was even a lawyer, but I got disbarred. (HE *searches his pockets again*)

GILL *comes in,* DELANEY *after him.*

DELANEY: It's all right. The Captain don't want Joe, yet. (HE *goes out to the street*)

MEYER (*Finding the paper* HE *had been searching for, handing* GILL *the paper*): See, Lieutenant. I got a release slip. Judge Wicks just approved the bond for this Scarsi boy.

GILL (*Tossing the paper to* SULLIVAN): Take care o' this. (HE *goes out right*)

SULLIVAN (*Beginning to draw up the release papers*): You runners for these lawyers have to be a little of everythin', uh?

MEYER (*After a worried look at his watch*): I got to be downtown at the Detective Bureau in an hour, for another one. Business is too good.

SULLIVAN *grunts.*

And when we got to serve habeas corpus writs, I'm a deputy sheriff, too. (HE *goes to the water-cooler and gets a drink*)

SULLIVAN: A hell of a lot o' good it does us haulin' in crooks.

MEYER: You shouldn't go monkeyin' with the big ones.

SULLIVAN: In the old days, crooks were hard all right, but they were dumb, an' you kind o' liked 'em. Now they're smart, an' you don't like 'em.

JOE *and* IRENE *come in right, followed by* GILL, *who goes to the desk.* IRENE *is carrying her coat, hat, fur and purse and stops by the desk, laying them there as* SHE *puts on her hat.*

JOE (*To* MEYER): Where've *you* been?

MEYER: Now, now. Your brother—

IRENE (*To* JOE): "I'll only be a minute!" Ha!

JOE (*To* MEYER): What's that outfit o' yours think Nick pays 'em for?

IRENE: A great drag you've got!

MEYER: Your brother—

IRENE: That punk!

MEYER: Lady, please!

IRENE (*To* JOE): Who's he?

JOE: He's none o' your damn business, you—

MEYER: Lady, I got to do this.

GILL: Here, here—

IRENE (*To* JOE): Does that brother of yours keep him to dry you off behind the ears?

MEYER: Lady—

JOE: Nick's not runnin' me.

IRENE: I suppose the rest of your nurses are lost, or you'd have been out of here before.

MEYER (*To* JOE): Nick didn't know about this till noon, but he said—

IRENE (*Taking up her things and starting for the street*): Let's go!

GILL (*To* MEYER): What've you got for her?

MEYER: Nothin'. She ain't goin' noplace.

HE *goes to the desk and signs the paper* SULLIVAN *gives him.*

IRENE (*Stopping*): What? (*Advancing on* JOE) Are you leaving me?

GILL (*Distressed*): We haven't facilities for women here!

JOE: Yes, and I hope you like it—high-hattin' *me* last night.

MEYER (*Grabbing* JOE's *arm*): Come on. (HE *pulls him on*)

IRENE (*Holding* JOE): Wait a minute. (*To* GILL) What am I booked for?

SULLIVAN: She's not booked, Lieutenant. Captain's orders to hold her, that's all.

IRENE (*To* JOE): They're trying to make me talk.

JOE: You better not.

IRENE: As long as they're holding me without a charge, can't you tell (*Indicating* MEYER) him to get me out with one of those writs they keep signed up?

MEYER: Please! Lady!

JOE: I could if I would, but I won't.

IRENE: Still afraid of Nick?

JOE: Damn it, I told you—*no.*

IRENE: I had you cured of being afraid of him, so there was something to you. But you get in a jam and cry for him, and leave me in with a lot of tarts!

JOE: Maybe they'll teach you not to be so touchy, so next time you're out with somebody you'll play.

IRENE: Not me, you cocky fool.

JOE: That's all I wanted you for.

IRENE: What?

JOE: Jeez, I kidded myself, thinkin' there'd be any excitement makin' you. *You* fool! Did you think I was goin' to *marry* you?

IRENE (*After a moment. Ripping the ring from her finger*): Take it, then. (*Throwing the ring at him*) There's your jewelry.

JOE (*Recovering the ring*): All right. Now shut up.

IRENE: No, I'll talk fast.

JOE: Go on. (HE *turns for the door*)

IRENE: I will—about what you spilled to me last night when you were tight.

JOE (*Turning*): What?

IRENE: The only thing you did talk about. What Nick did to—

JOE (*Hastily*): Lieutenant! (*Going to* GILL) The other fellow I told you about—he stole that car. But she was with him, so that makes her an accessory, don't it? (*To* IRENE) Tie that.

HE *goes out to the street.* MEYER *follows him.*

IRENE (*Looking after* JOE): You dirty rat.

GILL, *sighing, goes into* McQUIGG's *office.* IRENE *drops to a chair at the table.*

Men!

AMES *comes in down right, wearing a yellow slicker with the Greek letters of his college fraternity painted large on its back. His reporter's police card is stuck in his hatband.*

AMES: Oh, I was afraid you'd gone! (HE *goes to her*)

IRENE: Sweet of you.

AMES: What's the matter?

IRENE: If you hadn't told them who Joe Scarsi was I wouldn't be here, would I?

AMES: I told you how sorry—I didn't know they'd keep you!

IRENE: What did you think they'd do if they thought I knew anything about that car?

AMES: I didn't think.

IRENE: You ought to. Even at your age.

AMES: I mean, I did think it was right to tell them it was young Scarsi they had. I still do! Except that I'm sorry— (HE *stops*)

IRENE (*After eyeing him curiously a moment*): Listen, Boy Scout. If you keep on trying to do what's right—

AMES (*Belligerently*): Well?

IRENE: You're in for a lot of headaches, trying to figure out why everything you've been taught is right is wrong.

AMES: Oh, if you go by what other people say—

IRENE (*Rising*): I go by myself.

AMES: But just because this went wrong—

IRENE: "Just!" Nick Scarsi will frame me with that car, to protect this brother of his, he's so wild to make a *gentleman* of Joe.

AMES: Frame you?

IRENE: Yes, Joe threw that at me when they took him out, among the rest of his bouquets.

AMES: They took him— (*To* SULLIVAN) Then why don't you let her go? (*To* IRENE) They can't hang this on you! I'll see the Captain. (HE *starts for* McQUIGG's *office*) He'll have to let you go. It's my fault.

IRENE: Oh— (*Wearily*) Shut up.

AMES *stops confusedly.*

AMES (*After a moment*): Well—it's stopped raining, anyway.

IRENE: Doesn't it rain in Nebraska?

AMES: Sure. But not this dishwater. Now in New York— (*Enthusiastically*) I always get a kick when I see that skyline, or Fifth Avenue in the sunshine, in a newsreel. It'll be different there.

IRENE (*Looking up at him*): Marvelous!

AMES: It will be! When I get to be what I want to be, I mean.

IRENE: Darling, I don't know what will happen to you if you ever have a baby and no one's tipped you off about storks.

GILL *comes from* McQUIGG's *office.*

GILL (*To* SULLIVAN): Put her back in her berth. (HE *goes on into his office*)

IRENE (*Calling after him*): Well, this time get me a lower, that don't smell!

AMES (*To* SULLIVAN): Yes, you know some of those girls are sick down there.

IRENE (*To* SULLIVAN): And if you don't think so, take a sniff of this fur! (*Holding up her fur*)

SULLIVAN *nods her out right.* SHE *goes.* HE *follows her.* AMES *leans dejectedly on the desk, looking after her.* DELANEY *comes in from the street.*

DELANEY: Hello, kid. What's the matter with you?

AMES: I'm going to get the Department of Health after the conditions down there. (HE *bangs out after* IRENE)

McQUIGG *comes from his office with some reports, and goes to the desk.*

DELANEY: Captain, anythin' for me?

McQUIGG: No.

DELANEY: Then I'm goin' to go eat. (HE *goes out to the street*)

SULLIVAN *comes in and returns to the desk.* PRATT *comes from* McQUIGG's *office, followed by* MILLER.

PRATT (*To* MILLER): Oh, wait a minute. (*Going to* McQUIGG) Captain,—I've got another idea.

MILLER: Loud cheers.

PRATT: What about Taylor, the owner of that Rolls Royce?

McQUIGG: What about him?

MILLER (*To* PRATT): *What* about him? Jeez.

PRATT: Lie down. We're on LaSalle Street with this story now, not in the back room of some joint.

McQUIGG: Well?

PRATT: Will Taylor prosecute Joe Scarsi for that auto theft? What good's your getting the kid to trial if he won't?

McQUIGG: What's it to you?

PRATT (*Smiling*): Well, my paper's hot after this administration, and we're going to—

MILLER *makes a heartily indecent noise with his lips.*

(*To* MILLER) Oh it's not all politics, either. Just our characteristic snobbishness in feeling that there are people who resent being governed by a lot of goddamned hogs. (*After a moment*) Even the most sophisticated of us get tired of living in a privy, it's so monotonous. (*To* McQUIGG) Captain, there are a lot of rackets beside liquor, crap games and parking privileges in this town. Taylor's firm does most of the streets-and-alleys paving for the City Hall, and not without the proper connections. What if for Nick's sake they told him to lay off?

McQUIGG: You damn papers quit rockin' this boat till she gets ashore!

PRATT: We want it to get to shore. We're ungodly highminded about Civic Virtue on my paper, since we lost the last election.

McQUIGG: Yeh, no wonder the people think the newspapers are crazy, and kids play bandit after school instead o' policeman.

PRATT: Think Taylor over, Captain.

MILLER (*Wearily*): Oh—h—h—

PRATT: Come on. I'll explain it to you. (HE *goes out*)

MILLER (*Following him*): Write me an editorial. (HE *goes out*)

McQUIGG (*To* SULLIVAN): Get up that Hayes girl. Quick.

SULLIVAN: Yes, sir. (HE *goes to the door right*)

McQUIGG: If she'll talk—

SULLIVAN: She ain't been doin' anythin' else. She's sore. (HE *pushes the door open*)

McQUIGG: Well, maybe I'll get her sore enough to talk.

SULLIVAN (*Calling*): You, Bill! Get Hayes.

McQUIGG: By God, if she'll come clean and I get her story in print, Taylor'll have to prosecute this case.

SULLIVAN *returns to the desk. There is, again, the rumbling approach of a truck outside, and as it bumps past the door to the street a few tough voices rise in a yell of "Hi-i-i, McQuigg!"* McQUIGG *stiffens, and jumps for the door, jerking out his revolver.* HE *pulls open the door, but as the noise of the truck fades, replaces his gun.*

SULLIVAN: It's still too light outside for 'em to shoot.

FIRST PATROLMAN *brings* IRENE *in.* AMES *follows.* IRENE *is carrying her coat, fur and purse.*

IRENE (*To* McQUIGG): Listen, policeman— (SHE *starts for him*)

McQUIGG *gestures the* PATROLMAN *out.* HE *goes.*

McQUIGG: Good afternoon.

IRENE: What's good about it? (SHE *throws her things to the table*)

McQUIGG: So they took away your playmate?

AMES: Yes. So why don't you let her go?

McQUIGG: Who're you?

AMES: *City Press.* You know. I met you last night, for a minute.

McQUIGG: So you did. You're still fightin' other people's battles, uh?

AMES: Sure.

McQUIGG: Hasn't that general public o' yours even given you a nosebleed yet?

AMES: I'm more worried about my city editor than the public, now. I almost got fired because I didn't turn that story in last night, till later, I mean. And the position I'm in at my office, I've got to be here today, so—

McQUIGG (*A gruff bark*): So I'm to give you some "dope," uh?

IRENE: Let him alone.

McQUIGG (*Turning*): Ho! Transferrin' your affections already, uh?

IRENE: He's all right.

McQUIGG: What you can see in a newspaperman's beyond me.

AMES: She's not having any picnic with policemen.

McQUIGG (*Eyeing* IRENE): No?

AMES: You don't have to treat her like a drunk or something.

McQUIGG: I told you, there's no feelin' in this business.

AMES: That's the trouble with it.

McQUIGG (*His eyes pinched on* IRENE): Once your feelin's get into anythin', you *are* licked.

IRENE (*To* AMES): Don't you believe it.

McQUIGG: They're lickin' you, aren't they?

IRENE (*To* AMES): Let these Big Thinkers have the Ideas. You keep the heart-stuff. And if no one else wants it, give it to me. I can use it this season.

McQUIGG: Seems to me if anybody gave you any more feelin' right now, you'd bust.

AMES (*Patiently*): Do you have to talk to her like that?

McQUIGG: Run along, son. Run along. I've got to—ah—interview this young lady.

AMES *sighs and goes out.*

Well, Miss Hayes?

IRENE: Why put me in with those hookers? Even if you are McQuigg? Oh, I know who you are, now. (*After a moment*) One of those girls down there cried all night for her mother.

McQUIGG: I know who you are, too, now, Miss Hayes. You used to stall—tease along the come-ons—for Beauty Parker's mob. And since Beauty went down you've been singin' at Wieberg's, and seein' Joe Scarsi after the show. You weren't there last night—told one o' the girls you were goin' to marry Joe. Tryin' to cop off a rich guy for yourself.

IRENE: Why not?

McQUIGG: But you didn't marry him, did you?

IRENE: I'll get what I wanted without having to take on Joe Scarsi now.

McQUIGG: You can get out o' here if you tell me about that auto theft.

IRENE: I'll tell that to Nick.

McQUIGG: Tell it to me.

IRENE: I'm not stooling for policemen, yet.

McQUIGG: Goin' back to last night—what made the noise that caused the complaint about that Rolls?

IRENE: Joe, the little (*Contemptuously*) gentleman, tried to—beat the wedding bells, and when he discovered he'd have to wait he threw a fit. None of these foreigners can keep their temper. God, they drive you mad! If that big brother of his had seen me—

McQUIGG (*Interrupting*): Women talk too much for Nick.

IRENE: Nick! I've heard "Nick—Nick" from Joe, till I wanted to scream. You'd think Nick Scarsi was God and the Devil both, listening to Joe brag about what he pulls off.

McQUIGG: It usually takes a woman to beat a combination o' the Devil and God, Miss Hayes. But you haven't, have you?

IRENE (*Angrily*): I'll—

McQUIGG (*Cutting her short*): Nick's got you cold! And your Joe'll be home in a minute, dressin' for dinner in that exclusive North Side apartment o' theirs, laughin' with Nick at you—

IRENE: Nick's out here, at some brewery he bought. Joe told me.

McQUIGG: And you're here, too, aren't you? In a dirty cell. Why, the Scarsis 've shaken you, made a monkey o' you. You'll be laughed at—

IRENE (*Seething*): Yeh?

McQUIGG: Nick's laughin' at you now.

IRENE: Women talk too much for him. Ha!

McQUIGG: But you're afraid to, when it comes to him.

IRENE: I am not.

McQUIGG: Even with him turnin' this job on you, you're afraid—yellow, for fear of a braggin' wop.

IRENE: You're a liar.

McQUIGG (*Quickly*): Then who else was with you in that car last night?

IRENE: Nobody! Joe Scarsi stole it himself.

McQUIGG: Sullivan! Get that *City Press*.

SULLIVAN *goes out.*

IRENE: Tell that to Nick, and tell him I'll tell it to a judge.

McQUIGG: Not so afraid o' him now, uh?

IRENE: No. No! Not after what Joe's told me about him. "Women talk too much for him."

SHE *laughs sharply.* AMES *comes in, followed by* SULLIVAN, *who returns to the desk.*

It's Nick Scarsi's own brother who's talked too much for him. Tell him *I* know what happened to the secretary of this Old Man they talk about—Higgins— who "disappeared" last week, and then see if he'll try to frame *me* with this car his beloved brother stole.

McQUIGG (*Sharply*): What? (*Stepping quickly to her, seizing her arm and pulling her around*) What do you know about that?

IRENE: Enough to make Joe come through if you can find him again.

McQUIGG (*To* SULLIVAN): Is there a squad in?

SULLIVAN: Yes, sir. Anderson's.

McQUIGG: Jump 'em out. Tell 'em to pick up Joe Scarsi and bring him back. (SULLIVAN *goes out right*) Now let's go into detail about this, Miss Hayes, inside. (HE *goes to* GILL's *office, and opens the door*)

IRENE: Charmed. (SHE *picks up her things and goes into* GILL's *office*)

McQUIGG: Take a statement from Hayes, Lieutenant, about young Scarsi stealin' that car. Make carbons, and get 'em all witnessed and signed, this business is gettin' so damn legal now'days. (*To* AMES) Turn that in about Joe Scarsi stealin' that car. But not the rest of it till I tell you. Hear? (HE *goes into* GILL's *office*)

AMES (*Calling after him*): But, heavens, I've got to! It's my— (HE *glances at the phone, then goes to it, jiggling the hook*) State eight one hundred.

There is the sound of typewriting from GILL's *office.*

Give me the desk. . . . Mr. Brown there? . . . No, I've got to speak to Mr. Brown, personally, on this. . . . Well, it's Ames, then. . . . Ames. . . . You know! I work for you. . . . Mr. Brown, this Hayes girl— . . . At Captain McQuigg's station. . . . She just made a confession that Joe Scarsi stole that W. K. Taylor car. . . . I know, but—

WELCH *comes in right.*

Here's what's important. She knows what happened to that missing secretary, Higgins.

WELCH *stops and listens.*

She says young Scarsi told her. . . . Well, what if it is a rumor? The papers could print it if they found it was true, couldn't they?

WELCH *clears his throat and comes on,* AMES *glancing at him, then continuing despondently into the phone.*

All right, then (*Replacing the phone*) I'll keep on chasing your births and deaths!

WELCH: Won't they take your stuff?

AMES: Did you hear what I said?

WELCH: No. I saw your face.

AMES *snatches up his slicker and starts for the street.*

Don't let them get you, boy. It's all in the game. I was a reporter once, myself.

AMES *goes out.* WELCH *goes to the phone, looks up a number in his vest-pocket notebook, and then takes the phone.*

WELCH (*At the phone*): Beverly nine three three three. . . . Who is this? . . . (*Lowering his voice*) Scarsi? This is Welch. . . . At McQuigg's station. . . . This girl who was with your brother— . . . I know. But I'll take care of that. . . . I'm trying to find Taylor now. . . . Wait a minute! This Hayes girl has told McQuigg something about—Higgins. . . . She says Joe told her. . . . Of course he was simply talking. It's all insane. . . . But if any such rumors gain ground now— Hello! (*Jiggling the receiver hook*) . . . Nick! . . . Operator! . . . Get him back, then. He's got to stay there! Beverly nine—

PRATT *and* MILLER *come in right.*

(*Blandly*) All right, thank you. (HE *replaces the phone*)

The typewriting in GILL's *office stops.*

PRATT (*To* MILLER): Shall we interview this Hayes gal?
MILLER: No, she never shot anybody, did she? Anyway, (*Yawning*) Nick Scarsi'd sue you for libel.

AMES *comes in from the street.*

MILLER: Hi, Pr'fessor.
AMES: Hello.

WELCH *goes out.*

MILLER (*To* PRATT): Come on. Let's eat. (*To* AMES) Take that police card out o' your hat. What d'you think you're coverin', a parade?
AMES: I've been thrown out of a director's meeting, two weddings, and three inquests because I didn't have it. But (*Grinning*) it got me a story this afternoon, all right.

WELCH *comes in, followed by* TURCK.

MILLER: Where you eatin', Welch?
WELCH: That place at the corner of Western was good last night.
MILLER (*Following him*): Let's go.

WELCH *goes out to the street,* TURCK *after him.* McQUIGG *comes from* GILL's *office with typewritten statements and hands copies to* MILLER, PRATT *and* AMES.

McQUIGG: Miss Hayes's statement on your Scarsi stealin' that Taylor car. Spread that on a front page and see if Taylor'll dare throw this case.
MILLER (*Eyeing the statement*): And me with a ticket to the Chicago-Wisconsin game! (HE *stuffs the paper in his pocket*)

AMES *starts, ducks into the phone booth, and makes a call.*

PRATT: They'll get to Taylor, Captain.

McQUIGG (*Starting for his office*): To hell with even Taylor, if I can tie Scarsi with a new line I've got.

MILLER (*To* PRATT): Let's eat!

DELANEY *comes in from the street, chewing a toothpick.*

McQUIGG (*To* DELANEY): Jim, take Miss Hayes out for somethin' to eat. Keep everybody away from her, and bring her back.

DELANEY (*Going to the door right, hurriedly*): Just a second.

McQUIGG *goes into his office.*

SULLIVAN (*Opening* GILL's *door*): All right, you—Hayes.

IRENE *comes in.* SULLIVAN *returns to the desk.*

PRATT (*Following* DELANEY): Now what? Is Scarsi after Hayes?

DELANEY *goes out.* AMES *bursts jubilantly from the phone booth.*

AMES: Nebraska won!

MILLER (*Staring*): What?

AMES: Nebraska beat Harvard.

MILLER: Who hasn't? (*To* PRATT) Come on. (HE *opens the street door, sniffling*) The wind's from the north tonight, all right—just full o' the scent o' some mute, inglorious heifer's end. (HE *goes out*)

PRATT (*Following*): Coming, Dave?

AMES: No, I've got to pick up some shorts.

PRATT *goes out.*

IRENE: Short what?

AMES: Stories. We call the little ones like deaths, births, accidents, and that stuff, "shorts." And then this Scarsi story's important. But, Lord, it's all like a canful of angle-worms to me! What *I* don't understand is—

IRENE (*Smiling*): You don't understand anything.

AMES: I don't?

IRENE: No. That's why you get such a kick out of everything.

AMES: I'll get to understand it.

IRENE: No, you should have stayed in college longer.

AMES: I'm glad I didn't. I wouldn't have known anything. But I'll get *this* dope.

IRENE: Don't get too much. Just go on having Nebraska beat Harvard like that, all over the place. And don't let these other reporters shame you into being "wise"—crammed full of important, inside dirt. Or you won't.

AMES: Won't what?

IRENE: Be so full of breeze. Now, you're like a ride in an airplane. See?

AMES: Well, I have to—

IRENE: Be like everyone else, and know so much you can't believe in anything anymore?

AMES: You don't believe in much, do you?

IRENE: Oh, I did, darling. Till I got black and blue inside. And damn tired.

AMES (*Exasperatedly*): Of *what*?

IRENE: Men. And their— (*Wrenching irritably*) Why shouldn't I have used Joe Scarsi to get on the inside, safe? And when he was going to get me for that auto theft why shouldn't I get him first? Men live by this dog-eat-dog stuff. And when you're stuck in the middle of things that are run by men, you have to play their game. Or (*Dropping to the bench*) try like the devil. And then take a kick in the face because you can't. (*Lightly*) Said she!

AMES: Oh, you're not as hard-boiled as you think.

IRENE: Do tell! Give me a cigarette.

AMES (*Getting out his cigarettes*): Can you smoke these?

IRENE: If they're cheap enough.

AMES: They are.

IRENE *takes a cigarette.* AMES *lights it for her.*

IRENE: Listen. I'm sorry I took you so for granted last night.

AMES: That's all right.

IRENE (*Amusedly*): Thank you.

AMES: You're welcome. (*Sitting beside her*) I suppose you would think I was after you.

IRENE: Yes, *I* would. But don't you get so everyone can identify the kind you are by a glance. Just keep on being natural, youngster. (*With mock gaiety*) Be yourself!

AMES: I can be, with you.

IRENE: Go on.

AMES: I don't believe in much, either, except—well, standing up for what you do believe in, and getting someplace with what you want to do.

IRENE (*Smiling*): That *is* a little, anyway.

AMES: Yes. (*Rising*) But that's what they kid me for. What do *you* think?

IRENE (*Rising*): I think you—affect me like a mammy song! I—(*Laughing derisively*) My God!

DELANEY *comes in.*

DELANEY (*To* IRENE): All right, kid. Food.

SULLIVAN *comes from* GILL'S *office and returns to the desk.*

Come on.

IRENE (*Eyeing* AMES *reflectively*): It's a shame they have to grow up. (SHE *turns for the street*)

AMES: Coming back?

IRENE: Will you be here?

AMES: Sure.

IRENE: I'll be back.

SHE *goes out,* DELANEY *after her.*

SULLIVAN: "Anythin' doin'?"

AMES (*Starting*): What? Oh. (*Laughing*) There's plenty doing in my head.

McQUIGG *comes from his office, his cap on.*

McQUIGG: I'm goin' to supper, myself.

SULLIVAN: Yes, sir.

McQUIGG *goes out to the street.*

AMES: Who do you think will win Tuesday, Sarge—between these two Republican factions, I mean?

SULLIVAN: What's the difference?

AMES: There's another thing! Nobody even mentions the Democrats in this campaign.

SULLIVAN: Those donkeys're too busy fightin' among 'emselves to vote.

One of the desk phones rings.

(*At the phone*) Tenth District—Sullivan. . . . Yeh, right here. (*To* AMES) Your office wants you.

AMES: *Me?* (*At the phone*) This is Ames. . . . Yes, sir. (*Enthusiastically*) Yes, sir! (*Abruptly subdued*) Yes, sir.

JOHNSON *comes excitedly in.*

JOHNSON (*To* SULLIVAN): Where's the Captain?

SULLIVAN: You, uh? Why the hell didn't you wait'll I told you you could go out on a beat tonight?

JOHNSON: What's the matter?

SULLIVAN: You were supposed to stay in here till we got this Scarsi set. The Captain himself said—

JOHNSON: Where is the Captain? When he hears what I've just cleaned up— (HE *paces restlessly*)

AMES (*At the phone*): Yes, sir—I know.

SULLIVAN (*To* JOHNSON): You can report anythin' you got to me. Now get back there, and—

JOHNSON: I don't belong inside!

SULLIVAN: You belong where the Captain puts you.

JOHNSON: Listen, when I crash through with what I got, the Captain'll put me in a safe. (HE *goes to the water-cooler and gets a drink*)

AMES (*At the phone*): Writs of habeas corpus? . . . Yes, sir. I know what they are. They get people who've been falsely arrested out of jail. They've got one for— *Who?* . . . But before he's even *arrested?*

SULLIVAN: Johnson! Did you hear me?

JOHNSON: It'd look like I'm yellow, hidin' in here!

AMES (*At the phone*): No, the Captain went out to eat. But I'll find him. I'll tell him. . . . Yes, sir. (HE *replaces the phone, and ducks out to the street*)

SULLIVAN (*To* JOHNSON): Get in there! You bantam, you got a lot o' gall, but no brains—like all you young ones.

JOHNSON: No brains, uh? It took brains to grab off what I did last night and this afternoon. And then tellin' me to hide! That Scarsi mob ain't got any bullets that'll fit a hole in me! It's me that'll knock them, with this case I got. That ain't so dumb, is it?

There is the sound of a high-powered automobile coming up and stopping outside. GILL *comes in from his office.*

GILL: Schmidt's squad in?

SULLIVAN: He's on the way.

GILL: Get these raid orders for him.

HE *returns to his office.* SULLIVAN *starts after him.* A MAN *comes in from the street, hesitating at the door for a quick glance about the room.* HE *is a muscular, hard-bodied, Americanized Italian of thirty-eight, in a slightly form-fitted brown topcoat and soft hat.* HE *is smartly dressed, but under the knot of his necktie his soft, colored shirtcollar is fastened with a diamond barpin.*

SULLIVAN: Johnson, you wait here. (*To* THE MAN) Be with you in a minute, Mister. (HE *goes into* GILL'S *office*)

THE MAN: You the Johnson that picked up Joe Scarsi last night?

JOHNSON: What of it? (HE *starts for the door right*)

THE MAN: Wait a second.

JOHNSON *turns.*

I came to see a witness you got—girl by the name o' Hayes.

JOHNSON: See the Sergeant.

THE MAN: But I might as well see you, too. I'm a friend o' that Scarsi kid's.

JOHNSON: I just told his last friend to—

THE MAN: Choke it. We don't want any trouble with you. You did your duty, but—

JOHNSON: That's a lot o' manure about "duty," too. I get paid for my job. I like it, and so I do it. If I didn't like it, I wouldn't be doin' it. I don't like crooks for the same reasons I don't like a lot o' other people, and because they banged my old man, and because, generally speakin', I'm a better man than they are.

THE MAN: Don't take it so personal.

JOHNSON: There ain't much that amounts to anythin' that ain't personal.

THE MAN: You must be kind o' young, talkin' like that.

JOHNSON: I ain't used to it yet, that's all.

THE MAN: Joe Scarsi's not used to it yet, either. That's why he's got to be looked after for a while. That girl you got kissed him into sellin' his own car to buy her a ring, and then—playin' him for his brother's jack, that's all.

JOHNSON: Why don't that big brother o' his look after him?

THE MAN: He tried to.

JOHNSON: Do you know him?

THE MAN: Nick? Yeh.

JOHNSON: Everybody knows him. But nobody meets him. (*Jerking up his belt*) I'd like to meet the yellow—

THE MAN (*Cutting him short*): I thought Nick had lot o' guts.

JOHNSON: Guts, my can! These newspaper bad-men don't take the air without half a dozen armed guards stickin' to 'em. Catch one—two—three of 'em alone and you could slap 'em to sleep.

THE MAN: Yeh?

JOHNSON: Yeh.

THE MAN: Yeh?

JOHNSON: Yeh!

THE MAN: If Scarsi's so yellow, how do you happen to be hidin' inside?

JOHNSON (*Curtly*): Orders.

THE MAN: Afraid the witness'd get banged, uh?

JOHNSON: I ain't afraid—

THE MAN (*Interrupting*): You're cocky, for a kindergarten cop.

JOHNSON (*His fists clenching*): I ain't afraid o' Scarsi. Or any of his mob. And as for Joe Scarsi, no little wop's goin' to tell me who I can pinch, and grandstand around about what he's goin' to do to me, and get away with it.

THE MAN: No?

JOHNSON: No! And that goes for that big brother o' his, too.

THE MAN: Yeh?

JOHNSON: And if you're from Nick Scarsi, tell him I told you. And tell him to quit his braggin', too, because I know how that Higgins—this political Old Man's private secretary—disappeared.

THE MAN: What? Where'd you get that?

JOHNSON: From one o' Nick's own men who tried to scare me into layin' off Joe Scarsi's case.

THE MAN (*Quickly*): Who?

JOHNSON: And after I gave him the treatment he spilled all the dope—how Higgins got his head blown off, because he knew too much.

THE MAN *turns slightly away, his right hand slipping into his left overcoat sleeve.*

Yeh! And in another hour we'll have the evidence, (*Turning away*) because I know—

THE MAN *turns sharply, jerks a .38-caliber blue steel revolver from his overcoat sleeve and fires at* JOHNSON. AMES *comes panting in from the street.* JOHNSON *gasps, his shoulders wrench convulsively, and* HE *pitches on his face against the desk as* THE MAN, *jamming the revolver into his pocket, jumps for the door to the street.* AMES *comes to and springs at him.* THE MAN *smashes* AMES *in the face.* AMES *falls, but tries to tackle him.* THE MAN *jerks a leg away and kicks* AMES *in the face, then jumps into the entryway and out, down the steps, to the street.*

THE MAN (*Off, shouting*): Step on it!

AMES *lies stunned.* SULLIVAN, GILL, FIRST PATROLMAN *and* SECOND PATROLMAN *burst in. The motor of the automobile outside accelerates and tears off with a grinding of gears.*

FIRST PATROLMAN (*Shouting back through door right*): Glick!

SULLIVAN *pulls* AMES *up.*

AMES (*As* HE *sees* JOHNSON): Carl!

SULLIVAN: Who did it?

SECOND PATROLMAN (*Over* JOHNSON): For God's sake!

GLICK, *a plainclothesman, comes in door right. There is the sound of a flivver coming up outside.*

AMES: That man in here— (*Pointing to the door*) There! There was a car waiting—

GLICK *jumps for the street door.*

GILL (*Bending over* JOHNSON): What the hell—what the hell—what the hell—

GLICK (*Shouting from the entryway*): Schmidt! After that car.

There is an answering shout, and the flivver tears off.

SULLIVAN (*Shaking* AMES): Come out of it. Who—?

GLICK (*From outside*): Captain! Johnson—

AMES *turns, sways a little, and drops to a chair at the table.* McQUIGG *and* DELANEY *rush in from the street, followed by* GLICK *and* IRENE.

GILL: Somebody got Johnson.

McQUIGG *goes to* JOHNSON, *kneels beside him a moment, then rises and motions* THE PATROLMEN *to carry him off right.* THEY *do.* DELANEY *follows them.*

IRENE (*Going to* AMES): What is it? (SHE *goes to the water-cooler, soaks her handkerchief, and returning to* AMES *wipes the blood from his face*)

McQUIGG (*To* AMES): Did you see it?

AMES: I was just coming in—

McQUIGG: Who was it?

AMES *shakes his head.*

GILL (*Distressedly*): Unidentified man.

McQUIGG (*To* GILL, *indicating* AMES): Keep him here. (HE *starts for the door right*)

IRENE (*To* AMES): Are you all right?

GLICK: Schmidt's squad's after 'em, Captain.

McQUIGG: Which way?

GLICK: South.

McQUIGG: Call that county patrol at Ninety-eighth Street and tell 'em to block the road. (HE *hurries out*)

GILL (*To* SULLIVAN): Get me the Chief—personal—on this.

GLICK *starts for the desk phones.*

SULLIVAN (*To* GLICK): Use the booth.

GLICK *goes into the booth and calls.*

GILL (*To* SULLIVAN): Give me a phone. (*At the phone*) Box twenty-seven.

AMES (*Still dazedly*): I was just coming in— (HE *rises suddenly, and starts for the phone atop the partition*)

SULLIVAN (*At a phone*): The Tenth. Lieutenant Gill callin' the Chief, personal.

AMES *takes the phone.*

GILL: Here, you can't— (GILL *grabs at him*)

AMES (*At the phone*): Wire. State eight one hundred.

IRENE (*To* GILL): Let him alone!

SULLIVAN (*To* GILL): Chief's secretary on the wire, Lieutenant.

GILL: I'll talk to him. My office. (HE *goes into his office*)

GLICK (*Coming from the booth*): The patrol's on the road, Lieutenant.

AMES (*At the phone*): Give me the desk.

IRENE: Keep your head.

AMES (*To* SULLIVAN): Did you look at Johnson? Did you see if he was—? (*At the phone*) This is Ames, at the— . . . (*Desperately*) Wait! There's a— (*Frantically*) But listen! (*He stiffens, then slumps, and replaces the phone*) They hung up on me.

IRENE: Call them back!

AMES (*Seizing the phone*): State eight one hundred!

SULLIVAN (*Jerking the phone from him*): Don't turn that in.

DELANEY *comes in.*

DELANEY: Sullivan! Get—

AMES: Is he—*Is* he?

DELANEY: He's dead.

AMES *goes to the table and drops to a chair.*

(*To* SULLIVAN) The Captain's orders—no report on this till he gives the word. (*To* GLICK) Keep it quiet. (HE *goes out right*)

AMES (*Jumping up*): Do something. He's dead, you fools!

GLICK (*Pushing him down*): Sit down.

AMES: He oughtn't to be out there—just lying there—like that. (*His voice rising*) How do you know he's dead? Maybe he's bleeding to— (*Jumping up*) Isn't there even a doctor out here? God *damn* this town!

GLICK: What the hell's the matter with you?

IRENE (*Pushing* GLICK *aside*): Growing pains. (SHE *gets* AMES *into a chair*) They have to wait for the coroner.

AMES: I was just coming in—

GILL *comes from his office.*

GILL (*Over* AMES): Stand up. Now, who—?

AMES *gets up.*

Here! Don't be a baby about this.

GLICK: This ain't the first time. You better get used to it.

AMES: Used to it? Pretend I haven't got any insides? (*Pulling himself together*) All right. I'll get hard. I'll get hard-boiled. (*Turning to* GILL) Hard-boiled as hell's what I'll get! (*Abruptly going to* GILL) You get a doctor or—*Do* something! You hear me?

GILL *precipitately steps back.*

IRENE: Come on! (SHE *takes* AMES's *arm*) Some coffee. (SHE *starts him for the door to the street*)

GILL: You can't take him!

IRENE: Who says so?

GILL: Glick!

IRENE: I'll bring him back.

SHE *takes* AMES *out.*

GILL (*To* GLICK): You bring him back, yourself.

SCHMIDT *comes in, panting, from the street.*

SCHMIDT: Got one of 'em, Lieutenant.

GLICK *goes out.*

GILL: Oh, Schmidt! (*To* SULLIVAN) Get the Captain.

SULLIVAN *goes to the door right.*

SCHMIDT (*Pushing back his hat, and wiping his forehead with his sleeve*): What come off in here?

SULLIVAN (*Calling out right*): Schmidt, Captain.

SULLIVAN: We was just turnin' in, when—

McQUIGG *comes in, followed by* DELANEY. SULLIVAN *returns to the desk.*

Got one of 'em, sir. Clark and me. We was just drivin' in, when—

McQUIGG: Where's the other one?

SCHMIDT: Ross's after him.

McQUIGG: Where's the one you got?

SCHMIDT: Clark's bringin' him in. We was just drivin' in when one of 'em—I don't know which—comes down the steps with a yell at the driver in the car. The car lights out south, the one that come down the steps makin' a dive for the runnin' board, and they tear.

McQUIGG: Where'd you get 'em?

SCHMIDT: They got stopped by a freight at that crossin' at Eighty-sixth and Halsted, and jumped for a getaway. One of 'em flipped the freight. That's the one Ross's after. The other one cuts across a prairie. Clark and me got him.

GILL (*To* McQUIGG): I just talked to the Chief's sec—

CLARK (*Outside the entryway*): Get in there!

> CLARK *comes in, a sawed-off shotgun in each hand.* THE MAN *who shot* JOHNSON *follows him, his hat pulled down to shade his eyes.* SECOND PATROLMAN *is at his side.*

McQUIGG (*To* CLARK): Did you fan him? (*His eyes are pinched on* THE MAN)

CLARK: Yes, sir. If he had a rod he threw it away.

McQUIGG (*To* SCHMIDT): Take some men, Sergeant, with flashlights, and find it. You know the way they drove.

> SCHMIDT *and* SECOND PATROLMAN *go out right*

CLARK (*Handing the shotguns to* GILL): They had these in the car.

McQUIGG (*To* CLARK, *indicating the entryway*): Get on that door, and keep everybody out o' here.

> CLARK *goes into the entryway.*

(*To* GILL *and* SULLIVAN) Nothin' about this to headquarters till I give the word.

> HE *steps to* THE MAN *and knocks up his hat.*

Hello, Nick.

SCARSI: Good evenin', Mac. You like it out here?

McQUIGG: I'm beginnin' to. Thanks for not askin' me why I'm here.

SCARSI: You're not a gover'ment cop—dumb. What's the matter? That driver o' mine pull somethin' off in here?

McQUIGG: Somebody did.

SCARSI: What'd he do?

McQUIGG: Who?

SCARSI: "Breeze" Enright. My driver I sent in here.

McQUIGG: I thought Enright was down for some bank job.

SCARSI: He must've got paroled.

McQUIGG: Yeh. A lot do, since they equipped that penitentiary with revolvin' doors. What brought Enright in here?

SCARSI: I sent him to see that girl you got about how much she wants to lay off that brother o' mine. And—yeh, I told him to see that copper—Johnson—o' yours, too, since I heard you were keepin' him in.

McQUIGG: I wanted him in, knowin' what he was up against. But we haven't got this protection business down as efficient as you—big businessmen!

SCARSI: Big business runs this country. I'd get wise if I were you.

McQUIGG: I am.

SCARSI: What do you want him for?

McQUIGG: Who?

SCARSI: Enright.

McQUIGG: I don't want him.

SCARSI: Then if he didn't pull something—?

McQUIGG: Somebody did, and, by God, I got you!

SCARSI: Are you so sore about your transfer you're thinkin' o' hangin' somethin' onto me?

AMES *comes in from the street.* CLARK *tries to stop him.*

AMES (*Pushing* CLARK *aside*): Let me in! Captain, I know. That man who came in— (*Seeing* SCARSI, HE *stiffens*) That's him. He did it.

SCARSI: What?

McQUIGG: Now, Nick! How'll you alibi this?

AMES: Is *he*—?

McQUIGG (*To* DELANEY): Lock him up.

SCARSI: What's the charge?

McQUIGG: Same old thing for you. Murder.

SCARSI (*After a moment*): All right. I'll call my lawyer.

HE *starts for the phone on the partition.* McQUIGG *motions to* DELANEY. DELANEY *blocks* SCARSI.

McQUIGG: Forget who he is.

SAM MEYER *comes wearily in from the street.*

MEYER: Back again.

SCARSI: Where the hell've you been?

MEYER: I couldn't help it, Mr. Scarsi.

McQUIGG (*To* MEYER): Who're you?

MEYER: Sam Meyer, Captain, from Reilly, Platka and Cohn. But I'm a deputy sheriff now. (*Taking a paper from his pocket*) I got a writ o' habeas corpus to take him out.

AMES (*To* McQUIGG): I tried to tell you. My office phoned me—

SCARSI (*To* McQUIGG): "Efficiency." Do you imagine, for God's sake, I don't leave word where I'll be? They know what to do when I'm late reportin' in.

MEYER (*Handing the writ summons to* McQUIGG): All legal. Just issued by Judge—

McQUIGG (*To* DELANEY, *indicating* SCARSI): Take him down!

SCARSI: McQuigg!

McQUIGG (*Unheeding, indicating* AMES): Hang onto that boy.

SCARSI (*Shoving* DELANEY *aside*): Didn't you hear him about that writ?

McQUIGG: Try and serve it.

SCARSI: Are you trying to trick me?

McQUIGG: No, that's your way—in the dark, so's you can hide, and frame, and fix, and grab, till everybody's rotten with fear and don't-give-a-damn, and a man can't call his soul his own. It's the racket o' this whole damn town. But I'm through.

SCARSI: Not yet. (*Snatching the writ from* MEYER, *he extends it to* McQUIGG) You got to recognize a write. That's the law.

McQUIGG (*After a moment*): I'm licked again by due process o' law, uh? Well— (*Seizing and tearing up the writ*) I'm sick o' the law. We'll fight this out here.

SCARSI: You'll get contempt o' court for that. (*To* MEYER) Go phone that to the judge.

MEYER *turns for the door.*

McQUIGG: Jim!

DELANEY (*To* CLARK): Hi!

HE *trips up* MEYER *and as* HE *falls, pushes him to* CLARK, *who mixes with him and shoves him back to* DELANEY.

SCARSI: Look out! They're framin' you!

DELANEY (*Jerking* MEYER *up by the collar*): Pickin' a fight, uh? *Drunk*, uh?

McQUIGG: Lock him up till he sobers up!

DELANEY (*Getting* MEYER *to the door right*): Reilly, Platka, and Cohn resistin' arrest, uh? The Department's been wantin' a crack at that outfit. (HE *gets him out*)

End of Act Two

ACT THREE

The Captain's office a few minutes later—a narrow room, high ceilinged and finished like that of Acts I and II, with the same kind of high, arched window with an old cracked green blind pulled down at left; a door opening in from the outer room back center; and another door, opening out, at right. When the center door is open, SULLIVAN's desk and the light over it can be seen across the outer room. This side of the window is a radiator, its pipe running up through the ceiling.

A small, old-fashioned rolltop desk, and a swivel chair with an overstuffed black leather cushion is back left, a chair by the radiator up left, and back right a black leather overstuffed couch, its raised head toward the door right. On the wall over the couch is a large Board of Election Commissioners' map of Chicago showing wards and precincts only. On the desk is a telephone; on top of the desk old directories, and a pile of old newspapers; and over it a large calendar reading

NOVEMBER

3

SATURDAY

The pigeon holes of the desk are stuffed with a dusty accumulation of papers, envelopes, and files. There is a buzzer in the right side of the desk. A spittoon like that in the outer room is between the desk and center door. The chandelier hanging from the center of the ceiling, controlled by a push button in the wall left of the center door, is also like that in the outer room.

MCQUIGG *comes in center, followed by* DELANEY, *removes his cap, and tosses it to the desk.*

DELANEY: Nick's put the whole Organization in a trap with this job.

McQUIGG: Yeh. They'll have to be with me this time.

DELANEY *(Impatiently)*: What'll they do?

McQUIGG: What can they do?

DELANEY: What they always do—ride us down.

McQUIGG: No. This time, by God, I'll use their machine myself to push Scarsi to trial.

DELANEY: Even gettin' him to trial won't wash Nick up.

McQUIGG: It's as far as I can take him, bein' only a policeman. But that far he goes. (HE *pushes the buzzer on the desk*) Now get after Schmidt and see if he's found Nick's gun.

DELANEY: Yes, sir.

SULLIVAN *comes in center,* DELANEY *goes out.*

McQUIGG: Send Scarsi in. And a couple o' men.

SULLIVAN: Yes, sir. (HE *goes out*)

FIRST PATROLMAN *and* SECOND PATROLMAN *come in.*

McQUIGG (*To* FIRST PATROLMAN, *indicating door right*): Get on that door.

The FIRST PATROLMAN *goes to door right and out.*

(*To* SECOND PATROLMAN) You, there.

SECOND PATROLMAN *goes out center, standing back to let* SCARSI *in, then closes the door, remaining outside.*

McQUIGG: I finally got you, Nick. And I wanted to. But not for this.

SCHMIDT: So that copper o' yours got killed?

McQUIGG: Yeh.

SCARSI: What do you suppose he tried to do to that chauffeur o' mine?

McQUIGG: Still stickin' to that stall! So when that reporter made you, he mistook you for Enright, uh?

SCARSI: That's it.

McQUIGG: How much did that cost you, gettin' Enright out?

SCARSI: So long as we're bein' frank, plenty, these politicians got such a lech' for jack! (HE *sits in the chair, taking out and lighting a cigar*)

McQUIGG: They must think we're playin' ping-pong, battin' these punks back at us as fast as we bat 'em in.

SCARSI: Why don't you make a complaint to the Reform gang. It'd give 'em another statistic.

McQUIGG: Those old women've been gatherin' statistics for fifteen years!

SCARSI: It'd help you more if they'd furnish you juries, eh?

McQUIGG *grunts.*

The trouble the Criminal Court has in gettin' a jury now, it looks like the public imagined bein' a juror in these cases wasn't safe.

McQUIGG: It's not, is it, when if you don't like 'em they're liable to disappear.

SCARSI: Nobody's got any guts. I'm surprised "Breeze" Enright had enough to bang that cop.

McQUIGG: I didn't know Enright was a killer.

SCARSI: Times've changed. You can get by with it better now.

McQUIGG: Yeh. We've got to do (*Sarcastically*) thinkin', to keep up with you.

SCARSI: I'll take anythin' you four-thousand-dollar-a-year harps can think up for me.

McQUIGG: Shut up, you peacock, and get this! I've got a lot o' bones to pick with you.

SCARSI *laughs.*

Oh, I know you're powerful. You've got a lot o' political sluts on their backs.

SCARSI: And takin' candy.

McQUIGG: And they've got a lot of our leadin' businessmen on *their* backs, takin' candy from them. But I don't like that kind o' candy.

SCARSI: No?

McQUIGG: And when my job makes me swallow it, I'm sick till I get it up again. This time I'm goin' to get it up with such a commotion that hereafter it'll leave me alone.

SCARSI: Yeh?

McQUIGG: And I'm gettin' you out o' my system at the same time.

SCARSI (*Rising*): Gettin' *me* out o' your system. You got any idea they'll let you lock me up?

McQUIGG: Why, with you out o' the way I'll feel like a kid again.

SCARSI: You don't imagine I'm goin' to hang or anythin', do you?

McQUIGG: No.

SCARSI: Not these days.

McQUIGG: No, the (*Contemptuously*) law wouldn't let you. But there just might be even a chance o' that once this election's out o' the way and the powers-that-be quit shakin' at mention o' your name. Yeh, and prosecuted by Welch! (HE *laughs*) That'd give the whole department a laugh, and we could use some laughin' in this business now.

SCARSI: Don't make me laugh. Where is Welch? I know he's here, for raids.

McQUIGG: They can't fix this.

SCARSI: He'll have to.

McQUIGG (*After a moment*): H'm. They couldn't take the chance! (HE *abruptly rises and opens the center door*) Sullivan! (*To* SCARSI) All right. You asked for Welch.

SULLIVAN *comes to the door.*

Send around to the restaurant at the corner o' Western and get Mr. Assistant State's Attorney Welch. (*His eyes on* SCARSI) We'll see what he can do.

SULLIVAN: Yes, sir. (HE *goes out*)

SCARSI: He'll take care o' me.

McQUIGG (*Going to door right*): He'll take care o' himself. He'll take care o' me!

SCARSI *laughs.*

Go on. You'll laugh yourself to death. (*Opening the door. To* FIRST PATROLMAN *there*) Put him in the bullpen where he'll be handy.

SCARSI: You ought to be in the Marines. (HE *goes out*)

There is a commotion outside the center door. It flies open. PRATT *and* MILLER *trying to push past the* SECOND PATROLMAN *there.*

PRATT: Captain—

McQUIGG (*To* SECOND PATROLMAN): All right.

MILLER (*Shoving* SECOND PATROLMAN *aside*): Horses! (HE *gets in*)

The SECOND PATROLMAN *withdraws.* PRATT *comes in.*

PRATT: We called our office from the restaurant—

MILLER: Thank God.

PRATT: Who killed this cop?

McQUIGG: Did you give this shootin' out?

MILLER: Headquarters's got it, downtown.

McQUIGG: Now who the hell— (HE *goes to his desk*)

PRATT (*Following him*): And when we told Welch—

MILLER (*Following*): I thought he was goin' to faint.

PRATT: Have you identified your pinch?

McQUIGG: Who said I had a pinch?

PRATT: Half the neighborhood. The street out front's packed.

McQUIGG: Damn!

MILLER: Oh, nobody spilled the pinch's name.

PRATT: No one had to, this is such a typical Scarsi job. Welch saw that.

McQUIGG: Where is Welch?

MILLER: He stopped to phone.

PRATT: Captain, if you can nail Scarsi for this, the Organization won't sleep tonight. And if they try to spring him, the stuff we'll print may rouse a few of the last of the Anglo-Saxons into voting, anyway.

McQUIGG: I'll give you the story after I talk to Welch.

MILLER: Jeez, this time make it somethin' we can print.

PRATT (*Starting for the door*): We've got plenty of time.

MILLER (*Following him*): Yeh, it was nice of him to pull it so early.

PRATT *goes out.*

(To McQUIGG) You know, Captain, this one makes fourteen policemen killed so far this year.

FIRST PATROLMAN *comes in.*

FIRST PATROLMAN: Hayes, sir.

IRENE *comes in.* FIRST PATROLMAN *goes out.*

IRENE (*To* McQUIGG): I want to talk to you.

MILLER *stops interrogatively.*

McQUIGG (*To* MILLER): Travel.

MILLER *goes out.*

IRENE: Have you got to keep this Ames boy here?

McQUIGG: He's the witness.

IRENE: For you to tie Scarsi with. But I don't care about Scarsi. I do, him.

McQUIGG: So do I, if he can make his identification stick.

IRENE: Do you want him killed, too?

McQUIGG *sits down at the desk.*

You know what Scarsi will do to him.

McQUIGG: I'll take him through this.

IRENE: Can't you think of anyone but yourselves? You and Nick Scarsi both. So cocky you kill a policeman trying to get at each other's throats, and show this boy so much—

AMES *comes in center, a piece of adhesive plaster over the cut on his head.*

AMES (*To* IRENE): Listen, I told you not to look after me. I'm all right. But— Apparently nothing else is here! Captain, I saw Johnson. He's— (*Incredulously*) smiling! (*His voice rising*) Nobody seems to realize that somebody's been killed. And the one who did it giggling over it, and everyone calling him by his first name.

McQUIGG: Havin' a tough time of it, aren't you?

AMES: Aren't you—with the public hiring you to protect them and then not giving a damn whether you do or not?

McQUIGG: Yeh.

IRENE: They can't do anything. Not to Scarsi.

AMES: Maybe you can't do anything—the way things are, I mean. I don't know. I don't know anything, anymore. But somebody's got to try to, haven't they?

IRENE: Not you.

AMES: Yes, me.

IRENE: Because of your pride, or your honor, or whatever it is you men call your lack of sense? (*To* McQUIGG) You're in this. (*Indicating* AMES) Tangling him in these *manly* principles of yours until he's afraid to run away from even being killed. Make him go! (*To* AMES) Tell him you won't testify!

AMES: I've got to. I'll identify him, Captain. I'll testify.

McQUIGG (*Rising*): Good boy.

AMES (*To* IRENE): Oh, I *have* to!

IRENE: All right. (*After a shrug, to* McQUIGG) Count me in, too, then. I'll try fighting again, myself. (*Her eyes on* AMES) And if Scarsi tries anything, I'll do some testifying that'll put Dunn and Bradstreet themselves up on the stand.

GILL *comes in center, the raid order still in his hand.*

GILL: Mr. Welch is here.

McQUIGG (*Alert*): In your office.

GILL (*Distressed*): But what about these raids?

McQUIGG: Hold 'em up.

GILL: But the order says—

McQUIGG: Orders, flypaper! I'll give the orders tonight.

GILL: Yes, sir. (HE *turns for the door*)

McQUIGG: And from now on.

GILL *goes out.*

Now we are ready for Mr. Welch. (HE *goes out center*)

IRENE *sinks wearily to the couch.*

AMES: I wonder what they'll say to me at the office?

IRENE: Find out.

AMES *takes the phone from the desk.*

AMES (*At the phone*): State eight one hundred. (*To* IRENE) When I missed young Scarsi's arrest they told me the next time I was late— (*At the phone*) Give me the desk. (*To* IRENE) And then when I tried to phone in about Johnson, they hung up on me. (*At the phone—taking a deep breath*) This is— (*Blurting*) Ames, at the— . . . I know, Mr. Brown, but I did call and you hung up. . . . What? . . . You're taking me off police? . . . Now, listen! Just because I try to give you big stories instead of your damn newsnotes— Well, I won't go back to covering women's clubs . . . I've done that. . . . All you want's the same old stories with different names and addresses, anyway. You can take that *City Press* of yours and stick it in the lake. I'm through. I quit! (HE *slams up the phone*)

IRENE: You're getting that "experience" you wanted, fast.

AMES: All at once.

IRENE: You'll get another job.

AMES: Not here. If they won't listen to me, they can all go to hell. If I'm going to be a reporter, I'll be one! I'll go to New York. Here it's like working in a butcher shop.

IRENE: New York?

AMES: Yes.

IRENE: Right away?

AMES: They'll print my stories there.

IRENE: I'd print anything you'd say, to me.

AMES (*After a moment*): I wonder if I will be able to get a job in New York?

IRENE: If you can keep your mind on it longer than you can on—this.

AMES: This what?

IRENE: You and me.

AMES: What—

IRENE: We could talk to each other—couldn't we—if you'd be satisfied with this "experience" for awhile, and not have to make a flying tackle at New York? If you'd just tie to— (SHE *stops*)

AMES: The only thing you can tie to is yourself.

IRENE: And the girlfriend?

AMES: Girls? What do I care about gi— Oh. You. Sure, I can talk to you. (HE *sits down beside her*)

IRENE: I'm listening.

AMES: Well, a fellow can't just keep on talking to himself!

IRENE: Don't.

AMES: I mean, there's none o' this lovemaking stuff with you.

IRENE: Oh! (*After a moment*) No?

AMES: No. That's a lot of bunk.

IRENE: What's the idea?

AMES: I'm getting a lot of ideas. (*After a moment*) Everything you believe in and try to do—you can't! Nobody gives a damn. You learn to hold your head up for a lot of bunk.

IRENE (*Laughing a little*): You're so "experienced" now I suppose you wouldn't let yourself fall in love, even if you could.

AMES: What?

IRENE (*Rising*): I mean, if I wasn't so intimate with inside dirt, there wouldn't be such a ditch between you and me, would there?

AMES (*Impatiently*): There's nothing between you and me!

IRENE: No?

AMES: What's the *matter* with you?

IRENE: "A lot o' bunk." I—like you, you damn fool.

AMES: Well, I like you, too.

IRENE: Yes? (SHE *shrugs*) We'll let it go at that. (SHE *goes out center*)

WELCH *comes in right, pale, tight, followed by* McQUIGG.

AMES (*To* McQUIGG): Do you want me now?

McQUIGG: In a minute, son.

AMES *goes out center.*

WELCH: Where is Scarsi?

McQUIGG: He'll be here in a second.

WELCH: I'll see him. But, Mac! Don't give this to the papers yet. Let's get together on this. I felt it was Nick—

McQUIGG: You would, wouldn't you?

WELCH: I knew it was him, the minute I heard how it was done.

McQUIGG: You've been afraid o' somethin' like this, haven't you?

WELCH: Gall? God! But nobody saw it, did they?

McQUIGG: You'll find that out, too.

WELCH (*Unheeding*): The State's Attorney is out of town. I don't know where to reach him now. So—

McQUIGG: He wouldn't stand for their fixing this.

WELCH: He's not here, I tell you! So I had the Old Man on the wire. And I'll handle this, myself. If you'll turn Nick over—for questioning—to me—

McQUIGG: "Use *your* head"—like you told me last night. Can't you see your whole ticket would be (*Sarcastically*) criticized, for carryin' such an eminent murder now?

WELCH: I've been seeing it in my sleep.

McQUIGG: Then why don't you shake him off?

WELCH: I wish to God he'd— (HE *stops*)

McQUIGG: What?

WELCH (*Relaxing*): But I'll have to take him out, as soon as the Chief of Police phones you the release.

McQUIGG: Who's gettin' to the Chief?

WELCH: The Old Man.

McQUIGG: Yeh, the Chief's in a tough spot, too. But the Old Man, himself, can't hush this case. And if you try to spring Scarsi with what I've got on him, your opposition, and their papers, and this respectable public that's been keepin' you awake nights'd come down on you like a ton o' brick. (HE *opens the door right. To* FIRST PATROLMAN *there*) Get Scarsi in. (*To* WELCH) Release order or not, Welch, you can't afford to turn Nick loose. So I'm keepin' him, and without bookin' or bail, or writs, or any other o' the sleight o' hand performances that Old Man o' yours pulls off.

SCARSI *comes in, followed by* FIRST PATROLMAN.

(*Indicating* SCARSI) Tell him that.

HE *waves* FIRST PATROLMAN *out, and goes out center.*

SCARSI: Where've you been?

WELCH: Talking to the Old Man.

SCARSI: On this?

WELCH: Yes.

SCARSI: Then get me out o' here.

WELCH: You must have gone crazy to pull this.

SCARSI: Who says I pulled it?

WELCH: You were told to stay away from McQuigg.

SCARSI: And I told 'em where to go, didn't I—tellin' *me* to hide.

WELCH: You—

SCARSI: I didn't keep away from McQuigg, or *any*body, did I?

WELCH: No.

SCARSI: And I showed McQuigg, didn't I?

WELCH: He made you.

SCARSI: *Made* me?

WELCH: This is what he wanted—you in his hands. That's all he came down on your brother for.

SCARSI: Leave my brother out o' this.

WELCH: That's how McQuigg used this girl—to nag you wild.

SCARSI: Well, with the jimmies you old woman're in it's wonder you didn't phone McQuigg I was comin' into this district, and to please meet me, and show me picturebooks or somethin', till those scared grandmas o' yours could get out and sic me home again!

WELCH: Now, going back to your coming here—

SCARSI: Choke that cross-examination language with me.

WELCH: Did you leave word you were coming here? How did Reilly, Platka and Cohn get out with that writ?

SCARSI: They do that automatic with me when I'm late reportin' in to that switchboard o' theirs. What the hell're you gettin' so innocent about? But McQuigg'll get contempt o' court—he will get suspended—for that.

WELCH: For what?

SCARSI: Tearin' up that writ.

WELCH: McQuigg?

SCARSI: Tore it up!

WELCH: Then he saved me the trouble, that's all.

SCARSI: What?

WELCH: Do you think the Old Man would have stood for a writ, if he'd known the jam you're in?

SCARSI: If he wouldn't't've—

WELCH: He wouldn't have taken the chance. McQuigg knew what he was doing. Contempt of court? That's a joke! The judge who signed that writ will kiss him for getting rid of the damn thing. Now, about this brother of yours. If he hadn't bragged to this girl—

SCARSI: Lay off him, I tell you—Keep him out o' this.

WELCH: He is out of it, you— (*Controlling himself*) Didn't I tell you we'd take care of the owner of that car? I talked to downtown from the restaurant. W. K. Taylor left for Hot Springs tonight. Doctor's orders. Joe won't ever be prosecuted for that theft, so—

SCARSI: So what're you goin' to do for *me?*

WELCH: I'll take you out, for questioning.

SCARSI: Hurry it up.

WELCH: We're getting a release order now.

SCARSI: Then you can find "Breeze" Enright and tell him to take this rap. He was drivin' for me tonight. (HE *reclines lazily upon the couch*)

WELCH: Is he all the defense you've got?

SCARSI: He can swear self-defense, take a second degree sentence, and go back down. I'll buy him out again.

WELCH: Keep it quiet. (*His voice rising again*) If you just hadn't let this girl get you with that nonsense she said Joe told her about— (HE *stops*)

SCARSI: What?

WELCH: This Higgins thing!

SCARSI: I've taken care o' that.

WELCH (*Unheeding*): But, no, you had to break out and show them who you were.

McQUIGG *comes in center.*

SCARSI (*To* WELCH): Snap out of it.

McQUIGG: A break for justice, Welch. Such an influential citizen might force whoever was with him to take this rap, if that gent was handy at all. But I just heard from my man who was after Mr. Scarsi's chauffeur, and he's not handy. He's gone, got away, dropped off that freight in the dark. And we're not lookin' for him. So don't let (*Indicating* SCARSI) him worry the prosecution with that.

SCARSI: If you think that kid you got's goin' to do any identifyin' o' *me*—

WELCH (*To* McQUIGG): Did somebody see this?

McQUIGG: I told you you'd find that out, too. (HE *opens the center door*) Come in.

AMES *and* IRENE *come in.*

(*To* AMES) Now make your identification to Mr. Welch.

SCARSI (*Rising*): I been wantin' to hear if this loudspeaker o' yours was positive about that.

AMES: Yes. You—

WELCH: You're a minor, aren't you? (*Running down weakly*) Your testimony might not—be any good.

AMES: I'm twenty-three. And right now I feel about fifty. So what do you think of that? He shot Johnson!

SCARSI (*Jerking him around*): Take a look at me.

AMES: Just as I came in—

SCARSI: Maybe you'll change your mind.

AMES (*Knocking* SCARSI's *hand away*): I'm not afraid of you.

SCARSI: With what I got on a couple of fancy doctors downtown, they'll tend to you.

IRENE: Leave him alone, you *hero.*

SCARSI (*After a moment*): You're Hayes, uh?

IRENE: Yes. And you're Scarsi, the Awful—afraid of women, but death on kids. I've known enough men to realize that you couldn't be anything but just another one, so vain you have to play only with men because women would laugh, and you can't stand being laughed at, can you?

SCARSI: Nobody laughs at me.

IRENE: I thought you might be heroic, you're so damn bad. But you were scared stiff when I got in your brother's way.

SCARSI: You won't get in his way again.

IRENE: No, now I'm getting in yours.

SCARSI *laughs.*

I'll play you off the board. Anybody can trick you.

SCARSI: No woman has yet.

IRENE: Then why were you so afraid to see me when Joe wanted you to?

SCARSI: Now cut this stuff! Do you imagine I'd stand for you with Joe after what I made o' him? I educated him, East, didn't I? Yeh. He's a college man. He can go anyplace—mix with the high-class people—in this town. He's not in the racket, and he won't be, because I'm keepin' him out, d'you hear? And with the jack he'll have he can marry right—on the Drive—*high* class—and not you, you common—

IRENE *quickly slaps him across the mouth.*

SCARSI (*Rigid with fury*): I'll— (HE *starts for her*)

McQUIGG: Get back. (HE *seizes and spins* SCARSI *back*)

IRENE: Nobody ought to be afraid of you.

SCARSI (*Seething*): No?

IRENE: No. Not when you had to kick this (*Indicating* AMES) baby in the face.

SCARSI: What the hell'd he get in my way for?

IRENE (*To* McQUIGG): There's your confession.

SCARSI *stiffens.* WELCH *drops to the chair.*

If he was the one who kicked Ames, he was the one who shot Johnson, wasn't he?

McQUIGG (*To* SCARSI): Ha. Women are still poison to you. (*To* IRENE *and* AMES) Wait outside. (*To* AMES) You'll be all right, with her.

SCARSI (*To* AMES): I'll see *you* later.

IRENE *and* AMES *go out center.*

McQUIGG: You heard him, Welch. (*To* SCARSI) How'll you explain that?

SCARSI: How'll you explain anybody strollin' into your station and bangin' an officer—a public servant—a representative o' the people—under a lieutenant's, and desk sergeant's, and your nose?

McQUIGG: What?

SCARSI: The public'll forget this shootin' if it's turned on you.

McQUIGG: Oh, no it won't.

SCARSI: There's sob-stuff in a young policeman.

McQUIGG: After he's been killed.

SCARSI: The paper'll demand somebody's head for this.

McQUIGG: All right. (HE *goes to the center door*) Any head in a storm, Nick. (*Opening the door*) Boys! *Tribune!* (*To* SCARSI) I'm givin' 'em yours, first.

WELCH (*Desperately*): Mac—

MILLER *and* PRATT *push in past* SECOND PATROLMAN.

PRATT (*Seeing* SCARSI. *To* MILLER): I told you.

MILLER (*To* SCARSI): Hi.

PRATT (*To* McQUIGG): Do we shoot now?

McQUIGG: Fast, and quote me. Mr. Scarsi swaggered in here a half hour ago to scare Johnson and Hayes here into layin' off his brother's case. Johnson started to throw him out, and Scarsi killed him—"a public servant"—without even givin' him a chance to draw. Ames came in and saw him, and when I got him, made the identification, cold. And Miss Hayes just tricked him into admittin' the killin', himself.

MILLER (*Starting for the door*): Women and children first.

McQUIGG: I got Scarsi ten minutes after the shootin'. (MILLER *turns*) Get that part of it from Sergeant Schmidt, and give him and his squad the credit. And here's Mr. Assistant State's Attorney Welch, already on the job for the people o' the State of Illinois! What the state's goin' to do about it, you can get from him.

WELCH (*Rising*): I'll see you after I talk to the accused.

MILLER *goes out.*

PRATT (*Innocently*): Will you ask hanging for Scarsi, Welch? (HE *goes out center*)

MCQUIGG: No, Nick wouldn't like that, would he, Mr. Welch?

SCARSI (*To* WELCH): Get that release order!

WELCH (*Going to him*): I told you we're trying to. But the Chief has to sign it, doesn't he? And he's lost in some campaign meeting tonight, himself.

MCQUIGG: Yeh, they're all out bellowin' for the Organization, Nick, not thinkin' o' you. As long as your river wards are set for them for Tuesday what do they care for you? They didn't intend to marry you, and you've got too big to carry. Why, after this election they'll drop you, anyway. Because, o' course, they're goin' to win Tuesday at the polls.

SCARSI: It's not Tuesday yet. And the river wards can still be set the other way.

WELCH: Now—

SCARSI: Your faction don't win this primary if I don't give the word.

WELCH: Wait a min—

SCARSI: You're all lice, whichever side o' the pile you're on, so it don't matter to me who I'm with. What d'you suppose I gave fifty grand to *both* factions' campaign funds for? You didn't know I play both ends against the middle, uh? (HE *laughs*) Whoever's in has got to be with me. If I'd put this Reform gang in they'd play pretty, they're so dumb! Now get me out o' here. And quick (As WELCH *hesitates*) 'Ave you always got to wait for orders?

WELCH: No!

SCARSI: Can't you do anythin' but jump through hoops?

WELCH: Yes.

The center door opens, TURCK *appearing there.*

TURCK (*To* WELCH): On the phone.

WELCH: Who is it?

TURCK: The Old Man.

WELCH: In a minute.

TURCK: This story's out in the football extras downtown.

WELCH: Keep him on the phone.

TURCK *goes out.*

(*To* SCARSI) Now with this in the papers you may have to stand arrest till after Tuesday, anyway. (HE *starts for the door center*)

SCARSI: Me?

WELCH: Yes.

GILL *comes in center.*

GILL (*To* McQUIGG): The coroner's office called.

McQUIGG: Who gave them this?

GILL (*Distressedly*): Well, you see, before you gave the order not to, I had the Chief's secretary on the wire, so—

McQUIGG: So it was you, uh! (HE *drops to the chair at the desk*)

GILL: So the coroner's on the way himself, and—

McQUIGG: And prob'ly a carload o' those mahogany desks from headquarters, with all the reporters and photographers in town. All racin' each other to the scene o' the publicity.

GILL (*Hurriedly*): Well—a squad from the Detective Bureau, too.

SCARSI: Homicide dicks! (*To* WELCH) Get on that phone (*To* McQUIGG) Do you imagine I'm goin' to take a massage from dicks?

McQUIGG: These Homicide dicks won't wait to use the hose on you. They'll use their hands. This time it was a policeman who was killed. Oh, maybe you could get him out after election, Welch, if he'd take this rap till then. But after four nights and three days at the Detective Bureau you'd have to carry him on a stretcher. Because (*Rising*) if anybody takes him away from here it'll be these Homicide dicks, not you.

SCARSI: Are you tryin' to frame me?

McQUIGG: Yeh. In purple satin, under glass. (*To* GILL) Know anyplace you can call on Western Avenue about Seventy-ninth Street? (*His eyes on* SCARSI) That's about five minutes from here.

GILL: There's a fillin' station.

McQUIGG: Get 'em and ask 'em to call you when a Detective Bureau car comes by. They'll know it by that siren they use.

GILL: Yes, sir.

TURCK *comes in center.*

TURCK (*To* WELCH): His Nibs is gettin' restless.

SCARSI (*To* McQUIGG): Where's the washroom?

McQUIGG (*To* GILL): Lieutenant! (HE *sardonically bows and gestures* GILL *to the door right*)

SCARSI (*To* WELCH): Speed it up. I got to go to the theatre tonight. (HE *goes out with* GILL

DELANEY *comes in center, a .38-caliber blue steel revolver wrapped in a handkerchief in his hand.*

DELANEY: Well, Captain, here's his rod. (*Exposing the revolver*)

McQUIGG (*To* WELCH): Nick's.

DELANEY: Exhibit A.

WELCH: Christ! (HE *goes out center*)

McQUIGG: Take care of it till I come back. (HE *goes out center*)

TURCK *unwraps and chews a fresh piece of gum.*

DELANEY (*Exhibiting the gun*): In the ditch by that crossin' at Eighty-sixth Street. I knew he wouldn't lose it before he got stopped. (HE *breaks the gun and knocks out the cartridges into his palm*) One gone.

TURCK (*Picking up one of the bullets and scratching it*): Dum-dum bullets. Say, is it true they don't allow them anymore in war?

WELCH *opens the door center.*

WELCH: Turck.

TURCK *turns, and at* WELCH's *nod for him, goes out.* DELANEY *puts the revolver on the desk, takes an envelope from the desk, spills the bullets into it, seals it, pencils a notation on it, and puts it in a drawer of the desk, lightly whistling the tune of a popular song.* GILL *comes in right.*

GILL: Captain's orders. Wait for the coroner out back, and keep him there.

DELANEY: How?

GILL: *I* don't know.

WELCH *comes in center,* TURCK *after him.*

DELANEY (*Going out right*): I'll get these reporters to interview him. He'll talk for a week. (HE *goes out*)

GILL *goes out center.*

TURCK: So that's what the Old Man told you to do.

WELCH: Yes.

TURCK: Shall I get Scarsi in?

WELCH: In a minute. (*After a moment*) Fix the window. We'll need an alibi, for the press.

TURCK *goes to the window, pushes it up, pulls down the blind, weights it with a telephone directory, then strolls back to* WELCH.

But not unless I give you the word. Got it?

TURCK: Yeh.

WELCH: Get him in.

TURCK (*Opening the door right*): Send Scarsi in.

WELCH *paces.* SCARSI *comes in, his hat on, getting into his overcoat.* TURCK *leans against the door right, chewing lazily.*

SCARSI: Well? Did you talk to the Old Man?

WELCH: Yes.

SCARSI: Then you got your orders, didn't you?

WELCH: Yes.

SCARSI: All right, then! What're we goin' to do?

WELCH: Don't say "we"! You've got to take this rap till after Tuesday.

SCARSI: What?

WELCH: I can't take you.

SCARSI: Afraid o' two newspapers and the lilly vote?

WELCH: We *can't*—

SCARSI: Are you tryin' to shake me?

WELCH: You know the publicity you get.

SCARSI: Listen, you—

WELCH: We can't carry you and this primary both.

SCARSI: You take me out or—

WELCH: We're not going to be embarrassed out of votes!

SCARSI: You take me out, or I'll drown you for county judge in the river wards. Then where'll you be with the jack you owe? You know you haven't got a dime.

WELCH: This isn't personal with me.

SCARSI: Your wife's such a shopper she even runs through your graft.

McQUIGG *comes in center.*

McQUIGG: That Bureau car just passed Seventy-ninth and Western, Nick. You'll carry right through your trial the beauty spots this Homicide squad'll leave on you. Why, in the papers your picture'll look like a stockyard's beef.

SCARSI (*A snarl*): Yeh?

McQUIGG: They'll have to carry you to the scaffold—you'll still be too weak to climb. And you know it takes about twenty minutes to hang by the neck till dead unless the knot o' the rope's just right.

SCARSI (*To* WELCH): If anybody touches me I'll drown your whole ticket. You'll lose—

WELCH: We'll lose either way, with you.

SCARSI: *I'll* get the papers in here, and— Yeh, *I'll* give 'em a story! With names, and dates, and figures, that'll raise such a stink there won't be any prominent people left to handshake Queens. (*Starting for the door*) Examiner! Tribune!

McQUIGG *seizes him by the neck and flings him back.*

McQUIGG: I'll take care o' them. (HE *goes out*)

SCARSI (*In cornered fury*): I'll give 'em one o' their exposés of politics and business and crime that'll rip this town wide open!

SCARSI *jerks open the door.* FIRST PATROLMAN *starts for him.*

FIRST PATROLMAN: Keep in there!

SCARSI *slams the door in his face.*

WELCH: You won't get the chance.

SCARSI: All right, then. All right! The facts 'll spill easy after I been beat up by dicks. Who that Organization o' yours paid to get its names first on the ballot this time—

WELCH: Who'd believe you?

SCARSI: I got it on paper. Yeh, I got everythin' up my sleeve—ready for a double-cross by you. How you made that special investigatin' grand jury o' prominent high-hats fold up last month by condemnin' the elevators in a couple o' million dollar department stores! Yeh! And by remindin' some o' our leadin' citizens o' the extra apartments they keep!

WELCH: Stop!

SCARSI: How the Old Man had that kid in that treasurer's office accidentally killed by a train because his wife made him promise to squeal about the public funds grabbed there!

WELCH: You'll get—

SCARSI: How you framed the Civics Board, to get your own hogs in there, because *that* Board's got seventy-five *million* to spend next year!

WELCH: Keep qui—

SCARSI: I won't stop at blowin' up this town! I'll talk some o' your *state* politicians into court—makin' me pay ten grand a head for pardons and paroles. I'll talk some o' your Republicans in the Federal Building into committin' suicide over the liquor dope I got. Who do you suppose I pay for the breweries I own? Who do you suppose I pay for the alcohol I get? I'll knock your whole Organization cuckoo!

WELCH: Shut up! The Old Man thought you'd try that.

SCARSI: He did, uh?

WELCH: But you won't!

SCARSI: I won't, uh? I'll talk him into flyin' the country if I even whisper about what happened to that friend o' yours, Higgins, last week.

WELCH (*Struck, horribly*): What?

SCARSI: Who do you suppose ordered him out o' the way, so that my guns had to do the job?

WELCH *stares.*

The Old Man!

WELCH: You're lying! The Old Man wouldn't—

SCARSI: He knew too much for the Old Man!

WELCH: No. *No!* The Old Man wouldn't—

SCARSI: Higgins had been collectin' for him for years. Yeh! He was gettin' too big to carry, too. Christ, *you'll* be next!

WELCH (*Waving a limp hand at the window*): Go on. The window. It's fixed, for a getaway.

SCARSI: I thought you'd crawl when I spoke that piece. (HE *springs to the chair against the window, pulls the shade aside, sees that the window is open, then jumps down. To* TURCK) Here. Give me your rod.

WELCH (*Coming to, and hurriedly pushing* SCARSI *on the window*): Hurry up. There's an elevated two blocks north—that railroad—Hide in a basement, till you can get to your men.

SCARSI: Give me—

McQUIGG *comes in center.*

WELCH (*Grabbing* SCARSI's *arm*): Wait.

SCARSI (*Jerking away*): No.

McQUIGG: What're you up to?

SCARSI: Tell him.

WELCH: Wait!

SCARSI: Not me. (HE *backs to the window, his eyes on* McQUIGG) Did you imagine I'd let any lousy politicians who'd knock their own mothers over the head for a vote tell *me* what to do? (*To* WELCH) I'm off you worms! You haven't got a prayer for Tuesday now. I'm goin' to deliver the river wards to the Reform gang, for a laugh. And if you think you can steal this primary, fight it out with the mob, *I'll* have Tuesday at the polls. To lick you, we'll have an election for a change that's square! (HE *notices the revolver* DELANEY *left on the desk, snatches it up, holds it on* McQUIGG, *and puts one foot on the chair to spring to the window*)

McQUIGG (*Hunching*): Give me that gun.

SCARSI: In the belly if you don't get back.

McQUIGG *starts for him.* SCARSI *fires. The pin only clicks.* HE *fires frantically again. Realizing that the gun is empty.*

You bastards!

HE *flings the gun at* McQUIGG, *who ducks, and jumps to the window sill.*

WELCH: Turck!

TURCK *draws a revolver and fires at* SCARSI, *then again.* SCARSI *pitches to the floor. The* FIRST AND SECOND PATROLMEN *burst in right.* McQUIGG, *after a look at* TURCK, *then at* WELCH, *goes to* SCARSI, *bends, examines him and rises.*

McQUIGG: Out.

TURCK: It was the second one that got him.

McQUIGG *motions* THE TWO PATROLMEN *out, picks up the gun* SCARSI *threw and breaks it, inspecting the chambers.*

He didn't know it wasn't loaded! (TURCK *goes out right*)

McQUIGG *tosses the gun to the desk.*

McQUIGG (*Eyeing the body*): Well—uh—Judge, that issue's out o' the way.

WELCH *hands him* SCARSI's *overcoat.* McQUIGG *covers the body with the coat, then sits at the desk.*

The Grand Old Party here'll prob'ly run you for mayor, for that.

There is a commotion outside the center door. MILLER *and* PRATT *push in past* FIRST PATROLMAN.

(*To* MILLER *and* PRATT) Mr. Scarsi tried a getaway. Sergeant Turck o' the State Attorney's office got him.

MILLER (*Starting out*): Jeez, what a break for the Sunday papers! (*Indicating the body*) Is he—?

McQUIGG: He is.

PRATT (*Innocently*): Why, Mr. Welch?

MILLER (*Going out*): So that gover'ment o' the professionals, by the professionals and for the professionals, shall not perish from the earth.

PRATT (*To* WELCH): What were the events leading up to the tragedy?

WELCH: He— (HE *cannot go on*)

PRATT: That will do. An inquest's hardly legal anymore without a little perjury. (*Eyeing the body*) Well, that blows this election exposé of mine to hell. The long delayed rising of the upper classes will have to be postponed. (HE *goes out*)

WELCH: I'm going to—get—some—coffee. (HE *goes out right*)

McQUIGG (*To* FIRST PATROLMAN *outside the center door*) Send those two in. (AMES *and* IRENE *come in*) You can go now.

AMES: Thanks.

THEY *shake hands.*

McQUIGG: Good luck. Keep your feet.

AMES: Sure.

DELANEY *comes in right.*

DELANEY: Where you goin', kid?

AMES: New York. (*Eagerly*) Were you ever there?

DELANEY: Yeh. A hick town.

AMES (*Grinning*): Aw-w-! (*To* IRENE) Going downtown, Irene? Come on.

IRENE: Not your way, darling. Run along.

AMES: Well— Good-bye, then. (HE *goes out*)

IRENE (*After a glance at the body*): Dog eat dog to the last ditch, Policeman, eh?

McQUIGG: "Old dogs—," Miss Hayes!

IRENE: Yes. You and me both. (SHE *goes slowly out*)

McQUIGG (*Gazing at the body*): I thought they might have to do that.

DELANEY: I thought you did, when you sent for Welch. (*After a moment*) What now, Captain?

McQUIGG: I'd like some sleep.

DELANEY *goes out.*

But (*Rising and snapping on his cap*) by the time I get through with the coroner, and the papers, and headquarters, and the rest o' the public servants that'll be out here, it'll be time to go to Mass. (HE *pushes off the light, and goes out, closing the door*)

The room is still, and dark except for the night blue coming in through the open window and making SCARSI's *body faintly visible. Outside, there is again the careening rumble of a passing truck and a raucous shout of* "Yah-h-h, McQuigg!"

END OF PLAY

A SLIGHT CASE OF MURDER

A Comedy in Two Acts

by

DAMON RUNYON

and

HOWARD LINDSAY

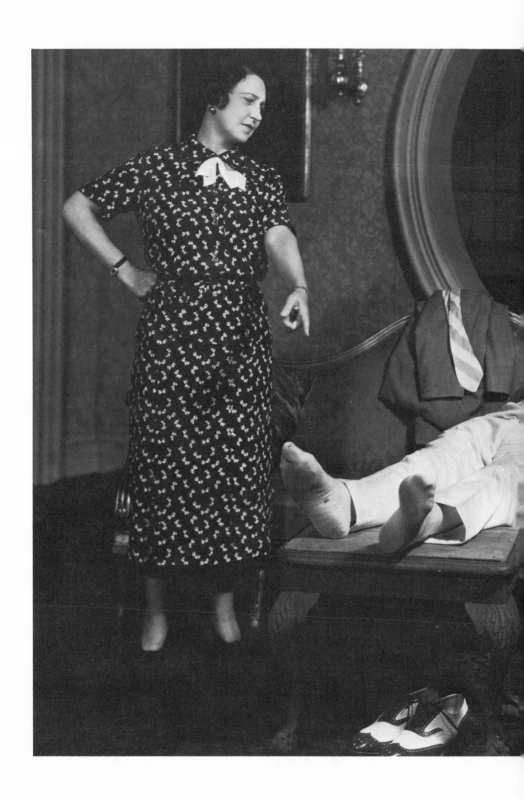

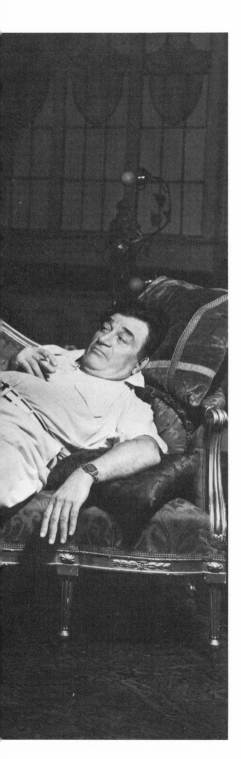

Damon Runyon, surrounded by Patrice Gridier and George Engel at Hialeah racetrack in Florida, 1931.

Howard Lindsay

A *Slight Case of Murder* premiered at the 48th Street Theatre, New York City, on September 11, 1935. Howard Lindsay was producer, and also directed, along with Damon Runyon. The sets were designed by Kate Drain Lawson.

Nora Marko (Georgia Caine) scolds her husband Remy (John Harrington) in the original production.

The Original Cast

Lefty . . . . James La Curto
Giuseppe . . . . Clyde Veaux
Innocence . . . . F. H. Day
Mike . . . . Joseph Sweeney
Douglas F. Rosenbloom . . . . Roy Le May
Chancellor Whitelaw . . . . John Griggs
The Singin' Kid . . . . Frankie Wheeler
Sad Sam . . . . Harry Levian
Remy Marko . . . . John Harrington
Commissioner Mahoney . . . . Percy Moore
Gammon Smith . . . . Sydney Booth
Mary Marko . . . . Phyllis Welch
Nora Marko . . . . Georgia Caine
Telegraph Boy . . . . Nick Dennis
Theodore Whitelaw . . . . Lawrence Grossmith
Ex-Jockey Kirk . . . . Richard Taber
Mrs. Ryerson . . . . Beth Franklyn
Loretta Paige . . . . Eleanor Brent
Pete Ryan . . . . Paul E. Burns
The Champ . . . . Ray Devlin
Mrs. Ritter . . . . Joy Hathaway
Calvin Ritter . . . . John M. Kline
George Hatch . . . . Charles Wellesley
Clyde Post . . . . Malcolm Duncan
Colonel Jake Schultz . . . . George Christie
Taxi Driver . . . . Walter Wagner
First Policeman . . . . Clyde Franklin
Second Policeman . . . . Jose Ferrer

Passers-by: Geoffrey Lind, Richard Courtney, R. Norvak, M. Miltos, James Kearns, J. Fitzgerald, E. Molenedyk, Marga Barbet, Winton Sears, T. Lynn Kearse, Irja Koski, Marion Frederic, Frances Levian, Annette Le May, Fred Steinway, Ted Levey, Eleanor Healy, Alice Frey, Dan Malloy, Mrs. Fralick.

Place

The living room of a large house in Saratoga Springs, New York.

Time

Toward dusk and later in the evening of August 1, the second day of the racing meet.

Characters

Principles:

REMY MARKO, ex-racketeer, now a legitimate brewer
NORA, his wife
MARY, their daughter
DOUGLAS FAIRBANKS ROSENBLOOM, an orphan (six to ten years)
LEFTY, Marko's chauffeur, formerly one of his henchmen
GIUSEPPE, his cook, formerly a henchman
MIKE, his butler, formerly a henchman
CHANCELLOR (CHANCE) WHITELAW, Mary's fiancé
COMMISSIONER (JIM MAHONEY), an important politician
THEODORE WHITELAW, Chance's father
THE SINGER, one of the "boys," a bookie
SAD SAM, a bookie
KIRK, an ex-jockey
CLYDE POST, a banker
CAL RITTER, a banker.

Minor characters:

INNOCENCE, a gangster, an Australian
SALLY, who sings
BATTLING WOLF (CHAMP), a fighter
PETE RYAN, fight manager
MRS. RYERSON
MISS SMITH, the Commissioner's secretary
MRS. RITTER
LORETTA PAIGE, old friend of Nora's
COL. JAKE SCHULTZ
MISS FRANKLIN, Mrs. Ryerson's sister
FIRST and SECOND POLICEMEN
MADELEINE, Nora's maid
(various guests and voices off stage)

Playwrights' Note

Among the roles listed above as principal characters, those of Kirk, Post and Ritter are relatively unimportant. It is possible in Act II to omit a few minor characters, and to add others to the party scene.

A certain amount of doubling is possible throughout the play.

The Play

ACT ONE

The living room of a large house in Saratoga, rented for the racing season by the Markos. It is a large square room. People entering it come through the arch from the Right. On the Left of the room is a door leading to the dining room and kitchen. It is furnished in the usual Saratoga manner—a mixture of old furniture, some Colonial antiques, some Victorian. Somewhere near the center of the room is a pile of several cases of beer from the Marko Brewing Co. On the front of one of these is pinned a note.

The time is toward dusk, and the room has an empty, deserted appearance until the servants enter and throw open the window curtains, or turn on the lights.

We first hear the sound of footsteps on the porch, then voices. We hear the voices in the hallway before the appearance of the characters through the arch, as THEY *are bringing luggage in from the automobile.*

LEFTY *comes in loaded down with baggage which* HE *dumps at the foot of the stairs with a clatter.* HE *steps into the room and looks around to find the phone, locates it on the table, goes and starts looking up a number in the phone book. It is too dark to see, so* HE *goes to alcove, throws open blinds and returns to phone.*

GIUSEPPE *comes in loaded with bags, dumps them carelessly and looks into the room toward* LEFTY.

GIUSEPPE: Another month of trouble fighting with the cook-stove in this old joint. (*Mops face*) I told the Boss to tell the Missus to get a different house this season. (*Throws paper on sofa and crosses out*)

144

LEFTY (*Calling off*): Hey, Mike, get Miss Mary's hatbox; it's on the trunk rack.

INNOCENCE *comes down the stairs watching* LEFTY *over his shoulder. As* HE *nears cellar door* HE *hears the stove lid offstage.* HE *stops, looks both ways and ducks into cellar.*

(LEFTY *goes to phone on table. In the phone*) Four two three. (*Sits on arm of sofa*) Hello . . . Jerry's Bar? What won the last? . . . No, you lug, not Narragansett. . . . Here at Saratoga. . . . Yeah! What price? . . . All right, thanks.

Enter GIUSEPPE *from kitchen.*

(LEFTY *calls out*) Hey, Mike! My Dandy won all right . . . two to one.

GIUSEPPE: That's a hell of a place to put that beer.

LEFTY: Why does the Boss take his own beer along when he's away from home? You'd think he'd be glad of an excuse to drink real, decent beer.

GIUSEPPE (*Sits, back to audience, on keg*): Somebody's gotta drink it.

LEFTY: It hasn't been any good since they went legit. He made the best beer in the country in the good old days.

MIKE *enters with two bags in one hand, which* HE *dumps with the other baggage. With his other hand* HE *is holding a boy aged anywhere between six and ten—* DOUGLAS FAIRBANKS ROSENBLOOM.

MIKE (*Pulling* DOUGLAS, *who resists*): Come on, Douglas. Come on . . . come on . . . come on. . . . (HE *throws him in front of him*) Now you stay there and behave yourself. (*To* OTHERS) That's a swell idea of the Boss's bringing this kid up here.

GIUSEPPE: Aw, he's a nice kid.

MIKE: You weren't in the back seat with him. He's been trying to get toeholds on me all the way from Yonkers.

DOUGLAS: I don't like you.

MIKE (*Standing over him*): That makes it even. I don't like you either.

DOUGLAS: I'll tell Mr. Marko on you. He likes me.

MIKE: Yeah, he likes a lot of funny things. (*Moves to* GIUSEPPE) What's that beer doing here?

GIUSEPPE (*Faces* MIKE): Look, here's a note stuck to it.

MIKE: What does it say? (MIKE *takes note and reads*)

LEFTY: Hey, Mike, I told you the guy that gave me that horse was plenty smart.

GIUSEPPE: What d'you have on him?

LEFTY: Two bucks. But I gave that horse to the Boss and he telephoned a thousand-dollar bet up here to Sad Sam.

GIUSEPPE: That's great. Maybe now the Boss'll pay us some wages.

LEFTY: Yeah, I never did come to Saratoga before as broke as I am now. I enjoy having a little of that old-fashioned spending money around here. The Boss has certainly tightened up lately.

MIKE *has finished reading note.*

GIUSEPPE: What's it say?

MIKE: It's for the Missus. Hoping she'll enjoy the house as much this season as other years . . . and the delivery man dumped this beer on her in the living room when she was out, and she ain't been able to move it herself.

GIUSEPPE: Who ain't? . . . The Missus?

MIKE: Naw. . . . Mrs. Thurston ain't . . . the lady that owns this house.

LEFTY: What do you think of the gall of that old pancake? She always leaves plenty of something to do.

DOUGLAS *wanders off into dining room.*

MIKE (*Picking up case*): Let's move the beer out on the back porch before the Missus gets here. They might drive in any minute. She'd raise hell about it.

LEFTY: I've seen the time she didn't mind seeing beer all over her house.

GIUSEPPE: Yeah, she's chucking a swell.

MIKE: I used to call her Nora once, but I wouldn't try it now.

GIUSEPPE (*Lugging out a case of beer*): My cooking isn't good enough for her any more. Trying to make me cook without garlic. (*Exits with beers*)

LEFTY: I suppose Mary'll be like the old lady since she come back from Europe.

MIKE: No, she's all right—she's hundred percent. When she got off the boat this morning, what does she do (*smiles, sighs*) but kiss me.

LEFTY: She couldn't have known it was you.

MIKE *and* GIUSEPPE *exit, each with a case of beer.* LEFTY *follows, rolling barrel lazily with foot. Enter* CHANCELLOR WHITELAW *in uniform of a state trooper—a tall, good-looking boy of twenty-three.* HE *enters diffidently, looking around, coming into the living room.*

(*Off*) I'm glad the weather's warm so I don't have to wrastle with that crazy furnace down in the cellar—(HE *reenters, sees* CHANCE *and shuts up*)

GIUSEPPE (*Follows behind* LEFTY): What a job! The Boss likes spaghetti—the Missus don't like spaghetti—(HE *sees* CHANCE *and shuts up*)

MIKE (*Behind other two*): A fellow who knew Jockey Workman's valet told me— (HE *sees* CHANCE *and shuts up*)

MIKE *walks down to* CHANCE. *As* CHANCE *circles around him, quietly and non-committally.*

Hello. (*Looks him over*)

CHANCE: How do you do? The Markos haven't arrived yet?

MIKE: No.

CHANCE: When do you expect them?

MIKE: I don't know.

CHANCE: Will they be here tonight?

MIKE: I don't know.

CHANCE: You don't seem to know a great deal.

MIKE: No.

CHANCE *turns and walks out.* THEY *look at each other.*

(*Perturbed*) What do you suppose that louse wanted?

GIUSEPPE: There can't be nothing wrong about the Boss *now?*

LEFTY: Whoever knows what a copper wants anyway?

GIUSEPPE (*To* LEFTY): You ain't done anything—

LEFTY: No—can't think of anything to do!

GIUSEPPE: Giuseppe ain't done nothing wrong. You, Mike?

MIKE: No, I'm all right.

GIUSEPPE: We ain't done nothing wrong—lately.

LEFTY: Come on. Let's get back to work on this beer.

LEFTY *and* GIUSEPPE *carry case out together.*

MIKE: I don't like the idea of that copper.

GIUSEPPE: I don't like the idea of *any* copper.

A knock on outer door.

SINGER (*Off*): Hello, anybody home?

MIKE: Come in!

Enter SAD SAM, *looking his name, and the* SINGER—*two bookies.*

Hello, Singer. How do, Mr. McGraw? (*Shakes hands with them*)

SINGER: Whaddya know? (*Goes down to chair by phone*)

SAD SAM: Whatsa good word, Mike? The Boss here?

MIKE: Expect him any minute. He left two hours after we did in the Lincoln with a friend of his.

LEFTY *and* GIUSEPPE *enter.*

LEFTY: Hello, Sam. Hello, Singer.

MIKE: You know how the Boss drives when he hits the road. Anything I can do for you? (*Moving* SAM *toward sofa*)

SAM: Well, no—I wanted to see him personally. (*Sits on sofa*) He beat me for a pretty good bet this afternoon and I just wanted to tell him I'd take care of it tomorrow when the insurance company settles with us.

LEFTY: You didn't get knocked out the first day of the meeting, did you, Sam?

SINGER: Haven't you heard about the stick-up?

MIKE: What stick-up?

SINGER: You know that armored truck that brings the bookies' dough from the bank to the track every day—?

MIKE: Yeah?

SAM: It was knocked off by five guys today and we didn't hear of it till just before post time, and nobody had no money to book with.

LEFTY: Musta been some busted horse players done that. I've often felt like sticking up somebody myself after a tough day.

SINGER: They got every bookie's envelope in the truck. Must have got something like half a million.

LEFTY: That's wonderful—wonderful.

SAM: There was twenty thousand fish in my envelope alone.

LEFTY (*Laughing*): Well, well, the bookies' money, eh?

MIKE: How could the bookies do business without any dough?

SINGER: They did business with IOU's, just the way we used to when we had oral betting. There's enough markers around this town tonight to paper Pennsylvania Station.

SAM (*Getting up*): Pennsylvania Station? I've got enough out myself to reach from here to Empire City.

MARKO (*Off*): Hey, Mike! Lefty! Get out here!

MIKE and LEFTY start on a run.

MIKE: It's the Boss. Lefty, let's get goin'. (*Crosses to hall*)

SINGER wanders over and joins SAM.

MARKO (*Off*): Get hold of this stuff. (*Calling to a neighbor*) Hello, Mr. Vogel!

NEIGHBOR'S VOICE (*Off*): Hello, Remy!

MARKO: What won the sixth?

NEIGHBOR'S VOICE (*Off*): My Dandy!

MARKO: My Dandy! Ha! That's me! I'm off to a good start! Come on in, everybody! Come in, Jim!

MARKO enters—a big bull of a man, bluff, hearty, loud-voiced, well-dressed on the loud side. HE is followed by JIM MAHONEY, the Commissioner, and his secretary, MISS SMITH, quiet, businesslike, bespectacled. DOUGLAS skips in from dining room.

Well, well, well! I didn't expect to see you till tomorrow. How you, Sam? How you, Singer? Shake hands with Commissioner Mahoney and Mrs.—er—Miss Smith. This is Sad Sam and the Singer. They're all right.

Handshakes and greetings.

Hello, Douglas! You have a nice ride?

DOUGLAS: No—that man pushed me.

MARKO (*Quietly*): What's that beer doing in here? Put some of it on ice.

DOUGLAS crosses to MARKO. MARKO and DOUGLAS are pummelling each other. MIKE and LEFTY each pick up a case and exit.

Douglas, come and shake hands with Sad Sam here. Sam has done us a big favor. He has contributed two thousand dollars to the Star of Hope Orphanage. I hung a good one on you, didn't I, Sam?

SAM: Yes, and so did everybody else, Remy. There was money for that horse even in China.

MARKO: You know, Commissioner, I chip in twenty-five thousand dollars every year to the orphanage, but I win it off these gamblers around here.

COMMISSIONER: What do you do if you lose?

MISS SMITH *busies herself inconspicuously with papers, and guardedly watches the strange people about her.*

MARKO: What you talking about? I never lose. That's a great place, the Star of Hope. Me and my two brothers was raised there. (*Holding* DOUGLAS *in front of him*) It turns out a lot of good men. Look at me; look at Douglas here— he's the prize pupil this year. Might be mayor of New York some day.

DOUGLAS: Naw! I'm going to make beer like you, Mr. Marko.

MARKO: This boy here is my prize.

DOUGLAS *hangs on his back for a moment, then drops.*

His mother, God rest her soul, named him after the great actor. He is Douglas Fairbanks Rosenbloom. I got to thinkin' I ought to reward the prize orphan every year with a little trip up here for the mountain air. Besides, he might bring me luck.

COMMISSIONER: Remy, you deserve a lot of credit for taking care of those orphans. They'll all be voters someday.

DOUGLAS (*Runs to sofa and jumps on it*): I can recite. Wanna hear me recite? "When you see a man in woe,
  Walk right up and say 'Hello' . . ."

SINGER (*Leaning against column of door*): I'd rather hear you say good-bye.

MARKO (*To* SAM): Sam, I need a little ready. I want to take that two thousand you owe me out to Reilly's tonight and run it up.

SAM: You'll have to wait till I get it from the insurance company.

MARKO: Is the insurance company making book, too? Listen, Sam, I need that tonight.

DOUGLAS *wanders off.*

SAM: Remy, I haven't got it. You couldn't find two thousand dollars around the town tonight. It was all in that truck.

MARKO: What truck?

MIKE *enters.*

MIKE: Say, Boss, what do you think? Some people knocked off the truck with all the bookies' dough in it—got away with a whole lot—half a million!

MARKO: Half a million? That's liable to cause talk. Who were those people? Anybody we know?

SINGER: There was five of them—and they all got away. There's a big story in the papers about it.

MARKO: The bookies got robbed, eh? (*Laughs; then thoughtfully*) You don't suppose those bookies would do a thing like that themselves, do you? Sam, stick-up or no stick-up, you still owe me that two thousand.

SAM: Everybody's protected by the insurance company. You'll get your money tomorrow.

COMMISSIONER: Remy, hasn't Col. Schultz a house near here?

HE *exits through alcove window, followed by* MISS SMITH.

SINGER: Yeah, you can see it from the porch, I think. Sam, isn't that the Schultz house up there on the corner. There's a green one, and it's two houses after that.

SINGER *goes through window to porch.*

SAM (*Following* SINGER *through*): Yeah, the one with the big lawn.

MIKE: Boss, the law was around here a little while ago.

MARKO: The law?

MIKE: Yeah!

MARKO: What kind—local?

MIKE: No—state trooper.

MARKO (*Laughs*): State trooper? You'd oughta thrown him out on his ear. We don't have to worry about the law anymore. Say, sometimes I wish we did . . . not much fun these days.

NORA (*Off; elegantly*): Harold, Michael!

MARKO: That's you, Mike.

COMMISSIONER *comes in through window followed by* DOUGLAS *and* SAM.

COMMISSIONER: I think this is Mrs. Marko, Remy.

NORA: Michael!

MIKE *races into action.*

MARKO (*Amused*): Ha, I bet her a new hat I could give her two hours and beat that old Rolls of hers up here.

MISS SMITH *reenters and sits arranging papers and briefcase at table.*

NORA (*Grandly*): Michael! (*Not so grandly*) Mike!

MIKE *is on his way.*

(*Off*) Get these bags upstairs. Is this any place for them? What have you been doing since you've been here? Put the Commissioner's bags in the large west room, and Miss Smith's on the second floor at the back. Put Mr. Marko's bags and mine in the same room we had last year. It seems to me you could have done that much.

NORA *continues ad-libbing off until her entrance into room a few moments later, accompanied by* MADELEINE, *her French lady's maid, carrying small bag.* MARY *enters.*

MARKO: Hello, Mary.

MARY: Hello, Dad.

MARKO: Commissioner, this is my Mary. This is my good friend, Jim Mahoney. Mary—be nice to Jim—he's the biggest man in Washington next to the President.

COMMISSIONER: How are you, Miss Marko?

MARY: I'm glad to see you, Mr. Mahoney.

MARKO: She'll be able to vote in another year. And that's Miss Smith.

MISS SMITH: How d' you do?

MARKO (*Crossing with* MARY *to join* DOUGLAS *and* SAM): You know Sad Sam and the Singer.

SAM: Lookit who's here!

SINGER: You're all grown up now. How did you find Europe?

MARY: Wonderful—but it's great to be back. How are things with you?

SINGER: What's the good kicking?

NORA *enters with* MADELEINE, *and crosses to* COMMISSIONER.

NORA: How d'ye do, Commissioner? We're so happy to have you here with us. Madeleine, take the bag up to our room.

MADELEINE: Veree well, Madame. Up here?

NORA: Yes, right up the stairs.

MADELEINE: Yes, Madame. (SHE *goes upstairs*)

COMMISSIONER: It's a pleasure, Mrs. Marko. May I present Miss Smith—

Mutual greetings, as MISS SMITH *takes off and puts on her glasses again.*

MARKO: Nora, here's Sad Sam and the Singer.

NORA: How do you do? (*To* COMMISSIONER) Have you met my daughter?

MARKO: Aw, sure. Commissioner, what do you know about my girl here—come back from Europe engaged to be married?

NORA: Yes, indeed.

MARKO: But she did all right by herself—I looked the family up—their name is Whitelaw, from Amsterdam.

NORA: Yes, *the* Whitelaws.

MARKO: They're hundred percent.

COMMISSIONER: Whitelaw hundred percent? Well, the Social Register and Dun and Bradstreet all agree with you, Remy.

NORA (*To* COMMISSIONER): I'm sorry you reached here before I did. Has Remy showed you your room? You must want to clean up. Remy, call Harold.

MARKO: Harold?—Hey, Lefty!

MARY: I'm going upstairs, Mother. Mike is up there, isn't he?

NORA: Yes, *Michael's* up there. My daughter will show you your rooms. Just make yourselves at home anywhere in the house.

MISS SMITH: Thanks so much. I'll be all right.

COMMISSIONER (*At doorway*): Don't worry, Mrs. Marko. We'll be all right.

Enter DOUGLAS *with bottle of beer.*

NORA (*Elegantly*): I'm afraid our cook hasn't had time to get organized, so we'll all go out to dinner. Remy! (*The old* NORA!) Take the beer away from that punk! (*To* COMMISSIONER) Hurry back down! We'll be waiting for you.

MARKO: Douglas! Come here! Give me that!

MARY, COMMISSIONER *and* MISS SMITH *disappear upstairs chatting.*

NORA (*To* MARKO): Listen! That's a swell idea lugging that orphan up here. As if our house isn't always overrun with funny people.

SAM (*Embarrassed, crossing to hall doorway followed by* DOUGLAS): Catch you tomorrow, Remy.

SINGER: Might see you on the late shift.

MARKO: Come in anytime, boys. Always glad to see my old pals.

SAM *and* SINGER *exit.*

DOUGLAS: Why can't I drink your beer, Mr. Marko? Ain't it any good?

MARKO: You shouldn't drink it out of a bottle. You tell the cook to give you a glass.

NORA: That child's too young to be drinking beer. (*Sits down by table*)

MARKO: 'S good for him. Make him sleep.

NORA: Put a case up in his room then. As far as I'm concerned he can sleep through the whole month of August. (SHE *calls off*) Giuseppe!

MARKO (*Pushing* DOUGLAS): Why, Nora, Douglas here is a fine boy. I figure he's going to bring me luck. And God knows I can stand a little right now.

Enter GIUSEPPE. MARKO *takes off coat and vest by chair near sofa.*

NORA: Giuseppe, take this prize out in the kitchen and give him something to eat.

GIUSEPPE (*Holding* DOUGLAS *at door*): I don't have to keep him out there, do I? I've got lots to do.

NORA: You keep him there till his bedtime. We'll put him to bed early. Let him finish the beer.

Enter MARY *down the stairs.*

MARY: Dad, has there been a phone call for me—or a telegram?

MARKO: Do you know, Giuseppe? (*During following* MARKO *takes off shoes, coat and tie*)

GIUSEPPE: No, nothing come. Hello, Miss Mary.

MARY: Giuseppe! How are you? When are you going to cook me some spaghetti with lots of garlic?

NORA: You better give up garlic now that you're engaged.

MARY: Nonsense! Chance loves it. We ate it all over Europe.

GIUSEPPE: Your boyfriend like spaghetti? Is he Italian?

NORA: Giuseppe, you get back to your kitchen, and take Mr. Marko's prize with you.

MARY (*Following* GIUSEPPE): Oh, Giuseppe, I went through your hometown in Italy . . .

Exit MARY, GIUSEPPE *and* DOUGLAS.

NORA: For Pete's sake, Remy, can't you keep your shoes on till we get Mary married?
MARKO: Nora, you know how my feet always hurt me when I'm worried.

Enter MIKE *down the stairs, and crossing to sofa.*

MIKE: Everything okay upstairs.
NORA: Michael.

MIKE *pays no attention.*

MARKO: That's *you*, Mike.
NORA: We didn't use the third floor at all last season, did we?
MIKE: No—ma'am.
NORA: I want you to put Mr. Marko's prize up there—in the room furthest away. Go up and see if it's in order.
MIKE: Right.
NORA: And when I ask you to do anything you say, Yes, ma'am.
MIKE: Okay—ma'am! (*Goes upstairs*)
NORA: Remy, when we get back to New York we get *new* servants. I'm sick and tired of putting up with hoodlums.
MARKO: Don't you call those boys hoodlums! They're my friends.
NORA: They may be your friends, but they're no good as servants.
MARKO: They're not servants. They're my friends. Say, Lefty got me out of a bad jam once in Halifax. And Mike went to jail for me.
NORA: Ssh! Why do you talk about such things?
MARKO: And I guess Giuseppe is a hude. Where would we get a cook like him?
NORA: I'm going to get an English butler and a French chef. (*Moves away from* MARKO)
MARKO: You're going to do nothing of the kind! That would hurt these boys' feelings. Mike butlers good enough for me. They're friends of mine—what's more, they're not particular when payday comes around. And besides, who would I have to talk to? You got your maid—and she costs me plenty!
NORA (*Returns toward sofa*): Listen, Remy, you're in a respectable business now. And I want a respectable household. We ain't living on Clinton Street, Brooklyn, anymore.
MARKO: I wish I was. I didn't have any troubles when I lived in Brooklyn—I mean nothing I couldn't handle.
NORA: You've been doing a lot of squawking lately. Now let *me* do some squawking. I don't want the uproar around this house that we usually have. Mary's fella's coming here tomorrow and I want you to be careful who you invite.
MARKO: Why, Nora, you know nobody waits to be *invited* to Marko's. They just come.
NORA: Well, we don't want the Whitelaws getting wrong ideas about us.
MARKO: Why, Nora, you know what Saratoga is when the races are going. Every

house is open house. Say, around here you meet millionaires and the boys in the same spots.

NORA: I don't mind the millionaires, but I don't want the boys.

MARKO: I can't play the chill for my old pals no matter who's coming here. Don't you be trying to play favorites on who's coming to this house right now. Because I've got to do some finaglin' around here. You can never tell who you can raise money from.

NORA: It's time you began to think of something besides money. You're all straightened out now and you're getting some standing.

MARKO: Look, Nora, if I'd 'a known this getting straightened out would put Marko in so much trouble I'd have stayed the way I was.

NORA: What trouble are you talking about?

MARKO: Well, Nora, you see it's like this . . . in the old days I did all my business out of my pocket—see—now I have to have an office, bookkeepers, books, regular hours and everything. My business used to be my own . . . nobody knew nothing about it, if I could help it. . . . Now the government, the state, everybody can look at Marko's books and ask you how much beer you sold and what you put in it. And you're always signing papers.

NORA: Why, Remy, you sign your name beautifully.

MARKO: I signed it once too often. Look, Marko needed a little money one time not long ago, so I signed a paper—what they call a chattel mortgage on the brewery. Now what you think? They say if I don't pay they can take my brewery. You know I didn't mean they could have my brewery—and what's more my own lawyer tells me I couldn't get it back. That shows you the difference. You remember in '29, Bill Ballard grabbed that brewery on me when I was away in San Pierre—but how long did it take me to get it back?—One night.

NORA: Yes, but now you've got to conduct yourself according to the law.

MARKO: That's just what I'm kicking about.

NORA: Who did you get that money from?

MARKO: Cal Ritter and Clyde Post.

NORA: But they're friends of yours.

MARKO: Yes, but it seems when you're legit you got no friends. That's what surprises me.

NORA: How much do you owe them? I've got nine hundred dollars in my bank account.

MARKO: Nine hundred dollars! And I've got to pay four hundred and sixty-two thousand dollars day after tomorrow.

NORA: Well, for gosh sake, why didn't you say so? We didn't need to come to Saratoga and spend all this money.

MARKO: I've got to keep chucking a front if I'm going to try to get an extension or raise the money. If I do I'll be all right in six months, but if people know I'm short I couldn't raise a quarter. And another thing, you know being in Saratoga is important to Mary just now.

NORA: Don't let that worry you, Remy. Something will happen.

MARKO: It don't seem to be worrying *you*. Anyhow, if I lose my brewery I can consider some very nice propositions that I've been turning down.

NORA: Remy Marko, don't you ever let me hear of you considering any propositions!

Doorbell rings.

Michael!

MARKO: Hey, Mike!

Enter MARY.

MARY: It's a messenger boy. I'll go. (MARY *exits*)

NORA: A telegram from Chance, probably, telling us when to expect him.

MARKO: I'll be glad to lay eyes on that fella of Mary's. He got back from Europe a couple of months ahead of Mary and he hasn't been near us.

NORA: You're going to meet him tomorrow and I hope you make a good impression on him.

MARKO: Listen, you better hope he makes a good impression on me.

Reenter MARY *with a stack of telegrams.* MARKO *crosses to coat on chair to get change.*

MARY: They're all for Mr. Mahoney. Got some change for the boy, Dad?

MARKO (*Gives bill*): Here's a dollar for him.

MARY goes out and returns in a moment. MIKE *has come downstairs.*

NORA: Michael, take those telegrams up to Mr. Mahoney.

MARY: I'm going up. I'll take them. (SHE *starts up*) Where are we going to dinner tonight, Dad?

MARKO: Maybe Arrowhead.

MARY disappears up the stairs. MARY *changes her frock here.*

NORA: Michael, get all that junk out of here. Is that room for Mr. Marko's prize all right? (*Sits on sofa*)

MIKE: No, I don't think we can use that room. (*By piano*)

NORA: Why not?

MIKE: There seems to be some—people in it.

MARKO: People? What people? How many people?

MIKE: Well, there's four—*fellas*.

MARKO: Four!

NORA: What are they doing there?

MIKE: Just sitting around—in chairs.

NORA: Did you tell them to get out?

MARKO: Wait a minute! Four people that don't belong here, you mean?

MIKE: No, I don't think they belong here *steady*.

NORA: *Did* you tell them to get out?

MIKE: Well, I'll tell you: I thought I'd speak to them about it, but to tell you the truth them people are in no position to listen to much. You see, they don't seem to be alive.

MARKO: You mean they're dead?

MIKE: Well, that's about what it comes to, Boss.

NORA: I never heard of such gall in my life! What does old Mrs. Thurston mean by going away and leaving four dead people in this house?

MARKO: Wait a minute! What was wrong with those fellows?

MIKE: Well, Boss, somebody shot 'em. Yes, sir, shot them right there in that room. Interrupted a card game. One fella had a king-full, too. They're sitting there just as natural!

NORA: You've got to get them out of there at once. I can't have people like that around my house. We've gotta get Mrs. Thurston on the phone and make a complaint. She was supposed to leave the place in good order.

MARKO: She wouldn't have left them if she'd known.

NORA: Then get the agent on the phone. (*Pushes* MARKO) They've got no right to rent a house with people like that in it. They've got to move them out. What would the neighbors think? What would Mary's Chancellor think if he came in while they were here?

MARKO *crosses to phone.*

MARKO: What would the Commissioner think? We better call the Board of Health and tell them we want to use that room.

MIKE: Boss, I don't think you'd better do that. I don't believe we want any outsiders in on this. I'll tell you. Who do you think those fellows are?

MARKO: Who?

MIKE: One of them's Black Hat Gallagher. Then there's No Nose Cohen and Little Dutch, and the other's a fella I never seen before—must be a total stranger.

MARKO: The hell you say!

NORA: What difference does it make who they are? I don't care anything about them, and I don't want them there.

MARKO: Listen, Nora, those three fellas used to be mobbed up with the late Bill Ballard—the fella that took my brewery that time—nice fella, Bill, but awful pigheaded.

MIKE: Old Bill was pretty game, too, Boss. Only trouble with him was he never could get over feeling he had some right to that brewery just because he started it.

MARKO (*Sitting on table*): My difference of opinion with Bill Ballard was pretty well-known. In fact the newspapers used to talk about it as a war. What do you think? . . . When Bill got cooled off his people thought I had something to do with it. And these fellas upstairs told it around they were going to see me about it.

MIKE (*To* NORA): They tried to see him a coupla times.

MARKO: Now the trouble is, some people might get the wrong idea about them being found in my house like this.

NORA: Remy, do you mean to say . . .?

MARKO: Oh, no-o! I haven't even thought of those fellas for a long time. I've missed them around.

MIKE: Boss, don't you remember they were sent away in Trenton a couple of years ago? They must have just got out of college.

MARKO: Say, the chances are they came up here to pay me a visit and some friend of mine happened to meet them. Wait a minute! Mike!

MIKE: No, no, Boss. I didn't see them. Lefty and Giuseppe and me got in just a little before you did.

NORA: My God, we don't want to get back in the papers now—of all times! Just as if we didn't keep Mary in Europe half her life to keep her away from those newspaper stories. Think what it would mean to the Whitelaws!

MARKO: The Whitelaws! Think what it would mean to Marko's Beer just when I got it established! This would be bad advertising.

NORA: All right then! Get those people out of the house. I don't care what you do with them, but get them out quiet. I'll keep Mary upstairs with me while I'm unpacking. We won't dress for dinner. You won't have time to dress and do that, too. (SHE *exits up the stairs*)

MIKE: They've got plenty of artillery, too.

MARKO: Hide it somewhere. Put it in the big closet in the front room. No one's going to use that. And get Lefty and Giuseppe in here quick.

MIKE *starts out.*

Mike, which one had the king-full? Black Hat Gallagher?

MIKE: Yeah. (MIKE *exits*)

MARKO (*Toward stairs*): I thought so. Lucky fink, that Gallagher. (MARKO *puts shoes and clothes on during following*)

LEFTY (*Off*): Gallagher and Cohen?

MIKE (*Off*): Yeah!

GIUSEPPE (*Off*): Little Dutch?

MIKE (*Off*): Yeah, and there was another fella there, too.

LEFTY (*Off*): What do you know about that?

LEFTY, MIKE *and* GIUSEPPE *come in.*

Say, Boss, this is a fine situation, eh?

GIUSEPPE: Just the kind of a dirty trick those fellas would pull—leaving themselves in that kind of shape around your house.

MIKE: I always knew Little Dutch was a wrong gee anyway.

MARKO: You're sure you boys didn't have a hand in this?

GIUSEPPE: No, no—wish I did. It 'ud be a pleasure.

MIKE: Why, Boss, we wouldn't keep it confidential.

LEFTY: I think I got it figured out.

MARKO: Let's hear it.

LEFTY: These must be the fellas that knocked off the bookies' truck.

MIKE: Say, that sounds right.

LEFTY: Then I figure they come straight here to take up that old matter with you, Boss, before they scattered. They probably thought you got in yesterday.

MARKO (*By phone table*): Can you imagine those fellas having such an idea—and me a square businessman for all these years?

MIKE: D'ye suppose they got in a fight over the card game?

LEFTY: There was five men held up that truck. There's four of them left upstairs. I figure the fifth guy musta given the others the business, and is probably plenty of miles away from here with the dough.

MARKO: Lefty, pull the Lincoln up alongside the back door. We'll take those people down and throw them away somewhere.

GIUSEPPE: Where we going to put them?

LEFTY: I know where I'd *like* to leave one.

MARKO: Where?

LEFTY: You know that Mr. Brent? The gentleman steeplechase jockey? I bet on a horse he rode at Belmont and I think he pulled that horse, though I hate to say anything against a gentleman jockey. He's got a house in the next block and I'd love to leave one of them on his doorstep. Might scare him into riding those horses right.

MARKO: Say, that's fine. I don't like gentlemen jocks myself. We'll give him Little Dutch. Now, let's see, we'll leave Black Hat Gallagher at the Steins' cottage around the corner. It's the second white house. Abe welched on me last year when he was making book at Jamaica.

GIUSEPPE: There's a fella I don't like runs an Italian restaurant downtown—his name is Giovannie Gambetti, and he's no good.

MARKO: We can't take any downtown. We'll leave one on Col. Jake Schultz's lawn.

MIKE: Yeah—the Gotham Brewery.

MARKO: He once circulated a report I was making chemical beer. We'll give him No Nose Cohen—he's the handsomest!

Telephone rings.

LEFTY: Say, Col. Schultz got a good stable here.

MARKO (*Into phone*): Hello. This is Marko. . . . Oh, just a minute. Mike, tell the Commissioner he's wanted on the phone.

MIKE: Okay. Say, that stranger *ain't* very good-looking. You ought to pick out a good place for him. (*Hurries upstairs*)

MARKO (*Hands over phone*): Now where can we leave this stranger? We don't want to waste any of 'em.

GIUSEPPE: Boss, please can't I keep one in the kitchen till late tonight? I'll leave him at Gambetti's myself without no bother to you.

MARKO: No, we got to get 'em out of here right now. Nora's getting sored up about this.

COMMISSIONER *comes downstairs.* GIUSEPPE *drifts off into kitchen.* MIKE *comes downstairs after* COMMISSIONER.

Here you are, Commissioner. Some fella—named Preston.

COMMISSIONER: Thank you, Remy. (*In phone*) Hello. . . . Yes, how are you, Mr. Preston? . . . Yes. . . . Yes. . . . Yes. . . . Thank you. (*Hangs up*) Remy, this doesn't go beyond this room—if Mr. Preston telephones again I'm not in.

MARKO: Sure. Mike, you hear that?

MIKE: Okay.

MARKO: You mean Marshall Preston, Commissioner?

COMMISSIONER: Yes. He's still hoping we'll forget he knifed the President with his newspapers.

MARKO: Knifed the President, did he?

COMMISSIONER: Yes.

MARKO: Where does *he* live?

COMMISSIONER: I think he has the Gaxton Cottage on Union Avenue.

LEFTY: I know that place.

MARKO: All right, Lefty. Get the Lincoln.

LEFTY *exits.*

Mike, you and Giuseppe get busy. Use the back stairs.

MIKE *and* GIUSEPPE *exit.*

Commissioner, are you fixed all right upstairs? Anything you want?

COMMISSIONER (*Opening telegrams*): Everything's fine, Remy. Very comfortable.

MARKO: Anything you want just holler for it. How about some Marko's Beer?

COMMISSIONER: Not now, thanks, Remy.

MARKO: I make pretty good beer. Don't you think so, Commissioner?

COMMISSIONER: None better.

MARKO: Marko Brewery ought to make a lot of money for Marko, hadn't it?

COMMISSIONER: Should make you a fortune, Remy.

MARKO: Commissioner, you know Cal Ritter and Clyde Post?

COMMISSIONER: Of the Manhattan Trust and Exchange Co.? Yes—very well.

MARKO: Your word ought to go a long ways with them, hadn't it?

COMMISSIONER (*Reading wire*): I don't know. I imagine it would.

MARKO: Well, I'm expecting them here any minute. And you might be able to do me a good turn: just tell them what you told me just now, that Marko's Brewery will make a fortune.

COMMISSIONER: You planning to do business with the Manhattan Company?

MARKO: I done business with them. I got some paper coming up with those people and they're pushing me. They're so tough about it I got an idea some of those big brewers are back of them. They'd like to put me out of business. I can clean it up in six months and you would be doing me a big favor, Commissioner, by asking them to give me that much time.

COMMISSIONER: How much is involved, Remy?

MARKO: Only 462 grand. Can you imagine Marko asking time on that? In the old days a lot of bankers would have been proud to lend Marko that kind of money, or I could have called up the boys in Chicago or Philadelphia and got it overnight.

COMMISSIONER: Well, you see, Remy, I don't think I know those men well enough for that. And besides, I can't afford to ask favors. It only means I get asked ten favors in return. You know I've got the toughest job in the administration.

MARKO: Commissioner, this is a desperate situation for Marko—it's a proposition of life or death. Of course, I don't mean really death—it's twice as bad.

COMMISSIONER: You'll get out of it some way.

MARKO: Listen, Commissioner, when you got me that permit for my brewery you made me legit. If I lose my brewery I'm just another fella with a lot of bad publicity behind him. Why, Nora would be awfully upset. She loves being legit. And think of Mary. We're meeting this fella of hers here—this Whitelaw. Well, that's all right. I'm Marko of Marko's Brewery—but supposing I didn't have the brewery?

COMMISSIONER: Why, Remy, everyone would feel the same toward you whether you had the brewery or not.

MARKO: Commissioner, if I didn't have my brewery would you be a guest in my house? You would not! You couldn't afford to be.

COMMISSIONER: Well, Remy, I'd like to help you. You know that. I'm afraid speaking to Ritter or Post is out of the question. Let's think . . . is there some other way?

MARKO: What about this money the government's lending around?

COMMISSIONER: I don't think they'd lend any on a brewery.

MARKO: Why not? It's better'n a farm. If they'd only lend me what they took away from me on back income taxes.

NORA *enters down stairs.*

NORA: There you men are—talking politics behind my back. Look out for my husband, Commissioner. He's a great hand at cajoling people into doing favors for him!

COMMISSIONER: I hope we're not going to be too much trouble to you, Mrs. Marko.

NORA: It's a pleasure to have you. I love a house full of people! (*Noticing his handful of telegrams*) My, they keep you busy, don't they—even when you're away from Washington.

COMMISSIONER: Yes. I have quite a lot to get through before dinner, and Miss Smith's a hard driver. So if you'll excuse me.

NORA: Make yourself right at home. We want to see as much as we can of you, but we know the government must go on.

COMMISSIONER: Yes—well, I'll be through in half an hour or so. See you later, Remy. (*Goes upstairs*)

NORA: Here I thought you were getting those people out of the house and I come down and find you wasting your time with the Commissioner.

MARKO: I'm afraid I *was* wasting my time.

NORA: Haven't you even started to move them yet?

MARKO: The boys are getting 'em downstairs into the Lincoln. Say, how do you think an English butler would have liked that job?

Enter MIKE *and* LEFTY.

LEFTY: We're all set, Boss.

NORA: Well, get started, Remy. You don't know how many hours it's going to take you.

MARKO: It won't take no time at all. We're leaving them right here in the neighborhood.

NORA: Where?

MARKO: We're putting these people to good use. We thought of some folks we don't like, and we're sort of spreading them around among them.

NORA (*Pleased*): Why, who thought of that?

MARKO: Marko. We're leaving one with Col. Jake Schultz—you know what he said about my beer? Then we're giving one to a gentleman jockey down the street here that done Lefty wrong. And we're placing one with a fella the administration don't like.

NORA: What administration?

MARKO: Why, the present administration! And the last is my personal present to Mr. Abe Stein.

NORA: No—you can't leave one there!

MARKO: Why not?

NORA: His wife's up here with him and she's going to have a baby.

MARKO: Well, the baby won't see it.

NORA: It might make Mrs. Stein nervous.

MARKO: It'll make Abe nervous, too, and that's what I want.

NORA: I don't care what you do to Abe, but Mrs. Stein's in no condition to appreciate it.

MARKO: Well, let's see . . . we have to think of somebody else.

LEFTY: I wonder if any of them blind racing judges live around here?

MARKO: *You* got one. That's enough for you.

NORA: You've got to get going quick.

MARKO: Well, but—

NORA: If you're going to Col. Schultz's you've got to pass by that Mrs. Wiler's—

MARKO (*Nodding*): Right! Lefty, Mrs. Wiler gets No Nose Cohen. Mike, you stay here. Me and Lefty and Giuseppe can handle this proposition. We won't be gone long. Come on, Lefty.

MARKO *and* LEFTY *exit.*

NORA: Well, I'm glad those people are out of the house.

MIKE: Yes—in this weather. (*Mops brow*)

NORA: Michael—Mike!—take these drapes down so we can get some air into the room—and move the piano over to that corner so people can get out on the porch. And I'd like to get rid of that chromo picture: Remy thinks it's bad luck. We took it down last year and Mrs. Thurston squawked about it. It's her late husband—told me *she* didn't like him either.

Enter GIUSEPPE *with* DOUGLAS, *whom* HE *shoves onto bench.*

GIUSEPPE: I gotta go with Mr. Marko, and this punk can't stay in my kitchen.

DOUGLAS: I want some more to eat.

GIUSEPPE: This boy et a can of sardines, a can of baked beans, a loaf of bread, a glass of milk and three bottles of beer. And every time I turn my back he throws an empty at me. Mrs. Marko, this boy is a mistake.

MIKE: In spades.

NORA: You run along, Giuseppe. We'll take care of him.

GIUSEPPE *exits.*

Michael, is that room upstairs in order?

MIKE: Yeah, I scattered some rugs around. Looks all right now.

NORA: Take Mr. Marko's prize upstairs and put him to bed. Get Madeleine to help you.

DOUGLAS: I'm not going to bed yet. I want more beer and sardines.

MIKE: Missus, I ain't had no experience puttin' punks to bed. You women know more about that than I do.

NORA: Michael!

DOUGLAS (*Jumping up on sofa*): I ain't goin' to bed anyway.—Wanna hear me recite?
"Half a league, half a league, half a league onward,
Into the valley of death rode the six hundred.
Cannons to the right of them—"

NORA: Michael!

DOUGLAS:
"Cannons to the left of them
Volleyed and thundered—
Rode the six hundred."

MIKE: Come, little boy.

DOUGLAS (*Jumping off sofa*): No, I don't like you. Your nose is too big.

MIKE: Come on. Come with Mike.

DOUGLAS: You gotta catch me first.

MIKE: Now be a good boy. We'll go beddy-bye (*To* NORA) My mother always said that to me.

DOUGLAS: You can't catch me—you can't catch me.

DOUGLAS *leads* MIKE *on a chase around the room. At a good opportunity* NORA *distracts* DOUGLAS's *attention.*

NORA: Oh, look!

DOUGLAS *makes mistake of looking.* MIKE *nails him.* DOUGLAS *makes his second mistake of struggling.* MIKE *shakes the liverlights out of him.*

MIKE: That's enough out of you, you little squirt!

MIKE *starts upstairs with* DOUGLAS, *when the doorbell rings.* HE *plants* DOUGLAS *on stairs.*

If you move I'll break your skull. (MIKE *comes downstairs and we hear him off as* HE *answers door*) What do you want?

CHANCE: Have the Markos arrived yet?

MIKE (*Off*): Who wants to know?

CHANCE (*Off*): I want to see Miss Marko—or Mrs. Marko.

MIKE (*Off*): Well, you can't see them.

NORA: Michael! Who is it?

MIKE (*Off*): You wait here and stay outside. (HE *enters. Loud whisper*) It's the law.

NORA: What?

MIKE: A johndarme—a copper. He was here before. I told the Boss and he said if he came back to throw him out.

NORA (*Whispering*): Do you suppose he's here about those parties that were upstairs?

MIKE: You never know what a copper wants.

NORA: Is he a local?

MIKE: No—state trooper.

NORA: Oh, that must be the fellow who was trying to catch us outside of Albany this afternoon. We weren't going fast. I'll take care of him—send him in here. (*Crosses to sofa and assumes pose*)

MIKE *goes into hall and calls.*

MIKE: Come in if you want to . . . in here.

MIKE *starts up the stairs and* DOUGLAS *hurries up ahead of him.* MIKE *disappears.* CHANCE *comes diffidently in and stands by door.*

NORA: So you had to follow us all the way here! Well, let me tell you something, young man. We weren't doing over thirty-five.

CHANCE: There's some mistake.

NORA: There's *no* mistake. That old Rolls of mine can't make over thirty-five. If you don't believe it, you can take it out and try it.

CHANCE: I'm not here to arrest you for speeding.

NORA: Then what *do* you want, anyway?

NORA *evidently sees* MADELEINE *at top of stairs and calls to her.*

Madeleine, help Mike with Douglas Fairbanks! (*Then* SHE *turns to* CHANCE)

CHANCE: This is Mrs. Marko, isn't it?

HE *advances toward her, hand outstretched.* NORA *backs away.*

NORA (*Brooklyn again*): What of it?

CHANCE: My name's Whitelaw. I'm Chancellor Whitelaw.

NORA: Oh, yeah? In that uniform?

CHANCE: Mary told me when I got back to America I had to do something—so this is it. It'll surprise Mary, don't you think?

NORA: Surprise Mary? Oh, my God! (SHE *calls off*) Mary! Mary! (*Returns to* CHANCE) Pardon my shouting for Mary, but my servants are all busy—Oh, how are you Chancellor? Such a shock—thinking I was going to be collared and then it turned out to be only you.

CHANCE: Oh, I understand.

NORA (*Sweetly*): Mary! Mary! (*Returns to* CHANCE) And don't mind our butler, Michael. He's always very *broosk*. Just an old family retainer. He treats us all that way, but we love it!

MARY *appears on stairs.*

MARY: Chance! Oh, Chance!

SHE *tears down and into his arms for a hug and a kiss.*

Why, look at you! What a grand uniform!

NORA: He's got bad news for you—I mean, a surprise, eh, Chancellor?

MARY: Don't tell me you're really a state trooper?

CHANCE: I certainly am.

MARY: That's swell! Have you arrested anybody yet?

NORA: He made me think I was arrested. I'm afraid I was a little sharp with him. Sit down, children, sit down.

THEY *sit on sofa.*

MARY: Chance, whatever put it into your head to become a state trooper?

NORA (*Sitting on chair by sofa*): That's what I'd like to know.

CHANCE: I hadn't been back from Europe two days before I was stopped for speeding. I was pretty mad at the time, but he was perfectly right. I *was* speeding, and that's very dangerous. Well, this fellow that stopped me turned out to be an old friend.

NORA: You mean you have *friends* that are policemen, too?

CHANCE: A college friend. He told me it was a great life—riding up and down the highways enforcing the law. . . .

NORA: What an idea *that* is!

CHANCE: Isn't it? It sounded adventurous, so first thing I knew I was trying to get in the troops and don't think it was easy, either.

MARY: I think it's grand. That uniform is wonderfully becoming. Why, I'll fall in love with you all over again.

NORA: What does your father think of this?

CHANCE: Oh, he didn't say much. I don't think he gives me long at it. But I'm going to stick until I get to be a sergeant at least. Father's here in Saratoga now.

NORA: He is? (*Gets up and moves away*)

CHANCE: He drove over from Amsterdam yesterday to meet Mary—and of course you and Mr. Marko, too.

NORA: Well you're going to have dinner with us—both of you. We have other guests—Commissioner Mahoney—do you know him? Or your father?

CHANCE: Dad might, possibly.

NORA: We're going to Arrowhead for dinner.

CHANCE: Well, my instructions from Dad were to bring Mary over to dinner with him at the United States. We could all arrange to meet somewhere later.

MARY: That's just what we'll do, Mother.

NORA: Then, Mary, bring Chancellor and his father right back here and we'll come home early. I'm going to leave you two alone while I change. Chancellor, you dear boy, I can't tell you how happy we are about you and Mary!

CHANCE: Thank you, Mrs. Marko. I'm pretty happy myself.

NORA: And Mary's father is so pleased with it all. He's very eager to meet you. (*Stops short for a second*) Have you any other clothes with you?

CHANCE: No, I'm just here overnight on leave. I haven't had a dinner jacket on since I got my uniform.

NORA: I didn't mean a dinner jacket—just *any* other kind of clothes.

MARY: Why, Mother, what do you mean?

NORA: I was thinking of your father. He—he doesn't like uniforms. (*To* CHANCE) He's—he's a pacifist.

MARY: Father's no pacifist—anything but.

NORA: Well, he just doesn't like *uniforms*. I remember I had a cousin—one of the O'Reillys—Terence—he was on the police force in New York and your father wouldn't even let him come into our block.

MARY: If Father doesn't like uniforms, it's time he learned. I like it, and that's enough.

NORA: You children run along to the hotel now. Your father won't be back for half an hour. He's gone out calling on some neighbors. Good-bye again, Chancellor. I'll see you later this evening—and your father.

CHANCE: Good-bye till then, Mrs. Marko.

MARY: I'll be up before we leave, Mother.

NORA: It will be *so* interesting to have a policeman right in the family. (NORA *goes upstairs*)

MARY: Oh, Chance, I'm so glad to be back with you.

CHANCE: Maybe you don't think I'm glad to have you!

MARY: Missed me much?

CHANCE: Have I?

> THEY *go into each other's arms.* MIKE *enters and turns on light on table by sofa.* HE *shows surprise and some horror at seeing* CHANCE *with* MARY. *Then* MARY *sees him.* HE *immediately exits. This leaves them a little constrained.*

Did you enjoy Vienna?

MARY: Not much. I wish I'd come home when you did—I wanted to.

CHANCE: I hope your mother liked me. I liked *her*.

MARY: You'll like Father, too, when you get used to him. I told you all about him when you asked me to marry you—I told you what he is and what he used to be.

CHANCE (*Sitting with* MARY *on sofa*): I'm not marrying your family, I'm marrying you. People don't look at things that way nowadays.

MARY: I know how you feel, Chance, but it's your father I'm thinking of. After all, the Whitelaws are the Whitelaws. If he objected to your marrying me— or into my family, I could understand that easily.

CHANCE: Will you wait till you meet him, Mary? I'm sure he'll be all right. Of course he's old-fashioned—about the importance of family and things like that, but he promised to wait till he met you and your people, and I know no one could resist you.

MARY: All right. Let's get it over. I'm going upstairs.

Both rise.

I'll be right down. (SHE *kisses him*) I'll bet you knew how good-looking you were going to be in that uniform before you joined.

CHANCE *laughs,* MARY *goes upstairs.* HE *takes a turn about the room happily, then stands looking off, his back to the arch. The door under the stairs leading to the cellar opens cautiously, and* INNOCENCE *comes quietly into the hall—a small furtive fellow, badly dressed. Looks up and down and is tiptoeing toward foot of stairs when* HE *sees* CHANCE's *back.* HE *decides to retrace his steps back into the cellar and does so, closing door softly behind him. We hear* MARKO *laughing uproariously off.*

LEFTY (*Off*): You shoulda seen him, Mike!

MARKO (*Off*): That was a corker! When Jake Schultz opens his door and Little Dutch falls in on him, won't he be nervous! Ha! Ha! Well, boys, that was perfect. Get Lefty to tell you about it, Mike.

CHANCE *has turned at the sound of* MARKO's *voice.* MARKO *enters from kitchen, laughing uproariously. When* HE *sees* CHANCE, HE *freezes.*

CHANCE: Good evening, sir. Mr. Marko, isn't it?

MARKO: Are you in this house on any business?

CHANCE: No, sir, I'm—

MARKO: Then get the hell out of here! You bulls have got plenty of gall walking into an honest man's house.

Laughter from BOYS *in kitchen.*

I don't have to stand for any coppers around me *now*.

MARY *appears on stairs, running down.*

MARY: Father! Father!

MARKO: Go on! Take your hat and get out of here! I ought to take a smack at you just for old times' sake.

MARY (*Runs between them, facing* MARKO): Father, this is Chance!

MARKO: I don't care who he is! I don't want no cops prowling my joint!

NORA *appears on stairs fighting her way into a kimono. Only one arm is in.* MADELEINE *follows, rather flustered.*

MADELEINE: But, Madame, permit me—!

NORA (*A step away from her*): I'll fix this myself, *Madalane!* You run upstairs and finish the unpacking.

MADELEINE: As Madame says, but if you would permit—

NORA (*Sharp*): Up! I can manage this myself.

MADELEINE *goes upstairs, protesting, "But, Madame, you should not," etc.*

Remy! Nix! Nix! That's Mary's fella!

MARY: Dad, this is Chance!

MARKO: Who?

MARY: Chance! Mr. Whitelaw, Father! This is my father, Chance.

CHANCE: Pleased to meet you.

NORA: Take it easy.

MARKO: What is he trying to do—make a sucker out of somebody? Coming around dressed up like that, making people nervous.

NORA: But Chance here really *is* a representative of law and order. Isn't it wonderful?

MARKO: Listen, I can take a joke as good as anybody, but just what is this?

MARY: Listen, Daddy, I told Chance when we became engaged that I couldn't marry a playboy no matter how much money he had, so he's joined the state police and I think it's wonderful.

MARKO: It's phenomenal!

MIKE *has drifted in.*

NORA (*Hurrying them out quickly*): Now you children run over to the hotel and have dinner. Your father must be waiting for you, Chancellor. Then after dinner we'll all meet back here and have a nice chat.—Michael!

MARY (*At door*): Yes, Chance, give Dad time to get used to the idea.

MIKE *enters.*

Come on.

CHANCE: Well, we'll be seeing you later. (HE *extends his hand in* MARKO's *direction. Exits*)

NORA (*Calling*): Tell your father how eager we are to meet him, Chancellor.

MARY *crosses to* MARKO *and gives him a quick kiss.*

MARY: If you don't want a family fight on your hands, you'll behave yourself.

MIKE *stands inattentive.*

NORA: Michael—Mike!
MIKE: Who? Me?
NORA: The door, Michael.

A look from NORA *and* MIKE's *spirit is broken.* HE *precedes* CHANCE *and* MARY *off.*

MARY (*Off*): We'll see you later.

NORA *watches them off until door slams.* NORA *crosses to end of sofa and plumps down wearily.*

MARKO: So that's what Europe did for our Mary, huh?
NORA: Mary didn't know anything about this. It was entirely the boy's idea.
MARKO: But she stood up for him. She doesn't think for one minute I'm going to let her marry a copper?
NORA: Why, Remy, you're on the side of law and order yourself now.
MARKO: Sure, I'm in favor of law and order, but you don't have to have it right in your own house! I won't stand for that.
NORA: Remy, you stop shooting off your mouth. This boy's coming back here tonight and bringing his father with him, and you're going to be nice to them. Mr. Whitelaw and the Commissioner are different kinds of guests than we had in this house last year. And we've got to think of Mary.
MARKO: I'd hate to tell you what I think of her now.
NORA: This job is just a whim on Chancellor's part. He won't stick at it.
MARKO: What do you suppose was his idea turning copper? That don't make him out so good. It's a bad symptom. Say, you don't suppose he gets a *pleasure* out of arresting people? You know there are coppers in this world like that.

The COMMISSIONER *comes downstairs with* MISS SMITH, *who has made an attempt to dress up.*

COMMISSIONER (*To* MISS SMITH, *as* HE *comes,* SHE *taking notes*): Get those wires off right away and speak to the telephone company about a private line for me here. I don't think I'll need you again before tomorrow morning, unless you want to come to the party tonight.
MISS SMITH: Thank you. Good night, Commissioner. (SHE *exits*)
MARKO (*Simultaneously with above, to* NORA): You better get upstairs and get your clothes on. Who do you think you are, Hedy Lamarr? (*Spanks her behind*)

The COMMISSIONER *comes over to them.*

NORA: Forgive my appearance, Commissioner. I'll be dressed in a minute and then we'll start.
COMMISSIONER: No hurry.

NORA *runs upstairs*

This is a comfortable old house, Remy. Pretty big, but you always do things in a big way.

MARKO: Yes, I try to go first cabin. Say, you were never a policeman, were you, Commissioner?

COMMISSIONER: Never.

MARKO: I thought not.

COMMISSIONER: Of course, policemen are necessary. The lawless element must be kept in check.

MARKO: That part of it's all right. I admit the government's got a argument. Commissioner, I got another favor to ask you—a big favor. Could you get a state trooper fired off the force?

COMMISSIONER: I don't know—what's he been doing to you?

MARKO: Doing to me?—He wants to marry my Mary.

COMMISSIONER: I thought your daughter was engaged to young Whitelaw?

MARKO: That's the fella I'm talking about.

COMMISSIONER: You mean to say he's got a job like that! For Pete's sake, why?

MARKO: That's just it! Why! Why? Can you imagine having my son-in-law around putting the arm on friends of mine?

COMMISSIONER (*Amused*): Why, Remy, I'd think the presence of the uniform of authority in your household would be a constant reminder to you of your thoroughly legitimate status.

MARKO: It'd remind me of some other things, too.

MIKE *enters, picks up paper on sofa and exits.*

Think what it would remind Mike of!

COMMISSIONER: What does your daughter think of it?

MARKO: Commissioner, I don't like her attitude. She thinks it's all right. Shows you no matter how careful you bring up children they're liable to cross you up. Getting that fellow fired should be no trick for you.

COMMISSIONER: Remy, that's a pretty solid organization. It's difficult to get in and I imagine pretty hard to get a man out without cause. It may work out all right. (HE *looks out of window*) This is a real Saratoga night. (HE *drifts out onto porch*)

MIKE *and* LEFTY *enter as though looking for a chance to talk to* MARKO. MIKE *has a stepladder.*

MIKE (*Putting ladder back by sofa*): Boss, can we speak to you a minute?

MARKO: Sure, get my shoes. What's eating you?

MIKE *kneels in front of* MARKO.

LEFTY: Boss, you know we wouldn't say nothing to you in a hundred years, but me and Mike . . .

MARKO *says "Ouch!" as* MIKE *puts shoe on his foot.*

. . . have just got to have a few bobs. You know we ain't seen no wages for six months.

MARKO (*Busy with shoes*): Don't you think I'm good for it?

LEFTY: Yeah, we know you're good for it, but we like to play the races a little and go around, and it's embarrassing not to have something in your pocket once in a while. We had to hock Mike's wristwatch to bet on that horse I gave you today.

MIKE: Yes, Boss, and Giuseppe said to say he wouldn't mind sending some money home to his mother and sister.

MARKO: Look, boys, I know it's been tough for you, but it's been tougher for me. I expected that money from Sad Sam tonight, and I'd of scattered some around. But you know what happened.

LEFTY: We'd like to have a couple of hundred as quick as we can, because we're going to have some good information around here on these races.

MIKE: Of course, Boss, we know things aren't so good—but we're eatin' and sleepin'. Boss, what you suppose became of all that money we used to have?

MARKO: All the boys are wondering about that. Listen, when I get ahold of anything you'll get yours. Here, split this fifty between you. (*Gives them bill*)

LEFTY: Well, that'll help. Maybe we can think of some way of raising some more.

MARKO (*Rising*): Say, don't you fellas be getting any ideas about raising money around here without consulting me. We don't want anything out of the way to happen here right now.

NORA (*Appearing on stairs*): Ready, Remy?

MIKE (*Taking ladder to alcove*): Don't tell the Missus we asked. She takes offense at people wanting money. Ready Commissioner?

LEFTY *exits. The* COMMISSIONER *comes in from porch.*

NORA: I'm ready if you men are.

COMMISSIONER: Yes, indeed. In fact, I'm a bit hungry.

NORA: Come along, Remy. Michael!

MARKO: Mike!

NORA: Tell Harold to bring the Lincoln around.

MARKO: We're using the Buick. The Lincoln needs a little—attention.

NORA: Oh, yes. The Buick, Michael.

MARKO: Tell Lefty, never mind. I'll drive us over. The Buick's out front here.

NORA: We'll be returning right after dinner, Michael.

MARKO: Take care of any of the boys that drop in—but tell *Madalane* she'd better stay in her room!

THEY *exit.* MIKE *returns into living room.* LEFTY *comes in.*

LEFTY: The folks gone?

MIKE (*On ladder*): Yes, Boss took them in the Buick. Tell Giuseppe to bring us in some beer—anything but Marko's.

LEFTY (*Calling*): Giuseppe, beer! (LEFTY *takes off his coat and lies down with the pink edition of* The Saratogan)

MIKE: I knew the Boss was pretty short, but I didn't know he was down that close.

LEFTY (*Lying on sofa*): Looks like we might be hunting jobs soon.

MIKE: Wish I could do something to help him out. Of course he said he didn't want anything to happen around here.

LEFTY (*Studying paper*): The chart shows that thing we bet on today won by just a dirty snoot. Let's see what's in tomorrow. (HE *consults the entries*)

MIKE: Fella in New York give me a right good thing in the third. Horse named Sleepless. (MIKE *gets this name from a slip of paper out of his pocket*)

LEFTY: Sleepless! Why, it's a mile race and that old alligator couldn't do a mile in a van. I like Sun Beauty.

MIKE *gets off ladder.*

MIKE: What's he carrying? (*Folds curtain* HE *has taken down*)

LEFTY: A hundred and twenty.

MIKE (*Puts curtains on piano bench and carries them below piano*): The handicapper might as well put Kate Smith on him.

GIUSEPPE *has entered with beer bottles.*

LEFTY: I wouldn't bet on Sleepless anyway, because jockey Bonito rides for that stable, and he's strictly a burglar. Say, that guy's as full of larceny as Dannemora.

MIKE *crosses to window in alcove.*

MIKE: They oughtn't to allow dishonest people around race tracks. It gives the game a bad name. But I can find out tomorrow if they're going with Sleepless, and if they are I'll let you know.

GIUSEPPE *gives beer to* LEFTY, *then crosses to bench and sits drinking from bottle.*

GIUSEPPE: You fellows are horse-crazy. Today is the first winner you guys have had since we were all at Auburn, and then you couldn't play 'em—See what that bladder says about the stick-up.

LEFTY: Say, here's an absolute stand out. They got Playful Joe in with a bunch of awful pigs in the sixth. Here's where we ought to get rich.

MIKE *sits on top of ladder, drinking from bottle.*

GIUSEPPE: Forget the horses awhile and read what it says about those people we just spread around.

LEFTY *reluctantly turns to front page.*

LEFTY (*Glancing through article*): Oh, they don't know any more than they did before. (*Sits up.* HE *keeps on reading, then ejaculates*) Fer Gawd's sake! (*Freezes*)

GIUSEPPE: Whatssa matter?

LEFTY (*Reading*): There's an offer of *ten thousand dollars* reward for each of the bandits, alive or *dead!*

Pause. Then GIUSEPPE *runs to door.* LEFTY *races after him, struggling into his coat.* MIKE *scrambles from ladder, dropping bottle on piano. Rushes to door—thinks better of it, dashes back for bottle. Exits grasping it tight in his hand.*

End of Act One

ACT TWO

It is two hours later. Sitting in a stiff high-backed chair near the alcove is THEODORE WHITELAW, *a dignified old aristocrat who is devoted to a quiet, well-ordered life and is pretty unhappy when* HE *doesn't have it.* CHANCE, *still in uniform, is sitting on the arm of the sofa, nervously snapping the snap on his holster.* WHITELAW *looks toward* CHANCE *and speaks quietly, but with parental authority.*

WHITELAW: Chancellor!

CHANCE: Yes, sir?

WHITELAW: I wish you wouldn't do that.

CHANCE: I'm sorry.

MARY enters brightly, with a glass of water, which SHE brings to WHITELAW.

MARY: Here you are, Mr. Whitelaw. Sure you wouldn't prefer something stronger?

WHITELAW: No, just this water, thanks. Anything stronger than water treats me very badly. (*Drinks*)

CHANCE: How've you been, Dad, since I was home last?

WHITELAW: A slight recurrence—one of my old spells.

CHANCE: I'm sorry.

WHITELAW: It passed as soon as I lay down.

MARY: Oh, is your health troubling you, Mr. Whitelaw?

WHITELAW: Oh, no—I'm all right. (*Hands her back the glass*) I have to keep quieter than most people—excitement seems to be bad for me.

MARY starts off with glass, sees MIKE off and calls to him.

MARY: Mike!

MIKE enters. SHE gives him glass.

Take this, please. Mike, how long have Dad and Mother been gone?

MIKE: About two hours, Miss Mary. (*MIKE exits*)

MARY (*Back to WHITELAW*): They should be back any minute then. I wish you would move over here to the sofa. You look so temporary on that chair, and the strain is beginning to tell on Chance.

THEY laugh.

WHITELAW (*Smiling*): How are you bearing up?

MARY: Oh, I'm my Dad's daughter—not afraid of anything.

CHANCE: Come over here, Dad, and be comfortable.

WHITELAW: I'm all right here. Mr. and Mrs. Marko should be along very soon.

MARY: Don't think you're just going to say how-d'ye to them and walk out. If I know my parents they'll want you to stay with us for the whole meeting.

WHITELAW: That would be nice of them, but impossible for me. It's quite important that I should be back in Amsterdam tonight.

CHANCE: Oh, the farm will get along without you, Dad.

MIKE *and* LEFTY *enter and go to porch, carrying card table, games, food, drinks, etc.*

MARY: What are you doing, Mike?

MIKE: We're getting the porch ready for the crowd, Miss Mary. (*Turns on porch light by window in alcove*)

WHITELAW: Is there going to be a crowd?

MARY: Wherever Dad is there's a crowd. And he always keeps open house in Saratoga. Mr. Whitelaw, wouldn't your chauffeur like a glass of beer while he's waiting?

WHITELAW: I imagine he would.

MARY: Oh, Mike!

MIKE *comes in with beer from porch.*

Take some beer out to Mr. Whitelaw's chauffeur.

MIKE (*Sadly, semi-confidentially*): We've only got Marko's Beer.

MARY: What's the matter with Marko's Beer?

MIKE: *Maybe* he'll like it. (MIKE *goes out*)

WHITELAW: Your father brews Marko's Beer, doesn't he?

MARY: Yes.

WHITELAW: How long has he been a brewer?

MARY: Oh, for years! That is, since repeal—as a matter of fact, for a long time before. It was repeal that made an honest man of Dad. You knew that, didn't you?

WHITELAW (*A bit at a loss*): I—I heard it spoken of—recently.

CHANCE: You know, Saratoga reminds me of Carlsbad.

MARY *and* WHITELAW *look at him.*

MARY: Does it? Why?

CHANCE: I don't know. . . . You know, Dad, I met Mary at Carlsbad. Her school class was making a tour, and as soon as I met Mary I joined on.

MARY (*Laughing, sits with him on sofa*): The Fräulein was pretty worried about us, Mr. Whitelaw.

CHANCE: Mary handled her. Mary could handle any of those people over there—especially waiters or policemen. You should hear her talk German, Dad, or French—or Italian, for that matter. (*To* MARY) Remember the argument we had with the Italian policeman in Milan? You certainly saved me from a lot of trouble.

MARY: Well, you're an officer now yourself, Chance, so who do you think was right in that argument, you or he? What do you think of your son being a trooper, Mr. Whitelaw?

WHITELAW: I think it's a little absurd, I'm afraid. I don't see how it's going to train him for the responsibilities he will have to meet later.

MARY: Well, if you don't approve of Chance being a trooper, you and my Dad have one point in common already.

A knock at outer door and we hear the SINGER's *voice.* HE *enters through terrace window. With* SINGER *are* SALLY *and* KIRK.

SINGER: Hello! Anybody home?

KIRK: Hi, Remy!

SINGER (*Coming into alcove*): Hello, Mary.

MARY: Hello, Singer.

THEY *appear in arch and notice* CHANCE.

SINGER: Jimminetti!

KIRK: What'sa matter? The joint pinched?

SINGER: This is ex-jockey Kirk.

MARY: How do you do?

KIRK: I'm all right. How's yourself? (*Pointing to* SALLY) And this is Sally. She sings, even if she can't talk!

SALLY (*Waving*): Hiyya! Pleased to meet ya, folks.

MARY: Mr. Whitelaw—this is—

SINGER: I'm the old Singing Kid himself, Pop.

KIRK: What's the matter? Your Dad in trouble again?

MARY: This is Mr. Whitelaw's son, Chancellor Whitelaw.

KIRK: Is that so? Looks like a cop to me.

SALLY: It *is* a cop, can't ya see?

SINGER: Pop, meet my friend ex-jockey Kirk. He's all right.

KIRK: How are ya?

WHITELAW (*To* KIRK): You were formerly a rider?

KIRK: A rider? Where you been all your life?

SINGER: This is ex-jockey Kirk. Where's the Boss?

KIRK: I wish he'd been out to the track today. I'd 'a' made him win a couple of big bets.

SINGER (*To* WHITELAW): Say, Pop, d'ya ever dally with the gee-gees?

WHITELAW: Gee-gees?

SINGER: If you're out to the track tomorrow look me up. I'll know plenty.

MARY: No, no, Singer. Dad isn't home yet. Don't you boys want to wait for him on the porch?

KIRK: Look, Singer, the piano.

SINGER (*Sits near piano*): I saw it.

KIRK (*Sits on piano bench*): Give us a tune.

MARY: No, no, Dad isn't back yet. Why don't you wait for the others?

KIRK: You can't keep him away from a piano.

Music starts—"Somebody Stole My Gal."

Al Jolson once told him he had a good voice and he's been a bum ever since.

WHITELAW *gets up, sees terrace exit blocked.*

MARY: Boys, there are sandwiches out on the porch.

KIRK (*Gets up, does a little buck and wing*): Aw, let's have a little music. Sit down, sit down, everybody. We'll entertain ya.

> WHITELAW *sits down, resigned. The* SINGER *is playing very loudly.* SALLY *comes to piano and joins singing. After a pause,* MIKE *enters from hall with two beers on a tray.*

MIKE: Hello, Singer. Hello, Jock.

KIRK: Hello, Mike. How's about some beer?

> MIKE *hands* KIRK *two bottles, one of which* KIRK *puts on piano for the* SINGER *and stands listening. At the end* MIKE *speaks.*

MIKE: Gee, that's good.

> SINGER *continues to play with one hand, drinking beer from bottle held in the other.* MIKE *exits through window. Off is heard sound of cars and distant ad-lib.*

WHITELAW: Is music his profession?

KIRK: Profession? Naw, he's a leading member of the N.T.A.

WHITELAW: N.T.A.?

> MIKE *enters with plate of sandwiches, which* HE *puts on piano, then starts to exit.*

KIRK: National Turf Advisers. He advises people how to bet on the races. I'm a member of the N.T.A. myself.

MIKE (*Over shoulder at door*): What the Pinkertons call 'em is touts. (MIKE *exits*)

> *Loud ad-libbing off. Enter* MRS. RYERSON *with a younger woman, her sister,* MISS FRANKLIN. MARY *crosses to meet them.*

MARY: How do you do? I'm Mary Marko.

MRS. RYERSON: How do you do? I'm Mrs. Ryerson. This is my sister, Miss Franklin.

MARY (*Crossing with* MRS. RYERSON *and* MISS FRANKLIN *to* WHITELAW): Mrs. Ryerson and Miss Franklin, may I present Mr. Whitelaw and his son Chancellor?

> MARY *crosses above sofa to* CHANCE *and* MR. *and* MRS. RITTER, *who have entered, and talks quietly with them during* MRS. RYERSON'*s scene with* WHITELAW.

MRS. RYERSON: How do you do, Mr. Whitelaw? I believe you're a friend of the Chandlers?

WHITELAW: The Sewell Chandlers! Yes, they're neighbors of mine.

MRS. RYERSON: I suppose you've come over to the Markos to see the fun?

MISS FRANKLIN: The party here. We always come. It's wonderful fun.

WHITELAW: FUN?!

MRS. RYERSON: The most entertaining house in Saratoga. Haven't you been here before?

WHITELAW: No, I haven't met the Markos yet.

MRS. RYERSON: Oh, they're a Saratoga institution. They supply most of the amusement for us. Mr. Marko is so picturesque—

Music starts offstage.

—a rare character, really. And his wife is priceless.

The SINGER *starts playing,* WHITELAW *looks pained. We hear the* CROWD *approaching.* LORETTA *and* PETE RYAN, *a jovial fellow, come first, followed by* BATTLING WOLF, *a fighter.*

LORETTA (*Laughing*): All right, Pete. I'll get back at you before the evening's over.
RYAN (*To piano, picks up sandwiches*): Well, I'm two up on you now. Hello, Jock, hello, Singer. Hello, everybody.

MARY *has gone up to meet the guests.*

LORETTA: You must be Mary Marko. I'm Loretta Paige.
MARY: How do you do?
LORETTA: And this is Battling Wolf—he's Pete Ryan's fighter. He's training out at Luther's. Pete's trying to teach him how to act in society.
RYAN: Hey, Champ!
WOLF: Hiya, folks!
RYAN: Sandwiches!

Enter NORA. MARKO *is talking as* HE *comes on, then sees* MARY.

MARKO (*Off*): Hey, Mary, Mary. (*Enters*) Hello, Mary. Have a good time? Did you bring that Whitelaw fella back with you?
MARY: Yes. Mother, Dad . . .

But MARKO *has picked out* WHITELAW, *and bears down on him.*

MARKO: Hello, there, Mr. Whitelaw. How are you? (HE *shakes hands, then slaps him on shoulder*) Come to look us over, eh? That's all right. We look *you* over, too.
MARY: Mr. Whitelaw, this is my mother.
WHITELAW: Charmed to meet you, Mrs. Marko.
NORA: This is a *great pleasure*, Mr. Whitelaw. We're very glad to have you in our house.
MARKO: This ain't our house. We just rent it for the meeting. You ought to see our place in New York. Yes, sir, when you see that place you'll see something, eh, Nora? Say, do you know these people? Hey, folks, I want you to meet Mr. Whitelaw. As far as I know, he's all right.

The RITTERS *enter from terrace.* MRS. RYERSON *exits same place. Several of the* YOUNGER PEOPLE *begin singing "Show Me the Way to Go Home."* MIKE *goes to piano and joins in, with backgammon board under one arm and a folding chair under the other.*

NORA (*Goes to greet* RITTERS): Mr. Whitelaw, this is Mrs. Ritter and Mr. Ritter.

MARKO (*Grabs* WHITELAW, *pushing him across stage*): Here's the fellow you want to meet—the next heavyweight champion—training up at Luther's.

RYAN: Greatest fighter in history. He can punch like Dempsey, box like Tunney, and is faster than a bantamweight. Hasn't got a bad habit in the world. Just a big boy.

MARKO: Now you know who *he* is—he's his manager—Pete Ryan.

RYAN: How are ya?

RYAN stretches out his hand to WHITELAW *but purposely misses, leaving* WHITELAW *embarrassed.* MARKO *roars.*

MARKO: Look out for Pete here, Mr. Whitelaw. Up to tricks all the time—funniest fella in the world. Mike, how about some beer and sandwiches?

NORA: Put everything on the porch, *Michael.*

MIKE *stops singing.*

(*To* WHITELAW) You'll have to excuse me till I get things organized. Then I'll come back and we'll all get acquainted.

MIKE *exits to terrace.*

MARKO: You boys like some drinks? Mike, take the orders for drinks out on the porch.

KIRK *and* RYAN *cross to porch, taking* SALLY *with them.*

NORA (*As the* RITTERS *start back*): Who wants to play bridge or backgammon? Everything's ready on the porch. Let's all go out there.

SAM *enters from the hall.* LORETTA *starts to shag near piano.* SAM *joins her, dancing en route.*

MARKO: Like some backgammon, Mr. Whitelaw?

NORA: No, Mr. Whitelaw is going to stay here with us.

MARKO: All right. (*Urging them out*) Out to the porch now, folks!

NORA: Excuse me, Mr. Whitelaw. Harold!—All of you go out on the porch. HAROLD!! (NORA *crosses to* WHITELAW)

The SINGER, LORETTA, WOLF *and* SAM *are grouped around the piano,* SALLY *having returned to join them.* MIKE *approaches* MARKO.

MIKE: Say, Boss, I want to speak to you.

MARKO: Not now. You get busy waiting on these people.

Music, soft.

MIKE: This is important.

MARKO: Getting drinks out to our guests is important, too. Say, Mike, have you heard if any of those parties've been found yet?

MIKE: That's what I want to talk to you about.

MARKO: Don't worry. You'll hear about it when they're found. You get busy. Get Lefty to help you.

Music stops.

NORA: Singer, run along now and join the others out on the porch.

WHITELAW *sits by phone table.*

LORETTA (*Back of piano*): Oh, I can remember when you used to like to hear the Singer. And here's Sally, too.

SALLY (*A bit peeved*): And you used to like to hear me—you *said* you did.

NORA (*By piano*): There are lots of things I used to like that I don't now.

LORETTA: You used to like to sing yourself when we worked at Coney Island.

NORA: Come, come, Singer, out on the porch. (SHE *exits*)

MARKO: Hey, Nora, let the Singer alone. Some people *like* music. (*Sits on sofa. To* WHITELAW) Got a great voice, eh? You know Jim Crawfoot?—Why, he sung for Crawfoot once for eight hours. Say, Singer, where's our old friend, Jim?

SINGER: He's sick, Boss.

MARKO: Sick?

SINGER: Yeah, some hospital in San Diego.

MARKO: Aw, that's tough. Say, I got an idea. (*Pushes* WHITELAW *off chair*) Let's call him up and say hello. It would cheer him up. (*Sits*)

Laughter offstage. LORETTA *crosses to porch.*

LORETTA (*Looking off*): Pete's up to something.

CHANCE *and* MARY *rise from window seat.*

NORA (*Coming in to* WHITELAW. *Crowd laughs*): There seems to be a little confusion around here.

MARKO (*Into phone*): Give me long distance. . . . Nice fella, Jim. He's all right.

LORETTA *enters and crosses to piano.*

LORETTA: Pete put some Limburger in the cards.

MARY *crosses back to piano and off.*

NORA: Mary, watch out for those people on the porch. See that they have everything they want.

CHANCE *and* MARY *exit to porch.*

MARKO: Long distance? Get me Jim Crawfoot—C-R-A-W-F-O-O-T. He's sick in some hospital in San Diego. . . . Yes. . . . San Diego, California. This is Remy Marko. (*Looks at phone*) One eight two. (MARKO *hangs phone up*)

MIKE *and* LEFTY *enter carrying drinks in tall glasses on trays, and beer mugs.* MIKE *exits to terrace.*

Lefty, serve a glass of beer to Mr. Whitelaw here.

LEFTY *crosses back to* WHITELAW *who is on sofa.* NORA *on other end of sofa.*

WHITELAW: No, thank you.

MARKO *takes two glasses from tray and tries to make* WHITELAW *accept one.*

MARKO: I make this beer. I want you to try it.
WHITELAW: I really don't care for any.

LEFTY *crosses through room and exits,* MIKE *after him.*

MARKO: Come on, drink it! Best beer on the market. Cleans you out good.

WHITELAW *has to take it and like it. Both* HE *and* MARKO *drink,* WHITELAW *just sipping, then sets down glass.*

Say, Singer, give us "I Lost All My Love for You."

Selection optional. SINGER *starts playing. Music gradually increases in volume,* VOICES *rising with it.*

Say, Nora, remember when we used to listen to this down at Kelly's on Sullivan Street? (*Dreamily meandering here and there*)
NORA: No, I don't remember!—Mr. Whitelaw, how long have you been in Saratoga?
WHITELAW: I just drove over yesterday. Chancellor wanted me to meet your daughter. I'm driving back tonight.
NORA: Indeed you're not. You're going to stay right here with us.
WHITELAW: That's very kind of you, but—
MARKO: No buts. You can't get away from us like that.
WHITELAW: I must be back tonight. My chauffeur is waiting out front for me now.
MARKO: We'll take care of the chauffeur, too.
NORA: Yes indeed. This is a large house—and very comfortable. I love the big closets in these old houses.

SAM *joins in, faking a muted cornet as music stops.*

Of course, I can't boast of this furniture. And they arrange it so badly in some of these Saratoga houses, don't you think?

WHITELAW *is annoyed by the loud music. Song ends.* NORA *is caught unawares by ending of music and continues to shout for a moment, then stops embarrassed.*

MARKO: That's great, Singer. Give us some more.
NORA: Mr. Whitelaw, let's go out on the porch.

MARY *enters, followed by* CHANCE.

MARY: I'm sure there must be some in the house. Mother, where are the bridge scores?
NORA: I'm sure I told Michael to get some. Excuse me just a moment, Mr. Whitelaw.

NORA *exits, followed by* MARY *and* CHANCE.

MARKO: Mr. Whitelaw, what do you think of that girl of mine?

WHITELAW: Very nice indeed.

MARKO: Nice? She's the best girl in the world. I spent fifty thousand dollars educating that girl. Of course, I understand you spent some money on that boy of yours, too. But what about this business of his being a policeman? Don't you think that's a bad sign?

WHITELAW: I don't think so. It so happens that the Whitelaws for generations have held offices of law enforcement. The boy's great-grandfather was sheriff of our county, and his great-uncle was the first warden of Auburn Prison.

MARKO: You don't say so? That's news to me.

SAM (*Entering*): Singer, let's have "Melancholy Baby."

Music starts and phone rings.

MARKO (*Crossing, glass in hand*): Hey, that must be Jim Crawfoot. . . . (MARKO *answers phone*) Yeah, put him on. . . . Hello, San Diego? Jim? This is Remy Marko. How d'you feel? . . . . Yeah, I know, that keeps you traveling, don't it? . . . . The Singin' Kid told me where you were. He's right here now, singin' to us.

MIKE *enters.*

. . . Oh, you would? I can fix that. Mike, bring me that piano . . . and a highball.

MIKE (*Calling off*): Hey, Lefty! (*To* SINGER) Got to move you, Singer.

SINGER: Go right ahead, don't mind me.

LEFTY *enters.* MIKE *and* LEFTY, *and the group around piano, start pushing the piano from alcove while* MARKO *ad-libs on phone. When* WHITELAW *sees piano coming in his direction,* HE *crosses rapidly in an attempt to escape to porch, but the piano is swung in front of him. Several guests lean on it.* RYAN *scares* WHITELAW *by quickly stepping on his toe.* WHITELAW *angry as* RYAN *bursts into laughter.* WHITELAW *turns and crosses rapidly away.*

NORA (*Entering*): What are you doing? What's going on here?

MARKO: Hey, Nora, Jim wants to hear the Singin' Kid. (*Into phone*) Just a minute, Jim, and we'll be all set for you. (*To* SINGER) I got Jim on the phone. Sing somethin' he likes.

SINGER: Oh, here's something he loves.

SINGER *starts singing and playing "Mexicali Rose,"* SALLY *joining him, and* MARKO *holds mouthpiece in front of* SINGER. ALL *listen a moment.*

MARKO (*Into phone*): Hey, Jim, ya listenin'? Does it sound natural? . . . You just hold on and we'll give you a concert.

MARKO *hands phone to* SAM *to hold for the* SINGER.

MARY *and* CHANCE *have entered.*

NORA (*Indicating bridge scores*): Mary, take these out on the porch.

MARY *and* CHANCE *cross to porch.* NORA *has come back to* WHITELAW.

WHITELAW: Mrs. Marko, is he singing to someone in San Diego, *California?*

NORA *nods.*

A sick man?

NORA: Once my husband had him sing to a man in Australia. Wonderful invention the telephone, don't you think?

WHITELAW: Yes, wonderful.

> SINGER *finishes singing. The* COMMISSIONER, *who came in with the others and went upstairs, now comes down and into room.*

NORA: Oh, Commissioner, I want you to know Mr. Whitelaw. This is Commissioner Mahoney. He's our house guest.

> MARKO *joins them.*

MARKO: I guess you know all about Commissioner Mahoney . . . big shot in Washington. If you're ever down there he might do you some good with the President.

COMMISSIONER: You're down in Montgomery County, aren't you, Mr. Whitelaw?

WHITELAW: Yes, I am.

COMMISSIONER: I believe you know the President.

> *Music very soft outside.*

WHITELAW: Oh, yes—for many years. How is he?

COMMISSIONER: Thriving.

MARKO: So you know the President? Know him well?

WHITELAW: He used to visit us when he was a boy.

MARKO: Was he the same kind of fella when he was a boy as he is now?

> SAM *joins the* SINGER *who begins to play and sing.*

WHITELAW: Well, he could always stir up trouble.

COMMISSIONER (*Laughing*): Shall I tell him you said so?

WHITELAW: Why not?

> *Enter* CLYDE POST.

POST: Hello, everybody. Hello, Commissioner. How are you, Mrs. Marko? Hello, Remy.

MARKO: Hello, Clyde.

NORA: Mr. Whitelaw, this is Clyde Post.

> POST *at hall door.* LORETTA *at terrace door up.*

SINGER: Come in, Loretta, and chirp a little.

LORETTA: Okay.

MARKO: Say, Clyde, I'm glad you're here. Cal's out on the porch. I want a little talk with you boys.

LORETTA *comes down to piano, and* SAM *hoists her up on it. Sitting there, and facing audience,* SHE *sings a song; phone receiver is held near her by one of the boys.*

NORA: We'll go out on the porch. I'll send Mr. Ritter in. Come on, Mr. Whitelaw. Coming, Commissioner?

MARKO: The Commissioner can stay here. He knows what it's all about.

COMMISSIONER: I'll go out on the porch, Remy. You can settle your business without me.

THEY *move toward porch,* MARKO *following.*

MARKO: Hey, Cal! Cal Ritter! Clyde's just come in. . . . (MARKO *disappears to porch after the others*)

POST *turns toward piano. The* SINGER *is now singing "Mother" into the phone.* MIKE *enters from hall, with* WHITELAW's *bags, and meets* LEFTY.

LEFTY: You had a chance to tell the Boss yet?

MIKE: He's too busy. We'll have to wait till we've got rid of these people here.

MARKO *comes in from porch with* RITTER, *sees* POST *listening to* SINGER.

MARKO: You know what we're doing? We're entertaining Jim Crawfoot!

POST: Why, Jim's sick on the Coast, isn't he?

MARKO: Yeah, that's where we're singing to him.

Goes to piano by LORETTA. *Stands listening appreciatively. Takes phone from* SAM *and listens.*

Jim's crying like a baby. This is giving him a lot of pleasure.

LORETTA *jumps down from piano and exits to terrace.* MARKO *gives phone back to* SAM, *who listens with a seraphic expression.*

I only wish we could get the Big Fella at Alcatraz. He'd love this. I don't suppose they'd let him come to the phone?

Enter COL. SCHULTZ *through hall.*

SCHULTZ: Hello, Remy.

MARKO: Hello, Colonel. How's everything?

SCHULTZ: Fine, Remy.

Music stops.

MARKO: You boys know Col. Jake Schultz.

POST *and* RITTER *sit on or near sofa. The* MEN *exchange hellos.*

Where'd you come from?

SCHULTZ: I just ran over from my house. I heard the Commissioner was here. Want to see him.

MARKO: Just come from your house? How's everything *around* your house?

SCHULTZ (*A puzzled look*): Everything's all right.

MARKO (*Also puzzled*): Is that so? Did you come out the *front* way?

SCHULTZ: Yes—across the lawn. Why?

MARKO: Oh, nothing.

SINGER *starts another song.* MARKO *looks toward* MIKE.

SCHULTZ: The Commissioner out on the porch?

MARKO: Yeah. Go right out. Sure everything's all right around your house?

SCHULTZ: Yes. (SCHULTZ *gives* MARKO *wondering look and exits to porch. Off*) Hello, Commissioner.

COMMISSIONER (*Off*): Hello, Colonel.

OTHERS (*Off*): Hello, Colonel.

MARKO *goes to* MIKE.

MARKO: You hear what the Colonel said, Mike? What about that?

MIKE: Yes, listen, Boss—I gotta tell you—

The expression on SAM's *face changes abruptly.*

SAM (*In phone*): Oh, is that so!

Music stops.

(*To the* OTHERS) Some broad says he's running a temperature. She's hung up.

SINGER: What do you know! And I was just going into "A Baby's Prayer at Twilight."

Sound of several police car sirens passing the house.

Say, maybe they got those truck stick-ups!

SAM: I hope they found my money on them.

Group at piano go out to porch.

RYAN (*Off*): Maybe somebody's in trouble.

MARKO (*To* POST *and* RITTER): Say, you fellows didn't pull that stick-up, did you?

THEY *laugh.*

From the way you're dogging me, you act like you need money.

RITTER *and* POST *sit, as* MARKO *stands.*

RITTER: Remy, we don't *own* that bank. We've got to do what the board tells us.

MARKO: Well, you gotta tell that board you gotta give me another extension.

POST: No, Remy, we can't go any further.

MARKO: Say, you boys don't think I can't pay it, do you? You don't think I'm going to let you take my brewery for that kind of money? Why, I could pay you in cash tonight if I wanted to.

POST: We're glad you've got it, Remy.

RITTER: Yes, we were a little worried about you. Our reports don't show that you have anything near that amount.

MARKO: Why, all Marko owes you boys is four hundred and sixty-two grand. That ain't even half a million.

RITTER: Well, Remy, it's due tomorrow. We planned to stay up here for the meeting. Do you want to turn it over here in Saratoga, or shall we go back to town?

MARKO: It's all the same to me—Saratoga or New York. But listen here, boys, here it is:

POST *rises.*

The reason I want an extension is I'm planning a big campaign for my beer over the radio. I'm going to need all the ready cash I can get my hands on for a while. In the old days you could push your beer, now you gotta make people *want* it.

POST: Well, Remy, the last time it was newspaper advertising.

MARKO: I did advertise and my beer is just commencing to go good again. Besides, I've made a connection with a Western outfit that'll be wound up in a couple of weeks that'll make my brewery the greatest proposition on the market.

RITTER: That's fine, Remy, but we can't go along with you.

MARKO: I tell you what I'll do for you boys—I'll give you an extra two percent on the interest on that thing for a three month extension. I guess that's pretty good news for you, eh?

RITTER, *behind* MARKO, *signs "No" to* POST.

POST: No, that won't do either. Let us know tomorrow what to expect.

MARKO: Just for that I got a good notion to pay you right now.

NORA *enters from porch.*

MRS. RITTER (*Off*): How about some backgammon? Cal will take my hand here.

RYAN (*Off*): Those fellows think that siren is a toy. They love to play with it.

NORA (*Off*): I'll get Cal for you.

MRS. RYERSON (*Off*): Why, is anything the matter?

NORA: Mr. Ritter, Clara wants you to take her hand. She's going to play backgammon with Miss Smith.

POST: I'll take on Miss Smith. I've got a score against her. (HE *starts out*)

RITTER: No, you don't. We need that Washington money more than you do.

NORA (*Smiling*): Don't fight about it.

RITTER: No, no, we won't.

RITTER *and* POST *exit to porch.*

MARKO *pulls his coat down viciously.*

MARKO: Sometimes I'm sorry we're respectable. There's no chance for action. (*Sits on sofa*)

NORA: What's the matter, Remy? (*Joins him on sofa*)

MARKO: Looks like those guys may own the Marko Brewery in a few days. They know I haven't got a quarter and they're all set to grab. People don't respect me anymore.

NORA: Take it easy, Remy. We've been in trouble lots of times before and we've always managed to get out. Anyway, this isn't the kind of trouble that used to have me sitting home wondering if you were coming back.

MARKO: Take it easy yourself.

NORA: Oh, you'll get out of this all right.

MARKO: I don't know how, unless you kick up a gold mine.

KIRK *comes in from the porch. Laughter offstage.*

KIRK: Hey, Remy, come here quick.

MARKO *starts over.*

NORA: Don't worry, Remy. (NORA *exits through arch*)

MARKO *joins* KIRK *and* THEY *look out onto porch at something that's afoot. There's an explosion followed by a burst of laughter.* KIRK *exits through hall.*

MARKO: Look, he jumped three feet. (MARKO *laughs heartily*)

WHITELAW *comes in from porch pretty mad.*

I told you to watch out for that fella. He got you again, eh?

MARY *and* CHANCE *come in.*

MARY: Dad, you tell Pete Ryan to get out of here. He set off a firecracker under Mr. Whitelaw's chair.

MARKO *exits to porch, followed by* MARY.

MARKO (*Off, laughing*): Hey, Pete, can those firecrackers. We don't want people to think we're having target practice around here.

WHITELAW *turns to* CHANCE.

WHITELAW: So this is the kind of family you want to marry into! A lot of imbeciles!

CHANCE: I'm not marrying the family. You haven't seen anything wrong with Mary, have you?

WHITELAW: Yes, I've seen her father and mother.

RITTER (*Off*): Two spades.

CHANCE: She's the girl I want to marry and she's the girl I'm going to marry!

WHITELAW: I don't think either of you will enjoy living on your present pay.

CHANCE: We don't mind that!

WHITELAW: I'm absolutely against your marrying this girl. I'm making that clear to you and I'm going to make it clear to these people.

CHANCE: Now, Dad, don't say anything to them, please!

WHITELAW: I shall enjoy doing so—I'm going to stay in this house just long enough to do that—and then go back to the farm.

MARKO (*Off*): Everybody has a good time at Marko's.

(MARKO *enters from porch*) Don't mind this fella Pete Ryan, Mr. Whitelaw. He's just full of fun. Great fella when you get to know him. Sit down, I want to talk to you.

CHANCE *exits to terrace.*

WHITELAW: Thank you, I should like a few words with *you.*

WHITELAW *crosses and sits on sofa,* MARKO *by his side.*

MRS. RITTER (*Off*): I'll double.

MARY (*Off*): What are trumps?

MRS. RYERSON *laughs, off.*

MARKO: Mr. Whitelaw, what did you think of that beer of mine? Marko makes pretty good beer, don't you think?

WHITELAW: I'm not an authority on beer, Mr. Marko.

MARKO: You ask the Commissioner. He told me just today—"Marko, that brewery should make you a fortune." I'll tell you what I'll do for you—

WHITELAW: I wish to speak of something else—of the attachment between your daughter and my son. Let me tell you something about my son.

MARKO: Listen, Mr. Whitelaw. He's your son and of course you've got to stick up for him. I understand that—sure. But this marriage thing, I've been giving it a lot of thought and I hate to tell you, but it won't do. I can't stand for it.

WHITELAW: What are you saying? (*Stands up*)

MARKO (*Pulls him down again*): I'll tell you: at first I thought this idea of your boy's of being a policeman was just a kid's notion and wouldn't last. But what you told me about his grandfathers and uncles shows there's a lot of police blood in your family all the way down, and I don't like it.

WHITELAW: I can understand *your* feeling that way, Mr. Marko. (WHITELAW *starts to rise,* MARKO *stops him*)

MARKO: I'm glad you're taking it like that. Look, I'll tell you why I gotta be particular. You see, I'm an orphan and I'm starting a new family and I want my family to amount to something in this country in years to come. (MARKO *slips his shoes off*) It's a big idea with me. I've had it for a long time. I've read a lot about these big old American families. There was a couple of years once—when I had nothing to do but read. All of them started just the way I did, only they had real estate and furs and railroads. I don't know how you Whitelaws got started, but way back some Whitelaw had the same idea I got about a family. He did pretty well and it might have worked out big, but somewhere that police blood got in and spoiled things for you. It's a sort of—(MARKO *searches for a word*)

WHITELAW (*Sarcastically*): Taint?

MARKO: Yeah, 'tain't so good. That's probably why the Whitelaw family's about washed out. No, Mr. Whitelaw, I can't consider it. Now, it's nothing personal, y'understand.

WHITELAW: Oh, isn't it? Well, I'm relieved to hear that.

MARKO (*Struck by a thought*): I'll prove it to you. I'm willing to let you put a little money into my brewery—not much—just enough to give you a rooting interest—say half a million.

WHITELAW: Did you say half a *million?*

MARKO: I might let you press it a little.

WHITELAW: Mr. Marko, (*Gets up*) I should like to say this is an experience I'll never forget.

MARKO (*Generously*): That's all right. (*Also up*) Maybe a couple of hundred thousand more, but that's all now.

WHITELAW: Mr. Marko, I haven't a penny to put into your brewery—and what's more I'm going to remove the Whitelaws and their police blood out of your house this instant.

MARKO: Don't do that. You'll make me think you're sore at me.

WHITELAW: Where can I find Mrs. Marko?

MARKO: For God's sake, don't tell her we talked about those kids. It would upset her. Let her find out gradual.

SINGER enters and goes to piano.

SINGER (*Speaking back toward porch*): I'll see if I can remember it.

WHITELAW: Miss Marko, I wish to speak to your mother. (HE *exits*)

MARKO (*Exiting to porch*): Don't get me into a jam with Nora.

RYAN (*Off*): Remy, you got anymore dice? We want to start a game.

MARKO (*Off*): I'll see if I can dig some up.

Ad-lib off continues a moment. The SINGER is playing. After a short pause, MARY enters, followed by CHANCE, and goes into hallway.

MARY (*Calling upstairs*): Mother! Mother! Mr. Whitelaw wants you. (*Crosses to dining room door. Calls off*) Mother! (*To CHANCE*) Your father looks very forbidding.

CHANCE: Dad suffers from spells—nervous indigestion, and maybe this is too much excitement for him.

MARY: I dreaded his being here tonight, but I thought we might as well get it over with. Has he said anything to you? (SHE *and* CHANCE *lean on piano*)

CHANCE: Well, I don't think Dad is feeling well.

MARY: Then he *has* said something. It looks to me, young man, as if you're on a spot.

CHANCE: The only spot I'm on is right beside where you're standing, and you'll always find me there.

MARY: You're sure of that, Chance?

CHANCE: You can bank on it.

MARY: I'm glad. I'd never want you to know how I'd feel if you weren't.

Enter WHITELAW *and* MARKO *from porch.*

MARKO: Mary, they tell me your mother is out around the grounds somewhere. See if you can dig her up.

WHITELAW: Chancellor.

CHANCE: I'll be back, Dad. I'm going with Mary.

> MARY *and* CHANCE *go out.* WHITELAW *remains in front of sofa.* DOUGLAS, *in his sleeping-suit, comes halfway down stairs and stands looking at people off. Music stops.*

MARKO: They'll bring Nora back with them, but when she comes, remember—tape! (*Puts finger to his lips*) Why, Douglas, why aren't you upstairs abed and asleep? Come on down here.

> DOUGLAS *starts down.*

MRS. RITTER (*Off*): Cal, I've just lost seventy dollars.

RITTER (*Off*): Lose all you want to. Nobody ever pays Clyde.

MRS. RYERSON (*Off*): It's your play, Mr. Ritter.

> DOUGLAS *runs down to* MARKO, *who picks him up.*

MARKO: See this boy, Mr. Whitelaw? This is Douglas Fairbanks Rosenbloom—the prize pupil of the Star of Hope Orphanage—that's where I come from. Every year Marko gives them twenty-five thousand dollars that I win from these gamblers around Saratoga. Yes, sir, these gamblers practically support that orphanage. Say, tell me, do you ever shoot craps?

WHITELAW: Do I what?

> At this moment DOUGLAS *pulls his right hand out from breast of his sleeping-suit, where he has been holding it. His fist is full of bills.*

What has that boy got in his hand? Why, there's a thousand-dollar bill! Do you allow the child to play with money like that?

MARKO: Why not? I always keep plenty of ready around. Douglas, where did you get it? (*Takes money from* DOUGLAS)

DOUGLAS: There's lots more under the bed.

MARKO: Here, hold Douglas!

> MARKO, *after forcing* WHITELAW *to sit down, tosses* DOUGLAS *into* WHITELAW'*s lap and tears upstairs.* DOUGLAS *begins to climb over* WHITELAW. *At the same time* RYAN *crawls in and along the floor toward* WHITELAW *with a book of matches in his hand.*

DOUGLAS: Who are you? What's your name?

> WHITELAW *is trying to recover his breath.* DOUGLAS *pulls at his mustache.*

What do you wear that thing for? (HE *ruffles* WHITELAW'*s hair and laughs with glee.* DOUGLAS *reaches into his sleeping-suit and pulls out a bookmaker's envelope*)

Look what I got—money! I'm going to buy candy with it tomorrow. (*Tosses envelope on floor*) Do you wanta hear me recite?

RYAN *has adjusted matches in* WHITELAW's *shoe and is lighting them. The* SINGER, *when* HE *notices what* RYAN *is about, stops playing long enough to signal people on porch.* LORETTA *and* KIRK *appear in upper window, expectant.* DOUGLAS *stands on sofa.*

"I hailed me a woman from the streets,
Shameless, but oh, so fair!
I had her sit in the model seat
And painted her picture there.
I hid all trace of her heart unclean,
I painted a babe at her breast . . . "

The heat has reached WHITELAW's *foot.* HE *yells and dances around, stamping. The* SINGER *accompanies him with Scotch hornpipe music. The* OTHERS *howl with laughter, all coming in from porch.* NORA, CHANCE, *and* MARY *come in from hall,* LEFTY *carrying two bags.*

NORA (*Mistaking what* SHE *sees for gaiety*): Well, Mr. Whitelaw, you're turning out to be the life of the party! (*Applauds him lightly*)

WHITELAW (*Slowing up*): I've never been so abominably treated in my life! Savages! Barbarians! Every one of you!

NORA: What's going on here?

LORETTA: Pete gave him the hot-foot.

All laugh again. MARKO *comes downstairs with a bag, which* HE *holds tightly.*

NORA: Remy, throw that bum out of this house.

MARKO, *thinking* NORA *means* WHITELAW, *starts for him.*

NORA: No, no, no. Ryan!

WHITELAW: I wish you a very good evening, Mrs. Marko. I'm leaving! (*Starts to exit*)

NORA: Please don't be offended, Mr. Whitelaw.

WHITELAW: I'm leaving.

NORA: But you can't leave.

WHITELAW: Can't leave? (*Coming back*)

NORA: I've sent your car back to Amsterdam.

WHITELAW: What!

NORA: But I've got your bags right here. I wouldn't dream of letting you leave us tonight. What would you think of our hospitality?

MARKO: That's great, Nora. (*To* WHITELAW) My Missus always gets her own way— even with Marko. (*Laughs heartily*)

WHITELAW: I'm feeling ill. I must lie down somewhere. (*Collapses on piano, strikes keys, jumps back*)

NORA: Why not in your room? It's the room right over this.

WHITELAW: Chancellor!

NORA: Yes, Chance, come and help your father upstairs like a good boy.

CHANCE *and* NORA *start to lead* WHITELAW *away.*

CHANCE: Feeling bad, Dad?

WHITELAW: I've never felt worse in my life.

NORA (*To* WHITELAW): Now you get a nice rest. It will be cool and quiet up there. (NORA *sees* DOUGLAS *with fistful of money*) Remy, where'd that punk get all the money? Whose is it?

MARKO: It's my money.

NORA: Here, Douglas, gimme that—and get up to bed.

NORA *slaps* DOUGLAS *on the behind.* DOUGLAS *cries and runs toward stairs.* DOUGLAS *steps on* WHITELAW's *foot in passing and* WHITELAW *yells.*

WHITELAW: Ouch! (*Sits down suddenly on piano bench*)

NORA: And Remy, when I said throw that bum Ryan out I meant it.

CHANCE, NORA *and* MARY *lead* WHITELAW *upstairs.*

MARKO: Better leave, Pete. The Missus is gettin' sored up.

RYAN: Aw, her chest is gettin' too big.

MARKO: What you say?

RYAN: You know yourself Nora's gettin' swelled up.

MARKO: Why, you . . . fink!

HE *slaps* RYAN *and keeps after him.*

RYAN: Hey, Remy, lay off! I didn't mean it. Hey, Champ!

LEFTY *drops* WHITELAW's *bags.* WOLF *steps in, a sandwich in his mouth.* MARKO *grabs both* WOLF *and* RYAN *and bumps their heads together. To do this* HE *has to drop the bag. It falls near* WHITELAW's *bags.* HE *kicks both* RYAN *and* WOLF *up through arch, following along out of sight down the hall, toward outer door. During the above* KIRK *has picked up bookmaker's envelope and been studying it. The* CROWD *follows* MARKO *off with excitement and laughter.* SAM *is upstage when* KIRK *calls to him.*

KIRK: Hey, Sam. Come here—quick!

SAM (*At alcove*): I'll be back in a minute.

KIRK: I got something important. (KIRK *holds up envelope*) Take a peek at this.

SAM: Where'd you get that?

KIRK: Under the sofa there.

SAM: Why, this is my envelope—there's my name and the amount—twenty-three hundred—my own handwriting.

KIRK: That's what I thought.

SAM: This was in the truck that was stuck up. How d'ye suppose it got here?

KIRK: Are you sure this was in that truck? I thought you said you had twenty thousand in the envelope.

SAM: You don't understand business methods. (*Sits*) That's my envelope; it was in the truck. And whoever was in that stick-up has been in this house. Why, it's a cinch.

KIRK: Who do you suppose it was? Do you think it could have been Ryan—he'd do anything—or maybe his fighter?

SAM: No—they were out at the training camp. I know.

KIRK: It couldn't be any of these swells—what about this fellow Whitelaw—you know his son's a copper?

SAM: No, they've got plenty dough.

KIRK: Well, you know where that leaves us. (*A pause. Sits on sofa*) And I heard Remy was troubled with the shorts.

At this point CHANCE *trips down stairs and looks around. Sees his father's suitcase and beside it the bag* MARKO *dropped when* WOLF *attacked him. Picks them all up and goes upstairs with them.* KIRK *and* SAM *play dead while* CHANCE *is doing this.*

SAM: Yeah, he dunned me for two thousand before I had more'n time to say hello to him. (*Gets up*) He ain't goin' to get that two thousand. I'm not going to pay over any money to a thief.

KIRK: If I was you I'd flash that envelope right under Remy's nose and ask him what about it.

SAM: Oh, you would, would you? Then you can be me. (HE *holds out envelope to* KIRK)

KIRK: Wait a minute! (*Gets up*) We got the law right here in this house. (*Crosses to hall door*) How about the state trooper doing it?

SAM: Why, Remy would swallow that poor kid without chewing. Maybe we'd better put this up to the Commissioner?

KIRK: That's a good idea. Let's get a hold of him. But he don't get any part of my reward.

SAM: What reward? Oh, yeah. No, we split fifty-fifty.

KIRK: I found the envelope.

SAM: But I can testify to its being in that truck. We split it fifty-fifty.

MARKO *and the* CROWD *come back laughing and talking.* MARKO *is wiping his hands together.*

MARKO: The next heavyweight champion of the world, eh? What does that make me?

MIKE *enters bringing slippers.* MARKO *steps into them.*

SINGER: That Wolf takes them good from behind anyway. Nobody's going to knock him out kicking him.

The CROWD *is now all in the room.* LORETTA, *singing, is joined by three or four* OTHERS, *including* MISS SMITH. MARKO *looks around for bag.* NORA *comes downstairs.* MARY *and* CHANCE *after her.*

NORA: Quiet, everybody, quiet. Poor Mr. Whitelaw is going to bed, so we can all go back to our games and quiet down. Let's all go out on the porch.

Herds them before her. SINGER *starts playing and singing.*

Singer, we've had enough of that for one night. You get out on the porch with the others.

THEY *start moving toward porch and exit.* COMMISSIONER *enters as others go out.*

SAM: Commissioner, can I see you a minute?

COMMISSIONER: Not just now, Sam.

SAM: It ain't a favor.

COMMISSIONER: I'll be down shortly. (COMMISSIONER *goes upstairs*)

NORA: Remy, if that heel Ryan shows up around this house again—

MIKE: He won't be out of the hospital till the meetin's over.

MARKO: Nora, have you seen a big black bag around here?

NORA: No, I've been upstairs.

MRS. RYERSON (*Off*): We'll just have to deal over again.

MRS. RITTER (*Off*): I want to get some of that seventy back.

NORA *exits to porch.*

MARKO: Mike, there was a big black bag I dropped here. Did you put it anywhere?

MIKE: What black bag? I didn't know there was a black bag around the house.

MARKO: Never mind what black bag. Where's it? We gotta find it. Do you suppose any of these guests of mine might of taken it? Get Lefty and Giuseppe and we'll search the place for it before any of these people start to go. It's very important to me.

MIKE: Listen, Boss, there's something more important—

MARKO: There couldn't be. There's nothing in the world more important than that bag right now.

MIKE: Yes, there is. The Missus shouldn't've put the old man in that front room.

MARKO: Why not?

MIKE: Because those parties are up in the closet in that room.

MARKO: What parties?

MIKE: Why, Gallagher and Little Dutch and—you know, those parties we found here.

MARKO: Those parties? Mike, are you drunk?

MIKE: No, Boss, they're up there.

MARKO (*Going to* MIKE): Jimminetti's sake, how did they get there? They didn't walk, did they? Is somebody trying to play a joke on Marko? That ain't funny!

MIKE: We boys brought 'em back ourselves, Boss. We didn't want to put 'em back in the same room with Douglas. We don't trust Douglas. So we put 'em in the front room closet where we put the artillery. It's nice and big and plenty of room for them. They're settin' around there as comfortable as anything.

MARKO: Well, for God's sake, what was the idea of bringing 'em back?

MIKE: The papers say there's ten thousand dollars reward for each one of them fellas, dead or alive. Why, they're practically as good *as* cash in hand for us. Of course, Boss, we've declared you in for your bit.

MARKO: Why, you dopes! You knew yourself I couldn't afford to have those parties found around here—especially the way they are. For a lousy forty thousand dollars you'd ruin my social standing.

MIKE: I don't see where you come off to be kicking about forty thousand dollars coming into this family.

MARKO: I don't have to worry about that kind of money if I can find that black bag. It's got ten times forty thousand dollars in it—and more.

MIKE: Say! Where did you make that score?

MARKO: It's the bookmaker's dough that was taken from the truck. Little Douglas found it for me under the bed.

MIKE: Douglas? Say, he's all right, that Douglas.

MARKO: Well, this is a fine situation. Those four parties back in my house and half a million dollars of my money gone somewhere. Do you suppose there's a thief in this house?

MIKE: You never can tell about people.

Enter KIRK *and* SAM *from porch.*

MARKO: I'll ask around among my guests, and you and Lefty make a search for it—the house, the grounds, everywhere. Don't stir up the old man in the front room.

MIKE: How about the Commissioner's room?

MARKO: Go through it—close.

MIKE *exits, having picked up* MARKO's *shoes.* MARKO *turns to* SAM *and* KIRK.

KIRK: Have you boys seen a big black bag around here any place?

SAM: What was in it, Remy?

MARKO: What you care what was in it? Have you seen it?

KIRK: Was it anything valuable?

MARKO: About as valuable as your tips on the races. Why, you applehead, what do you suppose I'm looking for it for if it wasn't valuable?

SAM: No, we ain't seen it.

MARKO: Well, don't go away till it's found. (MARKO *exits to porch*)

KIRK: What do you suppose is in that bag?

SAM: I'll tell you what I think's in it. I think it's that dough.

KIRK (*On his knees with* SAM *by sofa*): Well, maybe we better look for it ourselves.

COMMISSIONER *crosses downstairs.* SAM *and* KIRK *get up at once.*

SAM: Never mind that now. Here comes the Commissioner.

COMMISSIONER *comes up to them.*

COMMISSIONER: What's on your mind, Sam?

SAM: Commissioner, there's something you ought to know. And it's a matter you got to do something about.

COMMISSIONER: Well, Sam, there's a lot of things I've got to do something about, but somehow I never get round to doing them.

SAM: Commissioner, this is different. You got to do something about this to protect yourself. Remy was mixed up in knocking off that truck.

MRS. RYERSON (*Off*): But I thought hearts were trumps.

COMMISSIONER: That's silly. I'm surprised at you, Sam.

KIRK: We got evidence! We got Sam's envelope—the one that was in that truck and we found it here in this house.

SAM: We think it dropped out of his pocket when he was in that scramble with Pete and the Champ.

COMMISSIONER: It's out of the question. I drove up here in Remy's car with him. Don't you fellows realize you're making a very serious accusation?

SAM: We don't say Remy was there himself, but he was in it.

MRS. RITTER (*Off*): All right, but you'll be sorry.

KIRK: Mike and Lefty and Giuseppe didn't drive up in that car with you, did they?

COMMISSIONER: No, they were here when we arrived.

SAM: Commissioner, here's our evidence and you've got to get busy on it.

COMMISSIONER: Why, Sam, I can't go to my host and ask him if he helped rob a truck.

KIRK: I tell you what we'll do—we'll even cut you in on the reward.

COMMISSIONER (*Walking away*): You boys started this; you finish it.

Phone rings.

SAM: Okay, Commissioner, but what will they say down in Washington—especially if it comes out that you're fronting for this fella?

MARY *comes in from porch to answer phone,* CHANCE *loafing in at her heels.*

COMMISSIONER (*Back to* SAM): I'm not fronting for Remy! But I'm not a police officer. There's a state trooper right here in the house. Put it up to him.

SAM: Is that all right with you?

COMMISSIONER: I wash my hands of it.

MARY (*Pushing phone across piano*): This is for you, Commissioner—long distance from Washington.

COMMISSIONER: Oh, thank you, Mary. (HE *hurries to phone*)

MARY *goes to* KIRK *and* SAM.

MARY: Why aren't you boys out on the porch with the others?

SAM: We're talking over a little business here.

KIRK: A plan to raise some money.

COMMISSIONER (*Into phone—simultaneously*): Hello. . . . Yes. . . . Yes. . . . That's all taken care of. . . . Tonight. (COMMISSIONER *thinks over an idea*)

SAM: We'd like to meet this copper. Is he a friend of yours? . . . No offense.

MARY: Chance! This is Sad Sam and ex-jockey Kirk . . . my fiancé, Mr. Whitelaw.

KIRK: Your fian*say*?

THEY *shake hands and murmur greetings.*

COMMISSIONER (*Phone resting on piano*): Hold on a minute. (*Raising his voice to make sure* HE'*ll be heard on porch*) What! You mean I'll have to return to Washington immediately?

NORA *comes in to French window with concern.*

Well, that's bad news for me. . . . I'm having a wonderful time. . . . If he feels I should be there tomorrow I'll have to leave at once. . . . I'll explain when I see you. . . . Good-bye. (*Hangs up hastily*)

NORA: Commissioner, you don't have to go back to Washington tonight! You just got here!

COMMISSIONER: Isn't it a damn shame? I knew what the job was when I took it! I must tell Miss Smith to get my things ready. (*Starts off*)

NORA (*Heading him off*): Mary can do that. Mary! Tell Miss Smith the Commissioner wants to see her right away. She's in there playing bridge.

MARY: All right, Mother. (MARY *goes off*)

COMMISSIONER: I should see her myself.

NORA (*Taking him by arm*): Nonsense. We're so disappointed. You've got to spend every minute with us until it's time to go. (*Leads him to porch*) Boys! Clyde! The Commissioner has been called back to Washington.

POST (*Off*): That's too bad, Commissioner.

CHANCE *crosses toward alcove.* KIRK *and* SAM *surround him.* CHANCE *turns front in surprise.* KIRK *and* SAM *have backs to the audience.*

MRS. RYERSON (*Off*): Do you think you'll get back for any of the meeting?

On porch we hear the chatter of regrets.

KIRK (*To* CHANCE): Listen, pal, we got some business for you. You've got to make a collar.

CHANCE: I beg your pardon?

SAM: You gotta arrest a certain party.

CHANCE: What's the matter?

KIRK: You'll thank us when you hear about this. It's going to be a very important thing for you. You've got to put the arm on Remy Marko.

CHANCE: I don't quite understand what you mean?

SAM: We got evidence that Remy engineered that truck stick-up. All we want is for you to arrest him. We gotta have some justice around here. My money was in that stick-up.

KIRK: You get the credit and we get the reward.

CHANCE: Mr. Marko—in that? I can't believe it!

SAM: Do you know what was in that truck? Bookies' envelopes full of money. Do you see this—my envelope—my name on it—the same one that was in that truck. And where did we find it? Right here in this house.

KIRK: I saw it drop out of Remy's pocket.

SCHULTZ (*Off*): Well, I like to get to bed early up here.

MARKO: Don't go, Colonel! Don't break up the party.

CHANCE: Oh, that's terrible! Why, I don't . . .

MISS SMITH comes in from porch. SAM *sees her and touches* CHANCE's *arm.*

KIRK (*Finger to lips*): Tape!

COMMISSIONER *goes to meet* MISS SMITH. HE *sees* CHANCE *in conference with* KIRK *and* SAM.

MISS SMITH: Yes, sir! (*Puts on glasses*)

COMMISSIONER (*To* MISS SMITH): Just a minute. (HE *crosses to other group and addresses* CHANCE) Young man, I happen to know what these gentlemen are asking you to do. If anyone ever inquires as to my attitude in this matter it is this: I told you to do your duty.

Walks away. SAM *and* KIRK *unexpectedly push* CHANCE *forward toward him.* CHANCE *is brought up short as* COMMISSIONER *turns back.*

You don't have to hurry it, though. You don't have to rush into this. (*To* MISS SMITH) We've got to get out of here right away. Pack everything as soon as you can. Call a taxi. We don't want to use any of the cars belonging to this household. Make haste. (COMMISSIONER *goes out onto porch*)

MISS SMITH *goes to piano and phones quietly.*

CHANCE: I can't do what you're asking me to. I d-don't think Mr. Marko likes me.

SAM: What the hell has that got to do with it?

CHANCE: Mr. Marko seems a very impulsive man. I don't think I want to arrest him.

MISS SMITH (*Into phone*): Can you connect me with a taxi company? (*Talks quietly into phone*)

CHANCE (*In alcove, head in hands*): And besides, I'm engaged to his daughter.

KIRK: That makes it better for you. It's all right in the family.

CHANCE: I can't arrest the father of the girl I'm going to marry!

KIRK: Most fellows would be glad to put their father-in-laws in jail.

MISS SMITH *exits upstairs.*

SAM: Let's get down to cases. We've given you evidence. You're an officer of the law. You heard the Commissioner tell you to do your duty and you know who the Commissioner is. So get busy.

CHANCE: I suppose there's nothing else to do, but it's very embarrassing.

KIRK (*To* SAM): He ought to leave off that gun while he's doing it, don't you think?

SAM: Yes, he ain't got the sights filed down.

CHANCE: I should think I'd be safer with it.

SAM: Yeah? A deputy named Weinstein once had a gun when he tried to collar Remy, and Weinstein's still got dents in him.

KIRK: Remy's awfully funny about being arrested.

MARY *enters and goes to them.*

MARY: You boys been having a nice chat?

SAM: We chatted all right.

KIRK: We leave it to you, fella.

> KIRK *and* SAM *move away.*

LORETTA (*Off*): Hey, Sam, come here a minute, will ya?

SAM (*Off*): Sure! Excuse me.

MARY: What's the matter, Chance? You look unhappy.

CHANCE: I am. It seems I have to arrest your father.

MARY: What! What for?

CHANCE: He was mixed up in that truck holdup.

MARY: How dare you say such a thing? My father's an honest man now!

CHANCE: I'm awfully sorry, Mary, but I must perform my duty. You said yourself I should always do my duty.

MARY: Duty! Chance, do you believe my father had anything to do with that affair?

CHANCE: I've seen evidence.

MARY: Chance, do you believe my father had anything to do with that?

CHANCE: That isn't the question.

MARY: Then you do believe it. All right, Chance. Of course we're through.

CHANCE: Mary!

MARY (*Holding out her ring*): And I'll have to ask you to get out of the house.

CHANCE (*Ignoring her offer, has an idea*): I can't go till I've arrested your father.

MARY: Chance, let me give you some advice. Don't do it. . . . Don't do it alone, anyway. You better bring your whole state troop with you.

> *Enter* MARKO, *pretty mad.*

MARKO: Hey, young fella, I been looking for you. There's a thief in this house.

CHANCE: Where?

MARKO: You're a policeman. That's what you gotta find out. I've been robbed!

MARY: Father, what's missing?

MARKO: A big black bag full of important papers.

CHANCE: There's something else I'd like to talk to *you* about.

MARKO: We gotta find the rascal that stole my property. We got no time to talk about Mary.

MARY: We've broken our engagement, Dad.

MARKO (*Goes to hall door*): Broken the engagement? Good. Come on, Officer.

> WHITELAW *comes tearing downstairs in his pajamas.*

WHITELAW: Chancellor—Chancellor! Is this a madhouse? There's such a thing as carrying practical jokes too far.

> *People on porch come in the windows.*

MARKO (*Coming back in*): Is that fellow Ryan back bothering you?

MARY: What's the matter now, Mr. Whitelaw?

WHITELAW: I go to the closet to hang up my clothes and what do I find? Four of your friends sitting on the floor with guns.

LORETTA *drops on piano bench.*

KIRK: That ain't no joke.

CHANCE: Did they take a shot at you?

WHITELAW: No, but one of them aimed a gun at me and another shook his fist.

COMMISSIONER *enters from porch.*

COMMISSIONER: Remy, who are these men?

MARKO: How should I know? It's all news to me.

COMMISSIONER: Sam, give me the envelope.

SAM *does.*

Remy, this envelope was in the truck that was held up, and it was found here in this house. What do you know about it?

MARKO: I never saw it before in my life! Commissioner, you don't think I was in on that job, do you?

MARY: Some people here think you were.

NORA (*Entering from porch*): *Who* thinks he was?

MARKO: Does somebody want to get hurt? . . . Accusing me of a thing like that! I never stuck up a truck in my life! . . . A bookies' truck! I've been honest for quite a number of years and I wouldn't risk my reputation for all the money you could get in this room. Who mentioned Marko's name in this?

KIRK: Remy, it must be all a mistake about you. I guess those stick-up fellows just picked this house as a hideout.

RITTER: Do you think those men upstairs are the bandits?

WHITELAW (*Slumps, as* MARY *leads him to sofa*): Bandits!!

SINGER: They must be.

LORETTA: Let's get out of here. They're dangerous.

GUESTS *run out squealing, ad-libbing, etc.* COMMISSIONER *is the last one out.*

COMMISSIONER (*To* CHANCE): Young man, you're in charge; but you'd better get help.

CHANCE *goes to phone and calls.*

NORA: Remy, what do you make of this?

GIUSEPPE *enters followed by* MIKE *and* LEFTY. *Notices* WHITELAW *struggling to get up. Helps him up and to terrace door to get air.*

MARKO: Those parties are back.

NORA: Those same parties? How did they get back? Good God, we're ruined!

MARKO: Never mind now. Get outside with the others. Take Mary with you. We gotta think of what to do.

MARY *and* NORA *exit.*

CHANCE (*Into phone, wailing*): I want a policeman!

MARKO (*To* MIKE): You see what you done? You're so damn smart! You just got Marko into trouble—big trouble. Not only do I take the rap for the stick-up, but somebody stole the profits on me.

CHANCE (*Into phone*): Tell him to for God's sake hurry! (HE *hangs up*)

MARKO (*To* CHANCE): What the hell are you doing?

CHANCE: I called the police for reinforcements.

MARKO: We got trouble enough on our hands without reinforcements. I don't want any more cops around this place.

CHANCE doesn't answer, but takes out his gun and goes halfway upstairs, stands on guard.

What do you think you're doing?

CHANCE: I'm guarding this stairway.

LEFTY: He thinks they'd leave by the front door!

MIKE: Say, Boss, everybody thinks they're alive. Couldn't we shoot 'em all over again—before them cops get here?

MARKO: That ain't a bad idea! But we ain't got no guns.

MIKE: Borrow the cop's.

MARKO: Wait a minute. If we did that they might think we were crossing our own mob. I gotta better idea. (*To* CHANCE) Hey, young fella, come down here.

CHANCE: My place is on these stairs.

MARKO: COME DOWN HERE!

CHANCE comes down.

Do you want to make a big fella of yourself? . . . Walk right into that room and start blasting.

CHANCE: What?

GIUSEPPE, LEFTY *and* MIKE *in a huddle nearly convulsed during the following.*

MARKO: Those are the parties that committed that terrible crime and they're dangerous to be at large—especially to honest people. Now you're a copper—you wanted to be one—and this is your chance to become the biggest copper in the country all of a sudden. You go up to that room and order them to come out of that closet with their hands up—and if they don't—or even if they hesitate, start popping. Don't try to open the door or they'll shoot your ears off: they're *dead* shots!

CHANCE: I think it would be wiser to wait for reinforcements. We're instructed always to use our heads.

MARKO: Are you a cream puff? A coward? You're wearing the uniform of your country—your state, anyway—do you want people going around saying you disgraced it? And you a Whitelaw? Think of your father! Think of your grandfather!

MISS SMITH *comes downstairs with two suitcases and briefcase. Speaks blithely.*

MISS SMITH: Hello! Where's everybody? Where's the Commissioner?

MARKO: Probably in Albany by now. You better follow him.

MISS SMITH, *disconcerted, goes on out.*

CHANCE: I telephoned for the police. I think I ought to wait for them.

MARKO: No wonder Mary broke off with you. Do you think she'd marry a coward? And here's your chance to get her back. I know Mary. If you walk in there and grab those fellas, she'll be all over you. She loves people with moxie. I'll even withdraw my own knock against you. For Mary's sake, don't break my daughter's heart.

TAXI DRIVER'S *voice off.*

TAXI DRIVER (*Off*): Taxi?

MARKO: What?

TAXI DRIVER (*Off*): Somebody ordered a taxi.

MARKO: Get out of here and take your taxi with you.

TAXI DRIVER (*Off*): What?

MARKO (*Starting for him*): You heard me!

Sound of TAXI DRIVER *hurrying out.* MARKO *grabs* CHANCE.

Come on! I'll go with you! You're going to make a great rep tonight, young fella!

MARKO *starts leading* CHANCE *upstairs.*

CHANCE: You're hurting my arm. You're hurting my arm.

THEY *disappear.* MIKE, LEFTY *and* GIUSEPPE *move slowly toward stairway, looking at the ceiling. When* THEY *reach the foot of the stairs, five shots are heard.*

LEFTY: Well, he got 'em. They're gone.

INNOCENCE *enters with hands up. Then some running feet, then* CHANCE *tears down the stairs—into the room, faints and drops his gun.*

MIKE (*With* OTHERS *around him*): He's fainted. He must have been nervous.

LEFTY (*Picks up gun*): Say, shouldn't we take this gun and crease him up some to make him look good?

MIKE: Wait a minute.

Sirens heard in the distance. MARKO *comes downstairs carrying black bag.*

Say, Boss, where did you find the black bag?

MARKO: It was up in Whitelaw's room all the time. What d'ye think of that old burglar?

Throws bag to GIUSEPPE *who has been going over* INNOCENCE *for concealed weapons.*

Stash that bag upstairs in my room where no one can find it but you. (*Sees* CHANCE) What's the matter with this fella?

LEFTY: He folded up under the excitement.

MARKO: Say, this kid's got guts at that. He threw me off and walked in that room by himself. *I* wouldn't have gone in there alone. Not knowing them guys weren't already cooled off. He hollered at 'em to come out and when nobody come, he started blasting through the door. He hit it once, too—but the other shots ruined the chandelier. They ought to give those boys more target practice.

LEFTY (*Still kneeling*): Shouldn't we muss him up to make it look natural?

MARKO: No. I tossed those parties around the room. Anybody'd think there'd been a nice battle up there.

LEFTY *puts gun in* CHANCE'*s outstretched hand. The sirens grow very loud as they reach the house, then stop. We hear running of feet. Two motorcycle* POLICEMEN *come in with guns drawn.*

FIRST POLICEMAN: What is it?

SECOND POLICEMAN: What's going on?

LEFTY: It's all over now.

GUESTS *enter from terrace.*

MIKE: This fellow just got that stick-up mob.

LEFTY: They're upstairs.

MARKO: It's the greatest exhibition of nerve I ever saw.

SECOND POLICEMAN *runs upstairs.*

FIRST POLICEMAN: Did they get him?

MARKO: No, he ain't hurt bad. Got knocked out in the tussle.

FIRST POLICEMAN *goes upstairs followed by a few guests.* MARY *comes rushing in.*

MARY: Dad! Chance! (SHE *kneels beside* CHANCE. *Takes gun from his hand and lays it on sofa*)

GUESTS *come back with excitement and a little caution.*

COMMISSIONER: What happened? Did they get away?

MARKO: No, but they would of, but for the nerve of this young officer of the law. Most wonderful shooting I ever saw—and I've seen plenty. Commissioner, you ought to speak to the administration about this boy. He deserves some medals.

LEFTY *and* MIKE *calmly sit on sofa.* SINGER *comes running downstairs.*

SINGER: Hey, Remy, Remy!

FIRST POLICEMAN *comes downstairs shoving people ahead of him.*

FIRST POLICEMAN: Go on, get down there, get out of the way.

SINGER: Have you been up there yet? Do you know who these guys are?

MARKO: Yeah, I know.

KIRK: Who are they?

SINGER: Black Hat Gallagher, No Nose Cohen, Little Dutch and another guy.

KIRK: Little Dutch, Gallagher and Cohen!

SAM: Say, they must have been down here to get you, Remy.

NORA: Those dreadful men! My husband had trouble with them in the past.

SECOND POLICEMAN *comes downstairs.*

SINGER: Say, that explains them being here, Remy. They're just out of Trenton and they musta come here right away to get you and saw their chance to knock off the truck.

SAM: How about the money? Did you find the money?

MARKO: No sign of it.

KIRK: The fifth guy musta got away with it. He musta dropped that envelope going out this way. Wonder who he was?

MARKO *notices* INNOCENCE, *who still has his hands up.*

MARKO (*Knocking hands down*): What you scared of? It's all over.

FIRST POLICEMAN *at the phone.*

FIRST POLICEMAN (*In phone*): Hello. Give me headquarters. Send the coroner to— Huh? I got four stiffs here. . . . Oh! . . . Oh! (*Hangs up. To* SECOND POLICEMAN) The coroner's up at Lake Placid on a visit. We gotta let everything stand till tomorrow. (*To* GUESTS) Come on outside! Outside!

SECOND POLICEMAN: Everybody who doesn't belong here, outside!

NORA: Pete Ryan, what are you doing back in this house?

RYAN (*Entering from terrace*): It's all right. I never hold a grudge.

COMMISSIONER: Just a minute. This young man is entitled to ten thousand dollars reward for each one of those bandits—forty thousand dollars—and I'll see that his claim is properly taken care of.

WHITELAW: We Whitelaws do not accept rewards for duty performed. (HE *sneezes*)

KIRK: Why, the reward belongs to me! I found the envelope.

SAM: Why does it belong to you? I'm the one that identified it and told the Commissioner.

MARKO: So you're the guys that hollered copper on me, are you?

Chases SAM *and* KIRK *out to terrace.*

FIRST POLICEMAN (*Indicating* CHANCE): Get him out on the porch and give him some air. (*Ad-lib*)

CHANCE *rises.*

MARY (*Supporting him as* THEY *move toward alcove*): Are you all right, darling?

CHANCE: I'm all right.

MARY: I'm so proud of you.

CHANCE: Then everything is . . . ?

MARY: Don't ever leave me again. But if you think you're going on being a trooper, you're wrong. You don't know enough to keep out of danger.

Everyone exits except MARKO, WHITELAW *and* INNOCENCE.

MARKO: Hey, Whitelaw! We'll give these kids a wedding that'll make people sit up and take notice! Won't we?

WHITELAW: So you withdraw your objections to the police blood—er—er—(*sneezes*) in my family?

MARKO: Sure, as long as he quits making a business of it. Say, you're all right, too! I got a lot of respect for you. You didn't get away with it, but I respect you for trying.

WHITELAW *sneezes and exits to porch.*

INNOCENCE (*to* MARKO): I say, Governor, if they don't want the reward, I'll take it. I did in them four blokes myself.

MARKO: What? Who are you?

INNOCENCE: Innocence is the name, Governor. We stuck up that truck and then Black Hat insisted on our coming to this house—said he wanted to see a bloke named Marko.

MARKO: Oh, yeah?

INNOCENCE: After they got the money, they got greedy and decided they could save a share by getting rid of me. They was dealin' a poker hand to see who'd do it on me, but I nailed them first.

MARKO: So you're the guy! Say, that ain't bad.

INNOCENCE: I was waitin' till things quiet down and then I was goin' back after the money. But if I'm not goin' to get it, I ought at least to get the reward.

MARKO: Say, do you want to burn in the chair?

INNOCENCE (*Backing away*): I should say not.

MARKO: Then you better get out of here. Where you from?

INNOCENCE: Australia.

MARKO *reaches into his pocket and hands him a fistful of bills.*

MARKO: Here! Here's a coupla thousand.

Pushes INNOCENCE *out.*

You take the kitchen door back to Australia! And God bless you.

NORA (*Entering from terrace*): Remy, hand me my furs.

MARKO *quickly gets furs from porch and gives them to* NORA.

Mr. Whitelaw is catching cold in his pajamas.

POST *and* RITTER *enter.*

POST: We're running along, Remy, but congratulations. It looks as though you had a narrow escape from those men.

RITTER: Yes, congratulations.

MARKO: Well, it's too bad for you. If them fellas had 'a got me, you'd have had a two million dollar brewery for less than half a million.

RITTER: Well, remember, we still want that money.

MARKO: You'll get it tomorrow. What do you know about that?

POST: Now, Remy, stop bluffing.

POST and RITTER exit through window.

MARKO: I'm bluffing, am I? You'll get it!

NORA: Where are you going to raise that much money?

MARKO: It's all right; little Douglas arranged it for me. I told you he'd bring me good luck.

WHITELAW reenters, sneezing, and crosses to NORA, who puts furs around his neck.

NORA: Here you are, Mr. Whitelaw. I guess you're pretty proud of that boy of yours?

WHITELAW: He's a true Whitelaw. (*Sits on sofa*) We've always faced danger gallantly and unafraid.

MARKO (*To WHITELAW who has inadvertently picked up CHANCE's pistol*): Look, don't wave that gun, you might shoot the wrong fella.

WHITELAW (*Waving gun*): Why, we Whitelaws carried guns under Gates when we defeated Burgoyne on this very battlefield of Saratoga. (*WHITELAW sneezes, and gun goes off. WHITELAW falls back on the sofa in a faint*)

RYAN, who has been standing in door to porch, lets out a yelp, and hops in holding his foot.

RYAN: Hey! Who shot me?

MARKO: That's a pretty smart joke, eh, Pete? You'd ought to appreciate that one! Now it's time to go to bed, eh, Nora? We'll put Papa (*indicating WHITELAW*) to bed—get him another room for tonight—and tomorrow I'll fix things up with Ritter and Post.

NORA (*Concerned*): Remy, you're not going to use that money in the black bag?— Remy, are you?

MARKO: Sure I am.

NORA: Remy! That's crooked!

MARKO: All I got to do is show 'em a fistful of bills and offer to pay the note and they'll be glad to give me that extension. Why, they'll go down on their knees asking me to sell 'em stock in the brewery.

NORA: That's all right, Remy, but you can't keep the money—there's half a million in cash—

MARKO (*Taking her hand*): I'm giving back every nickel of it to the law soon's I show a little of it to my banker friends.

NORA: You mean, give it to Chance?

MARKO: Who else? Isn't that legitimate, eh? Say, this legitimate racket's not so bad after all, is it?

END OF PLAY

THE GHOST OF YANKEE DOODLE

A Tragedy

by

SIDNEY HOWARD

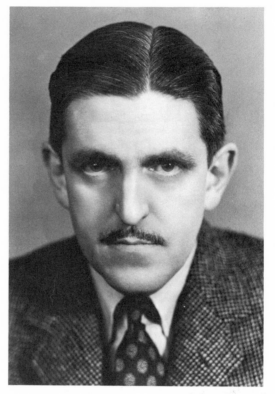

Sidney Howard

The play was first produced by the Theatre
Guild, and tried out in Rochester and Buffalo
before its formal opening at the Wilbur Theatre
in Boston on November 1, 1937. After two
weeks there, it moved on to the National
Theatre in Washington, D.C. for one week; it
then opened in New York City at the Guild
Theatre on November 22. The production was
directed by John Cromwell, with sets by Wood-
man Thompson.

*Sara Garrison (Ethel Barrymore) consoles Clevenger
(Dudley Digges) in the original production of* The Ghost
of Yankee Doodle.

The Original Cast

Sara Garrison . . . . Ethel Barrymore
John Garrison . . . . Frank Conroy
Patience Garrison . . . . Marilyn Erskine
Michael Garrison . . . . Jack Kelly
Senator Callory . . . . George Nash
Doris Garrison . . . . Kathleen Comegys
Roger Garrison . . . . John Drew Devereaux
Joan Garrison . . . . Barbara Robbins
Robert Garrison . . . . Eliot Cabot
Martin Holme . . . . Richard Carlson
Mary . . . . Ethel Intropidi
James Madison Clevenger . . . . Dudley Digges
Ockleford . . . . Don Costello
Steve Andrews . . . . Russell Hardie
Buck Anson . . . . Donald Black
A Police Sergeant . . . . Edward Butler
Policemen . . . . Arthur Davison and
                                                                                George Goss
Burke . . . . Lloyd Gough
Dr. Miller . . . . Howard Roberts

Place

The library of the home of the late John Garrison, now occupied by his widowed daughter-in-law, Mrs. Paul Garrison, in one of the older western American cities.

Time

Scene 1: The morning of Christmas Day.
Scene 2: Mid-afternoon of Christmas Day.
Scene 3: Just before Christmas dinner.
Scene 4: The morning of the day following.
Scene 5: Noon of the last day of the year.
Scene 6: New Year's Eve. After dinner.
Scene 7: New Year's Eve. Just before midnight.

In the original production an intermission of five minutes was placed after the first scene and an intermission of twelve minutes after the fourth scene.

210

Characters

(In order of appearance)

SARA GARRISON, formerly Sara Fithian, actress. Widow of the late Paul Garrison.

JOHN GARRISON, 45, her brother-in-law. Chairman of the Board of the Garrison Tool and Die Company.

PATIENCE GARRISON, 12, his daughter.

MICHAEL GARRISON, 10, his son.

THE HONORABLE EDWARD CALLORY, 75, banker and one-time United States senator.

DORIS GARRISON, 37, John's wife.

ROGER GARRISON, 19, Sara's son.

JOAN GARRISON, 21, Sara's daughter.

ROBERT GARRISON, 40, called "Rudi." John's brother. Publisher and editor of *The Morning Globe*.

MARTIN HOLME, 30, lately instructor in economics at a California university.

MARY, 28, the parlormaid.

JAMES MADISON CLEVENGER, newspaper publisher.

OCKLEFORD, 38, his secretary.

STEVE ANDREWS, 29, his illegitimate sone, now serving him as his pilot.

BUCK ANSON, 47, factory superintendent for Garrison Tool and Die.

A SERGEANT and two POLICEMEN.

BURKE, 26, a reporter.

DR. MILLER.

This play is dedicated to my mother and father, who raised an American family.

The Play

SCENE ONE

The library in the Garrison mansion. Christmas morning. The room stands almost exactly where it stood on the day when the last of Stanford White's decorators placed the finishing touch upon it and found it good. The walnut bookcases have lost none of their walnut solidity, and the tooled Cordoban leather—of both walls and chairs—has lost none of its depth and richness of texture. If carpets or hangings have been replaced, their replacements have been accomplished with truly archeological respect for the past. The room does also present a fairly comprehensive pictorial biography of the late John Garrison, to whose private requirements and idiosyncrasies it was dedicated. Steel engravings, mezzotints and photographs—there is just enough wall space free of books to permit a crowded display—include Thomas Jefferson, Abraham Lincoln (framed with an autographed letter), Grover Cleveland, William Jennings Bryan and Woodrow Wilson (also with autograph); and "The Last Spike" of the transcontinental railroad is being driven in oils over the mantel.

As to furniture, there is a large table desk and some of the chairs are large, too, particularly those with leather backs, and a sofa facing the fireplace is large.

One of the chairs, hereinafter referred to as "Sara's big chair," is placed so that it commands the room with the utmost comfort to its occupant.

As to doors and windows, there is only one group of the latter, and it is built into a bay, and there are two doors and both of them are double, heavy, and handsomely in keeping. One pair gives on the hallway. When this pair stands open it is possible to see, in the hall, a portion of the stair and, beneath the stair, the door

212

to the pantry. The second pair of doors gives on the parlor which, to judge from the glimpse afforded, was done at the same time as the library and in the style of the First Empire.

This visible corner of the parlor should be large enough to show the keyboard of a grand piano, placed against a window, with the right hand properly out.

There must be space in the hall and width on the stair to permit of some considerable playing in that part of the stage. The hall, furthermore, is furnished with a narrow hall table, long enough to take hats and overcoats when required to do so.

The season is observed by a fine Christmas tree—and it is a tree, too, and not one of those evergreen shrubs which serve as trees in city apartments—decorated with much more than oriental splendor. The gifts for an ample and present-giving family are piled beneath, the varied parcels all caparisoned in the gayest accessories of ribbon and cellophane. Fire glows in the fireplace and a heavy snow is falling on the garden out of doors.

Both doors are closed and the room is empty. Silence for a moment. Then, suddenly:

JOHN (*From the front door*): Merry Christmas, Sara!

Then voices unintelligible.

JOAN (*Nearer*): Mother! Mother! They've got here!

RUDI: By God if they haven't! Merry Christmas!

SARA (*Coming down the unseen stair*): Merry Christmas, John! Merry Christmas, Doris! *And* Patience! *And* Michael!!

Then a confusion of VOICES: *"Merry Christmas, Aunt Sara," from the* CHILDREN. *"How did you ever make it?" from* ROGER. *"We did get stuck once or twice!" from* DORIS. *"Take off your things at once!" from* SARA. *"Living in the country's no joke in this weather!" from* JOHN.

JOHN (*Clearly*): You haven't waited for me?

SARA: Of course we've waited! Have you had breakfast?

DORIS: We've had everything, Sara!

MICHAEL: Everything but our presents!

SARA: You shall have those at once, Michael. We'll go right in this minute and . . .

JOAN: We must have a march! A grand march in!

RUDI: A march? Just you leave that to me! They used to call me "the March King" even before Sousa . . .

A piano, from the parlor, now breaks into the refrain of "Over There" played very loudly and very incompetently. A chorus of protests puts an immediate stop to it.

VOICES: Uncle Rudi!
No!
Stop it this minute!
Not that!
That isn't for Christmas!

SARA (*Topping them*): Never mind the piano! We'll sing something and join hands and . . .

ROGER: You lead the choir, Mother!

And SARA *takes over with "God Rest Ye, Merry Gentlemen." Then, the* OTHERS *joining,* SHE *opens the door and the Garrison family circle invades the room.* SARA *first; then, holding her hand,* JOHN; *then, likewise hand in hand,* JOHN'S *children,* PATIENCE *and* MICHAEL; *then* SENATOR NED CALLORY *and* JOHN'S *wife,* DORIS, *and* SARA'S *son,* ROGER, *and his sister* JOAN, *and, finally,* RUDI.

SARA GARRISON *rejoices in a wise, humorous, human and humane fullness of beauty at its mature height and* SHE *exercises her own benign and balanced power, after her own indolent fashion, over all those who enjoy the agreeable experience of her influence.* SHE *is alight, now, with the excitement of this Christmas moment and her simple frock becomes her and the room almost equally.*

JOHN GARRISON, *the substantial member of the family, is in his late 40s, but apart from hair which will turn in spite of conscientious golf and healthful summer holidays, does not look it. His attitude towards life is apt to be easy and philosophical. His mood, at the moment, is serenely happy.*

PATIENCE *and* MICHAEL, *the two children, are just two children. Aged 12 and 10 respectively,* THEY *are neither more attractive nor less objectionable than other children of good family.* SENATOR CALLORY, *at 75, and still every inch the old guard Republican, has preserved a wondrously bright eye and prancing step.* DORIS *will always be the Southern belle God meant her to be and a delight to the eye, if not to the mind, in any company.* SHE *has retained her hat and fur neckpiece.* ROGER *is a personable young party of 19, probably a heart breaker in the society of his female contemporaries, certainly at his intellectual top on a tennis court.* JOAN, *his sister, seems at once somewhat more of a person.* SHE *is lovely and grave, has her own ideas, and a heart with real depths in it and* SHE *is thoroughly at peace with the world* SHE *knows because there has never been anything about that world to disturb her peace.*

RUDI GARRISON, *some years younger than* JOHN, *has taken less care of himself and worn less well.* HE *is keen, sardonic, lively and, one regrets to say, dissolute. All these things show in a hunted and irritable nervousness which is growing on him. Even his Christmas celebration has about it something cerebral and not wholly stable.*

The Christmas ritual consists in circling the tree to song. Only JOHN *and* JOAN *do clearly by the words. The others range from passable to frank la-la-la except* DORIS, *who smiles too brightly without making a sound. When the song is ended the circle breaks.*

MICHAEL: That's for me! I can tell by the shape.

RUDI: Shh, kids! Better wait till your Aunt Sara gives the signal.

JOAN: Always wait for the signal. It's good for your character.

PATIENCE: Oh, look at all the lovely hair ribbons!

JOHN (*Over this chatter*): There now, Doris! Wasn't that worth the drive in from the country?

DORIS: You can't give me too much Christmas ritual, John dear. It's the seamy side I object to. The wear and tear of shopping and . . .

ROGER: What is Christmas anyway, Aunt Doris? It's the festival of the Persian deity Mithra that the early Christians took over to cramp competition in the religion racket. And Christmas trees: what are they? Aboriginal, Teutonic fecundity charms!

RUDI: And that's anthropology 101!

JOAN: Somebody crown him with a wreath of holly!

DORIS: Really, Roger! After all the trouble your mother's gone to . . .!

But SARA *is laughing.*

SARA: Oh, you can't stop me on Christmas, Doris! I love it all: including the seamy side! The year has no climax to it with Christmas left out and the family that can't rise to Christmas is no family worth mentioning! But we must get down to business now.

MICHAEL: Presents?

SARA: In a jiffy, Michael. First we've all got to find ourselves chairs.

THEY *proceed loosely to obey,* DORIS *supervising the* CHILDREN.

JOHN: While your Aunt Sara reads aloud from *A Christmas Carol.*

SARA: There'll be no *Christmas Carol* this year!

Sensation.

DORIS: Sara!

JOAN: Mother! What's the matter?

ROGER: We love our *Christmas Carol*! We love our Dickens!

SARA: If you kids hadn't been right about Dickens, I should have left you both on a windy doorstep!

RUDI: My father will rise right up and haunt you if you go changing his Christmas routine on him!

SARA: We're having a Christmas sermon this year instead!

General alarm.

ROGER: Good Lord, Mother! Think what you're . . .! }
JOHN: A Christmas what? } (*Together*)

SARA: And Ned Callory's the preacher!

CALLORY: I, Sara?

SARA: You, Ned dear. It came to me trimming the tree last night. Roger and Joan were sticking that Star of Bethlehem there on the top. Those Woolworth stars all want to be comets. This is a solemn anniversary! It's Ned Callory's fiftieth Christmas with the Garrison family!

A general spontaneous rising.

DORIS: Now isn't that just wonderful!
ROGER: You must be a glutton for punish-
    ment, Senator!
                                       (Almost simultaneous)
JOHN: You're only beginning, you know!
JOAN: That does make this Christmas worth
    celebrating!
RUDI: Pioneers! O pioneers!
SARA: Don't embarrass him! Let him embarrass us! (SHE *sits in her big chair*)

CALLORY: I'll do what I can, Sara. But I'm blessed if I know how to begin a Christmas sermon!
JOHN: "To be honest, to be kind, to earn a little and to spend a little less . . ."
CALLORY: "O Pioneers" makes a better text for me. Fifty Christmases! Lord! You Garrisons have been generous!

A politely deprecatory murmur.

There was one of the fifty I came near to missing. '96, that was, the year of McKinley's election. (*This to* JOHN *or* RUDI, *and* HE *continues, addressing first one, then another of the company as his ideas turn him from one to another*) There I am out in that hall with my arms full of presents, listening to your father's voice. "You can tell Ned Callory we want no full dinner pails in the house this Christmas!"

The laughter of those who have heard this story before.

I've told that story before.
RUDI: Can't tell any family anecdote too often.
CALLORY: Well, there never was any sense to this family politically speaking. Why, I've heard Jim Hill go after your father till the sweat came out on Jim's neck and wilted his collar! And old John just grinning there in that chair of Sara's. And the vipers he took to his bosom! Single Taxers, the Populists, the Non-Partisan League! If he'd lived he'd have been a New Dealer sure as sin! How he could reconcile his ideas with the money he made! And the same for you coupon-cutting Socialists these days! Yes, I mean you, Rudi, with your pesky, trouble-fostering, labor-lopsided newspaper . . .

HE *puts such hate into this last adjective that* RUDI *cannot but bridle.*

And you, too, John Junior, emasculating your country's manliness with your Unions for Peace, and where have *they* got you?
DORIS: Good for you, Senator!

Protests from JOHN *and* RUDI.

CALLORY: I've affection enough for both of you as men, but I never could understand your carryings-on! The pair of you squandering the wealth your father left to you on the enemies of the system by which you live! Biting the hand that feeds you so you can feed the hand that bites you—that's what I'd call it! Liberalism, you call it, I know! Well, your father's to blame with the example he set you . . .!

JOHN *and* RUDI *are up and at him but* SARA *calls a halt.*

SARA: Children! Children! I know arguments are the Garrison family's weakness, but let's try to get through Christmas without one!

CALLORY: What's this got to do with Christmas anyway? (*And* HE *resumes*) There's another Christmas day this room won't forget. Old John's last one on earth. There was a world war then. There's a world war now. Only we were in that other war. I remember you two boys coming home from camp. Only your brother Paul was missing. What was it old John wrote in his diary? "Three generations of Garrisons at our tree this morning would have made this the richest Christmas I have ever known if only Paul could have got home from France." We didn't know then that Paul had been killed.

A general movement, accentuated by SARA'S *stillness, to indicate that the family could do with more tact on the preacher's part.*

And a fine lot of Christmas cheer my sermon's spreading! I can't help it! What is Christmas when all's said and done? It's a day set aside for families to get together and make sure that joy and grief balance each other. God love you, Sara, for holding this family together! Could you find such another gathering this day in England or France or Germany or Russia, or anywhere on that distracted continent? A family complete and no single member of it in peril after eighteen months of war? You paid your share last time when you lost Paul. A brother taken from you two, a husband from Sara, and from Sara's children a father whom Joan can't remember and Roger never knew. Praying's better than preaching in this house today. God give us the strength to see our troubles through and keep this nation and its families safe from this war and lead the world back into its suitable ways.

JOHN (*Low*): Amen to that, Senator.

CALLORY: My Christmas sermon! Lord! I've made you all sad.

SARA: You made us seem important and significant people instead of the thoroughly commonplace American family that we are! I liked that even though there's nothing in it! Who wants to be typical?

His reply is a warm hug.

JOHN: You said things we all wanted to hear. ⎫
RUDY (*Sourly dry*): Only we didn't know that ⎪
till we heard you say 'em. ⎪
ROGER: And I think it made a nice change ⎬ (*Almost simultaneous*)
from Tiny Tim. ⎪
DORIS (*Dominating*): Of course, Senator, I ⎪
find your patriotic convictions more ⎪
sympathetic than . . . ⎭

But SARA'S *hand is raised and* SHE *restores order.*

SARA: No! Wait! This *was* a solemn anniversary but the solemn part's over! You kids don't have to hold back any longer now!

The CHILDREN *rush to the tree.*

MICHAEL: Oh, boy, do I get what I wanted!

DORIS *follows to the tree.*

SARA: I've really been economical this year, John, and done all my grown-up shopping upstairs in the attic! In those old trunks marked "Sara Fithian, Theatre!"
PATIENCE (*Cutting in*): That's *my* pile!
DORIS: Children! Don't disgrace me!
SARA (*Continuing, to* JOHN): You'll see when you try looking grateful . . . (*And* SHE, *too, turns to the tree*) There's a pile for each!

MARY, *the parlor maid, enters with the mail and paper.*

MARY: They just got round with the paper, due to the snow . . .
JOHN: Oh, let's see the paper, will you, Mary?

SHE *surrenders it to* JOHN, *who opens it, the other men gathering around.*

MARY (*Continuing*): And the postman got stuck in the snow way down the street, so the mail just came, too.

JOHN *is immediately struck by something* HE *sees in the paper.*

SARA (*To* MARY): Just dump it there on the desk.

MARY *obeys and goes.* SARA *turns to* JOAN.

Don't you think we might get the maids' presents out to them?

And, as JOAN *bends to gather up the maids' presents:*

Oh, dear, I've forgotten the fundamentals! Where's my check book? (SHE *finds it in the desk. To* JOAN) Take 'em all out. Tell 'em the checks are coming.

JOAN *goes with the maids' gifts, returning presently.*

JOHN (*Intent on the paper*): What's all this, Rudi?

RUDI: That? Oh, that's our Christmas cartoon. Got to put something in the paper where the ads used to be!

CALLORY (*Inspecting over* JOHN'S *shoulder*): What's it signify?

RUDI: Well, it's a kind of a Christmas angle on the war. Here are the two teams. Germany, Italy and Japan. And France, England and Russia. Here's the American people. They're hard to draw. That's Santa Claus.

CALLORY: I recognized him.

JOHN: What are all those diplomas he's handing out?

RUDI: Can't you read? The blessings of isolation. Trade at your own risk. The usual crap. This big one's our National Honor. See? It's marked "Keep Me Home." That may be a little subtle.

CALLORY: Pity Santa Claus wouldn't hand out a few jobs and something to eat!

RUDI: Now would it be tactful to bring that up at Christmas?

ROGER *has joined the* MEN.

JOHN: Both your teams seem to be taking the holidays easy.

The MEN *concentrate on the news.*

ROGER (*Pointing*): So the French really did sink that freighter of ours?

RUDI: The *Farragut*, yes. That came through last night.

CALLORY (*Reading*): "Steamship *Farragut*. Bound for Athens, Greece, with a cargo of spark plugs . . . " (*And* HE *bursts out*) Athens is a neutral port in a neutral nation! It's a damned outrage and if we don't take a stand . . . !

RUDI: Aren't a good many cargoes clearing for Athens these days? Don't a good many stop over in Naples? Say "howdy" to Mussolini and just unload without meaning to? And don't the British and French know . . . ?

CALLORY: An American ship's an American ship!

RUDI: And contraband's contraband!

CALLORY: And trade's trade!

JOHN: We trade at our own risk in this war, Senator!

CALLORY: But I'm blest if I see why we can't trade in spark plugs! They're not munitions of war!

RUDI: Neither is cotton cloth. But cotton makes uniforms and you can't run a munitions truck without spark plugs, can you? Foreign trade's a fine thing, I know, and business can't do without it, but we're not taking chances on war just to earn money for you businessmen and . . .

CALLORY: How many American flags have they sent to the bottom? How many young American sailor boys . . . !

RUDI: We're not bringing that up on Christmas either.

SARA (*From the depths of her check book*): Children!

CALLORY: Neutrality!

JOHN: That's it, Senator! (*And* HE *explains himself with complete good humor*) We're not satisfied with the way things are going, either. We're not just Christian pacifists, you know. Till the nations can learn how to behave themselves, though, neutrality's cheaper than any alternative. As somebody said: Life is the only wealth.

ROGER: John Ruskin said it.

CALLORY: He was a liberal, too. And he lived on the proceeds of the liquor business!

RUDI: Liberals! You hate the breed, don't you, Senator? (HE *takes* CALLORY's *arm*) You haven't made your annual eggnog yet.

THEY *go into the pantry.*

JOHN: Sit down, Roger. I haven't had a good look at you since you got home.

THEY *sit.*

How are you boys taking this war back at Harvard?

ROGER: We take it or leave it alone. You know, Uncle John.

JOHN: No, I don't know! First year of the last war was my last at law school. Heard nothing but war talk around Harvard then. Boys running off to put on uniforms and drive ambulances and . . .

ROGER: Didn't you know that undergraduates are more enlightened now than they were in your day?

JOHN: I'm delighted to hear it.

ROGER: Oh, they are! We give the question a lot of time and thought. And I'll tell you what we've concluded, Uncle John. This isn't like your war.

JOHN: My war?

ROGER: You know what I mean. No martyred Belgium or *Lusitania* this time. They were great stuff! Made you boys want to fight! (*But* HE *sees a dangerous glint in* JOHN's *eye and quickly remembers to speak his piece*) Oh, I know! What did we get out of it but Allies' debts and the soldiers' bonus! And this war's between Hitler and Karl Marx and those of us who've no use for either of 'em hope it ends with both of 'em out of business, and let's us, for God's sake, stay clear of it! I agree with you, Uncle John! That's how the rest of the country feels too, I expect.

JOHN: I hope it is. I believe it is.

But ROGER *cannot quite control natural emotions.*

ROGER: This ship *Farragut*, though! She's the seventh they've sunk since college began! I've counted, Uncle John!

JOHN: Only you can't say "they," Rog. The Germans got the last one. And the British the one before that and the Japs and Italians . . .

ROGER: I wish the French hadn't got the *Farragut!* I wish it didn't ever have to be France or England!

JOHN (*Not as immune as* HE *would like to be*): So do I, Rog. So do I. But war's war. And we have to watch our sympathies. Because our real responsibility's keeping this country out. I thank God France and England are holding their own. If they weren't it might be harder to keep out.

ROGER (*A bit wistful*): And you think it would be wrong to go over and drive ambulances again, with the real will to peace that this country's got?

JOHN: The *will* to peace. That's the main thing, Rog!

DORIS, overhearing, has drawn near.

DORIS: Isn't it just too awful for John to have a patriot wife, who just hates hearing him talk that way to a young boy and he knows I hate it and if he'd only get over this idea of being his brother's keeper . . .

SARA: People who use that quotation, Doris, never seem to remember that Cain had just murdered Abel when he said it.

SARA rises, handing her checks to JOAN, who takes them out.

DORIS: John knows what I mean and Roger does, too, and coming as I do from a whole family of Confederate veterans, it just makes my blood boil to see France and England fighting democracy's battle! They're France and England! Oh, I know you're going to throw Russia at me because she's fighting with them! I can't help that! I remember Kitchener's Mob and the old Lafayette Escadrille, so I'm willing to overlook Russia!

JOHN: Do you want us to fight the French? They just sank the *Farragut*!

DORIS: They wouldn't have sunk her if we'd been in on their side!

JOHN: Oh, Doris!

DORIS: They're our old allies!

Her eyes blaze defiance. But CALLORY enters from the pantry at this moment carrying a tray covered with eggnog cups.

CALLORY: It's a beautiful eggnog, Sara!

RUDI follows him in, carrying the bowl.

RUDI: Oh, it's perfection! Where do you want me to put it before I drop it?

SARA: Don't you think it might be less crowded in the parlor?

RUDI is carrying his burden across to the parlor door.

We want some perspective on it.

RUDI: She's slipping! She's slipping! Lend a hand with a table, John!

JOHN hastens into the parlor, reappearing at once with a small table which HE places just inside the door. RUDI sets the bowl upon it and CALLORY the tray of cups. ROGER would go to help but DORIS takes his arm.

DORIS: I recall so well the day my father took his regiment to France in the last war . . . (*Her voice rises to hold ROGER's attention*) "That nation," he said, "that nation which lets slip . . . " (*But SHE must defer to SARA at this point*)

JOHN: There!

RUDI: Thank God. (*As the bowl is settled*) Now, Sara . . . (*HE is filling cups*) I shall . . .

SARA: You don't think it's too early to start drinking eggnog?

CALLORY: How could it be?

SARA: Well, you know how you feel when you start too early!

But none of the MEN *remembers feeling bad.*

DORIS (*Takes advantage of the silence around the punchbowl*): " . . . lets slip its opportunity to make the supreme sacrifice for its honor . . . "

SARA: The most awful condition sets in about three in the afternoon!

CALLORY: It's nothing! I've had it for years!

ROGER (*Simultaneously*): Wouldn't you like some eggnog, Aunt Doris?

The eggnog is tasted and approved with a long "AHHH!"

DORIS (*Forte and furious*): No! I would not!

Sensation.

CALLORY: God bless my soul!

DORIS: What's the use of my being in this house at all if nobody listens to what I've got to say?

SARA: Doris, I'm sorry. (SHE *comes back into the library*)

DORIS: I was saying something to Roger for Roger's good!

ROGER *backs away, frightened.*

But it doesn't agree with what you Garrisons think and you never listen to anyone but yourselves!

JOHN: Doris, please!

DORIS: Oh, you can take Sara's side but you know it's the truth!

SARA (*Low to* ROGER): Get the kids out, can you?

ROGER *proceeds to move* PATIENCE *and* MICHAEL—*with presents*—*into the parlor. As part of this transfer, phrases are dimly audible: "Come on, kids, into the parlor." "Why?" "Don't you like wrecking parlors?" But* DORIS *continues over them.*

DORIS (*To* SARA): Sometimes I wish your Garrison Tool and Die Works would just blow up! (*Then, to* JOHN) So you wouldn't be able to afford to waste all your time on stupid old meetings for peace, and committees for civil liberties, whatever they are! (*And* SHE *switches to* RUDI) And so you'd have to get out a nice successful paper that decent people could read without being upset! What good does all your fussing and fuming do?

RUDI (*Dismayed good humor*): I wish I could tell you, Doris, but I can't. (*And to the* OTHERS) Doris has the might of numbers on her side so she can afford to be magnanimous to us. You know what the giant said when his wife beat him: "It amuses her," he said, "and it doesn't hurt me, so why not?" You're all right, Doris! (*His arm goes around her waist in spite of her irritable resistance*) And I'm going to give you a special Christmas present of a subscription to

Mr. James Madison Clevenger's *Morning Eagle*, which ought to be hundred percent enough even for you!

CALLORY: Hundred percent or not, Mr. Clevenger's *Eagle* pays its own way, Rudi.

JOHN (*To* ROGER): This time we're really off!

SARA (*A low protest*): Please! Please!

RUDI's *smile continues, but his teeth are bare.*

RUDI: Oh, she'll have the best of the bargain, Senator! Mr. Clevenger's *Eagle's* a much better paper than mine, with lovely features I couldn't dream of affording, because Mr. Clevenger gets out so many papers in so many towns and I've only got my own here!

DORIS: I accept your offer, Rudi! I shall enjoy . . .

ROGER: Aunt Doris! Why, we don't even let the cook take the *Eagle!*

RUDI: That doesn't matter, Rog. The senator takes it!

CALLORY: Yes, Rudi, I do!

RUDI: I knew it!

JOHN *is laughing.*

SARA (*A wail*): Children! Christmas!

CALLORY: Because Mr. Clevenger's papers remain the last bulwark we conservatives have against you so-called . . .

RUDI: Oh, there's no name too low for the *Eagle* to call the Garrison brothers! Why, if she believes the *Eagle*—and she will believe it—we feed on the flesh of democracy's daughters that we roast over fires of burning constitutions! (*And* HE *swings savagely on* CALLORY) You think it isn't pretty of me to run a liberal newspaper on what I get from a conservative business! Maybe you know how to make enlightenment pay in the world we live in! We're going to start Christmas over at this point. Go out and come in again on a new foot. Roger, take your Aunt Doris in to the eggnog and get her stinking.

General delighted relief.

DORIS: I don't see what I've said to provoke . . .

ROGER *is already pushing her towards the parlor door. But* MARTIN HOLME—*hat and overcoat—appears in the hall.* HE *is a serious, stocky, sensitive young man of thirty, careless about his dress, travel-worn at the moment, easily at home in the present company.*

MARTIN: Merry Christmas. May I come in?

SARA: Martin!

JOHN: Well, if it isn't the professor!

RUDI: It can't be!

ROGER: It is! } (*Almost simultaneous*)

SARA: I don't believe it! I don't believe it!

MARTIN: It's true.

HE *enters the room to kiss* SARA's *proffered cheek.*

SARA: You can't have come all the way from Los Angeles?
MARTIN: Well, I started from there and I'm here now . . .
SARA: Joan! Where are you, Joan? Here's your young man come home!

JOAN *returns from the pantry.*

JOAN: Martin! Dear Martin!

SHE *is folded in his arms.*

MARTIN: Glad to see me?
JOAN: Yes, very!
MARTIN: Good! I'm glad to see you.
RUDI (*Handshake*): You must be feeling rich.
MARTIN: Not so rich as reckless.
ROGER: Fly?
MARTIN: No. Train. Eight hours late. Snow.

And HE *is shaking* JOHN's *hand.*

ROGER: That's not so reckless. You should have flown.
MARTIN: I wanted to think. Can't think in airplanes. Now I'm here I feel giddy.
JOHN: Well, well. . . .

HE *seats* MARTIN *on the sofa.*

Rog! Get this man some eggnog!
MARTIN: On an empty stomach? I forgot about breakfast this morning.

THEY *are all around him.* JOAN *sits on the sofa beside him.*

JOHN: If thinking ruins your appetite you'd better give up the academic life.
MARTIN: I have.

The family stops astonished, but HE *goes quickly on.*

And I forgot to wire I was coming. Forgot everything but just getting here. Well, it's all as it should be. There's Senator Callory! Merry Christmas, Senator.
RUDI: You remember Joan's young man, Senator?

HE *does. But* SARA *and* JOAN *are both looking closely at* MARTIN.

JOAN: You haven't been ill, have you, Martin?
MARTIN: Ill? No. Why?
SARA: Well, aren't you in just a bit of a state or something?

MARTIN: You don't know how it feels to escape from Los Angeles.

SARA: Oh, don't I?

JOHN: What did you mean, though, by saying you'd given up the academic life?

MARTIN: Just that. Aren't you glad you won't have to be a professor's wife, Joan?

JOAN (*Bewildered*): Well, I don't know.

A general exchange of glances.

SARA: When did you reach this decision, Martin?

MARTIN: It couldn't have been very long after they fired me.

Sensation.

JOAN: Who fired you?

MARTIN: The university did the actual firing. (HE *is on his feet again and moving about uncomfortably*) Now, I didn't want that to sound solemn. That's what I've been thinking hardest about. How to make it sound casual, you know, and . . .

SARA: But they couldn't have fired you!

MARTIN: They did. The bounced me right out on my ear.

JOAN: Just like that?

RUDI: What for?

MARTIN: It's so hard to say without sounding solemn. (HE *stops himself in distressful embarrassment, then*) But I just don't know how to teach present-day economics without some mention of the late Karl Marx. So I came right out and spoke that four-letter word to a lot of our American boys and girls. And that was enough. Now John Haynes Holmes and Rabbi Wise'll hear about it and . . . (HE *shudders*)

JOHN: Do you mean to tell me that a university . . .

RUDI: Well, a Los Angeles university . . . ⎫

ROGER: That wouldn't have happened at ⎬ (*Together*)
Harvard. ⎭

SARA *sits.*

MARTIN: Oh, you can't blame the university! After all, when the Clevenger papers get after a man . . .

RUDI: What's that?

ROGER: The Clevenger papers!

JOHN: It isn't true!

MARTIN: Get this last month's file of his *Los Angeles Eagle* if you don't believe me and see what a beating Mr. Clevenger gave me! They had to fire me! They couldn't do any less! Don't let it spoil Christmas, though. I came here to get cheered up.

RUDI: You haven't spoiled Christmas for me! I'll cheer you up! Come into the parlor and I'll give you an eggnog bath!

HE *goes into the parlor. The others, except* SARA *and* CALLORY, *are following him.*

JOHN: Of course it's quite characteristic of Clevenger ...

DORIS: I'm sorry for Martin! But I don't see why he had to teach such ...

ROGER: Wouldn't he like some solid food with his eggnog?

The voices die out in the parlor. JOAN *has linked her arm through* MARTIN'S.

JOAN: All the presents we sent out to you! You never got them!

MARTIN *looks at her.*

MARTIN: I'm spending Christmas with you. That's enough for me.

SHE *smiles up at him. Then, as* THEY *begin walking.*

How does your Christmas thing of Milton's go? You know ...?

JOAN (SHE *remembers*): "The shepherds on the lawn
      Or e'er the point of dawn
      Sat simply chatting in a rustic row ..."

MARTIN: I get you ...
"Perhaps their loves or else their sheep
Was all that did their silly thoughts so busy keep ..."
It's the ending I like, though.

JOAN: "But, see, the Virgin blest
      That laid her Babe to rest ...
      And all about the courtly stable
      Bright harnessed angels sit in order serviceable."

THEY *have gone into the parlor.*

SARA: Families are work. They're like farms. You have to work 'em to keep 'em.

CALLORY: The family's a mirror. One of those old-fashioned, bull's-eye, convex mirrors that reflects a whole room reduced and concentrated. You can see all civilization in the family. You can see what's wrong with the world.

SHE *smiles. Her hands go out to him.*

I love you, Sara. (HE *bends over her hands in the most courtly fashion*)

SARA: You can't leave without your present from me.

CALLORY: Do I get a present from you?

SARA: You get a walking stick. (SHE *has gone to the Christmas tree for a silver-capped walking stick*) Not that you haven't fifty others already, but this one's rather special. Because it's descended from Paul's and my honeymoon in the Southwest, from the desert and sandstone and the wide, dry rivers Paul loved, from an Indian pueblo where the chief was a friend of Paul's, and this was his wand of office from Abraham Lincoln. You can see the signature. "A. Lincoln," engraved here on the top. And that's because, back in the Civil

War—families were splitting on an issue then—the Confederates tried making Indian trouble for Lincoln. And Lincoln sent these walking sticks, one to each chief, like a feudal king swearing vassals to loyalty. And the tribes didn't make trouble and the chiefs still hand their staffs on to their successors. . . . One day, long after Paul's death, this came through the mail. There weren't any more Indians left in that pueblo. I like to think that Lincoln would have given the Indians a more generous deal than the senators of your generation gave them, dear Ned. (SHE *holds the walking stick out to him*)

CALLORY (*Much moved*): Are you sure you want me to have this?

SARA (SHE *smiles*): It's pioneer stock! It's old American!

CALLORY: If I'd had it in time it would have walked me straight into the White House!

SARA: In whose place?

CALLORY: Harding's. Thank you and God bless you, Sara.

HE *goes into the hall.* JOHN *and* RUDI *have appeared at the eggnog bowl.*

SARA: Now I'm started on this . . . (SHE *turns back to the Christmas tree for two more parcels, one a book, the other a framed picture*) John, my dear brother-in-law, and much better than any brother I've known about, will you accept this treasure I'd forgotten I owned? It's the very rare, very first edition of *Huckleberry Finn*, with the accidentally dirty picture in it that got it suppressed when it first came out, and that makes it what's called a collector's item, though I can't find any picture we'd call dirty now! Your father gave it to me on my first Christmas here. To make up for the row he raised when Paul married an actress. I'd told him how Mark Twain wanted me to play Joan of Arc, and you know how your father worshipped Mark Twain.

JOHN (*Unaccountably troubled*): You shouldn't be giving your treasures away now, Sara!

SARA: But I believe in passing the past along and making it somebody else's future! (*Then, to* RUDI) I want you, Rudi, as the companion of my baser nature—don't misunderstand me, John, will you?—to have George Bellows's report on the immortal wallop Firpo handed Dempsey. I used to creep round with this print at night and hold it up to the walls and say to myself: "My God, what a sock that was!" But these walls never seemed to do Bellows justice! Here it is, Rudi dear, in memory of the journey we made to see Schmeling knock out Joe Louis. (SHE *is suddenly angry*) And how he knocked him out! And how he should have had his crack at Braddock! (*Then*) Come in here, Joan, and get your Christmas present!

JOAN *enters to meet the large box* SARA *is holding out to her.*

JOAN: From you, Mother?

SARA: Oh, very much from me!

JOAN *drops to her knees and tears the box open.*

From the very gizzard of the old theatre trunk in the attic!

JOAN (*Pointing to the label*): From Jaeckel!

SARA: It came from Jaeckel a great many years ago, and it's just been back there having its face lifted.

JOAN *sits back on her heels to display a most beautiful evening coat of ermine.*

JOAN: Mother!

SARA: I don't want to be thanked! I've never felt right about that piece of goods. A man gave it to me once as the price of my virtue. I kept the virtue but didn't send back the coat. Let's see if it suits you.

JOAN *is on her feet and into the coat.*

Yes, I think it does. It makes you look less like a lover of poetry. Now, go dazzle Martin and Rog.

JOAN (SHE *runs into the parlor, calling*): Martin! Rog! Aunt Doris! Look at what mother's given me for . . .

Confused exclamations from those called upon.

DORIS (*Off*): Joan, how beautiful!

JOAN (*Off*): Mother gave it to me! It's an old one of hers made over!

ROGER (*Off*): Let's go right out to a party! I wouldn't mind taking my sister out in that!

MARTIN (*Off*): It's not ermine, is it?

SARA: I like my daughter, if she is a bit serious. I like Martin, too, and they'll live a perfectly rapturous life together, never seeing the funny side of anything. (SHE *is back in her big chair again*) Only we've got to pull the boy over this brutal deal Mr. Clevenger's given him. We can't just leave him to join the persecuted professor's club. Bring me some eggnog, Rudi, and we'll think what to do.

RUDI *fills two cups of eggnog at the bowl.*

Martin needs two things: a wife and a job. The wife's all fixed.

RUDI *delivers one cup to* SARA *and offers the other to* JOHN. JOHN *refuses.* RUDI *sits, sipping it himself.*

And there shouldn't be any trouble about the job. One has to find room for family in a family business. What else is a family business for except to live on?

JOHN: Oh, I see your point, Sara.

SARA (*To* RUDI): I'm not getting the encouragement I expected. Rudi, you'll have to make room for him on the *Globe*. And I'll build them a little home. Out in one of those new "developments" where young couples start life in old

English bird houses. House, lot and furniture: what should that come to, John? Don't scream, I shan't need it all at once.

JOHN (*Mournfully humorous*): The question isn't getting it all at once. Do you get it at all?

SARA: Now, John!

JOHN: The concept of free will, Sara, has been fun to philosophers for centuries and in times of peace we're allowed to enjoy the illusion.

SARA: Where's your toga, John? Don't tell me it's gone to the wash?

JOHN (*Good humor unshaken*): You *are* reckoning without Hitler and Mussolini, Sara. And now that those two paranoiac playboys have seen fit to wash the world in blood for despair of their prestige as dictators, all of these private things that mean so much to us and so little to anyone else are conditioned . . .

SARA (*Really vexed*): Oh, it's too bad of you on Christmas, John! I won't listen! (SHE *rises*) I won't listen!

JOHN: You've got to listen.

SHE *turns annoyed.*

I'd intended keeping my counsel till Christmas was over. I know you once you get an idea, though. And I know how Rudi always aids and abets you. So I'm compelled to put a simple choice up to you both. Between saving our extremely serviceable family business and letting it go to the wall. If it does that, of course, your plans haven't much chance of . . .

RUDI (*On his feet, thunderstruck*): Holy God!

JOHN: There's nothing so startling in that possibility these days, is there? After all, Garrison Tool and Die's no . . .

SARA (*Sits, deeply shocked*): But you can't let it go to the wall! It's your father's business that he built up and left to you to look after!

JOHN: This neutrality's turned out more costly than we expected. Even those of us who are most wholeheartedly for it. A good many concerns have collapsed in the eighteen months since this war began. In the last week two of our most valued customers. Both of 'em leaving large, undelivered orders for us to dispose of. And yesterday, while we were still groggy from that blow, a third valued customer cancelled a third large order, with the friendly advice to sue if we want to and good luck to our suit. We needed those three, because we haven't any others worth mentioning. And because we happen to have a note coming due the 15th of January. A big note, for a modest company. With interest, seven hundred and thirty odd thousand dollars. The prospects of meeting it are a bit complicated.

A pause, then suddenly a burst of laughter from the parlor and, on SARA's *signal,* RUDI *closes the parlor doors.*

SARA: You have to go very slowly and be very clear when you're talking business with me, John.

RUDI: Strikes me you've had your nerve to keep this to yourself!

JOHN: It's all happened pretty fast. You fight fans might call me a trifle punch-drunk.

SARA: What's it likely to mean?

RUDI: That we'll be in receivers' hands ourselves in about three weeks!

JOHN (*Maintaining his smiling calm*): It's true that we've no funds. It's true that our creditors won't give us any more time . . .

But SARA *laughs at this idea.*

SARA: How ridiculous, John! Creditors always give time! Do you think an old actress doesn't know about creditors?

JOHN: My dear Sara, these aren't the type of creditors you remember. They're the Pioneer National Bank.

SARA: That's Ned Callory's bank!

RUDI: That won't make any difference.

SARA: Don't be silly! You let me talk to Ned and . . .

JOHN (*Quickly*): That you mustn't do, Sara! I'm sorry, but you really mustn't.

RUDI: It would only embarrass the senator.

SARA: But he was here, singing around our tree this morning! (*Then*) Did he know all the time that we . . . that he . . .?

JOHN: I expect he wanted to spare Christmas, too.

RUDI: Holy God! (HE *sits again*)

A pause, then:

SARA: There was a time—wasn't there?—when the state of the world was something to read about and discuss in the village tavern? And when wars came, countries really could keep to themselves and families were secure to go their ways? Or was there ever such a time? Was that just another of our ancestors' delusions?

JOHN: I'm not as desperate as I might be. And that's because . . . (*A deep breath, then*) Because the Italian Government's prepared to take these cancelled orders off our hands. For considerably more than we should have realized on the original contracts.

RUDI *looks up sharply.*

We seem to have made precisely what they need.

RUDI *is on his feet again.*

RUDI: Well, I'll be goddamned! You, chasing war profits! You, with your convictions!

JOHN *winces but manages to maintain self-control.*

JOHN (*Crescendo*): What else can I do with no orders at home?

RUDI: What else? Anything else!

JOHN: Shut down? Throw the men out of work? When you've got a business to run, you can't let go your hold on it! It won't let go its hold on you!

RUDI: But we're not permitted to sell our wares to belligerents! They're contraband!

JOHN (*Really uncomfortable over what* HE *has next to say*): It appears the legal side can be got 'round. The sale would be made to some Greek or Guatemalan or other irreproachable neutral in New York and the shipment cleared for some irreproachable neutral port . . .

RUDI: Oho! Another *Farragut!*

JOHN: If the ship's destination's changed later by radio, we've nothing to do with that.

RUDI: Nothing except some pretty cagey conniving!

SARA: Rudi!

JOHN (HE *strikes back at last*): I've kept Sara's house and your *Globe* going through these bad times without laying off a single man or cutting a penny of union wages! I knew last summer we'd have to come to this, though I've held off till I couldn't borrow another dime, praying those armies in Europe would mutiny or their peoples revolt! Well, they haven't done either and I can't hold off any longer! There's your choice! Between salvation at a price we hate like hell to pay and shutting up shop!

SARA *rises suddenly and* HE *breaks off.*

There are firms with nerve that have taken the chance already. It's just one of the penalties of property, that's all.

RUDI: If you're not ashamed of yourself, I'm ashamed for you!

JOHN: I've learned an important lesson these last four days: that we liberals have to live in two opposite worlds. Our beliefs in one, our experience in the other.

RUDI: That sentiment sounds like an *Eagle* editorial signed by Clevenger himself.

JOHN: So? Well, speaking of newspapers, you have to think of how you'll feel about giving up the income that pays *The Globe*'s deficits.

This scores a hit on RUDI.

As for Sara's plans and responsibilities . . .

SARA: You can't hide behind me! I won't have that! I vote no. And without the slightest.hesitation. I won't build that house for Joan! They can move in here! It'll be much better than living in an apartment and going to bed in an elevator.

JOHN: Try to understand, Sara.

SARA: Is there more?

JOHN: You won't have any income at all. Not a penny. There won't be any more business. You'll be absolutely cleaned out. So will Joan and Roger. It's the end of everything. Including this house.

A pause.

SARA: I've loved this house. (*Her head turns slowly as her eyes range the room*)

RUDI (*Almost to himself*): Because we obey the law and live up to our principles . . . (*And* HE *turns to* SARA *in a plea almost of despair*) But self-preservation! That's a kind of principle, too! What's anything but a compromise with what should be? Father bought me *The Globe!* I've made it the best liberal paper in the country! I can't let it go!

JOHN: You don't have to apologize, Rudi. I've got my old law practice to fall back on so I'm the one with the least to lose. Whereas you and Sara . . .

But SARA *shakes her head.*

SARA: They must have some reason for making deals like this Italian thing illegal. I can only see how we'd feel if any deal of ours were to involve this peaceful country in war—I don't know how. I can only see that I've a son just at the fighting age whose father was killed in the last war. (SHE *smiles*) This isn't the first time I've seen notice put up on the call board.

RUDI: She's perfectly right, of course.

JOHN (*Heaves a sigh of relief*): Thank God she is.

SARA: I mean to see Christmas through now if it kills me. (SHE *turns back towards the parlor doors*) So I'll ask you not to speak about this to the others. Just for today. January 15th, you said? Well, there's oil enough to keep the oil burner going! (SHE *throws open the door*) I need a great deal more of that good eggnog!

But JOAN, *still in her ermine wrap, enters quickly and tensely, followed at once by* MARTIN, *in the same mood.*

There isn't anything else the matter?

MARY, *the parlor maid, enters.*

JOAN: Mr. Clevenger's here to see you, Mother.

This is a real sensation. ROGER *and* DORIS *enter.*

RUDI: Who? ! ! !

SARA: Did you say Mr. Clevenger, Joan?

MARY: Mr. James Madison Clevenger. I'm to say that he's come to wish you a Merry Christmas. You in particular, Mrs. Garrison.

ROGER: He's waiting in the hall.

RUDI: But what on earth's he doing in this town? The papers had him in Palm Beach for Christmas!

JOHN: What's he want with us? You ever meet him, Rudi?

RUDI: No! Nor do I feel the least desire to!

SARA: Mary, ask Mr. Clevenger to come in. ·

JOAN: Mother! . . . Just a minute, Mary! . . . Mother, you can't let that man into this house!

SARA: He seems to have got in already!

JOAN: Then send him word he's not welcome!

SARA: Please, Joan! He'll hear you!

JOAN: After what he's done to Martin, I want him to hear!

MARTIN: I never expected to meet him in this house!

RUDI: I'll be damned if I stay in the same room with him!

SARA: Rudi, please! Mr. Clevenger's coming in, of course. I hope we can keep him for lunch. After lunch is over, if it seems worthwhile, I'll throw him to the lions.

DORIS: *You* don't know Mr. Clevenger, do you, Sara?

SARA: Well, it's been a long time, but he still seems to feel some claim on my friendship. After all, he did give me an ermine coat. (*And* SHE *goes out into the parlor, calling off*) Where are you, Jim? Let's see you! Are you looking older?

The OTHERS *stare after her, stunned.*

End of Scene One

SCENE TWO

The room has been cleared of its Christmas litter. Only the tree remains to maintain the atmosphere. The fire glows in the grate. The snow is still falling. It is the afternoon of the same day. The doors to both hall and parlor are closed.

MR. JAMES MADISON CLEVENGER *sits on the sofa submitting to a massage treatment for stiff neck.* HE *is impressive and impudent, with an ample supply of romantic allure still at his disposal. His secretary,* OCKLEFORD, *who administers the massage, is a bright-eyed bruiser of forty, a bit of a gunman, a bit of a bouncer, but altogether a livewire.* HE *stands over and behind his chief and manipulates the neck muscles.* SARA, *still wearing the frock of the previous scene, sits quietly in her big chair.* RUDI *stands beside her. A cry of pain from* CLEVENGER.

OCKLEFORD: Now, it's all right, Chief. It's all right.

CLEVENGER: No, it isn't all right! A stiff neck's a damn painful thing!

OCKLEFORD: As Socrates said: Pleasure's so close to pain, if you go after one you're likely to get the other.

CLEVENGER: Where did you get that, Ockleford?

OCKLEFORD: Off some headache tablets an acquaintance of mine takes for sluggish liver.

CLEVENGER: Might make a good text for a Sunday page.

OCKLEFORD: Sounds pretty cynical to me for Sunday.

CLEVENGER: You may be right. Go on with your report.

OCKLEFORD: There's no more news of the *Farragut* sinking yet. I got through to the White House but the President's resting. They didn't want to disturb him. I wasn't sure you'd like being disturbed in here.

SARA'S *glance appeals for* RUDI'S *sympathy.* RUDI *gives no sign.*

He's up in the air and will be till you get there. I told 'em we're doing our best, only this isn't what's known as flying weather. Ceiling zero, visibility zero all the way to the Lakes. Ready, Chief?

CLEVENGER: Ready.

OCKLEFORD *bends for the grip on* CLEVENGER'S *neck which is the climax of all osteopathic treatment.*

OCKLEFORD: You're resisting me.

CLEVENGER: How can I help resisting when I know . . .

The jerk and the neck is cracked. CLEVENGER, *released, sits up and moves his head carefully.*

That feels better. Always been susceptible to stiff necks. (*Then, sentimentally*) You remember, Sara?

SARA: I'm afraid you concealed that side of your nature from me.

CLEVENGER: Yes, of course. I would have. A young man's vanity in physical fitness. Ah, well . . . (HE *rises*)

OCKLEFORD *hands him his collar.*

Unusual combination of talents Ockleford's got. First rate secretary. Downright genius at massage. Began his career with the six-day bicycle races. Came to me first as a bodyguard. Like two-in-one combinations. Makes fewer around me. The fewer the trustier. (*To* OCKLEFORD) Tie.

OCKLEFORD *delivers.* CLEVENGER *proceeds to put himself in order.*

We'll lay over tonight. And I'll accept your invitation to put me up, Sara. I didn't like that hotel. They don't keep their steam under control. (*To* RUDI) Send down for my bags, Garrison.

RUDI *starts to go, but* SARA's *hand stops him.*

Vest.

OCKLEFORD *delivers.*

Might be a bang-up feature in steam heat and how it's softening our national stamina. Call Curry in New York tomorrow morning. I want figures in Washington on what our American Radiator advertising's worth to us. Start calling at nine and tell me what time you reach him. (*To* SARA) Always try to keep track of when my executives get to their offices. (*To* OCKLEFORD) Coat.

OCKLEFORD *delivers.*

And I wish you'd get through to our boys in Rome and Paris. I want the real low-down on this *Farragut* business. (HE *stands frowning a moment, then, to* RUDI) What is it they call you? Rudi?
RUDI: That's right, Mr. Clevenger.
CLEVENGER: If your name's Robert, why don't they call you Bob?
RUDI: I couldn't say.
CLEVENGER: Was your name ever Rudolph?
RUDI: Never.
CLEVENGER: Damn peculiar. (*Then to* OCKLEFORD) That's all, Ockleford. (*Then to* RUDI, *as* OCKLEFORD *goes into the hall, closing the door after him*) That's all for you, too. I came here to renew old times with your sister-in-law. Don't you think her connections by marriage might give me a chance?

SARA's *hand is again out to stop* RUDI's *departure, but* RUDI *goes nonetheless and in a rage, closing the door after him.* CLEVENGER *continues meanwhile and regardless.*

(*To* SARA) Only fair to tell you I didn't enjoy my lunch. Who was that young fellow who wouldn't speak to me?

SARA (*Self-controlled*): Martin Holme is the son of a dispossessed farmer and the grandson of a pioneer friend of Rudi's father and I brought him up as an elder brother to Roger. Now he's going to marry my daughter Joan and I'm pleased about that because he's a very fine and very brilliant young man. With good reason for feeling coldly towards you.

CLEVENGER: Don't tell me about it. I only wanted to get the family straight. I've got the Booth Tarkington background: the fine old American house . . .

SARA *feels the hurt of that.*

. . . more than adequate income from a nice little family business. Call no man master, no, nor partner, even!

SARA *is on her feet.*

Did I hear you speak of entertaining tonight?

SARA: Haven't you heard about Christmas dinner on Christmas?

CLEVENGER: I suppose it's too late to call that off?

SARA: I don't want to call it off!

CLEVENGER: I only meant that it seems a pity to interrupt this reunion of ours with a lot of outsiders.

SARA: They're not outsiders to me! You can have your dinner alone in here if you want! Why did I let you into the house this morning?

CLEVENGER: To see what I'd be like after all these years.

SARA: You haven't changed much. You come hurtling across the continent in a plane and drop down out of a blizzard and for what? You've done nothing since you came but jump from bright object to bright object like a baboon!

CLEVENGER: That's my vitality that I'm famous for.

SARA: Vitality certainly is God's gift to lightweights!

CLEVENGER: Me?

SARA: I don't suppose anyone's ever called you a lightweight before! I was thinking of you, though, a few years ago in Milan in Italy. They were having a public dance competition and we went to pass the evening watching it, and the prize was won by a dapper, elderly Austrian nobleman. Winning dance prizes was his life's passion, he told us. His name was Von Berchtold. Do you remember his name?

CLEVENGER: He was the Austrian prime minister who wrote the ultimatum to Serbia and started that other war in 1914.

SARA: It's when one sees the leaders of millions like Von Berchtold and you that one's heart grows heavy for trusting humanity, Jim. I wish you'd go on to Washington and leave me in peace.

Blandly, HE *takes her arm and seats her on the sofa beside him.*

CLEVENGER: It's exactly what I knew it would be to see you again. Like Napoleon coming back to Josephine.

SARA: I shouldn't be good in the part. Need I say more?

CLEVENGER: You were in love with me once!

SARA: Don't I remember?

CLEVENGER: Well, I thought you would, but I didn't expect you to say so.

SARA: That's the past. I'm involved in the present now.

CLEVENGER: You don't fit in, Sara! This isn't for you!

SARA: You know I just might be the best judge of that.

CLEVENGER: It's not for you, Sara! It's not for you!

SARA: I've had both public triumphs and private peace. Enough of both to know which I like best.

CLEVENGER: I can't believe you! I don't want to believe you.

SARA: You've waited twenty years for your chance to patronize me and I shan't be petty enough to spoil your fun. Only you forget I was put on the stage before I was six and got my picture of life from the plays we played then. They were nice plays and about nice people who lived in big houses in peace and security.

This hurts again, but CLEVENGER *does not notice.*

CLEVENGER: Is that any excuse for living out here in the sticks?

SARA: You call it the sticks. I call it America.

CLEVENGER: That has the sound of civic-mindedness!

SARA: You should know I'm too lazy to be civic-minded. Except the symphony. I *do* work on that. I fall innocently in love with all the conductors and make them engage Rachmaninoff every season.

CLEVENGER: I remember your weakness for music.

SARA: You never shared it.

CLEVENGER: Oh, I don't know! (HE *clears his throat and performs*)
"And when I tell them
  How wonderful you are,
  They'll never believe me!
  They'll never believe me!"
(*Then*) You remember Julia Sanderson?

SARA: With the utmost affection and pleasure. For herself, though. Not because you paid for the tickets.

HE *is dashed.*

CLEVENGER: What have you done with your great gifts, Sara?

SARA: I've lived the life I wanted to live and liked it, and learned quite a few things you wouldn't know are important. How pleasant an evening alone can be, for example, with a long book and a great deal of coffee. That it's a great mistake to carry a watch, because no time matters except time to one's self. I've been singularly and completely contented here. (*Again the room and her troubles overcome her*)

CLEVENGER: Do you never regret what you gave up for this?

SARA: If I read that melting eye correctly, I do not regret you.

CLEVENGER: Why didn't you marry me, Sara?

SARA: Jim, how boring! You haven't thought of me for . . .

CLEVENGER: Now I've seen you again. . . . You're the only thing I've ever wanted that I couldn't get.

SARA: That's fairly cheap of you.

CLEVENGER: We *were* in love. Why didn't you marry me?

SARA: Well, if you must go digging into the past, you never asked me to marry you!

CLEVENGER (HE *is shocked*): You can't be right about that!

SARA: I am, though. The idea was to add my latchkey to quite a collection. I had my own waiting line at the box office then. I couldn't see myself standing in yours after the show.

CLEVENGER: But I did ask you, Sara! I remember!

SARA: The night I told you I was marrying Paul. I didn't count that. The gong had already gone.

CLEVENGER: You never cared for your husband as you did for me.

SARA (*Honest indignation*): That isn't true!

CLEVENGER: You only married to get away from me.

SARA: Oh, that's really annoying!

CLEVENGER: You didn't marry again after he died.

SARA: And what does that prove?

CLEVENGER: Don't the happily married always try it again?

SARA: All this wit and wisdom! I should hate you to think, though, that I haven't had chances. Now, isn't it about time for another osteopathic interlude?

CLEVENGER: You should have married me, Sara. I should have given you all this and more.

SHE *turns furiously on him.*

SARA: You couldn't have given me any of it! Nor understood why I wanted its peace and permanence! And if you've turned up here today for no better reason than an impulse to sort through old valentines, I'm sorry, Jim, but I'm just not in the mood!

CLEVENGER: I'm not here to sort old valentines. I'm here because, once I'd got safely down out of this storm, I thought of the curious gift you used to have for setting me straight in almost any dilemma. You're still the strongest and clearest person I've ever known.

SARA: And what am I expected to say to that? That I'm afraid I've become just a mousy widow lady? I haven't! Go to Washington! We've all got dilemmas of our own these days!

CLEVENGER: You and I share the same dilemma, Sara.

SARA: I doubt that somehow.

CLEVENGER: As people of property we're both preoccupied with self-preservation.

This startles her. For a moment SHE *thinks* HE *may know about her predicament. Then* SHE *recovers herself.*

SARA: But not in the same sense. I've been through that once today and solved it, what's more, so . . .

JOAN *enters from the hall, leaving the door open.*

JOAN: Mother . . .

CLEVENGER: We're very busy in here!

JOAN: But Mr. Clevenger's pilot's come.

STEVE ANDREWS *enters, with an appreciative glance at* JOAN *as* HE *passes her. In his late 20s,* HE *is handsome, romantic, thoroughly sure of himself and quietly flashy about it.*

STEVE: How do you do?

SARA *would greet him, but* CLEVENGER *interferes.*

CLEVENGER: What are you doing here?

STEVE: I didn't like that hotel any better than you did. You had a dreamy kind of look when you left there this morning. If you can improve your conditions, why can't I? So when that chauffeur came for the bags just now . . .

CLEVENGER: Whose bags did you give him?

STEVE: Yours and mind both, Chief. All there were to give.

CLEVENGER: But you can't plant yourself on Mrs. Garrison!

STEVE: Why not? They told me down there it's a great big, comfortable house. And it is. And I'm always welcome wherever I go. (*His smile is the more charming for his impudence*) It's peaceful out here, too. Any idea what goes on downtown?

JOAN: What?

STEVE: There are those who'd call it a riot. Maybe they're only celebrating not having any work to do these days. I've been known to celebrate a bit of leisure myself. Not quite that way, though. There I am in the hotel dining room, sitting quietly over my tea, when a brick comes crashing through the plate glass window and knocks the Old-Fashioned right out of my hand.

CLEVENGER: .Things weren't so bad downtown that you had to . . .

STEVE: Oh, no! I just brought them up as an excuse for joining you in the comforts of home.

SARA: You're welcome here, Mr. Andrews. I read every word that's printed about you famous flyers. Your father must be very proud of you.

STEVE: My father's dead.

SARA *is surprised to hear it.*

CLEVENGER: Of course I'm proud of him.

STEVE *is surprised.*

It's all right. She knew all about your mother and me.

STEVE: There's a young girl in the room. I don't think it's right to talk about things like illegitimacy with a young girl in the room. (*To* SARA) Might as well as call me "Steve," though. Everyone does.

SARA: That's the hallmark of great, great greatness, these days, isn't it? To be "Steve" to the public. Will you tell me a lot about flying in China and what Lhassa looks like? I've always had a weakness for mysterious, faraway cities. Without any ambition to see them for myself.

STEVE: Shall I tell you now or later?

But ROGER *appears excitedly from the hall—ski knickers and galoshes plastered with snow—accompanied by* PATIENCE *and* MICHAEL, *both in tears.*

ROGER: Have you seen what's going on in the street?

SARA: No. What?

ROGER: Shut up, you kids! You're all right now.

The CHILDREN *clutch one another and subside somewhat as* ROGER *comes into the room.*

I was dragging the kids in their sled and all of a sudden there they were, all around us . . .

JOAN: Who?

ROGER: The unemployed by the look of 'em! They must be the unemployed! And out here in this part of town, too! Can you beat it?

HE *has gone to the window. The* OTHERS *are following.*

STEVE: I'd keep back from those windows, Mrs. Garrison. Those are the boys who just got my Old-Fashioned.

DORIS *enters from the parlor, followed by* JOHN.

DORIS: Where are the children?

JOHN: Are they all right?

DORIS: They're terribly frightened!

JOAN: Listen! You can't hear a sound!

STEVE: That's the snow underfoot.

JOAN: The snow doesn't seem so peaceful now.

STEVE: You'd think they'd be singing or carrying placards.

JOAN: There's one with a placard. I can't read what it says.

DORIS (*From the hall*): They shouldn't be permitted in this part of town!

JOHN: Oh, I don't know! Not a bad idea for 'em to show themselves out here, to the people who've got the money.

DORIS *flashes an angry glance at him as* SHE *starts the* CHILDREN *up the stair.* RUDI *and* MARTIN *enter from the parlor.*

RUDI: I'm on my way down to *The Globe*, Sara. Don't want to miss too much, even on Christmas. (HE *has got his hat and coat from the hall table*) Back in time for dinner. (HE *goes towards the front door*)

JOAN: They're not even asking for food. Just marching by. Can't we do something, Mother?

SARA *turns as though to ask what.* JOHN *has come back into the room.*

At least give them what food we've got in the house.

STEVE: What would we eat for dinner?

MARTIN: That's not the way, Joan.

STEVE: I'd organize those boys into an army and rent it out. Mercenaries, you know. Keep 'em out of trouble.

JOHN *eyes him darkly.*

I suppose there'd be feeling against it.

MARTIN: I should think there might be.

STEVE: There always is against anything practical.

JOAN: There weren't many of them. That's the end.

DORIS *has paused on the stair, the* CHILDREN *going on up and out of sight.*

DORIS: There may be more! Pull down the window shades, Sara.

JOHN: That's not the way either.

SARA: We can't shut it out. We could board up the windows and seal over the doors, but the world's sickness would seep down the chimney like fog and up through the floor like smoke.

CLEVENGER: You're right, Sara. It would. (*Then suddenly, and very loud*) Ockleford!

Sensation. Silence. OCKLEFORD *enters.*

Where in hell's the news I wanted on that ship?

OCKLEFORD: The story in Rome as confirmed by the two survivors of the *Farragut's* crew is as follows: At noon yesterday she was stopped by a French submarine. The French must have known she was carrying contraband to the Italians. An Italian plane comes out of the clouds, so the French let go a torpedo without waiting to search. The *Farragut* broke all records on her way to the bottom. Two survivors were all the load the Italian plane could carry.

CLEVENGER: Two saved and how many lost?

OCKLEFORD: Seventeen.

JOAN: How awful! How perfectly awful!

JOHN: We just have to remember not to let ourselves . . .

DORIS: It doesn't seem like I could stand to hear any more . . .

STEVE: Seventeen! Say, we stepped into it that time!

(*Almost simultaneous*)

CLEVENGER: Quiet, for God's sake!!!

> *Quiet is restored.* SARA *looks at him, amazed.* HE *catches her eye.*

(*Then*) I couldn't hear myself think.

> *The* COMPANY *is not unnaturally offended.* DORIS *goes on up the stair and out of sight.*

That's all for now, Ockleford. I'll call you when I want anything else.

> CLEVENGER *moves away, smoking nervously.* OCKLEFORD *goes.*

SARA (*Low*): Joan, don't you want to take Mr. Andrews up and find him a place to sleep? There are all those bags, too. Roger will lend a hand.

> ROGER *is in fact just starting up the stair.* HE *pauses, hearing his name.* JOAN *turns back into the hall with* STEVE.

JOAN (*To* STEVE): This is my brother Roger. Mr. Andrews is Mr. Clevenger's pilot.
ROGER (*Comes down to shake hands*): Andrews? Not *Steve* Andrews?
STEVE: I'm afraid so.

> ROGER *is overwhelmed.*

ROGER: Well, for God's sake!

> *Then, as* STEVE *has picked up two airplane suitcases.*

Here, give me those! (ROGER *takes one of the bags, leading the way up the stair, chattering back over his shoulder*) You're the best Christmas present I've had this year! How many more great men does Mother know?

> *In the meanwhile, however,* SARA *has signed to* JOHN *to leave and* HE *goes now, closing the door after him, shutting the young people out and leaving* SARA *with her eye fixed hard on* CLEVENGER.

CLEVENGER: Thank you.

> HE *resumes his restless movement about the room.* SARA *draws a deep breath.*

SARA: Why is the sinking of this ship of such extreme interest to you at this moment?
CLEVENGER (*Evasive*): I'm a newspaper publisher. This is news. She was flying the American flag and named for an American naval hero and the French sank her the day before Christmas and seventeen young American sailors went down with her.
SARA: Everything but the ship and the sailors is sentiment. The ship had no business in the war trade, had she? And the sailors must have known she had none.
CLEVENGER: If we can take this, we can take anything.

SARA: We can take it, can't we?

CLEVENGER: I don't know.

SHE *is alarmed but can still think craftily.*

SARA: I can't help suspecting that you want an excuse for leading us into worse trouble, Jim.

CLEVENGER (*His eyes narrow a little before* HE *answers her*): Leading's one thing I've never attempted, Sara. I've built up my power by following. I was born with a gift for guessing what my readers want and with too much shrewdness to offer them anything else. (*But* HE *concludes murkily*) Now my power and I have been summoned to Washington. And I don't know what my readers want of me now.

SARA (*Very clear*): They don't want to fight.

CLEVENGER: They want only the right that we've taken from them—and don't call me a cynic for quoting Jefferson—to "fatten on the follies of the Old World." (*Then, violently*) We can't stand much more of this neutrality, Sara! Sooner or later, sooner or later, someone . . . (*His dilemma again moves him restlessly about the room*)

SARA (*Increasing alarm*): Someone, Jim?

CLEVENGER (*Almost to himself*): Nor would it take much . . . It would take very little . . .

SARA, *though steady, is watching him sharply.*

SARA: To push us into this war?

CLEVENGER (HE *is startled*): I didn't say that! I didn't say anything!

SARA (*Now thoroughly alarmed*): What are you going to do in Washington, Jim?

CLEVENGER: God in his wisdom may know—I wish I did! If you think they make any more sense in Washington than your idealistic brothers-in-law make here! The same confusion, here, there and everywhere! The same halfway, half-baked, half-assed thinking! (HE *recovers himself*) I beg your pardon. I forgot myself. (*But his fury bursts out again*) By God, though, I mean to prevent the President's using me and my power any further until I've determined a few things for myself!

SARA: You don't want us at war, do you?

CLEVENGER (*Moves quickly to his own defense*): No man hates war more than I do, Sara! Eighteen months ago, when your pacifist friends were passing resolutions on the horrors of war, I was making my plans for the horrors of peace. I knew their neutrality didn't stand a chance, with the depression it was sure to bring on us, if the country were told half of what would be going on. So I built up a dike around the country. Not only in my own papers but in every paper where I could make my influence felt. My fellow publishers loathe me but listen to me, because they know I'm a great newspaperman! And the President's grateful to my dike and me for the news and propaganda we've kept out of print. So it's my work that we've no war party here! (*But the pride of his tone falters*) That was all in the beginning, though. When there was no doubt what the readers wanted.

SARA: There should be no doubt now of what they want.

CLEVENGER: There may be some of what's best for them. (*And* HE *breaks out*) Those men out there! They're the price of this neutrality on parade! (*Then* HE *pulls himself up*) I don't know. I don't . . .

SARA (*Once again the deep breath* SHE *needs to steady herself. Then*): Do you know the look of the landscape just at twilight? When all the colors are clear and easy to see and the distance is sharp to the horizon? If we could hold that moment I think we should go wrong very seldom. (SHE *goes to him passionately*) I'm sorry for the easy, cheap things I've said today. If I have, as you say, some gift to make you see clearly—I don't know what it can be, but make use of me now! Not just as the woman you once loved, who once loved you! There are millions like me who find life too good for violence! Oh dear, it all sounds so trite. It's been said so often!

Her hands are reached out to him. Genuinely moved, HE *takes them in his own.*

CLEVENGER: I'm not making love to you, Sara, when I tell you that my only impulse is to let Washington wait and sit here in this house until looking at you makes my course clear to me. Will you give me guidance and an omen?

SHE *shakes her head, worried, yet smiling at him.*

SARA: If you'll heed any guidance or omen you get from me, Jim . . .

CLEVENGER: I promise to.

SHE *smiles.*

SARA: You know, Jim, there's something appealing about you, after all.

HE *looks up quickly.*

End of Scene Two

SCENE THREE

The lamps are lighted but the curtains are not drawn across the windows and the snow out of doors falls through the blue of a northern twilight.

CLEVENGER *is seated in* SARA's *big chair asleep, a handkerchief over his head.* JOAN *stands over him, watching him gravely.* MARTIN *stands in the parlor door. A pause.* CLEVENGER *stirs.* JOAN *glances towards* MARTIN *to make sure that* HE *is still there.* CLEVENGER *awakens, removes the handkerchief from his face, sees* JOAN *and is not pleased.*

JOAN: I thought I'd make myself felt if I stared long enough.

CLEVENGER (*With great dignity*): Whenever I have something peculiarly difficult to think out I sleep to give my subconscious a chance.

JOAN: Now's your chance, Martin. You'll be sorry your whole life if you don't take it.

CLEVENGER *turns as* MARTIN *comes forward.* CLEVENGER *is surprised,* MARTIN *embarrassed, but* JOAN *continues with complete steadiness.*

Martin thinks it isn't good manners to bring up his grudge while you're under our roof. But you're not staying under our roof more than a few hours longer and Martin's grudge is every bit as important as the fact that you once gave Mother an ermine coat.

CLEVENGER *looks from one to the other in bewilderment.*

CLEVENGER (*To* MARTIN): So you've got a grudge, have you?

MARTIN: Only for having me fired from my job.

CLEVENGER (*Shakes his head*): I never heard of you till this morning, Mr. Holme.

JOAN: Doctor Holme.

CLEVENGER: Then I'm sure you're wrong, because I don't employ doctors.

MARTIN: I'm an economist, not a physician. And I was teaching in the University of Los Angeles till your paper there forced me out as a Communist.

CLEVENGER: Oho!

JOAN: You do remember him now?

CLEVENGER: No. But I begin to see what he's driving at.

MARTIN (*Makes himself clear with undismayed good humor*): I don't want you to think I minded about the job. Teaching economics is really a kind of racket. Unless one's prepared each year to retract half the gospel one handed out the year before. And that only adds to the general confusion.

CLEVENGER: Your scientific attitude does you great credit, Doctor. You can't be a very orthodox Communist.

JOAN: But he's no Communist at all!

MARTIN: I wish I were. It would make both living and thinking a whole lot simpler.

CLEVENGER: Well, after all, communism's only a kind of trade name for all kinds of thinking one doesn't happen to relish. Unless of course one happens to *be* a Communist. In which case the term fascism may be employed for the same purpose and with the same poetic disregard for making sense.

MARTIN: But we teachers consider ourselves rather special people, Mr. Clevenger—chock full of the free, inquiring, critical spirit. And specially privileged, no matter whose corns we tread on.

CLEVENGER: This doesn't mean you've been attacking me?

JOAN: You know he has!

CLEVENGER: I'm more than embarrassed, but this is the first I've heard about that, too. (*Then, back to* MARTIN) Why don't you tell me what you want of me?

MARTIN: Well, I don't know.

JOAN: He wants satisfaction!

CLEVENGER: What kind? An apology? It's made. A published retraction? I'll arrange it tomorrow. I'll call Ockleford. (HE *is on his way and moving towards the door*) I'll give you a job.

MARTIN: Oh, no! No, thank you!

CLEVENGER (*The best of good humor*): Men of your type often like me to make the offer so they can have the satisfaction of turning it down.

JOAN: It's emotional satisfaction that he wants!

CLEVENGER: Won't he get more of that from you than he would from me?

MARTIN: I could wish you hadn't come here, Mr. Clevenger. And the same for your famous aviating son. Neither materialist nor hero is good for us here.

CLEVENGER: I never thought to hear an educator say that! Don't you know that every fresh contact opens a new mental door on life? You've still a great deal to learn. You think you're a victim of my political bigotry. Or of some desire on my part to get even with you. You're no such things. Your quarrel's with legitimate business enterprise. My Los Angeles paper has been losing circulation. At an alarming rate for such an inferior paper. My readers out there are acutely interested in a thing called Americanism. That's a kind of trade name they use for everything their taxes go to support. Up to the point where the taxes become a burden. (HE *ventures to buttonhole* MARTIN) And a Red raid, particularly on a university faculty, can be made to provide all the gladiatorial action the modern taxpayer seems to require before he'll read the paper I want him to read. And the worst that can possibly be said against me is that I interpret our civil liberties in the classic American way: that is, to my own private advantage as a conservative member of a conservative society. And the difference between me and the rest of my kind is that they're afraid to admit what they are and I'm not. Now, if I've explained myself with sufficient candor, I'll go dress for dinner and leave Steve the task of completing our joint educational program.

And HE *goes up the stair. But* JOAN *leaps into the breach.*

JOAN: You stood up to him! I don't think he's used to men standing up to him!

MARTIN: Am I still on my feet?

JOAN: You're ten thousand times the man he is!

MARTIN: He doesn't know that.

JOAN: Why did Mother ever let that pair into the house? Such people spread poison wherever they go!

MARTIN: He's right, though, about my having a lot to learn. And I thank him for teaching me quite a bit of it.

JOAN: Martin!

MARTIN: He's shown me that our kind can't stand in the middle of the road much longer. Sooner or later we'll have to choose one of the sidewalks.

JOAN: We're young! We'll make out all right!

MARTIN: Where? With those men marching by just now?

JOAN: We don't belong with them!

MARTIN: With Clevenger then?

JOAN: Oh, no! (*Then*) Martin! I'm frightened, Martin! Let's go away! Some place where we'll be safe from everything that pair stands for! And from everything else!

MARTIN: Run away, Joan? Shame on you!

JOAN: Far away! Let's get married next week and go to . . . to Fairbanks, Alaska!

Now MARTIN *is laughing.*

MARTIN: What would we do in Fairbanks?

JOAN (*Who can't imagine*): We . . . we could plant trees there! They must need trees in Fairbanks! I see Fairbanks without any trees! And that would give you something to do with your hands while you're thinking things out and . . .

But his arms are around her.

MARTIN: Oh, Joan! My darling Joan!

ROGER *enters from the pantry with cocktail glasses on a tray.*

ROGER: How about a drink to get dressed on, lovers?

MARTIN: Why not? Drink deadens the mind and makes trouble less troublesome.

ROGER: So Steve says.

JOAN (*Surprised and not pleased*): Steve!

STEVE *enters, also from the pantry, and shaking a very large cocktail shaker.*

ROGER: I've turned the bar over to Steve for the evening. This is his arrangement of rum, vermouth and cointreau. It's called a "Steve Andrews," isn't it, Steve?

STEVE: Only by the select public I make it for. Martinis still hold their own with the mob.

ROGER: It has to be made in Steve's own shaker, too. Look, Martin! He's carried it with him every place he's flown and every time he shakes 'em up for a party he has the place and date engraved on the side!

MARTIN: That will come in handy when you write your autobiography.

STEVE: Got the idea from an old war flyer. A fellow from Pittsburgh.

ROGER: My father was a war flyer. Did I tell you that?

STEVE: That's what planes were meant for. War. The rest of it's just endurance and navigation. War's real flying.

ROGER: Steve's got me all hopped up about flying. Doesn't see why I wouldn't make a swell flyer. Says any man with my nerve for winter sports . . .

STEVE: Sure. Why not?

> JOAN *finds herself disconcerted by the direct admiration with which* STEVE *persists in regarding her.* MARTIN *has been examining the shaker.*

MARTIN: Look, Joan! Here's your old stamping ground. Cairo. Luxor. Khartoum.
STEVE: What? Oh, yes! Egypt.
JOAN (*To* MARTIN): Some day, Martin, when the world's all straight again and licking its wounds, you'll take me back to Luxor and we'll ride horses out over a pale brass morning desert and sail up and down the Nile under the moon and drink marvelous gin fizzes at the Winter Palace and say how much better the social system is now than it was when the pharaoh rode in his barge to the temples at Karnak.

> *But* STEVE *lounges towards them.*

STEVE: Think so?
MARTIN: Don't you?
STEVE: You write books, don't you?
MARTIN: I? Well, I've written a couple.

> STEVE *seats himself comfortably on the sofa.*

STEVE: I like seeing things for myself better than reading about 'em. What are your books about?
MARTIN: Well, about the changing social system.
STEVE: Well, knocking around, I've picked up a few ideas on that. Egypt, now. That was a trip I took for the papers. To look for the Lost Oasis.
ROGER: Bet it isn't lost anymore! Bet you found it, Steve!
STEVE: We found a rock pile no one ever noticed before. Way out in the Libyan desert. All blighted flint and sand for hundreds of miles. No water at all, so there couldn't be any life there. We didn't see so much as a scorpion. But the funny thing was that the rocks were all full of caves. And the walls of the caves were all covered over with drawings. Eight, maybe ten thousand years old. And a lot of the drawings showed the old natives swimming.
JOAN (*In spite of herself*): How fascinating! How perfectly . . .
STEVE: What I meant, though, was those prehistorics swimming in a lake that's gone the way of all good geology. Because I can't see that social systems change much. Whether you ride to Karnak in a barge or to Wall Street in a Rolls Royce, we're still pharaohs, thank God! It's Nature does the changing in her own good time. From glaciers to great lakes. From lakes to desert.
MARTIN: Oh, it isn't that slow! It really isn't that slow.
STEVE: That's how it looks when you're high enough up to get a load of the works.
ROGER: I can see that! That's how it's looked to me when I've been up!
JOAN (*To* STEVE): Didn't I hear Mother saying you'd been to Tibet? To Lhassa? (*And* SHE *sits on the sofa beside* STEVE)
STEVE: I went there for the papers, too.

ROGER: There's more in the shaker. Can I pour?

STEVE: Sure. Go ahead.

JOAN: What's it like in Lhassa?

STEVE: Well, now, I'll tell you. That was a long flight to Lhassa, an awful long flight. And personally I was disappointed. It's a filthy town. Cold and bare. No trees.

JOAN (*Surprised*): No trees!

JOHN appears in the hall—dinner coat—followed by BUCK ANSON: *short, husky, up from the ranks of skilled labor, forty-five—hat and overcoat.*

JOHN: We can talk in here, Buck. You kids had better be dressing.

MARTIN: Is it that late already?

JOAN: Come along, Martin.

THEY go out and up the stair. JOHN *continues to* STEVE *and* ROGER.

JOHN: Won't that thing be of more use in the parlor?

SENATOR CALLORY—tails and white tie—enters from the parlor.

See? Your mother's customers are beginning to gather.

ROGER and STEVE take the shaker into the parlor.

Come in, Buck! Come in! You know Senator Callory, don't you?

BUCK: I've had the pleasure.

CALLORY shakes hands, but does not recall the meeting.

JOHN: Buck's been our general manager down at the plant—how long is it now, Buck?

BUCK: Well, it's twenty-five years since I first went to work there.

CALLORY: And you've let 'em break in on your Christmas, Mr. Anson?

BUCK: Holidays never was much in my life, Senator. Never took a day off I wasn't glad when it was over.

RUDI—also evening dress—has come down the stair and into the room.

RUDI: Hello, Buck! Merry Christmas.

BUCK: Guess we'll leave that part out this year, Mr. Garrison.

JOHN: I've already told Buck the worst.

RUDI: Then the rest is soon over. (*And to* CALLORY) Well, Senator, I see you're in on this, too.

CALLORY: Oh, I'm here tonight as a friend of the family . . . (RUDI's *glance is so sharp that* HE *adds*) For Christmas dinner.

RUDI: That's so. Fifty Christmases. And in three weeks—you'll have digested your Christmas dinner by then—you'll go into court, get your receivers appointed and take over. Still as a friend of the family, I suppose?

CALLORY does not answer.

JOHN: We don't have to take Buck's time up with this.

RUDI: No. Sorry, Buck. No judgment at all. Proceed with the proceedings.

JOHN: I've got Buck to come over because we'll have to begin laying men off at the plant tomorrow. I couldn't let him wait to hear the bad news with the whole gang in the morning.

RUDI (*Horrified*): Do you mean that when our men go to work tomorrow, the day after Christmas, there won't be any work?

JOHN: Saturday's payroll already looks pretty big.

CALLORY: You wouldn't be playing fair with your creditors, Rudi, to let it get any bigger.

RUDI: You ought to know. Objection withdrawn. Go on.

JOHN: It's said. That's always the way. You dread these moments and they're over before you know it. (*To* BUCK) Better get your plans for tomorrow lined up tonight. I'll be down early to see you.

BUCK: Will that be all for now?

JOHN: I can't think of anything more.

BUCK: I guess I'll be going then.

RUDI: Can't we give you a drink?

BUCK: Any drinking I do tonight I'll do alone. I wish I was ten years younger. Not so easy to find a new job when you're past forty.

RUDI: At least I'm in the same boat with you.

About to pick up his hat and coat, BUCK *pauses to speak his only protest.*

BUCK: We weren't laying off men in the last war. Your father didn't like fighting any better than you, but he was a practical man and he took his profits. And our men'd be better off in the trenches than they'll be in the breadlines. I'll say this, though. I know you wouldn't have got in so deep if you hadn't been so hell-bent to keep the men working. You'd be better off now if you'd shut down and waited for good times like other firms done. It's tough tittie, that's all.

HE *goes out.* JOHN *follows him.*

RUDI (*To* CALLORY): It's worse than tough tittie! When John told us about this this morning, Sara wanted to go to you and ask you for time. We told her she mustn't. Now I wish I could think of some way to . . .

CALLORY *will not let him continue.*

CALLORY: Why say that to me? Garrison Tool and Die's of no use to us! We won't realize fifty cents on the dollar! We're paying the forfeit, not you, if the truth be told! What can I do! My obligation isn't to John or you, or even Sara! It's to our stockholders and depositors!

RUDI: What's become of the old-fashioned family banker? Has he gone the way of the family doctor?

CALLORY (*Cuts him off*): Let's go to the party!

RUDI: Right. Sorry if I was tactless.

CLEVENGER *is shouting from above stairs.*

CLEVENGER: Ockleford! (HE *comes running down the stair—dressed, like the* OTHERS, *for dinner, but in a state of considerable excitement*)
RUDI: Pipe down about this.

CALLORY *is surprised.*

Let Sara keep up her front while he's in the house.
CLEVENGER: Ockleford! Where are you, Ockleford? (HE *enters the library*) The snow's stopped! Have you noticed?

HE *goes to the window to push back the curtain. The snow has, in fact, stopped completely.* CALLORY *signals for* RUDI *to introduce him and draws himself up.*

RUDI: Here's the leading citizen of our town, Mr. Clevenger. The Honorable Edward J. Callory, former United States senator and . . .
CLEVENGER (*The briefest handshake*): Oh, yes! (*Then to* RUDI) Where's that pilot of mine?

CALLORY, *mortally offended, goes into the parlor. Opening the door,* HE *releases the sound of a company of guests. This happens—the sound increasing as, presumably, the guests arrive—whenever the parlor door is opened from now on.*

RUDI: He should be in drinking a cocktail with the rest.

OCKLEFORD *enters.*

CLEVENGER: Well, get him in here! We can be getting off!

RUDI *goes into the parlor.* CLEVENGER *turns to* OCKLEFORD.

Get out in the street. Take a look at the sky. I can't see from indoors.

OCKLEFORD *goes out into the hall.* STEVE—*dinner coat—enters from the parlor.*

STEVE: What's going on?
CLEVENGER: We're going on! Have you looked out the window? The snow's stopped! Get on the phone to the airport! I want up-to-the-minute weather from here to the Lakes.
STEVE: Now? Before dinner?
CLEVENGER: We don't stop for dinner if we can . . .
STEVE: I was making my plans to take off at daybreak!
CLEVENGER: *Your* plans!
STEVE: Your old girl's got a damn pretty daughter!
CLEVENGER (*Angry*): Didn't I tell you not to get tight tonight?
STEVE (*Also angry*): Who's tight?
CLEVENGER: You've been drinking cocktails?

STEVE: What's that got to do with getting tight?

CLEVENGER: Stand on your hands!

STEVE: Why should I stand on my hands?

CLEVENGER: If you can't stand on your hands you're not sober enough to take me up in the air!

With the ease of the accomplished gymnast STEVE *is already standing on his hands. But* SARA, *most beautifully dressed for the evening, is coming down the stair.*

STEVE: Does that satisfy you?

CLEVENGER: Does that what?

STEVE: I can't talk! My mouth's full of spit!

SARA: I should think it might be.

STEVE *returns to normalcy.*

Are you all right?

STEVE: I was just demonstrating how all right I am!

SARA: I'm told that's the only way to look at a sunset. (SHE *turns to* CLEVENGER) I'm sorry to hear you're leaving. But I couldn't help hearing. Well, my poor little dinner started off without lions. It can go back now to its former simplicity.

OCKLEFORD *returns.*

OCKLEFORD: Can't see the sky on account of the street lights, Chief. Feels steadier, though, and colder.

But CLEVENGER, *his eye fastened on* SARA, *waves him back.*

CLEVENGER (*To* STEVE): Never mind the airport. We'll stay over after all.

STEVE: Then I can go back to my vital interests.

HE *returns to the parlor.* OCKLEFORD *retires to the hall.*

CLEVENGER: You're looking more than usually beautiful, Sara.

SARA *smooths her dress.*

SARA: I did my best for you. I'm glad you noticed.

CLEVENGER: Let's sit right down again and go on talking about the good old days.

SARA: Jim! All those people in there!

CLEVENGER: Oh, hang those people!

SARA: We covered the good old days this afternoon.

CLEVENGER: Yet they seem as real as ever to·me tonight. Why don't you feel more sentiment about them?

SARA: One can leave things in the icebox just so long.

CLEVENGER: You win! I can't stand ridicule!

SARA (SHE *softens*): Have I hurt your feelings? Shall I show you something?

CLEVENGER: What?

SHE *goes to a drawer in the desk for a photograph which* SHE *brings to him.*

SARA: It's what's known as a faded old photograph. I found it in my theatre trunk in the attic. That's a very affectionate inscription, Jim. I hope you meant it.

CLEVENGER (*Of the photograph*): That's a strong chin, Sara.

SARA (SHE *is looking at him*): Which? (*Then, back to the photograph*) Oh, that one!

CLEVENGER: The years have been kinder to you than they have to me.

SARA: You were a very attractive young man, Jim. I told you you haven't changed.

CLEVENGER: You weren't being very complimentary when you said that.

SARA: And I might so easily have been! It's rather nice, I find, to be with a man who isn't suffering from ideological jitters.

CLEVENGER: In this house, that must seem very restful.

SARA: It does.

ROGER *appears in the hall to call up the stair.*

ROGER: Mother! Where are you, Mother?

SARA *turns, startled out of her moment of sentiment.*

Everyone's waiting! What terrible manners, Mother!

SARA (*Too much on her dignity*): Really, Rog! I don't need you to remind me of my manners! (*Then, tossing the photograph into the desk,* SHE *turns back to* CLEVENGER) Are you ready to make your entrance?

HE *takes her arm.* THEY *move together towards the parlor.* ROGER *goes ahead to open the door.* VOICES *greet them.*

VOICES: Merry Christmas, Sara! . . .
      Sara, where have you been? . . .
      Don't you know you're having a party here tonight? . . .
      Sara, how lovely you look! . . .
      Merry Christmas, Sara! . . .

STEVE'S *cocktail shaker is loud as the scene ends.*

End of Scene Three

SCENE FOUR

It is the day after Christmas. The tree as before, but no fire now and out of doors the shine of a brilliant bitter morning.

JOHN, *back in civilian clothes again, is pacing to and fro across the room.* DORIS— *hat and fur coat—sits nervously on the edge of a chair. From the street beyond the parlor windows comes the diminishing clamor of shouts and cat-calls, through which the bell of a police patrol fades into the distance. Then* MARY *enters, followed by a police* SERGEANT.

JOHN: Well, officer, what was it this time?

SERGEANT: Had to run another one of 'em in, Mr. Garrison.

JOHN: What had this one done that you ran him in for it?

SERGEANT: He come out with a placard that you wouldn't of cared for.

JOHN: What did the placard say?

The SERGEANT *hesitates.*

Did you see it, Mary?

ROGER *appears in the parlor room.*

MARY: It said: "Step out of your fine warm house into the cold with our children and us."

SERGEANT: It was rougher than that.

JOHN: Those men out there are the old employees of our company, officer, who've lost their jobs through no fault of their own. And if it gives them the least satisfaction to picket this house they are not to be interfered with!

MARTIN *appears in the parlor door.*

SERGEANT: You're making things pretty tough for us, Mr. Garrison. This picketing private homes in the residence district ain't a precedent we can afford to encourage!

JOHN: We pay the taxes on this property. When we want police protection we'll ask for it.

SERGEANT: Okay, Mr. Garrison.

JOAN *has come tumbling down the stair.*

JOAN: What is going on outside, Uncle John?

JOHN: It's nothing to get anyone excited! We've had to lay off a few men down at the plant. For business reasons.

RUDI *enters from the parlor.*

And they quite naturally resent being laid off and they've every right to show their resentment.

The SERGEANT, *having gone into the hall and disappeared towards the front door with* MARY, *is now, as presumably* HE *appears in the street, greeted by a fresh outburst of cat-calls.*

RUDI: And I hope they can stick it long enough to . . .
ROGER: To what? Watch us walk out of our fine warm house forever?
MARTIN: That might give them some satisfaction.
JOAN (*Frantic*): What are you all talking about?
JOHN (*His nerve breaking*): Take her someplace out of here and tell her!
MARTIN: Come into the dining room, Joan, and get your breakfast.

THEY *go out into the hall and turn past the pantry.*

DORIS: You're beyond me! All of you just beyond me! (SHE *is on her feet, shaking*) I'm going home to the country and get my children where they'll be safe!

And she makes for the stair. But MARY *has returned from the front door, followed by the* SERGEANT *and two other* POLICE OFFICERS. *The sight of them is a red rag to* JOHN.

JOHN: What do you cops want now?

Before THEY *can answer,* CLEVENGER *has entered from the hall.*

CLEVENGER: They've come in at my invitation, Mr. Garrison. It's cold guarding a house on a morning like this. I've suggested that Sara's cook serve the officers coffee.
JOHN: Aren't you taking a good deal on yourself?

CLEVENGER, *ignoring him, has gone to the* POLICEMEN.

CLEVENGER: I asked for the sergeant in command outside.

The SERGEANT *steps forward.*

SERGEANT: That's me, sir.
CLEVENGER: I'm J. M. Clevenger. In case you don't know my name, I own *The Morning Eagle.*

But the SERGEANT *has already touched his cap.*

How many men have you got on duty here?
SERGEANT: Six including me, sir.
CLEVENGER: I want that force doubled and kept on night and day.
RUDI: Damn it, Mr. Clevenger, you must have heard my brother!
CLEVENGER: I haven't the slightest objection to your wet-nursing those pickets, but I reserve the right to feel uneasy for your sister-in-law. And in view of the fact that my paper owns the police force in this town . . .

He is waving the POLICEMEN *out. But* JOHN *has his counter proposal ready.*

JOHN: Mary, ask Anna to make a lot of coffee, please, and to turn all the bread in the house into sandwiches.

MARY *goes, the* POLICEMEN *following her into the pantry.*

Rog, you go out into the laundry and build up a big fire in the stove. Then, when the room's warm and refreshments are ready, ask our men in the picket line to come in.

DORIS (*From the stair*): Into the house?

RUDI: That won't really help, John.

JOHN: It'll help me! (*Then, hard to* CLEVENGER) I'll stand for a good deal of interference, but I will not have our men saying we do things for the cops that we don't do for them!

CLEVENGER *shrugs and turns away.*

Go on, Rog!

ROGER *goes into the pantry.*

DORIS: Well, this settles things as far as I'm concerned! (SHE *runs up the stair, calling*) Sara! Sara!

CLEVENGER (*To* RUDI): I can't think what you can do to express your liberal emotions, except to write an editorial in *The Globe*. Don't hesitate to say anything that occurs to you about me that might put you and your brother in a more heroic light.

RUDI *turns back into the parlor.*

(CLEVENGER *calls*) Ockleford!

OCKLEFORD *enters from the hall.* HE *wears gloves and coat and carries his hat in his hand.*

OCKLEFORD: Right here with the bags, Chief. That was Steve on the phone from the airport just now. Ship's all tuned up and ready to take off.

CLEVENGER: Did you give my message to Mrs. Garrison?

OCKLEFORD: She told me to tell you good-bye and she's sorry she's too tired to get up.

CLEVENGER: Go back upstairs and knock on her door again. Tell her I shan't leave this house till I have seen her. Tell her I'll come up if she doesn't care to come down. And explain that I can arrange to wait through the summer if need be. And certainly until after January 15th.

Needless to say, this last startles JOHN, *but* OCKLEFORD *goes obediently into the hall and up the stair.* CLEVENGER *turns to* JOHN.

I've picked up enough around this house this morning to piece out the rest. You needn't be afraid of my spreading rumors. I sympathize too deeply with your predicament.

JOHN *bows without answering.*

You make tools and dies, don't you?

JOHN: And lathes and drills. All such.

CLEVENGER: That wouldn't be such a bad wartime business, would it?

JOHN: We're not at war.

CLEVENGER: I might say that's unfortunate for you.

A renewed outburst from the street. CLEVENGER *looks out through the parlor.* OCKLEFORD *comes down the stair and into the room. The outburst subsides.*

OCKLEFORD: Mrs. Garrison prefers coming down to your going up.

CLEVENGER: I expected she would. Wait outside till I call you.

OCKLEFORD *goes.*

(*To* JOHN) Will you do me a very great favor, and leave me to talk with your sister-in-law alone? After all, you are entertaining this morning. You should supervise your preparations!

Without answer, JOHN *turns toward the hall, but* SARA, *dressed now in another simple and suitable morning frock, is coming down the stair.*

SARA: I entirely approve of the coffee and sandwiches, John. Doris is in rather a state. I'd go help her pack if I were you. (SHE *comes into the room*)

JOHN *goes up the stair.*

You've fine weather for flying, Jim. After yesterday, almost miraculous.

CLEVENGER: Why didn't you tell me about all this, Sara?

SARA: This what? (*Then, with a nod towards the window—and a bit too careless*) That? Don't let that alarm you.

CLEVENGER: You're cleaned out, aren't you?

SARA: A little tact on your part would have told you that I might be sensitive on the subject. I told you we'd solved our property dilemma.

CLEVENGER: Call this a solution? Reminds me of the Christian Scientist who jumped overboard due to religious scruples against being seasick.

SARA: That's an extreme example.

CLEVENGER: Don't you see this is the end of the world for you, Sara?

SARA: That's just the trouble. It isn't. I'm healthy and I've still got a long time to live.

HE *agrees.*

CLEVENGER: With me.

SHE *turns, astonished.*

Marry me, Sara.

SHE *gasps.*

And come with me to Washington.

SHE *is properly stunned.*

SARA: Now, why should I even consider . . .?

CLEVENGER: Whatever opinion you may hold of me, and you were pretty clear about that yesterday, I'm just as clear about what I feel for you today. History might have been different if you'd married me! History may still be different if you marry me now!

SARA: We'll leave history out of this if you don't mind.

CLEVENGER: I've seen the life you've made for yourself, Sara. All the strength and peace and privacy of it. And I see my own life as I've lived it without you. No center to it, unsettled and frantic. Doesn't that make you the least bit sorry for me?

SARA: Not enough to prescribe myself as a sedative.

CLEVENGER: We came together again on a white Christmas. I can't make love to you as a young man could . . .

SARA (*Completely off her guard*): You're not doing badly. That "white Christmas" is rather nice. (*In spite of herself, the energy of his pleading is stirring her*)

CLEVENGER: Sara, I could go into court and take my oath on the president's fifteenth-century Dutch Bible that you want to say yes!

SARA: Is it conceivable that I'm being tempted?

CLEVENGER: Why not?

But a sudden outburst from the pickets outside recalls her to her predicament.

SARA: I should have to be very sure, shouldn't I?

CLEVENGER: You can be sure of me.

SARA: But I might be using you as a way out. And that wouldn't do at all! Why didn't you go last night?

CLEVENGER: If I had I should have missed what looks like an opportunity this morning.

Her eyes flash.

Yes, Sara. To open my suit for your heart and hand. Under circumstances which, to my practical mind, make your acceptance . . .

SARA: Look at him with his head up and his tail over the dashboard!

CLEVENGER: You don't like being taken advantage of? Rise above it, Sara. Say to yourself: I'm fond of this man who's dropped back into my life out of the sky and come to care for me the second time . . .

SARA: No.

CLEVENGER: Put on your hat and coat and we'll go get the license.

SARA (*Crescendo vehemence*): How can I be sure of what I feel for you when I'm flying in the face of providence if I don't take you? Why didn't you drop down out of the sky a month ago? I could have seen you clearly and humanly then! With my life before me as it would have been if "all this," as you call it, hadn't happened! I should have seen Joan going out to get married to Martin and Roger following her in a few years and myself left here alone and Mr. Stanford White's architecture getting bigger and bigger and my trips abroad lasting longer and longer and winding up on a world cruise in a white serge suit! I should have seen that my function here was ended and jumped at the chance of a new function with you! But instead you appear just as I've had to give everything up, and offer me a suitcase full of millions and a way out of everything I've got myself into! How can I trust my feeling for you now?

CLEVENGER: If I say I'll take my chances . . .

SARA: No, it's no good! Come back in a year! If you really have got to care for me twice, you ought to be able to work yourself up a third time! And if I've made a go of my hat shop by then—or whatever I do decide to turn my hand to—I'll be less confused! But it's no good now, with all this around my neck! So go on if you're going and leave me to lie on the bed I've made for myself. Alone.

CLEVENGER: Oh, Sara, my Sara! You *are* mine, you know. And I'm damned if I let you . . .

Her hand stops him and at the same moment JOHN *reappears on the stairs.* HE *carries two bags and the two* CHILDREN, *in their hats and coats, follow him, and* DORIS *brings up the rear and* SARA *and* CLEVENGER *are interrupted by a resumption of the family argument.*

JOHN: The trouble is . . .

PATIENCE: But I don't want to go home to the country! You said we could stay with Aunt Sara the whole week!

MICHAEL (*Practically at the same time*): Aunt Sara promised to take us to see Pluto tomorrow! And Roger's promised to give me a lesson on skis!

DORIS: Be quiet!

THEY are down the stair and turning the corner towards the dining room.

If you want me to drive myself and your children through this riot . . .

THEY have disappeared.

SARA (*To* CLEVENGER): I've got to straighten that out. (*Then, pleadingly to him*) Will you do something for me? Morgan's out in front with my car waiting for you. Those men of ours won't trouble you, really they won't!

HE smiles, but SHE *concludes.*

Be gone before I come back.

CLEVENGER: Will you do something for me?

SARA: What is it?

CLEVENGER: Kiss me good-bye.

SARA: I don't see why there'd be any harm in that.

SHE offers her cheek. HE *takes her in his arms and kisses her hard on the lips. It is not a prolonged motion picture kiss, but* HE *means it and* SHE *likes it. Then, still holding her in his arms,* HE *looks down at her.*

CLEVENGER: Will you remember a farewell message, Sara? That in any choice ever made by any man, between the leveled balances of his interests, there's always a feather's weight to tip the scale. A feather's weight. Will you remember that?

SARA (SHE *is puzzled*): As long as you know what it means.

CLEVENGER: I do.

SARA: All right. Good-bye.

CLEVENGER: Good-bye.

There being nothing more to say, SHE *goes out after* JOHN *and* DORIS.

(*When* HE *is sure that* SHE *is gone,* HE *calls softly*) Ockleford!

OCKLEFORD *enters.*

Shut the door. (*Then, as* OCKLEFORD *obeys*) Come here to me.

His throat is dry, his whole body rigid with the excitement of his resolution. OCKLEFORD *comes to him.*

I want you to go down to *The Eagle* and get on long distance to Curry in New York. I want all the best men taken off what they're doing to round up the families of the captain and crew of the *Farragut*. Pray God that captain left a widow and children! I want interviews and detailed descriptions of each set-up here in my hands within forty-eight hours. That's Wednesday. I want Curry himself out here by Thursday. And he'd better bring Phelps from Washington and Green from Atlanta. And I want Bronson from Seattle, and someone from San Francisco or Los Angeles, and Bailey from Dallas and Cope from . . .

OCKLEFORD (*Completely bewildered*): Chief, what's the idea?

CLEVENGER: We're opening the dike and letting the floods cut loose! This neutrality had to stop sooner or later, Ockleford! I've found my good reason for stopping it a bit sooner!

OCKLEFORD: If we're just taking off for Washington, though . . .

CLEVENGER: Oh, that's all changed! I've been vouchsafed an omen and guidance, Ockleford! I'm staying right here in this house . . . (HE *sits smiling, in* SARA'S *big chair*) With a feather's weight and an old ermine coat! (HE *leans back happily, singing to himself*)
"And when I tell them
  How wonderful you are!
  They'll never believe me!
  They'll never believe me! . . .

End of Scene Four

SCENE FIVE

The library again. The tree has been removed. The fire as before. The Morning
Globe *has been left untidily spread out on the sofa. Out of doors the same brightness
of brilliant cold.*

In the hall, MARY *is helping* JOAN *to shed cold weather equipment of the best quality.* STEVE *peels off lined trench coat and muffler for himself.*

MARY (*As the scene begins*): . . . relieved to see you home safely, though I'm sure
with a flyer of Mr. Andrews' reputation . . .

A beaming smile for STEVE *as* HE *enters the library.*

STEVE: Thank you, Mary. Thank you.

HE *ambles idly to the sofa, picks up* The Morning Globe *and looks through it
without interest.* MARY *drops on her knees to negotiate* JOAN*'s galoshes.*

JOAN: You might tell Mother we're back. She may have worried.
MARY: She's up in her room throwing old trash away and generally getting ready
to move out. Mr. Roger he's just drove down to the bakery for more bread
to feed the picketers in the laundry. And there's messages from all your New
Year's parties tonight asking will you bring Mr. Andrews along with you,
which is only right that you should.

Again the beaming smile for STEVE. *But* JOAN *has come into the library, leaving*
MARY *to dispose of the hats and coats.*

JOAN: We ought to have waited till tomorrow and flown into the New Year.
STEVE: Flying the old one out wasn't so bad. Don't you think some hot coffee
might go pretty well now?
JOAN: Can we have some, Mary?
MARY: Easy, Miss Joan. There's always hot coffee on the stove these days!

MARY *goes into the pantry.* JOAN *is smiling dazedly at* STEVE.

STEVE: Ears feel funny? That's the change in air pressure coming down. Hold your
nose and swallow and push out inside.

SHE *obeys.*

Did they pop?
JOAN: How did you know my ears felt funny?
STEVE: The way you were acting.
JOAN: That wasn't my ears. I was trying to fix this morning in my memory. That
wizened, red-nosed sun that came up and turned the eastern slopes to pink
satin. And the sharp, northern look the pines had between the clearings.
And those boys we saw skating in front of that schoolhouse. That was like
looking down on a picture by Breughel.

STEVE: I'm not artistic. Can't be everything.

JOAN *smiles.*

JOAN: It seems to me that only two things in the world really matter. The shining space and light we've just been up in . . . and this here.

STEVE: What here?

JOAN: Hearth and home it's called.

STEVE: I never gave 'em a fair trial myself.

JOAN: They can be pleasant. And painful to lose. I can take hold down here now I've been up there.

STEVE: I know what you mean. I've often gone up like that. With a hangover. Pumped myself full of good, clean oxygen. Down in ten minutes. Head clear as a bell. That wouldn't be quite your problem.

JOAN: In principle.

STEVE: I should be more careful how I put things to you.

JOAN: How depressing!

STEVE: Not to me.

JOAN: Thanks. I'll try being brighter, though.

Has a mutual attraction developed? But MARY *has returned with a breakfast tray which* SHE *sets on the cigarette table.*

STEVE: Here's coffee.

MARY *goes.* JOAN *sits down to the tray. But* STEVE, *his eye fixed on her, closes the hall door after* MARY.

(*Comes back to the coffee almost too casually, saying as he does so*) I take sugar in mine. Two lumps in summer. Three in winter. That's science. Great heating properties in sugar.

JOAN: Get a lift with a Camel.

STEVE: I did that. They asked me to and I did it.

SHE *has delivered his cup.* HE *sits beside her.*

JOAN (*Uncovering the toast plate*): There's toast, too. Hot, buttered . . .

STEVE: I can eat it. (HE *takes a bite*) How do you like your butter? Fresh or salt?

JOAN: Fresh.

STEVE: Salt.

JOAN: I'll tell Anna to . . .

STEVE: No! I'm interested in characteristics, that's all. Been reading up on psychology. Things like different tastes in butter are only skin deep.

SHE *finds this touching.*

JOAN: Then there's no reason why we shouldn't get on very well.

STEVE: There are other things, though.

JOAN: Such as?

STEVE: Which shoe do you put on first?

JOAN: I haven't the faintest notion.

STEVE: That's not the answer.

JOAN: It may not be the answer, but it's the truth.

STEVE: You've got to learn to observe yourself. That's what I'm doing. I find I start everything on the right.

JOAN: I suppose that means you're just constitutionally right-handed?

STEVE: It might mean that.

JOAN: That's a good thing to find out before it's too late!

STEVE: You're kidding me.

JOAN: Have some more coffee.

STEVE: I've had enough coffee. You have a cigarette.

SHE *shakes her head.*

JOAN: I don't want to spoil the feel of that good, clean oxygen.

STEVE: Right. (HE *looks at her somewhat less casually than before*) Then tell me what you were thinking about up there.

SHE *is surprised.*

Besides art and nature, I mean.

JOAN: I was up with one of the world's most famous flyers who's completely unlike anybody I've ever known. What do you suppose I was thinking about?

STEVE: Me. How?

JOAN: At your Lost Oasis. In Lhassa. You live half in another element, don't you? You're like a centaur, aren't you?

STEVE: You keep pulling these on me. What is it?

JOAN: It *was* in the myths. Half man, half horse. You're half airplane.

STEVE: Two-thirds.

JOAN: What's the other third?

STEVE (*How does* HE *know?*): Oh, God!

JOAN: I expect flying's an old story to that lesser third.

STEVE: It gets monotonous.

JOAN: Not that last bounce when the wheels really leave? You said planes were meant for fighting. I hate that idea.

STEVE: You're wrong.

JOAN: Flight's too beautiful!

STEVE: So's air fighting beautiful! To shoehorn yourself into one of those little things and go up and look for that other guy and find him with your guns set right there in front of your nose! Man, plane, guns, all one animal then: one bean, one eye!

JOAN (*A pause, then, low*):
"She loved me for the dangers I had passed
 And I loved her that she did pity them."

Then, at once, because HE *looks sharply at her,* SHE *is extremely sorry that it slipped out.*

STEVE: What's that?

JOAN: *Othello.* (SHE *pushes the table from her and rises*) I don't know what made me quote it.

STEVE: Othello. That name strikes a chord. Coon, wasn't he?

JOAN: He was a Moor. He lived in Venice.

STEVE: I've been to Venice.

JOAN: Venice sounds tame for you.

STEVE: It was all right. It's full of fairies.

JOAN: Fairies in Venice? (SHE *draws back*) Oh, you mean . . .

STEVE: My God!

JOAN (*Feeling foolish,* SHE *takes refuge in dignity*): We don't talk about such things as much as some people.

STEVE: I didn't know there was a girl left on earth who would have thought I meant anything else!

JOAN: I'm sure there are plenty!

STEVE: I told you I'm too free spoken.

JOAN: It's not your fault if we're a bit old-fashioned in spots.

STEVE (*Suddenly surly*): Don't spoil it by apologizing to me, for God's sake!

JOAN: Steve!

STEVE: What?

JOAN: What does get into you?

STEVE: You wouldn't understand if I told you. I act the way I feel. If you don't like that, this is as good a time as any for saying so.

JOAN: Really, Steve! (SHE *picks up her coat and is moving towards the hall door*)

STEVE: Going?

JOAN: I don't seem to be doing so well here.

STEVE: Go ahead. Don't let me stop you.

SHE *turns back to the door.* HE *speaks without looking at her.*

Still planning to marry that school teacher, I suppose?

JOAN: He's not a school teacher any more!

STEVE: He hasn't changed. And you're finished with him. You must be or you wouldn't have fallen for me.

JOAN (*Panic*): Because I happen to think of a couple of lines of very famous poetry— and they *are* famous whether you've ever heard them or not!

STEVE: I knew what was what this morning up in the plane.

An exclamation of dismay from JOAN.

Don't worry. You've got me where you want me. In three days without lifting a finger. You say you've never known anybody like me. Well, I've never known anybody like you. I guess that explains it. I could have told you what that remaining third of me is. It's just plain, low-down, gutter-bum male. And you're not the cold-blooded party you think you are. (HE *has gone close to her*)

JOAN: Please don't.

STEVE: Oh, I'm not proposing to you! I'd ask no girl to marry an aviator. We could get some place, you and I, at that. Want to know what I wish about you? I'll tell you what. I wish to Christ almighty you weren't a virgin. I'm old-fashioned that way.

A sound from JOAN *but no words will come.*

Shocked, are you? Sure. But nothing like as shocked as you'd like to be. Well, are you?

HE *takes her in his arms and kisses her soundly. Then* HE *releases her.* SHE *backs away unsteadily.*

Sorry if I was rough. But that's how it is when it really happens. Can't you say something?

SHE *shakes her head and goes slowly to pick up her bag where* SHE *let it fall on the floor.* SHE *totters as* SHE *stoops and* HE *picks it up for her.* SHE *takes it from him and goes unsteadily to the hall door.*

Now listen to me, Joan. You don't want to take this too . . .

A look from HER *stops* HIM. *Then, opening the door,* SHE *discovers* JOHN, *where* HE *is shedding his coat in the hall.*

JOHN: Aren't you looking a bit seedy this morning?

STEVE (*Quickly*): I had her up in the ship to see the sunrise.

JOHN: Well, that would account for something.

HE *has come into the room, apparently weighed down by some new burden of care.* HE *slips the newspaper into the side pocket of his coat.*

JOAN: I'll tell Mother you're here.

JOHN: You needn't. I've come to see your Uncle Rudi.

JOAN: I'll tell him.

JOHN: Mary's already done it. (HE *sees the paper where it is lying on the sofa.* HE *picks it up quickly. Then, with relief*) That's the morning paper. (HE *drops it*) Everything seems quiet enough around here.

JOAN *gives an intense look at* STEVE, *unperceived by* JOHN, *and goes out and up the stair.* STEVE *is following her.*

Your father's an extraordinary character. A damned extraordinary character! You may have noticed that.

STEVE: What's he up to this time?

JOHN: You don't know?

STEVE: I never pay much attention.

JOHN is drawing his newspaper from his pocket. But ROGER is in from the pantry with MARTIN close after him.

ROGER: The damnedest thing's happened!

JOHN squares off for a blow, but it does not come.

MARTIN: Rog had to go out and buy food for the men in the picket line . . .

ROGER: When I got back they'd gone!

MARTIN: Decamped!

ROGER: The whole lot of 'em!

STEVE: They were there on duty when Joan and I came in!

MARTIN: And the cops don't know any more than we do! They saw the men in a huddle, then the whole works ran off down the street!

ROGER: Cheering!

RUDI is coming down the stair, pajamas, bathrobe and slippers, his hair still tousled.

RUDI: Don't you know that morning papers keep men up late?

But JOHN has drawn his paper from his pocket.

JOHN: Mr. Clevenger's *Eagle's* come out with a noon extra. He's written a little essay on our National Honor that isn't staying home any longer. It's going places.

RUDI: Holy God!

STEVE: Let's have a look at that, will you?

RUDI (*Reading*): "Honor is not a dead word in a dead language. We are not yet dead to our National Honor. Though we hate war, let us serve notice on these warring nations . . ."

DORIS is calling wildly from the front door.

DORIS: Sara! Where is everybody? (SHE *enters, brandishing another copy of* The Eagle) Have you seen the paper?

RUDI: If that's what's brought you here . . .?

DORIS: Oh, not to crow! Truly not to crow! But we ran into Sara's car in front of the post office and . . . (SHE *continues her excited chatter ad lib*)

SARA is coming down the stair.

MARTIN (*Over* DORIS): "In a deeper sense, these seventeen sailors are all America as Nathan Hale was all America . . .

ROGER: "Every ton of our fleet, every ounce of powder in our arsenals . . ."

DORIS: You won't believe what this means to me, but . . .!

SARA: Doris, where have you come from? John! What are you all . . .!

DORIS: Oh Sara, your wonderful friend Mr. Clevenger!

RUDI: Your wonderful friend's done as much as any man could to involve this country in war!

DORIS: And I love him for it! I just love him for it! Let her read for herself!

SHE *thrusts her paper upon* SARA, *who stands reading.*

Every newsboy's got another tagging after him! Handing out free American flags! And trucks are roaring up and down all the main streets with banners and radios . . .

JOHN: And the same show must be going on in every town where Clevenger's got a paper!

RUDI: Seattle, Birmingham, Boston, Salt Lake City . . .

JOHN: Oh, it's National Honor Day for the seventeen dead American sailor boys of the *Farragut!*

MARTIN: What's the President say to this?

RUDI: He's wondering what in hell to say just as I am and who'll listen when he says it!

MARTIN (*Reading*): "The weak can only submit to humiliation. But we are not weak . . ." (HE *takes the paper apart*)

STEVE *leaves.* RUDI *is pacing the room.*

DORIS: And all we needed was to be told we're not! And he's told us, thank God! Thank God for France and England!

RUDI (*Stops his pacing to snarl at her*): The French sank the *Farragut!!!* This is aimed straight at the point of France's chin!!!

DORIS: America's awake! That's all I care about!

RUDI *resumes his pacing, clutching his head, or the equivalent.*

ROGER: I'm going downtown! (HE *goes out, shouting*) Steve! Wait for me, Steve!

DORIS: Save room for me! I don't want to miss a minute of this! It almost makes me wish I were a man! (SHE *goes after* ROGER)

RUDI (*A new aspect of it strikes him*): And the cleverness of it, Holy God! The cold-blooded cleverness of breaking a thing like this in a noon extra! Too late for the evening sheets to come back at him! But just in time to turn New Year's Eve into a patriots' jamboree! Think of the liquor they'll be . . .

SARA: You're taking this too hard!

RUDI: Too hard? They may be doing things now that can't be undone! And how am I going to answer this tomorrow? What have I got to say that people aren't sick of hearing? That's the weakness of reason in a time like this! He's got a whole brass band he can play on! I can play one note on a bloody bassoon!

SARA: But why do you have to rush into print?

RUDI: You don't expect *The Globe* to take this lying down?

SARA: How do you know what there is to take?

JOHN: Good God, Sara!

MARY *enters.*

SARA: I want to be fair!

MARY: Here's Mr. Anson come to see you, Mr. John.

BUCK *enters—a very different* BUCK.

BUCK: It's a great day, Mr. Garrison!

JOHN: Great for what, Buck?

BUCK: Well, for Garrison Tool and Die, among other things! Isn't this just what we needed?

JOHN *has not thought of this aspect of the situation.*

Guess you've noticed the boys aren't out there in front anymore.

JOHN (*Horrified*): They haven't gone back to the plant?

BUCK: Where would you think they'd gone? And they're asking when do they come back to work!

JOHN: Damn! Oh, damn!

BUCK *turns, leaving* JOHN *stunned, to* RUDI.

BUCK: It's a great day for the whole, entire American labor movement that's had its bellyful of neutrality!

RUDI: Do you hear that, Sara? Do you want to hear more of what to expect now the lid's off?

SARA: I've heard enough, thanks!

BUCK (*To* RUDI): Well, it's you I've come to see. We'll have a big crowd down at Labor Temple tonight and ringing resolutions to put across. And it's them we want to read in *The Globe* tomorrow and no word of any trouble we may have between the local radical element and the strong arm squad we've assembled to handle it!

MARTIN: The A. F. of L. isn't coming out for war, too!

SARA: *The Eagle* said nothing whatever about war!

RUDI: Go back to our old rights of trade it said!

BUCK: Organized labor asks no more than that. Garrison Tool and Die asks no more!

JOHN *is barely able to control himself.*

We're for peace and organized labor's for peace! With honor, though, and on a paying basis!

RUDI: It's war he's offering you! Don't kid yourself, Buck! Once we go back to trading and protecting our trade! Once we start writing notes and taking sides . . .!

BUCK: Well, I can't forget the strides organized labor made in the last war!

Sensation.

MARTIN: Well, that's certainly taking the practical angle!

JOHN: What would you expect? Organized labor doesn't have to fight!

RUDI: And this is the boy who once stumped for Gene Debs and did time with Bill Heywood!

BUCK: We all have our own interests to look after!

SARA: Please! Please don't! I can't . . .

All this almost simultaneous and at full voice. MARY *has entered.*

RUDI: Well, I'm going to fight this son of a bitch and his *Eagle* as long as I've got a punch left in me!

MARY: And a young gentleman from your newspaper, Mr. Robert.

RUDI: Who? Where?

BURKE *enters—sharp young reporter, hat and overcoat.*

Oh, Burke . . .

BURKE: They thought you might want to hear the lowdown, so I . . .

RUDI: I do want to hear it! But I want you down at the Labor Temple tonight and if any man in that crowd shows the guts to stand up against what is going on today I want him played up for all that's in him tomorrow!

BURKE (*Delighted*): Do I take my brass knuckles with me?

RUDI: Take whatever you've got! And come upstairs and tell me the rest while I'm dressing.

BUCK *is after* RUDI *and* BURKE *as* THEY *go towards the stair.*

BUCK: I never believed I'd hear a Garrison . . .

RUDI: And you get out!

HE *goes up the stair with* BURKE. BUCK *goes towards the front door.*

SARA: "National Honor." That's a ringing phrase, John.

JOHN: It is that, Sara.

SARA: What's it all going to mean?

JOHN: He's trying to give us a new *Lusitania*, Sara.

SARA: Oh, I don't believe that! The *Farragut* isn't that! We couldn't fight France and England!

JOHN: He must think we could! He's the breed, you know. Mussolini's and Hitler's breed!

SARA: And I don't believe that!

MARTIN (*Shakes his head*): No. He's too shrewd to think we'd fight with the dictators!

JOHN: Then why does he choose this ship just at this moment, when he could count on the Germans or Japs or Italians to give us another any day?

MARTIN: I don't believe he cares about anything except putting an end to this business depression. If war's the result—well, war's good for business, too. And this *Farragut* at least puts us in a receptive frame of mind, gets us properly de-neutralized so that when the Germans or Japs or Italians do . . .

JOHN: That may well be.

SARA: Men aren't that cold!

MARTIN: Aren't they? You'd be surprised. I believe I'll have a look downtown myself. (HE *goes out*)

SARA: I could wish I'd lived more in the world and thought more about it. I shouldn't be coming to with such a jolt now. (SHE *rises*) I'll telephone Jim. He ought to know what it's going to mean.

JOHN: Hasn't he given you any hint of this?

SHE *stops on her way out.*

SARA: No. None.

JOHN: Not in all the hours you've spent with him this week?

SARA: We've talked about . . . not about world affairs.

JOHN: Doesn't it seem damn peculiar to you that he's stuck on here as he has in this backwater when he had such a move as this up his sleeve?

SARA: He makes the world come to him wherever he is.

JOHN: You know him pretty well, Sara.

SARA: I know him. Yes.

JOHN: I should think you might be sorry for that now.

A pause.

SARA (*A good deal less than assured*): It's not like you to judge a man without hearing him, John. He wants us to stand up for our national honor again. You may not believe in that, but many men do. Sincere men. Fine, trustworthy men. Not your type or Rudi's, perhaps, but . . .

JOHN: Not your type, either.

SARA: Oh, I'm not any type. I . . .

JOHN: Sara!

This is stern and SHE *flinches.*

SARA: What?

JOHN: Why are you trying to make excuses for him?

But RUDI *and* BURKE *are coming down the stair.*

BURKE: . . . and the streets downtown are all broken out in flags and the drunks are away ahead of New Year's Eve schedule. And there's telegrams coming in from bankers and editors and chambers of commerce and patriotic societies. As fast as he reads 'em he puts 'em out on the wire to the rest of his papers. You'll see the cream of 'em on the front page tomorrow. Under the heading "The Country Behind Us!"

SARA: Oh, dear!

THEY *have entered the library.* RUDI *still buttoning his vest and adjusting his tie, though* HE *is also wearing his overcoat and hat.*

RUDI: You both want to get this. Burke's my star reporter on *The Globe*. He's been buying drinks for the boys from Clevenger's *Eagle*. (*Back to* BURKE) Go on, Burke.

BURKE: He's got a string of mass meetings scheduled for this coming Saturday night in fifteen key cities. He's hired the arena for the one in this town.

SARA: But that's hockey night!

RUDI: It was hockey night. And he's got a competition for recruiting posters coming up. First prize ten thousand bucks. Under the slogan: "Let us be ready when our country calls!" Oh, yeah! And they're making a movie called *The Farragut's Daughter*. It seems the captain of the *Farragut* did leave a daughter. She's been through two divorces and runs a pet shop in Atlantic City, but she's going to be Shirley Temple on the screen!

JOHN: I think I'll ask Mr. Burke to go along, Rudi.

RUDI is surprised, as JOHN holds the door open for BURKE. BURKE goes. JOHN closes the door.

We've got to get to the bottom of something here. (*And to SARA*) Sara, will you give Rudi and me your authority to ask Mr. Clevenger to move out of this house?

SARA: Certainly not!

JOHN: Why not?

SARA: Why should I?

JOHN: You *are* trying to find excuses for him, you know. You *are* taking his side against us.

SHE falters. Then, at last, JOHN's suspicions come home to RUDI.

RUDI (*Low*): Holy God!

SARA (*A deep breath, and SHE speaks quite simply*): I'm going to marry him.

A pause. RUDI, being unprepared, is rocked. JOHN stands steady.

RUDI: I'll have to admit I hadn't thought of that.

SARA: First I thought I would. Then I knew I couldn't. Then I decided I might as well.

RUDI: You can't care for him, though!

SARA: I know it seems strange, but I do. (*Then*) It's only an exceedingly lucky woman who gets a second chance at her second choice. (*Then*) I'd rather not talk about it.

RUDI: But we can't take the Prince of Darkness into the family without some discussion!

SARA stiffens, offended.

SARA: Better say he's taking me out of the family.

This is a blow to both of the BROTHERS.

RUDI: I suppose that is what it comes to.

JOHN: You can't expect us to be happy about this, Sara. We wish you every happiness, though.

And, for him, the barrier is up already. RUDI, however will not abandon the fight.

RUDI: You get used to a family setup. It's been the three of us for a long time. Now it won't be the three of us any longer. Oh, I don't mean that we've any claim on you! (*But a new thought occurs*) Joan and Roger have, though. Have you thought of them?

SARA: I'm going to think of myself, if you don't mind.

RUDI: We were here in this room, the three of us, Christmas Day. Deciding to let the business go to the wall. And you said: "I've a son just at the fighting age whose father was killed in the last war!"

SARA (*Bursts out wildly*): You can't make me believe Jim Clevenger wants us to fight! He's neither a fool nor a criminal, and I refuse to believe until I have to . . .

RUDI: Please, Sara! We know how you feel. (*Then*) Well, if that's all . . . (HE *goes to the hall door*) There's something in making a clean sweep while you're at it. The business, the old house, *The Globe*, now Sara. I'll keep my mind on *The Globe*. Go down and get out the old anti-war rubber stamps and put one more editorial together. Then, in a few days, just at the height of *The Globe*'s real reason for being. . . . But why look ahead? Maybe Sara's new husband will give me a job! (*The last is venomous*)

RUDI *opens the door, to discover* CLEVENGER *in the hall, just in the act of shedding his overcoat. A deadly pause, then* CLEVENGER *enters smiling.*

CLEVENGER: I take it the liberal front's drawn up against me.

RUDI: Whatever I may think of you as a fellow citizen, Mr. Clevenger, as a fellow publisher I must congratulate you on the effect of the job you've done today. You might have shown more originality, perhaps, but . . .

CLEVENGER: Originality's of no use with mass emotion. The old standbys serve better with that. They would have risen to a tenth of what I've given them.

JOHN: It's good of you to find time for us today.

CLEVENGER: Oh, but I've made time for you! I've been busy in your behalf as well as the country's. Don't go, Sara, please. Deceptive though appearances may be, I'm here as the harbinger of glad tidings. "Harbinger"—that sounds like a piece of agricultural machinery, doesn't it? I ring in a golden New Year for you Garrisons. I've just come from your venerable senatorial banker. He's agreed to extend your company's note indefinitely.

Sensation. MARTIN *has appeared in the hall and now comes into the room to listen intently to what follows.*

National Honor's made a good risk of the tool and die business.

The GARRISONS *are too stunned to comment.*

I've seen people more grateful for financial salvation.

JOHN: We weren't asking for any kind of salvation from you, Mr. Clevenger.

CLEVENGER: You don't seem to realize that what I've done today would have been done sooner or later by somebody else. (*But he adds*) Too late for you to have profited, however.

RUDI: We're free to reject our profit, aren't we?

CLEVENGER: Oh, yes! You can go out on the street and give your business away. Medieval mystics did that sort of thing. You won't though.

JOHN: You feel plenty of contempt for us, don't you, Mr. Clevenger?

CLEVENGER: Not contempt but compassion! And for all loose thinkers like you! Holding your foggy faith in your smug ideals up as a light for mankind to follow!

RUDI: When have we ever done any of that? When have we even pretended to be more than we are: a decent American family with faith in the things we've been trained to believe?

JOHN: Mr. Clevenger must have been trained to believe in them, too! Yet he finds us ridiculous . . .

CLEVENGER: Well, I ask you! Is there a more ludicrous figure on earth than the man whose convictions are such he can't fight to uphold them?

Now RUDI *really explodes.*

RUDI: We've got no convictions that keep us from fighting you! I'll fight you as long as I've got a punch left in me!

A chuckle from CLEVENGER.

(*To* JOHN) We'll find a way out of this! He thinks he's trapped us! He hasn't! We'll find a way out without hauling our colors down!

JOHN: What way! He has saved the business. And the house and *The Globe* with it. We can't throw 'em away or get rid of 'em even. And what would it prove if we could. A solemn, Sunday school gesture! Nothing more.

HE *sits on the sofa, accepting his fate. But kindliness comes to* CLEVENGER, *and* HE *sits beside* JOHN *to administer consolation.*

CLEVENGER: I see nothing for you to be downcast about. We can all of us use salvation these days. Why, day before Christmas, at my Idaho paper mill, I watched a small army of out-of-work lumberjacks attack my company stores. And they weren't driven off till my guards had killed twenty-three of them! How long can we let that kind of thing go on?

MARTIN: Property, eh?

CLEVENGER (*Surprised*): What's that?

MARTIN: I said "property." (*Then*) Didn't John and I tell you, Sara? We're walking ourselves right into a world war to look after a mess of property.

CLEVENGER: Aren't you rather jumping at conclusions? We're not at war yet.

MARTIN: No. But you're ready to take your chances on war to look after your property.

CLEVENGER (*Outraged*): Not mine! Yours, too, if you've got any! Everybody's! Whether it's the circulation of newspapers for me or a widow's income from a family business for Sara . . .

MARTIN: Oh, sure, sure! Liberals own property, too. (*Then, to* JOHN) What are you going to do about it, though? Sit tight? Keep on seeing both sides of the question and getting nowhere? Or will you come down to the Labor Temple with me and stand up with the Reds and see what we can start?

The GARRISON BROTHERS *are mutually dismayed, but* SARA *goes quickly to* MARTIN.

SARA: You're not going there!

MARTIN: I don't want to go there. I'm likely to get the daylights beaten out of me! But I'm damned if I see anywhere else to go!

RUDI: Holy God, he's gone Communist on us!

SARA: I was afraid somebody would before we got through!

MARTIN: Maybe I have. (HE *points to* CLEVENGER) I've noticed extremes breed each other in this life! But you've got to fight dogma with dogma! And this is the dogma of property here! Call it patriotism! Call it any damn thing! Well, history's always turned its corners on dogma and saved reason for the straightaways between! If we're past the choice between fighting or not, I mean to fight to the root of the matter.

RUDI: What root, for God's sake?

MARTIN: Clevenger's root, for God's sake! Property, for God's sake!

JOHN: You're talking like a damn fool!

MARTIN: Well, what is to blame for this if property isn't? The business, *The Globe*, Sara's house, the whole cockeyed . . .

SARA: There's no good in violence, Martin!

MARTIN: Clevenger's rather won me around to thinking there may be. (HE *turns back to* RUDI *and* JOHN) You two may be right to let things ride. My patience has damn well run out on me. Clevenger wants results! Well, I want 'em, too! I suppose this washes this family up on me. (HE *turns back to* SARA) I'm sorry for that. I'm fond of this family.

HE *goes quickly into the hall and out of sight, snatching his coat and hat as* HE *passes the table.* SARA *turns after him, then desperately back to the* GARRISON BROTHERS. *But* RUDI *is already on his way after* MARTIN.

RUDI: Now, you don't want to do anything you'll be sorry for, Martin . . .

And JOHN *follows* RUDI *into the hall.*

JOHN: Keep your shirt on, Martin! You've always been levelheaded and . . .

SARA (*At the same time*): Stop him! You've got to stop him! (*And, unmindful even of the slam of the front door,* SHE *turns wildly on* CLEVENGER) That boy! I brought him up! Here in this house as one of this family! You've driven him out. What is this horrible thing you're trying to do?

CLEVENGER: Nothing, I tell you, that someone else wouldn't have done!

SARA: You don't *know* that! You needn't have done it! You did ask me for guidance!

CLEVENGER: And you gave it.

SHE *is stunned.*

SARA: I gave it? For this?

CLEVENGER: I saw those pickets in front of this house and understood why you'd called me your "way out!" There's always a feather's weight, remember, Sara! I did choose between delay and action then, because I could, then, save your pride with your property and clear away the barrier between us!

SARA: You fool! You blind, uncomprehending ninny! What do you call this that's between us now?

CLEVENGER: There's nothing between us now!

SARA: Oh, isn't there!

CLEVENGER: You love me, Sara!

SARA: I know what I am to you, though! You were on your way to robbing the mint and you picked a penny out of a blind man's plate and I'm the penny! You've wound your cords 'round and around this house . . .

CLEVENGER: Good stout cords! No idealistic weak spots in 'em!

SARA: Now you're twisting 'em into a hangman's noose for me!

CLEVENGER: Step on the trap, Sara! It won't be painful!

SARA: How can you talk about any of that now? How can you ask me to think about that now? I can only see that Joan may be standing where I stood when Paul went to France! And that Roger may be just where his father was! That's what you've put between us now, you dolt! I was a woman in love with a man this morning! Look at me now! I'm the Great American Mother!

HE *laughs delightedly.*

How can you laugh! You've a son of your own, Jim! Have you no thought for him? Oh, I didn't know I could ever be afraid of you but I *am* afraid of you now!

HE *stops laughing abruptly.* HE *goes to her.*

CLEVENGER: Of me, Sara? Not of the world as it is in spite of you? It's odd, though, your saying that just then. Because I've always been the least bit afraid of you. And I'm not afraid of you now.

Her gesture waves him away. SHE *sits, dismally, in her big chair.*

I'll be going now. I've done what I had to do here.

SARA: I hope so. I hope so.

HE *goes out, leaving her staring into the dark portent of the future.*

End of Scene Five

SCENE SIX

The lamps are lighted and the curtains drawn. The doors to both hall and parlor stand open.

CLEVENGER *sits by the fire, his after-dinner coffee and a glass of brandy on the cigarette table in front of him.* HE *sips first one, then the other, and reads a sheaf of telegrams which* OCKLEFORD *hands him. Some of these* HE *drops into a wastepaper basket placed alongside the table. Others* HE *piles neatly beside his coffee cup. The radio is on in the parlor. The sound is a confusion of patriotic band selections, choruses and oratory, one shifted brutally into another.*

OCKLEFORD: Can't complain of the radio program, Chief. Wonderful how the commercial hours took such quick advantage. Of course it's as much to their interest as ours. And there's no royalty charge for patriotic material.

JOHN *and* DORIS *enter from the parlor,* HE *dressed as before;* SHE *very much got up for the evening and with quite a touch of red, white and blue about her costume.*

DORIS: I do think it's mean of you!

JOHN: I'm just not in the mood for parties tonight.

DORIS: Not in the mood? And the most thrilling New Year's Eve that's ever been? You'd better learn to get in the mood, my dear! And stay in it! If you don't want everybody turning against you! Everybody but your beloved Rudi and Sara, that is! (*And* SHE *appeals*) You tell him, Mr. Clevenger! Here we've come in from the country, with four parties to go to and . . .

JOHN: Don't bother, Mr. Clevenger. I'll go up and dress. (HE *starts towards the door*)

From the radio in the parlor another outburst of patriotic oratory which is quickly dimmed by whoever is operating the volume control.

(*To* CLEVENGER *and* OCKLEFORD) I'll say this for you, Mr. Clevenger. At least you don't make any pretense of believing that hogwash yourself.

CLEVENGER'S *eyes flash a signal to* OCKLEFORD, *who draws himself up.*

OCKLEFORD: The Clevenger papers never ask the public to believe anything they don't believe themselves. That's a policy almost amounting to a motto.

Disgusted and angry, JOHN *turns and goes up the stair.*

DORIS: I just can't wait for the Red Cross drive to start. And all those more intimate little committees! (*And, over her shoulder as* SHE *leaves*) You don't know about the spy I caught last time!

SHE *goes into the parlor, passing* CALLORY *as* HE *enters, dressed for the evening.*

CALLORY (*Over the radio, which takes a sudden crescendo spurt*): You're the only one I haven't said good night and Happy New Year to, Mr. Clevenger. My heart, as both banker and patriot, is pouring out thanks for the job you've done today! Not that you aren't hearing that pretty generally. (*A gesture towards the telegrams in* CLEVENGER's *hand*) Sara's concerned for her children. That's not unnatural. I've advised her to turn to you for help with them.

MARY *enters with the regulation after-dinner tray of ice water, glasses, whiskey and soda.* SHE *sets the tray on a side table and goes.* CLEVENGER *rises.*

CLEVENGER: I'm glad you did, Senator. And I can assure you as a friend of this family's that those children of Sara's have never been safer. As for the boy, I'm ready to guarantee that he won't be permitted to get himself into danger, no matter how he may beg!

STEVE *chooses just this moment to enter,* ROGER *following.* STEVE's *manner is both wary and impudent,* ROGER's *breathless with excitement.*

STEVE: How busy are you?
CLEVENGER (*Surprised*): Did you want something?
STEVE: Any idea of when we'll be pushing on?
CLEVENGER: On?
STEVE: To points East.

SARA *has followed the boys in.* SHE *is dressed now in a simple but most beautiful house evening frock.*

CLEVENGER (*A smile for* SARA): I don't think the most blatant optimism would justify my leaving for a few days yet.
STEVE: Then you'll have to get yourself some new flying arrangements.

The briefest pause.

CLEVENGER: Really? Why?
STEVE: Because if I don't get to New York some time tomorrow I don't catch the boat on Saturday.
CLEVENGER: What boat?
STEVE: I forget the name. It's one of the French ones.

This really stops CLEVENGER. *Then* HE *turns, holding his telegrams out to* OCKLEFORD.

CLEVENGER: We'll answer these in the morning. The rest don't matter. That's all for now.

OCKLEFORD *goes, replacing the wastepaper basket by the desk on his way.*

And good night to you, Senator Callory. And let me thank you for what *you've* done today, in Sara's name.
CALLORY: I don't want any thanks. My old friend's business, Sara's security, this house where I've spent fifty Christmas Days . . .
CLEVENGER: And a Happy New Year, Senator . . .

And HE *has got the* SENATOR *on his way. Then* HE *returns to* STEVE.

Now where do you think you're going on a French boat?

STEVE (*Steady as a rock*): To Paris. Where the old Lafayette boys went in 1915. We new Lafayettes like French food and blue uniforms, too.

CLEVENGER's *eyes narrow.*

CLEVENGER: You new Lafayettes?

STEVE: That's me. And nine others just as good as I am, only they haven't had the breaks I've had. Must have dropped two hundred bucks on the long distance this afternoon. Don't worry, Mrs. Garrison. I went to the hotel. (*Then, back to* CLEVENGER) The old Lafayettes had two lion cubs for mascots. We've got everything set but the cubs and I'll have them tomorrow.

ROGER: I'll bet you will, Steve!

Startled, SARA *turns her attention to her son.*

CLEVENGER: What did you expect me to say to this?

STEVE: That's a question I haven't thought about much. All I know is I'm washed up on pushing you around. I'd as soon drive a milk route as do your kind of flying.

CLEVENGER *controls his anger.*

CLEVENGER: Do I have to remind you that you're under contract to me?

STEVE (*His most impudent grin*): Don't I always give the other party his chance to tear up the contract before I tell him to go to hell and sue?

CLEVENGER: I signed that contract because I wanted you with me. It isn't unnatural that I should want my son with me.

STEVE: And it isn't unnatural that you never thought about it till I'd made damn good publicity of my name!

CLEVENGER: I might remind you, then, of an act of Congress to keep our boys out of foreign armies.

STEVE: That law's a dead letter. You killed it today.

CLEVENGER: You'll lose your citizenship!

STEVE: I never voted yet.

CLEVENGER: I'll sue you! I'll slap a summons on you at the dock! You'll never get on that boat!

STEVE: And I'll tell the papers how you stopped me because you want us fighting on Hitler's side and what do your Jewish readers say to that! No answer. I guess everything's covered. (*Going into the hall*) I'll pack my stuff now. I'm going tonight so I've got to pack my stuff now.

HE *is on his way up the stair.* CLEVENGER *turns desperately to* SARA.

SARA: You see, Jim? It's all happening all over again.

CLEVENGER *turns and goes up the stair.*

CLEVENGER (*Calling*): You think you've had the last word, young man, but I'm not done yet! I am your father! And there are some things a boy owes his father! I don't expect either loyalty or obedience from you . . .

STEVE: That's lucky for you, because you wouldn't get 'em! They wouldn't be in your line anyway!

A door slamming above cuts them off. But SARA's *interest is on* ROGER, *who closes the hall door and turns uneasily towards the window.*

ROGER: It's snowing again.

SARA: Is it?

ROGER: The paper said snow. A big storm moving east. Put a kind of a damper on the excitement, won't it?

SARA (SHE *sits in her big chair again*): If it would snow all over the country. . . . Steadily now, for weeks and weeks. And bury all the excitement under a thick, wet blanket.

ROGER: You don't think I'm falling for it?

SARA: No!

ROGER: Steve's got the right idea. Be hard-boiled about it. What is there in it for him, Steve says. I don't know, though, which is the right way to go at it. To fall for the bunk and put your heart into it, or Steve's way, just for the hell of it. (HE *has to recover himself*) If you're going at it at all.

SARA *has grown very wary with him.*

SARA: We're not at war yet.

ROGER: I'm selfish enough to hope we don't go to war.

SARA: What makes you call that selfish?

ROGER: You wouldn't want people calling me a slacker?

SARA: There's only one thing that could make you a slacker, Rog. That would be staying out for any reason except your own conviction.

ROGER: You're not asking me what I'm going to do.

SARA: To do? What about?

ROGER: When . . . *if* we go into this war.

SARA: Do you want me to ask you?

ROGER: Yes, I think I do.

SARA: I thought you might. That's why I thought I wouldn't.

ROGER: Putting it up to me, are you?

SARA: I don't see anyone else to put it up to.

ROGER: Don't worry. I'll stick by our guns. (HE *laughs*) Well, not "guns." (*Then*) That word "pledge," though. It's a lousy, Sunday school word!

HE *gives up and opens the hall door to leave. Once again voices—now distantly muffled—are audible above stairs:* CLEVENGER *and* STEVE *still at it.*

CLEVENGER (*Off*): When I lay down a policy in my papers, I consider it my son's duty to subordinate his weakness for morbid excitement . . .

STEVE (*Off, at the same time*): Forget it! Dry up! Go sell your papers someplace else! (*Then, riding him down*) I'm starting for Paris tonight!

ROGER *closes the door, his resolution revived.*

SARA: That sounds like Steve's round.

ROGER (*Low*): I want to go with Steve, Mother.

SARA (*Very cool*): Straight off to France?

ROGER: A man of my age isn't satisfied just to read about life!

SARA (*A deep breath, then*): I can understand that. I might get Mr. Clevenger to send you over for one of the papers.

ROGER: That wouldn't be the real thing.

SARA: Want the real thing, do you?

ROGER: If a man doesn't get into the real thing sometime!

SARA: You've still got a few years, you know.

ROGER: A few years of what? We've got the business back again. Four years of college. Forty of the business. What's that add up to against learning to fly? If we do go in, wouldn't you like me all trained and ready to take my part as my father did?

SARA: You're terribly like your father at the moment.

ROGER: Am I?

SARA: Terribly!

ROGER: Why put it that way?

SARA: If I mean it that way?

ROGER: You loved my father!

SARA: I love you.

ROGER: That isn't fair! In a year and a half I'll be twenty-one! I'm a man!

SARA: And you've got to be manly and fall in line with . . .

> JOHN—*now in his dinner coat—enters from the hall. The opening of the door admits a fresh burst of the argument above stairs.*

CLEVENGER (*Off*): You'll start nowhere tonight! You'll stay here in this house! That plane's my property!

STEVE (*Off, at the same time*): If you scream that way you'll burst another blood vessel in your eye and get out of this room and leave me to pack!

JOHN: What in God's name goes on between those two upstairs?

SARA: We'll let them fight it through to a knockout and you referee this bout between Roger and me?

ROGER: Now, none of that!

SARA: Let your Uncle John take you on! (*To* JOHN) The war fever's caught up with the Garrison family, John!

ROGER: I don't give a hoot in hell for my Uncle John! All he does is spout about the horrors of war!

JOHN: You don't believe in 'em?

ROGER: I'm sick of hearing about 'em! You men of your age had your war! This is *our* war! Maybe you're right about yours! What do I want to do that's so different from . . .

> *But* JOAN *is down the stair and into them—the tumult above stairs still continuing—before* HE *can finish.*

JOAN (*Wild*): You've got to stop him!

JOHN: Stop whom?

SARA (*Simultaneously*): Joan, what's the matter?

ROGER: You're talking about Steve, too?

JOAN: He's going away and I can't get at him because that awful father's in there with him and I haven't got any time! Do something, Mother! (SHE *is very close to tears*)

ROGER: My God, if she hasn't fallen in love with Steve!

JOAN: What if I have? What's it to you if I have?

ROGER: It's okay with me! It's great!

SARA (*Stunned*): I wasn't prepared for this! John, will you please . . .? (SHE *motions him out*) And see that no one gets in here till I . . .

ROGER: But you haven't told me yet what I can . . .

JOHN: Your problems can wait!

ROGER: They can't wait! Steve's leaving!

JOHN: They're going to wait!

HE *has* ROGER *with him out in the hall and the door closes after them. Meanwhile* SARA *has seated* JOAN *on the sofa beside her.*

SARA: What is it you want me to do?

JOAN: Stop him! Stop him!

SARA: But I'm thinking of Martin! You might think about him!

JOAN: I can't think about Martin! I won't think about him! Steve's going away! I can't let him go, Mother! You've got to stop him! You're being no help at all!

And SARA *sees that her daughter's case requires even more tact and wariness than her son's.*

SARA: Joan, darling, I can't just pull this straight like a string trick! What's he want to do?

JOAN: Go away!

SARA: It's no fun having a husband away at war.

JOAN: But he doesn't want to get married!

SARA: Did he suggest any alternative?

JOAN: That's as far as we got.

SARA: Well, that's somewhere. (*And* SHE *becomes more hopeful*) Isn't it, though, a sign that he may not be quite as serious as you are?

JOAN: He loves me! I don't care about being married! I can't let him go! Can't you talk to him, Mother?

SARA: What can I say to him? Except that I shan't be sorry to see him go? And I do think you should talk to Martin before . . .

JOAN: Martin isn't here and I haven't got any time! And why can't you try to help instead of objecting! And making things harder for me and . . . (SHE *is very near breaking*)

SARA: But it's nothing unusual for a girl to love two men at once! I've done it often! It's complicated, I know! But it doesn't mean that you don't love Martin as much as . . .

Then JOAN *does explode.*

JOAN: What do you know about me or the way I feel? You've forgotten what it means to be in love! If you ever knew!

SARA: I wish I had never known! Because then I should know what to do about this!

JOAN: You don't know Steve! You've never seen him in his plane!

SARA: You wouldn't be living with him in his plane.

JOAN: I'll never live anywhere with him if he gets away! You will talk to him, won't you?

SARA: I wish I knew what to say! (SHE *calls off*) Rog! Rog, come in here a . . .

ROGER *opens the door.*

Will you ask your friend Steve Andrews to come down?

ROGER (*Calls up the stairs*): Steve!

STEVE (*From above and muffled*): What?

ROGER: Come down here, will you? My mother wants you.

A pause.

STEVE: Right.

SARA (*To* JOAN): You can't stay here, you know!

JOAN: I may never see him again if I don't!

STEVE *is coming down the stairs.*

SARA: But I cannot stand your young man up on the carpet to ask him if his intentions are honorable with you sitting there looking as dishonorable as . . .

JOAN (*On her feet*): He's coming now!

SARA: Oh, Joan, my dear Joan, he isn't the first hero to ride off to the wars!

STEVE *enters.* ROGER *follows, sneakingly, and closing the hall door after him.* SARA *rises.*

I asked you to come down here, Mr. Andrews.

A movement of protest from STEVE.

I'm sorry, but I can't call you anything more intimate and get through what I have to say. Whatever that is. (*Then, to* JOAN) Joan, won't you please . . .?

JOAN *sits decisively.*

Well, if you don't find this embarrassing, I don't see why I should! (*Then, back to* STEVE) You've succeeded in causing quite an emotional disturbance in this house. Now you're off to France, wreathed in palms of glory, to lead a flying squadron into battle, in spite of the fact that something seems to have happened between you and Joan. I'm interested to hear any helpful observations you may have to offer.

STEVE: I don't think of any.

SARA: You love Joan?

STEVE: Yes.

SARA: That's serious, is it?

STEVE: It is with me.

SARA: And still you're going away to France tonight?

STEVE: She says herself I'm two-thirds airplane. I couldn't love anybody enough to give up what I can't help doing.

SARA: Thank God for the one-track mind!

JOAN (*To* STEVE): You know I wouldn't want you to give it up!

SARA (*Overwhelmed*): Oh, dear, oh, dear! You should have taken her to Lhassa with you!

STEVE: I didn't know her then.

SARA: Do you want to say anything to her alone before you go?

STEVE: What?

SARA: Well, I don't like to make suggestions, but . . . "good-bye."

STEVE: Better not.

A sob, just one, from JOAN.

SARA: That may be, too. (*To* ROGER) Rog, will you tell Morgan he's wanted to take Mr. Andrews to the station? And get his bags down?

ROGER: Now? Right off?

SARA: The sooner the better. Much the better, I think.

STEVE: Only it's the airport, not the station, if that's okay.

ROGER: Flying in this snow?

STEVE: I've flown in worse. I get carsick on trains.

ROGER *goes, troubled, by the pantry door.* SARA *holds out her hand to* STEVE.

SARA: You can say good-bye to me at any rate. I've precious little use for what you're up to, but that doesn't blind me to your other attractions!

STEVE: Thank you. (HE *takes her hand*) Good-bye.

But JOAN *is on her feet.*

JOAN: Don't take Rog with you . . .

SARA: He's not taking Rog!

JOAN: Take me!

SARA: Joan!

HE *is startled.*

STEVE: Would you want to come with me?

JOAN: I shan't ever see you again if you don't take me!

SARA: Joan! My dear Joan! (*Then to* STEVE) If you've any sense of anything, Mr. Andrews . . .!

STEVE: You can leave this to me, Mrs. Garrison.

JOAN: Why do you listen to her when she's just said she's against you? I'm not against you and you don't want to give me up! And I promise to keep out of the way in New York and not even to try talking you out of sailing!

SARA: Joan, you don't know what you're saying!

ROGER *comes down the stair with* STEVE'*s bag, leaves it in the hall and comes into the room.*

JOAN: I don't care what I'm saying! Do you expect me to let the man I love go off to war and sit back and say nothing? And he loves me! And I'd follow him to Paris if he'd let me! Just to be there and see him when he gets leave and . . .

ROGER: You with a lot of us flyers in Paris?

JOAN: You keep out of this, Rog!

SARA: I won't have any more of this, Joan!

JOAN: He might not come back! Father didn't! You ought to understand! I never thought you'd let me down!

SARA: I'm not letting you down! This is what happened to me with your father! And it's not going to happen to you if I can help it!

JOAN: I don't care about that! I don't care!

ROGER (*At the same time*): You *can't* help it! You may keep Joan here, but you can't keep me!

SARA: You'll do as your legal guardians say for a while yet!

STEVE *is already on his way, but* JOAN *goes after him.*

JOAN: Not yet! You can't go yet!

*Voices—*RUDI'*s and* JOHN'*s—are audible in the hall from the front door.*

STEVE: Joan! For God's sake! I do love you! You're right about that! And I'll come back if you'll wait for me . . .

SARA: Will you go, if you're going?

STEVE: Right.

Going, STEVE, *runs into* JOHN *and* RUDI *as* THEY *enter talking excitedly and* BOTH *together.* THEY *stop to watch* STEVE *leave.*

JOAN: (*A wild cry*) Steve! No!

SARA: Joan, I'm ashamed of you!

SHE *has gripped* JOAN'*s arm. The door is heard to slam.*

JOAN: Let me go, please.

SARA *releases her.* SHE *goes weakly up the stair.* SARA *and both brothers looking after her. The radio in the parlor has been for some time broadcasting a military march. Now it switches suddenly to a mellifluous female voice in a recitation.* SARA *turns listening, disgusted, until* SHE *hears the words: " 'Shoot, if you must, this old gray head, but spare your country's flag,' she said." This is very much too much for her and* SHE *is charging the parlor.*

JOHN: I'm sorry, Sara, but . . .

SARA (*Distracted*): What is it now?

RUDI: Martin's got himself hurt.

> SARA *turns. The radio recitation continues.*

JOHN: He did go to that labor meeting. He did stand up and the Reds did get behind him and Buck's strong arm squad . . .

SARA (*Loud at the parlor*): Shut that damn thing off! (*Then, as silence falls on the radio*) Is he badly hurt?

> DORIS *enters.*

DORIS: Really, Sara, I don't think you've any . . .

RUDI (*Cuts her off*): Not badly. No. They took a few stitches in his head, that's all.

SARA: And Joan . . . (*Then*) I'll go to him. Where is he?

JOHN: That's it. He's locked up in a cell in the city jail.

SARA (*This is a jolt but* SARA *controls herself*): I'll go to him there.

RUDI: I wouldn't. It's a nasty place. Stinks of creosote. The thing is to get him out.

SARA: Can't you do that?

RUDI: You don't know the temper of this town tonight. I'm not the respected citizen I was. And tomorrow's a holiday and he won't even get his hearing till the day after. So I thought. . . . Well, I came here thinking . . .

DORIS: That you'll have to turn to Mr. Clevenger.

> A pause.

JOHN: Again?

RUDI: He really does own the police, you know.

> SARA *goes to the stair and calls up.*

SARA: Jim! Will you come down here a minute, Jim?

> A strained pause: SARA *immobile,* DORIS *triumphant, the* GARRISON BROTHERS *miserable. Then, suddenly,* RUDI *turns to make himself a whiskey and soda and* CLEVENGER *is coming down the stair.*

CLEVENGER: I'm sorry, Sara, for the disturbance Steve and I . . . (HE *looks around him*) Or is this something else?

SARA: We've had our first war casualty already, Jim. Martin Holme's been saying what he believes and got himself beaten up and arrested for it. Will you get him out of jail for me?

CLEVENGER (*Smiles, then*): You're sure jail isn't a good place for him? He'll only get himself into more trouble, you know.

SARA: I thought Paul's death had cured me of hero worship. I'm not sure I'm cured.

CLEVENGER: I'll get on the phone to *The Eagle*. (HE *goes out*)

RUDI: Can you trust him, Sara?

> A look, then SARA *follows* CLEVENGER *out.*

JOHN (*To* RUDI): Can we trust Sara?

RUDI *is shocked.*

Not to let him put anything over on her, I mean.
RUDI: We might just stand around.

THEY *follow* SARA *out.*

DORIS: Of course if young men will try to stand out against the inevitable. I've always said Martin was his own worst enemy. Don't you make any such mistake, will you, Roger?

SHE *goes into the parlor where the radio presently resumes martial music.* ROGER *lifts two desperate hands to heaven. Then* JOAN *is coming furtively down the stair.* SHE *wears her ermine coat and carries a small dressing case.* SHE *enters the room.*

JOAN: Lend me your car?
ROGER: Where do you think you're going?
JOAN: I've packed a bag. (SHE *shows it*)
ROGER: You'll be sorry!
JOAN: Will you lend me your car? I haven't got any time!
ROGER: Pipe down! (*Then, as* HE *is producing his car keys*) You'll be sorry, I tell you.
JOAN (*Frightened, obsessed, pathetic*): You can come if you like.
ROGER: You know I'd like, all right.
JOAN: Will you come? Or had you rather stay here in this . . . this . . . (SHE *can find no name for such stuffiness*)
ROGER: Jesus!

SHE *takes the keys from him.*

JOAN: Well . . . (SHE *starts towards the pantry door*)
ROGER: Hold it. My coat's right here in the . . .

HE *follows her to the hall, where* SHE *stands waiting quietly in the open pantry door.* HE *disappears and reappears at once, struggling into his coat.*

I ought to pack a bag. I ought to take . . .
JOAN: There isn't time for that! Do you want to miss him?
ROGER: No. But it's a hell of a thing to go to war in a dinner coat!
JOAN: I'm taking my ermine.

THEY *slip out through the pantry door. The radio swells.*

End of Scene Six

SCENE SEVEN

The lamps and fire as before.

SARA stands at the window, the curtain drawn back to show the blizzard outdoors.
JOHN and RUDI sit side by side on the sofa. The bottle of whiskey is nearly empty
on the coffee table before them and three or four empty pints of White Rock stand
on the floor.

RUDI (*As the scene begins*): I can't help feeling sorry for myself. Life may begin at
forty for professional grandfathers but panic begins at forty for professional
writers. The day comes when you have to admit the piece you've just written took twice as long as it would have a few years before.

MARY enters from the pantry with a tray of coffee—large thermos pot and large cup—
which SHE sets on a small table. SHE moves the table to place it beside SARA's big
chair. RUDI continues throughout.

And you buy a new pencil sharpener to speed things up and pin your ideas
on the wall so you won't forget 'em. Or will forget where you read 'em! And
what you need is a professional home! Where you can be sure of print for
a few years longer. Have you ever known an ex-liberal editor? (HE *shudders*
and empties his glass)

SARA (*To* MARY): What time's it getting to be?

MARY: Close on half past eleven.

SARA: Miss Joan's still quiet?

MARY: As a mouse, Mrs. Garrison.

SARA: That's all, Mary, thank you. You can go to bed.

MARY: Good night, Mrs. Garrison.

SARA: Good night.

MARY leaves. SARA goes to her big chair, sits and pours herself a cup of black coffee.

RUDI: If they want to fight, all the *Globes* in the world can't stop 'em. But I can
have a lot of fun trying to. Oh, no! I couldn't have given up *The Globe*!

HE is mixing another drink. JOHN *sweetens his.*

JOHN: *The Globe*'s saved now. And the house and the business with it. And Sara's
marrying Clevenger.

SARA's head comes up. SHE *frowns.*

SARA: We agreed not to talk about Sara and Clevenger.

RUDI: Right.

JOHN: The truth about us is: we're afraid of Clevenger. He makes the world as
men have messed it up more valid than the world as it ought to be. That's
part of the power of evil in men like him. They can make what's sound and
good seem senseless folly. And men like you and me sound like solemn fools.

SARA: Have another drink.

RUDI: You have one.

SARA: Coffee's my vice, thanks.

JOHN: You're waiting up for Clevenger to come back from the airport?

SARA: Why not wait up? It *is* New Year's Eve. And I'm at least interested to see if he brings Steve back with him.

JOHN laughs.

JOHN: I don't want to be nasty, but I did enjoy his howls when he heard Steve was gone.

RUDI: Now *I* want to forget about Sara and Clevenger.

JOHN: Right.

RUDI: I think I'll marry my girl.

JOHN: You'd better go out and get yourself some air.

RUDI: In this snow? I'll open my window . . . (HE *illustrates the size of the opening with thumb and forefinger*) But that's as far as I'll go.

JOHN, rising, knocks over one or two of the White Rock bottles.

JOHN: I haven't got so I knocked things over for years.

RUDI: I can knock anything over when I'm tight. Including women.

SARA: Really, Rudi!

This is the tolerant boredom which drink induces in the sober.

You ought both of you to be ashamed of yourselves!

RUDI: Why?

SARA: Oh, I don't know. The state of the world for one thing. Poor Martin upstairs in bed with his broken head. (*A shrug. It is all too distressing*)

RUDI: Martin had the wrong idea. Too violent.

JOHN: If I believed property really is to blame . . .

SARA: The evils of property are apt to be clearer to those who don't own any.

But JOHN, being troubled again, sits to pour just one more small one.

JOHN: We don't seem to be very clear about things, though, do we?

SARA: There's this much merit in confusion: if you stay confused you'll never be orthodox.

JOHN sees her point. So does RUDI.

RUDI: The truth about us is we're both in love with you, Sara.

SARA smiles.

(HE *continues to* JOHN) I've always known that. I asked her to marry me once. Not so long ago.

SARA: I should have laughed at all the wrong times.

RUDI: I thought maybe you would, so I gave it up. (*To* JOHN *again*) Now I wish I hadn't. She might not be marrying Clevenger now if . . .

JOHN: He's taking her out of our lives and a great store of our balance and humanity with her.

SARA *frowns.*

SARA: At least I'm taking him out of your lives.

JOHN: Only you aren't. We'll never be free of him. Every day I'll remember how the business was saved. You'll be running an anti-war paper on war profits.

RUDI: Well, Nobel earned his peace prize off dynamite.

JOHN: What's the answer? Or did Martin find the answer?

RUDI: He found one answer. Clevenger's got the other. We haven't got any.

JOHN: Us liberals! (*And* HE *shakes his head with melancholy humor. Then, however,* HE *turns with a new seriousness to* RUDI) Reason, though. And "the good life" and "live and let live" and "both sides of the question": somebody's got to worry about 'em! Damn it, Rudi, when the shouting's all over and done with, whom will they have to clean up the mess but us liberals?

The Scotch mist clears a little for RUDI.

RUDI: Search me!

JOHN (*His conviction growing*): No, I'm serious, Rudi! Our Yankee ancestors made our kind the guardians of man's faith in himself! Not in leaders or dogmas or governments, but himself! That's what we mustn't forget!

RUDI: I won't forget.

JOHN: Liberalism: a goal man's never been able to attain, a hope man's never been able to abandon.

RUDI: Democracy.

The word sticks.

JOHN: Don't laugh.

SARA: He wasn't laughing. That's the White Rock.

RUDI: Neither Hitler nor Marx. Just . . . (*With care*) Democracy. Foggy or not. (HE *rises. His stance is none too steady as* HE *moves away from the table*)

JOHN: It isn't easy to walk the middle way.

RUDI: It isn't easy for me to walk at all. (*But* HE *turns back to answer* JOHN) Oh, I'll stick to the middle! And not only because you can see both sides from the middle. You see further ahead from the middle, too!

JOHN: And if the time comes that we have to choose . . .

RUDI: Between standing in line thus . . . (*The Nazi salute*) Or thus . . . (*The Communist salute*)

JOHN: We can die, can't we?

RUDI: Or go to the island of Bali.

Then, the front door buzzer sounding.

There's the great lover back.

JOHN *rises.*

No, I'll let him in. I'd like him to see me at my best. (HE *goes into the hall and towards the front door.*)

JOHN: Oh, Sara! Sara!

SARA: What?

JOHN: Can you build for a better world in irony?

SARA: Better in irony than in violence.

Then, suddenly, SHE *is on her feet and turned towards the hall door—*JOHN *with her—as the entire house is shattered by the sound of* JOAN's *hysterical sobbing. It is the most complete possible letting go of uncontrolled agony. Through it the sound of voices—*RUDI's *and* ROGER's*—then* RUDI, *sobered or as good, meets* SARA *and* JOHN *in the hall.*

RUDI: Holy God, do you hear that? She's just . . .

Then ROGER *supports his sister to the foot of the stair and, almost at once,* DORIS *is down to them from above and* MARY *after her.* MARTIN, *in pajamas and bathrobe, an unbecoming plaster over one ear, trails after them.*

SARA: Joan! Joan, darling! What is it?

ROGER: It's Steve! Crashed! Crashed right in front of her eyes!

SARA: She wasn't going with him!

ROGER: We were both going with him!

The remainder, of course, comes with a rush.

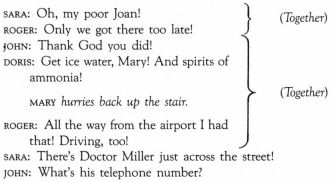

SARA: Oh, my poor Joan!
ROGER: Only we got there too late! } (*Together*)
JOHN: Thank God you did!
DORIS: Get ice water, Mary! And spirits of ammonia!

    MARY *hurries back up the stair.*

ROGER: All the way from the airport I had that! Driving, too!

} (*Together*)

SARA: There's Doctor Miller just across the street!

JOHN: What's his telephone number?

RUDI: The hell with the telephone! I can run across!

    HE *goes.*

SARA (*At the same time*): Try to stop it, Joan! Try! Take hold of yourself! . . .

SHE *has put her arm about her daughter's shoulders. But* JOAN *shakes loose and things are clear for a moment.*

JOAN: Not you! Not you! I don't want you to touch me!

SARA *recoils involuntarily.*

It wouldn't have happened if you'd stopped him!

SARA (*The deepest distress*): Joan, darling!

JOAN: I'd be with him, now, if you hadn't stopped me! (*And* SHE *turns into her aunt's arms*) Oh, Aunt Doris! Aunt Doris!

DORIS: Joan, I know! I understand!

JOAN: It burned him! It burned him!

Then confusion again.

JOHN: Get her up to her room! (*And to* JOAN) And lie down on your bed and try to . . .

THEY *are trying to get her up the stair but her collapse on the first step makes things difficult.*

JOAN (*Throughout*): But Mother stopped me! That's what I can't forget! I could have been with him! I'll never forgive . . .

SARA: Oh, my poor Joan! My poor Joan!

JOHN (*At the same time*): Now, it's all right, Joan! It's all right!

HE *is carrying her up.* DORIS *preceding them.* RUDI *returns and with him* DOCTOR MILLER—*any age at all—in the dinner coat of his New Year's party.*

SARA: This is very bad, Doctor. Thank you for coming over!

DOCTOR MILLER: Rudi told me. I think we can get her quieted down.

JOAN (*At the same time*): Don't leave me, Aunt Doris!

DORIS (*From above*): I won't, Joan. I'm just . . .

The PROCESSION *disappears above, leaving* ROGER *and* RUDI *below. A moment more of the sobbing and voices, then everything is shut off as though by the closing of* JOAN's *bedroom door.*

ROGER: What do they do to stop a thing like that?

RUDI: Opiates, I guess. Put her to sleep. (HE *comes back into the room*) What the hell happened and did she see it happen?

ROGER: Just as we got there, I tell you!

HE *comes into the room as* RUDI *proceeds to move the whiskey and White Rock empties to a side table.*

We got there just as he taxied out into the snow. They'd tried to stop him. I don't believe anyone could have stopped him. The snow hid him. God knows what happened then! They guessed he must have skidded on his takeoff. We only heard the crash. Then the flames shot up. You couldn't even see them for the snow. A red brightness, that's all. And a roaring that made even the snow feel hot! We saw 'em bring him in on the truck. I couldn't look.

RUDI (*Under his breath*): Holy God!

SARA *and* JOHN *are coming back down the stair.* THEY *enter the room.*

SARA (*To* RUDI): She won't let me near her. Doris is the one she wants with her now. I haven't forgotten how she feels, so thank God for Doris. Somebody give me a cigarette.

JOHN: How about a spot of brandy?

SARA: Just a cigarette.

JOHN is delivering. SHE *sees* MARTIN.

Martin!

None of the OTHERS *had noticed his presence. Now* THEY *all realize the blow* HE *has sustained.* SARA *goes to him but can think of nothing to say and merely touches his arm with her own warm sympathy.*

You should be in bed.

MARTIN: I'm all right. (*Then*) Who would have thought our sedate little Joan could have had a mess like this in store for her? (*Then*) You don't have to have me on your minds! (*Then*) All war seems to have got itself crammed into these few hours. The hero and the dissenter both picked off. And each in the way most suitable to him. (*Then*) Well, good night. (HE *goes up the stair again*)

SARA: It's hard to know what to do. I ought to be out at that airport now!

JOHN: Sara, what for?

SARA: Jim must be out there!

ROGER: He is.

SARA: I can't leave him alone out there with that . . . (SHE *stops herself, then*) Rudi, as soon as the doctor says Joan's all right, I'll ask you to take me . . .

The doorbell. A pause. JOHN *goes. Then* CLEVENGER *appears in the hall.* HE *moves heavily, a man still groggy from the impact of horror.* OCKLEFORD *joins him to help him off with his coat.* JOHN *comes last.*

CLEVENGER (*Orders, but effort behind every word of them*): You'd better get on the phone to *The Eagle.* Warn 'em against giving the accident too much space. The fact of its having occurred at the local airport is not—I'm most particular about this—to interfere with the National Honor campaign. Make sure the railroad has a car for me on that nine-whatever-it-is out of here in the morning.

HE *comes into the room as* OCKLEFORD *goes.* HE *is darkly but fully possessed of himself.* HE *looks about him.* SARA's *eyes are downcast. Likewise* RUDI's. JOHN *waits in the hall. It is* ROGER *who steps impetuously into the silence.*

ROGER: I want to tell you I'm sorry, sir. Steve Andrews was just God Almighty to me!

HE *goes out and up the stair.* CLEVENGER *turns to the* BROTHERS.

CLEVENGER: If you're reading some damn pacifist lesson into what's happened, there's none to be read! The boy himself was to blame! He had no business trying to get to France! None flying in this weather!

A gesture from SARA, *and* RUDI *goes into the parlor, closing the door after him.* JOHN *likewise closes the hall door.*

Thank you.

SARA: Flying in the air over the earth—that's an unreal and unhuman thing, isn't it? Even death from flying doesn't seem like death.

CLEVENGER: It's the earth taking its own back.

SARA: If I can do anything that will help at all . . . What do you want me to do?

A look at her and HE *goes to sit down.*

CLEVENGER: I think you know that.

SARA *is distressed.*

SARA: I couldn't very well leave Joan now, could I?

CLEVENGER: How quickly can you come to me, Sara? If I can know that—just that, just a date . . .

SARA (*A plea*): Don't try to pin me down!

CLEVENGER: Sara, you're not . . .? (HE *darts a sharp look of suspicion at her, then*) No, you couldn't do that to me now! (*But* SARA *cries out, almost in physical pain*)

SARA: Oh, please! I'm tired.

CLEVENGER: I don't mean to press you. But I'm afraid to be alone . . . with that poor burned body.

SARA's *eyes close to shut out the picture.*

SARA: Try not to think about that.

CLEVENGER: I'll always reproach myself. I said things to him that I'll always be sorry for.

SARA: Better not think about that either.

CLEVENGER: They tell me people get over blows like this. But I've nothing left now that I've lost the boy. You see that, don't you?

SHE *looks away.*

SARA: Yes. Oh, yes. I see.

CLEVENGER: You, only you, can heal me and fill my loneliness! Pity me, Sara! Pity my loneliness!

SARA (*The deepest conceivable unhappiness*): I pity you, Jim! I do pity you!

CLEVENGER: Then you'll come with me tomorrow, won't you? The boy's death in those flames must have sealed things for us! And we'll take him to Washington together! To Arlington! They wanted to bury him here on the field where he fell, but we'll bury him there with full military honors! (*His head is up and his eyes are blazing*) I shall acknowledge him to the world as my son now, Sara! I don't have to say he was rushing to fly with the French. Let 'em think he was on his way to offer his life for his own country! That way they'll never forget him! I'll keep his name alive to the day of my death! Steve Andrews who was really Steve Clevenger! The greatest flyer of all time and my son! My son and the first hero of the new war!

This is much too much for SARA, *but* HE *notices nothing.*

Ockleford! Ockleford!

SARA (*Low*): Don't, Jim! Please don't!

OCKLEFORD *returns from the hall.*

CLEVENGER: Get on the phone to *The Eagle!* Stop the presses! Tell 'em I'm coming down to tear the front page wide open!

OCKLEFORD *goes.*

I've found how to tie Steve's death in with National Honor! I'll get a memorial edition of every damn one of my papers and acknowledge the boy in facsimile of my own handwriting spread all over every front page! By God, Sara, I'll . . .

But all this is now far too much for SARA.

SARA: Of course you don't have to think such things out! You do them by instinct, don't you?

CLEVENGER: Now what do you mean by that?

SARA: Your instinct to use everything, even that poor, burned body, to your advantage.

HE *lurches angrily at her, but her steadiness holds him.*

CLEVENGER: I hope you may some day forgive yourself for saying that!

SARA (*Shakes her head*): I shall have forgotten tomorrow that I said it. It's odd that I should have let you use what you have used this week and made excuses for you and that I should stick now on this!

HE *goes to her, shaking with fury.*

CLEVENGER: You make me wish we hadn't met again and that this past week had never been!

But SARA *is equal to him.*

SARA: Your week hasn't been wasted! You've done what you had to do supremely well! You found us a family unafraid even of the disaster you saved us from! You'll leave us a zoo of prosperous lost souls! Twenty years of my dreams were invested here! Well, you've brought my investment off bankrupt! You've made shoddy melodrama of my daughter's life and given my son a mission of destruction! And all that's only incidental, I know! You'll go on! There's no one with the strength or vision to stop you! But you can't ask me to compromise with you now! Those who've nothing to offer can't compromise! And you've left me in command of a total wreck! (*And* SHE *calls off*) Rudi! John!

But RUDI *and* JOHN, *alarmed by the clamor of her outburst, are already standing at the parlor door.*

It's all right! I only wanted the interruption!

CLEVENGER *does not welcome the interruption, but* HE *manages to laugh it off pleasantly.*

RUDI: I didn't hear anything funny.

CLEVENGER: I know how you both feel but I don't give her up. And she won't be such a fool as to let me go. These are my times! That's my star up there!

SARA: What does a woman do, under your star, who can't look at life from your side of the river?

CLEVENGER: One thing you three will come to realize some day: that my creed holds water for the world we live in. I can't see that yours holds water even for you.

OCKLEFORD *has come into the hall for* CLEVENGER's *hat and coat.*

OCKLEFORD: Ready to go down to *The Eagle*, Chief?

CLEVENGER: I think so.

With the best of good humor, HE *drops an affectionate arm around* SARA's *shoulders.* SHE *looks up at him.*

SARA: Take care you don't catch another stiff neck.

HE *frowns because* HE *does not like jokes at the expense of his health. But* HE *is too surely in command of things to let* SARA *feel his annoyance.*

CLEVENGER: You'll still be up when I get back. You've got packing to do.

A final affectionate pat and HE *goes out towards the front door.* OCKLEFORD *following with the hat and coat.*

JOHN: He doesn't realize he's out.

RUDI (*Quickly*): He *is* out?

SARA: Twenty years ago I loved him and told him he wasn't good enough to love. Now I've loved him again and can find nothing better to say about him. That's a little sad. (SHE *smiles*) It's sad, too, for a woman to hear the last call from the dining car—and pass it up.

RUDI: I can see that.

HE *sits timidly, as it seems, not knowing what to say next.* JOHN, *too, is silent and ill at ease.*

SARA (*To* RUDI): Don't let it depress you. (*Then*) Is there any more coffee in this thing? (SHE *sits and refills her cup*)

RUDI (*To* JOHN): Remember how they used to give us our supper in here after Mother died? And the old man sitting there in that chair of Sara's glaring at us?

JOHN: How often we three have sat here like this!

SARA: Where were we ten years ago, before Joan came home?

JOHN *sits.*

JOHN: Discussing the irony of our predicament.

RUDI: So we were!

SARA: And I was about to say that it doesn't matter.

JOHN: I'd like to know what does!

SARA (*Her strength is returning to her*): I can't tell you that. But I can't feel too sorry for you! Oh, I know he's confused you now and set you back! But I read in a book once: "Stone the idealist—no flint can reach his thought. Bury the dreamer—his dreams will color the sky above his grave. Imprison the philosopher—his philosophy will wander free in the market place."

From far away the horns and sirens welcome in the New Year.

Listen! Happy New Year!

RUDI *rises and* JOHN *sits up, both in protest.*

Oh, not this year or next, I grant you. Or, perhaps, any that we shall ever see. Some year, though. . . . Some year . . .

The horns continue. SHE *sips her coffee. The scene ends.*

END OF PLAY